MOBILIZING IN UNCERTAINTY

MOBILIZING IN UNCERTAINTY

Collective Identities and War in Abkhazia

Anastasia Shesterinina

CORNELL UNIVERSITY PRESS   ITHACA AND LONDON

Copyright © 2021 by Cornell University

All rights reserved. Except for brief quotations in a review, this book, or parts thereof, must not be reproduced in any form without permission in writing from the publisher. For information, address Cornell University Press, Sage House, 512 East State Street, Ithaca, New York 14850. Visit our website at cornellpress.cornell.edu.

First published 2021 by Cornell University Press

Library of Congress Cataloging-in-Publication Data

Names: Shesterinina, Anastasia, 1986– author.
Title: Mobilizing in uncertainty : collective identities and war in Abkhazia / Anastasia Shesterinina.
Description: Ithaca [New York] : Cornell University Press, 2021. | Includes bibliographical references and index.
Identifiers: LCCN 2020014614 (print) | LCCN 2020014615 (ebook) | ISBN 9781501753763 (hardcover) | ISBN 9781501753770 (ebook) | ISBN 9781501753787 (pdf)
Subjects: LCSH: Group identity—Georgia (Republic)—Abkhazia. | Abkhazia (Georgia)—History—Uprising, 1992–1993. | Abkhazia (Georgia)—Ethnic relations. | Abkhazia (Georgia)—History.
Classification: LCC DK679.A25 S55 2021 (print) | LCC DK679.A25 (ebook) | DDC 947.58086—dc23
LC record available at https://lccn.loc.gov/2020014614
LC ebook record available at https://lccn.loc.gov/2020014615

ISBN 9781501778964 (pbk)

In memory of Lee Ann Fujii

Contents

List of Illustrations	ix
Acknowledgments	xi
Note on Translation, Transliteration, and Spelling	xiii
Introduction: The Puzzle of Mobilization	1
1. Studying Civil War Mobilization	18
2. A Sociohistorical Approach to Mobilization	47
3. Collective Historical Memory	68
4. Prewar Conflict Identities	88
5. From Uncertainty to Mobilization in Four Days	123
6. From Mobilization to Fighting	156
7. Postwar Abkhazia	177
Conclusion: Uncertainty and Mobilization in Civil War	201
Notes	213
References	225
Index	239

Illustrations

Figures

0.1. Map of Abkhazia   xiv

1.1. Research sites   22

1.2. The road connecting research sites   22

1.3. Prewar demographic composition in research districts: east   23

1.4. Prewar demographic composition in research districts: west   26

2.1. The concept of mobilization   49

2.2. Collective action continuum   56

2.3. Collective threat framing   64

2.4. Wartime mobilization continuum   66

3.1. Demographic changes in prewar Abkhazia: 1886–1989   78

3.2. Timeline of cultural Georgianization: 1920s–1940s   80

4.1. Demographic composition of Abkhazia by district: 1989   91

5.1. Military structure of the Abkhaz Guard   129

5.2. Locals guarding a village   151

6.1. Front lines: August 18–October 6, 1992   158

7.1. "Ten years of Victory"   187

7.2. The Order of Leon   188

7.3. A public memorial in Bzyb/Bzipi   188

Tables

1.1. Research participants   27

3.1. Prewar political status of Abkhazia: 1810–1992   70

Acknowledgments

This book is a result of deep commitment to people affected by violent conflict and war and to academic research on these persistent social problems. It would not have been possible without the support of many to whom I am indebted.

The generous financial support that I received for this project gave me the opportunity to conduct extensive fieldwork in Abkhazia, Georgia, and Russia in 2010–2013 and the essential time needed to analyze the vast amount of materials I collected during my field research. Support from the Social Sciences and Humanities Research Council (SSHRC) of Canada; Canada's Security and Defence Forum program; the Faculty of Arts, the Department of Political Science, and the Liu Institute for Global Issues at the University of British Columbia; the MacMillan Center for International and Area Studies at Yale University; and the Department of Politics and International Relations at the University of Sheffield made this project possible.

The Program on Order, Conflict, and Violence (OCV) at the MacMillan Center at Yale University provided me with an intellectual home as an SSHRC post-doctoral fellow in 2015–2017, when I was able to read deeply in the fields of mobilization, political violence, and civil war; share my research with three cohorts of OCV fellows and colleagues from a wide range of universities; and benefit greatly from the guidance and mentorship of Elisabeth J. Wood and Stathis N. Kalyvas. It was at Yale University that I began drafting this book.

For the invitation to present parts of this book and for intellectual exchange that influenced my thinking, I would like to thank participants in the Politics and Protest Workshop at the Graduate Center at the City University of New York; the Political Violence Workshop at the Weatherhead Center for International Affairs at Harvard University; the Post-Soviet Politics Seminar at St. Anthony's College at Oxford University; the Russia Institute Seminar Series at King's College London; the Central and East European Studies Seminar at the University of Glasgow; the Centre for Global Constitutionalism Speaker Series at the University of St. Andrews; the Asia-Pacific Centre for the Responsibility to Protect Seminar Series at the University of Queensland; Séminaire Sociologie des guerres civiles at Panthéon-Sorbonne; and the School of Governance Research Seminar at the Technical University of Munich.

I am grateful for invaluable comments provided at different stages of this project by Consuelo Amat Matus, Séverine Autesserre, Adam Baczko, Erin Baines,

Shane Barter, Regina Bateson, George Bennett, Tim Büthe, Jeffrey Checkel, Dara Kay Cohen, Gilles Dorronsoro, Jesse Driscoll, Vujo Ilic, James Jasper, Nino Kemoklidze, Peter Krause, Juan Masullo, Omar S. McDoom, Theodore McLauchlin, William Reno, Pilar Riaño-Alcalá, Lee Seymour, and Lisa McIntosh Sundstrom.

Brian Job believed in me from day one of my doctoral studies and invested enormous effort and time into helping me find a voice as an academic. I thank Elisabeth J. Wood for laying the foundation for scholars like myself to undertake field research on mobilization in civil war and Stathis N. Kalyvas for challenging me to think beyond the context of my case study. I am deeply indebted to the late Lee Ann Fujii, who during precious years of intellectual exchange helped me articulate my argument on mobilization in uncertainty. Sarah Parkinson has been a constant source of inspiration and support.

The generosity that I experienced during my field research cannot be forgotten. I thank all participants in my research and individuals who made my research possible in Abkhazia, Georgia, and Russia. Nearly two hundred men and women dedicated significant time in their busy lives to share their personal, often traumatic stories with me. I would not have been able to carry out this research without their trust. In Abkhazia, Liana Kvarchelia, Manana Gurgulia, Zinaida Paptsava, and Guguza Dzhikirba helped me reach out to research participants from across Abkhaz society. In Georgia, Ghia Nodia, David Darchiashvili, Yuri Anchabadze, and Timothy Blauvelt offered indispensable academic support. The Zaridze family were the most welcoming, caring hosts. Nikolai Silaev, Andrey Sushentsov, and Alexander Skakov helped me contextualize the case study and complete my research in Russia.

At Cornell University Press, Roger Haydon guided me through the process of writing, offering invaluable comments and advice along the way. I thank anonymous reviewers for their careful reading of and insightful input into the manuscript and the Cornell University Press team for copyediting and assistance in the production process.

An earlier version of some of the material in this book was previously published in "Collective Threat Framing and Mobilization in Civil War," *American Political Science Review* 110, no. 3 (2016): 411–427, © 2016 by American Political Science Association. I thank the publisher of this journal for the permission.

Finally, I am forever grateful to my family, friends, and colleagues for their persistent encouragement during the long life of this project. No one has supported me more in the years of writing this book than Paolo Sandro, whose unwavering care and daily motivation kept me afloat in the course of this journey.

Note on Translation, Transliteration, and Spelling

Unless noted otherwise, all interview excerpts are from interviews that I conducted in Russian. Interview excerpts and cited texts from Russian sources are presented in English translation. All translations are my own.

Where deemed significant, I transliterate Cyrillic into Latin script and italicize the term. I present the English translation of the term in square brackets. If a particular transliteration of a term or an author's name has become common in English sources, I use that transliteration. Titles of Russian texts are transliterated in the bibliography.

The English spelling of proper nouns differs in Georgia (e.g., "Sokhumi") and Abkhazia (e.g., "Sukhum"). Except when quoting from interviews or cited texts, I use the spelling common in academic research (e.g., "Sukhum/i"). Both "Abkhaz" and "Abkhazian" appear in academic research. I use the former, unless spelled otherwise in a cited text, to refer to the Abkhaz group and use the latter to refer to the Abkhazian language.

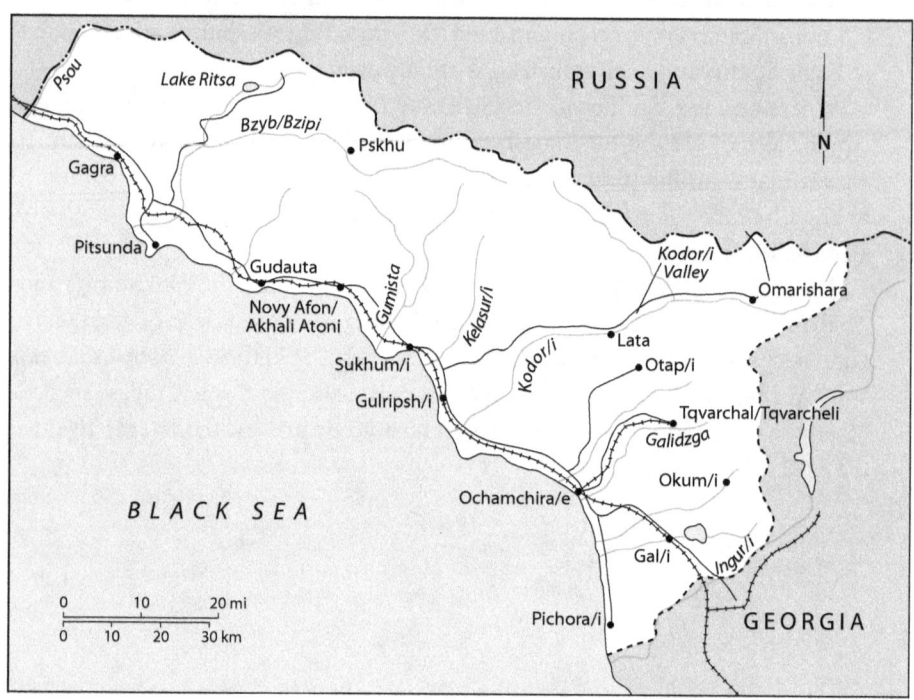

FIGURE 0.1. Map of Abkhazia.

Introduction

THE PUZZLE OF MOBILIZATION

> When the war started, I was at home. I had a day off. It was summer, hot. In the morning, we learned that the Georgian forces were already in Sukhum, there was fighting at the Red Bridge. First I was in shock, then we began gathering with friends, relatives, deciding what to do, what's next. We gathered at the administration. No one understood what was going on—how serious it was, how long it would last, whether it was a war.
>
> —Abkhaz fighter, Gagra, 2011

On August 14, 1992, Georgian troops crossed the Ingur/i River into eastern Abkhazia, a breakaway territory of Georgia located in the South Caucasus region neighboring Russia, and swiftly advanced toward the capital, Sukhum/i. The following morning, Georgian marines landed from the Black Sea in the west, encircling the small territory of Abkhazia in the span of a day.[1] For most ordinary men and women in Abkhazia, the events that marked the beginning of the Georgian-Abkhaz war of 1992–1993 were characterized by intense uncertainty.[2]

"Was this a war?" "Who was threatened, by whom, and to what extent?" "How should we act in response?" These were the dilemmas of the first days of the war for the Abkhaz. Many soon gathered the hunting rifles they kept in their homes, armed themselves at the former Soviet military base in Abkhazia, or joined Abkhaz mobilization unarmed. Others hid in Abkhazia, fled to nearby Russia, or in rare cases defected to the stronger Georgian side. They illustrate the question that motivates this book: How do ordinary people navigate uncertainty to make mobilization decisions in civil war? In particular, how did the Abkhaz go from the uncertainty created by the events of mid-August 1992 to a range of decisions about whether and in what capacity to mobilize? Why did some join the war effort, while others escaped the fighting?

Argument

The puzzle of mobilization in civil war is commonly framed in terms of the risks that individuals assume in voluntarily joining armed groups.[3] Explanations of mobilization focus on what drives individuals to accept the high risks, isolating the grievances that social groups develop before the war, the social pressures and incentives that armed actors provide to increase risk acceptance, and the in-process benefits of participation.[4] In other accounts, where fighting is not seen as riskier than nonparticipation, the skills and resources available to armed groups make joining an attractive option for survival-oriented civilians.

Both explanations are based either on the assumption of ordinary people's knowledge of the risks involved in mobilization or on observation of the patterns of violence, often long after mobilization had taken place. Such premises may be theoretically necessary and empirically valid, but they miss a central feature of mobilization: the perceptions of anticipated risk, or threat, by potential participants that shape their decisions. Why some potential participants join the fighting and in what capacity, but others do not, cannot be grasped without knowing their interpretation.

I argue that people come to perceive threat in different ways, affected by earlier experiences of conflict and by social networks at the time of mobilization. They act differently based on whom they understand to be threatened and mobilize to protect their own safety, family and friends, or broader segments of society. When faced with war, individuals do not simply choose to fight or not to fight based on a given notion of risk. Rather, they call on shared understandings of conflict and their roles in it—what I call *collective conflict identities* that develop before the war through observation of and participation in everyday confrontation, political contention, and violent opposition—to make sense of violence. As these appeals travel across society, people consolidate mobilization decisions with immediate social networks, whether to flee, hide, provide indirect or direct support, or join the fighting in the back or front lines, alone or together. I call this information filtering mechanism *collective threat framing*. Threat perceptions and mobilization decisions have lasting effects on how conflicts unfold and how individuals continue to mobilize during and after the war.

Underlying this argument is the recognition that ordinary people experience intense uncertainty when war breaks out in their communities. This experience differs from the ongoing uncertainty in protracted fighting, where people develop expectations about the occurrence of violence and how to act in response (Arjona 2016). In contrast, the onset of war disrupts "everyday routines and expectancies" in major ways and poses with urgency the dilemmas of mobilization (Snow et al. 1998, 2). In a context where violence can have different meanings, ordinary people rely on shared history and familiar social networks to understand who is threatened, by whom, and to what extent and how to act in response.

This argument has two analytical parts. First, it is a historical approach to mobilization. Most studies of civil war bracket prewar processes, but I argue that the history of engagement with intergroup conflict shapes collective conflict identities that relate individual actions to the group.[5] I stress that these identities evolve through observation of and participation in collective action to situate individuals at the onset of civil war.

Second, my approach is relational, in line with that of Mark S. Granovetter (1985, 487) and Lee Ann Fujii (2009), who analyze individual actions as "embedded in concrete, ongoing systems of social relations." Organizational studies of mobilization focus on prewar social networks as conduits between armed groups and the wider population (Staniland 2012; Parkinson 2013). By contrast, I find that social networks play a critical role in providing information at the time of uncertainty that generates different threat perceptions and mobilization decisions.

Mobilization does not take place in a vacuum, absent shared conflict history and the social networks that feed everyday life. It is an *ongoing process involving organization of and participation in collective action* in which earlier experiences of conflict and immediate social networks at the time of mobilization interact. Analyzing how these factors interact under conditions of uncertainty to produce a range of mobilization decisions among potential participants in civil war is my core contribution. In this book, I develop this sociohistorical approach to mobilization.

Field Research on Civil War Mobilization

To understand how people make difficult decisions under conditions of uncertainty brought on by war, I turn to face-to-face, immersive research with the actors in Abkhaz mobilization. We cannot grasp people's conflict experiences or their social networks by relying solely on elite interviews, archival and news sources, or secondary materials. These sources are essential to an overall understanding of conflict, but they rarely document how the participants themselves perceive the reality they face.

To get at the decades-long organization of and participation in intergroup conflict from the perspective of the ordinary Abkhaz, the interaction between prewar and wartime factors in their mobilization for war, and continued postwar contention, I conducted fieldwork over eight months in 2010–2013, primarily in Abkhazia, but also in Georgia and Russia. This fieldwork explored the Georgian-Abkhaz conflict during the Soviet and post-Soviet decades, but I focused on the first four days of the Georgian-Abkhaz war, August 14–17, 1992. I collected 150 in-depth interviews in Abkhazia and 30 in Georgia and Russia and also extensive secondary and archival materials.

I conducted fieldwork in four locales in Abkhazia selected for variation in patterns of territorial control and access to conflict resources in the war of 1992–1993. In each locale, I interviewed people across a wide range of prewar, wartime, and postwar political backgrounds and roles in mobilization to gather a broad variety of responses beyond the master narrative of conflict. Interviews underlie my analysis and are substantiated and contextualized with participant observation in national and local war-related events, meetings of mothers' and veterans' organizations, communal celebrations and everyday life, original news and document archives, and secondary data, including comparable interviews collected by other researchers.

To address issues of memory and potential bias in accounts of a war that took place two decades earlier, I paid careful attention to how respondents spoke about events, I cross-checked interview responses within and across interviews and with everyday conversations, and I addressed events from different angles using narrative and event questions. I compared responses to those I collected from Georgians displaced by the war and from experts in Georgia and Russia and those collected by other researchers, often with the same participants, at the time of the war in 1992–1993 and thereafter, as well as to archival and secondary materials. These strategies helped me verify the patterns that emerged in my interviews and increased confidence in interview responses, both individually and in the aggregate.

People who spoke with me at length about their conflict experiences used to be engineers and miners; doctors and nurses; teachers, professors, and university students; writers and journalists; security and party officials; tourism and cultural workers; and farmers and housewives. Some of these people maintained their positions after the war, but others became involved in the government, the security apparatus, nongovernmental organizations, and the business sector. It took many years of postwar poverty and destruction—deepened by an economic blockade by the Commonwealth of Independent States that isolated Abkhazia—before day-to-day life returned to normality for many of my 150 respondents. One half, including women, participated in the war in different ways. Many were injured and lost family members and friends. The other half escaped the fighting in or outside Abkhazia.

My semi-structured interviews walked through respondents' life histories in the context of conflict. Questions on childhood brought up family stories of repression, respondents' early memories of intergroup friendships and enmities, and history as they learned it at school. Reflections on prewar adulthood focused on daily interactions with Georgian family members, friends, classmates, and colleagues and whether, how, and with whom respondents participated in conflict-related events before the war. Combined, these responses conveyed how respondents understood the conflict and their part in it, or collective conflict identities that situated respondents at the war's onset.

The interviews then covered in great detail the first days of the war—where respondents were, how they learned about the war, whom they talked to, what actions they took. Beyond step-by-step recollections of mobilization trajectories, I gathered narratives on whether people anticipated a war, how they viewed Georgian forces, and what motivated them to act. These responses reflected how uncertainty at the war's onset was channeled into different mobilization decisions through collective threat framing. Reflections on wartime and postwar mobilization concluded the interviews, capturing long-lasting effects of threat perceptions and mobilization decisions for how the conflict unfolded into a full-fledged war and how people continued to mobilize during and after the war to protect the segments of society that they perceived to be threatened.

These rich data present the process of mobilization as understood by the participants themselves, isolate its social mechanisms, and shed new light on the understudied case of Abkhaz mobilization. In the next sections, I draw on these data to outline how intergroup conflict developed before the war in Abkhazia, how individuals went from uncertainty to a range of mobilization decisions at the war's onset, and what this tells us about alternative approaches to mobilization in the Abkhaz case. I conclude with implications of this analysis for future research on mobilization.

Intergroup Conflict in Prewar Abkhazia

Before the Georgian-Abkhaz war of 1992–1993, Abkhazia was one of the most visited tourist destinations in the Soviet Union. Its coastal resorts were bustling with activity. Russian, the common language in the Soviet space, but also Georgian, Abkhazian, Armenian, and Greek could be heard on the streets, reflecting the demographic makeup of a multiethnic republic. According to the All-Union Census of 1989, the last taken before the war, in the population of 525,061, Georgians and Mingrelians, a Georgian subgroup, constituted 239,872 (45.7%); the Abkhaz, 93,267 (17.8%); Armenians, 76,541 (14.6%); Russians, 74,914 (14.3%); Greeks, 14,664 (2.8%); and others, 15,959 (4.8%).[6] The population of six of Abkhazia's seven districts, Gagra, Gudauta, Gulripsh/i, Ochamchira/e, Sukhum/i, Tqvarchal/Tqvarcheli, and Gal/i, was mixed; the district of Gal/i, located close to Georgia, was predominantly Georgian. Shared education, employment, and social activities tied individuals and families from different groups in institutions of neighborhood, friendship, and intermarriage. Familial and communal celebrations, assemblies, and elders' councils allowed for preservation of a distinct Abkhaz heritage. Abkhazia was a diverse and highly integrated prewar society.

But underlying the relative calm in Abkhazia were tensions that characterized everyday intergroup relations. Public gatherings, protests, and clashes took place periodically in the Soviet period. These tensions have a long history, going back to the mass deportations of the Abkhaz by the Russian Empire in the nineteenth century and the repopulation of Abkhazia, which over time produced a near majority of Georgians. The political status of Abkhazia also changed in the Soviet period. Both Georgia and Abkhazia entered the Soviet Union as Soviet Socialist Republics (SSR) in 1921 but soon established special treaty relations, and in 1931 the status of Abkhazia was downgraded to an autonomous republic of the Georgian SSR. Social policies that favored the Georgian language and culture were associated with these changes and created a sense of Georgianization among the Abkhaz.

Abkhaz men and women vividly remember uncomfortable silences and confrontations that emerged when their classmates, coworkers, neighbors, and even friends raised the issues of Georgianization and in particular Abkhazia's political status in day-to-day conversations. They tell family stories that they heard as children of the closing of Abkhaz schools in the 1940s–1950s, when their parents or grandparents could not study in their native Abkhazian language, and the rewriting of Abkhaz history in the 1960s–1970s, diminishing the role of the Abkhaz in Abkhazia's past. They recount street jokes, restaurant brawls, the inability to buy bread if they did not speak Georgian in the 1980s, and the split in society around the first violent clashes of 1989, when intergroup divides appeared in regular jobs, university, and government offices. Armed groups, the Abkhaz Guard and the Georgian paramilitary Mkhedrioni (Horsemen), were formed and became active in Abkhazia.

Many Abkhaz participated and most knew family members or friends who took part in the clashes of 1989 and other events that preceded the war of 1992–1993. As early as 1921 and repeatedly thereafter, the Abkhaz political elite and intellectuals sent letters and telegrams to Soviet authorities in Tbilisi and Moscow requesting that their group's concerns be addressed. Popular mobilization unfolded in coordination with and parallel to elite efforts, taking the ordinary Abkhaz to the streets and traditional gathering places in nearly every decade of Soviet life. In 1921, after a period of Georgian military presence in Abkhazia, Abkhaz political leaders urged the population to join the revolutionary organization Kiaraz (Self-Help), which fought to establish Soviet power in Abkhazia together with Russia's Red Army. During the Stalin era in 1931, up to twenty thousand Abkhaz gathered in the Abkhaz enclave village of Duripsh/i to protest Abkhazia's status change. Mass protests took place during de-Stalinization in 1957, Brezhnev-era economic reforms in 1965 and 1967, and stagnation in 1977–1978, as the Abkhaz sought to reclaim their language, education, and history.

During perestroika in the 1980s, broader segments of Abkhazia's population joined Abkhaz mobilization. Aidgylara (Unity) emerged as an umbrella organization of the Abkhaz national movement that united non-Georgian minorities, coordinated public activities, and was active in the government of Abkhazia. Members of Aidgylara were central to the organization of the largest gathering in Soviet Abkhazia that brought over thirty thousand Abkhaz and other minorities to the Lykhnashta field in the Gudauta district in 1989 to demand the restoration of Abkhazia's SSR status "as proclaimed in 1921." The gathering and the resulting letter to Moscow that called on Soviet authorities to address the Abkhaz demand played a catalyzing role in events leading to the Georgian-Abkhaz clashes of 1989. Yet the trigger of violence was the opening of a Sukhum/i branch of Tbilisi State University, which Georgian professors and students initiated but non-Georgian professors, students, and the broader public vigorously protested. Clashes started in an attempt to prevent entry exams and escalated into the greatest violence between ordinary people on both sides before the war of 1992–1993.

Soviet troops stopped the violence, and an investigation was launched in Georgia. The response in Abkhazia was dramatic, a general strike of up to forty thousand workers across the republic coordinated by Aidgylara. Strikers claimed that Georgian and Abkhaz authorities were biased. They demanded that the investigation be transferred to the Soviet center in Moscow and were successful. Abkhazia thereafter was relatively calm. Minor intergroup violence broke out in the following years, but nothing comparable to that of 1989.

Political institutions became the epicenter of conflict. Zviad Gamsakhurdia, the leader of the Georgian national movement that pursued independence from the Soviet Union, and his party, Round Table–Free Georgia, won multiparty elections in October 1990 and consolidated power in May 1991 when Gamsakhurdia became the first president of Georgia. In December 1990, Vladislav Ardzinba, a fervent supporter of the Abkhaz cause promoted by Aidgylara, was elected chairman of the Supreme Council of Abkhazia. These leaders took simultaneous steps to break away from and to preserve Soviet structures, respectively. Georgia proclaimed its independence in April 1991, while the non-Georgian part of the government and the population of Abkhazia sought to remain in the Soviet Union through a referendum in March 1991, which Georgia banned. In this context, Abkhazia's strengthening ties with Russia and the North Caucasus and Georgia's war in South Ossetia in 1991–1992 pushed Gamsakhurdia to strike an electoral compromise that prioritized the Abkhaz in Abkhazia's government. The Abkhaz bloc comprising non-Georgian minorities thus won a majority in the October–December 1991 elections, and the government was subsequently divided along Georgian and non-Georgian lines.

The Soviet Union collapsed, and in December 1991 the National Guard, which formed the basis of the future Georgian army, together with the Mkhedrioni ousted Gamsakhurdia in a coup d'état, to pave the way for Eduard Shevardnadze's return to lead Georgia after his service as minister of foreign affairs of the Soviet Union. The new Georgian government was engaged in a war with pro-Gamsakhurdia forces, called Zviadists, until 1993. The Georgian-Abkhaz war of 1992–1993 took place in this context of social polarization following the clashes of 1989 and the political volatility surrounding the dissolution of the Soviet Union.

Futility of Abkhaz Resistance

An outside observer would not have expected the Abkhaz to mobilize in the Georgian-Abkhaz war. There was little chance that "a group with the structural characteristics . . . of the Abkhaz would have engaged in separatist mobilization" (Beissinger 2002, 222). The individual costs of mobilization gravely outweighed its potential benefits. The Abkhaz were at a significant disadvantage in manpower and arms when the war began. The population of 5 million in Georgia and the 240,000 Georgians in Abkhazia greatly exceeded the 93,000 Abkhaz. Georgia did not have a functioning army in 1992, but its forces, which included armed units from outside Abkhazia and local supporters in Abkhazia, were more numerous than any resistance the Abkhaz could have mounted, even with other non-Georgian minorities in Abkhazia.

A state successor of the Soviet Union, Georgia inherited a large share of Soviet weapons in the South Caucasus. The former Soviet military base in Gudauta did not provide comparable access to arms to the Abkhaz. Right before the war, Abkhaz authorities had collected weapons from the population in an attempt to halt criminal activity. The only weapons the Abkhaz had when the war began were hunting rifles that some hid in their homes and arms that others took, bought, or were given at the Gudauta military base. An inflow of foreign fighters and armaments strengthened the Abkhaz force in the course of the war, but this support cannot explain mobilization at the war's onset, when Georgian forces immediately captured most of the territory of Abkhazia.

When the war began, 2,000–5,000 National Guard and Mkhedrioni troops marched into the Gal/i district, equipped with tanks and artillery and supported by helicopter fire (Baev 2003, 138; Pachulija 2010, 27; Zürcher 2007, 131). They besieged a part of eastern Abkhazia around the mining center of Tqvarchal/Tqvarcheli, along the single major road connecting the territory; entered the capital, Sukhum/i; and "shelled the parliament, forcing the Abkhaz leadership to retreat to Gudauta" in central Abkhazia (Cornell 2000, 159). As the eastern advance progressed, 250–1,000 Georgian marines landed in seaside Tsandrypsh/Gantiadi in the west (Baev 2003, 138; Pachulija 2010, 77; Zürcher 2007, 131). Joined by a local branch of the Mkhedrioni and other supporters, they "block[ed] Abkhazia's border with Russia" and moved toward the western tourist center of Gagra (Baev 2003, 138). All but central Abkhazia was soon under Georgian control.

The Abkhaz thus ran substantial risks of repression, injury, and death if they mobilized on the Abkhaz side—risks that are common in cases of mobilization against superior state forces (Wood 2003). These risks were evident as early as July 1989, when clashes that broke out in Sukhum/i spread across Abkhazia and attracted thousands of Georgians from Abkhazia and Georgia over two days. Witnesses recall that "Abkhaz leaders were writing to Russia the whole night [of July 15 and] appealed to save us: 'If you do not send the army, there will be no Abkhaz people.'" Indeed, the Soviet army's intervention, the last in Abkhazia before the dissolution of the Union, prevented further escalation. But the dominance of Georgians and the repressive capacity of the Georgian state were demonstrated: up to four hundred people were injured or killed in the clashes (Sagarija 2002, 45). Many Abkhaz participants, particularly party officials, were removed from office and criminally charged (Sagarija 2002, 60; Hewitt 1996).

Once the fighting broke out in August 1992, witnesses recount, immediate casualties occurred on the Abkhaz side, first among the Abkhaz Guard and then among ordinary people who had mobilized. Formally the Special Regiment of the Internal Forces (SRIF) of Abkhazia, the Abkhaz Guard was formed in 1991, modeled on the so-called Eighth Regiment of the Soviet army, which suppressed violence in Abkhazia before the Union's collapse. Former Soviet officers were invited to serve in the SRIF. Members of Aidgylara were active in recruitment into the force, which over a year enlisted one thousand fighters, including one hundred regulars. The guards met Georgian forces twice before the war, in an attempt to prevent their crossing the Ingur/i River in February and April 1992. However, most reservists were dismissed on the war's eve, and the post near the Ingur/i River was left largely unmanned. The few remaining guards near the entry to Abkhazia were instantly captured and imprisoned as Georgian forces crossed the Ingur/i. Fighters further along the route to Sukhum/i who opened fire and the ordinary Abkhaz who joined the Guard or mobilized spontaneously incurred the first losses as Georgian forces surrounded the territory. The Abkhaz thus "joined the armed struggle in spite of the apparent futility of resistance" (Brojdo 2008, 51).

Uncertainty at the War's Onset

Although the futility of Abkhaz mobilization may have been obvious from the outside, for the participants themselves the nature of potential violence and the risks involved were not well understood when Georgian forces entered Abkhazia. Time and again respondents in my interviews recall feeling at a loss on the day of the Georgian advance. The events came as a shock for both the Abkhaz who were part of the Abkhaz Guard and those who had not been previously recruited into its armed units. Most men and women were occupied with regular daily activities and were deeply confused as helicopters appeared over Abkhazia and thousands of troops broke into Sukhum/i and Gagra. "Tanks entered all of a sudden on August 14," witnesses say. "People were at work, at the beach. It was like thunder in the middle of a sunny day." Three questions emerged with unprecedented urgency and intensity for the ordinary Abkhaz.

Was this a war? People could not make out the meaning of the Georgian advance. Many did not believe that a war could start in Abkhazia and interpreted the events as a clash similar to that of 1989, hoping for protection from the disintegrating Soviet troops, as in the past. "We thought it would be over right away, that it was like another clash," the regular Abkhaz explain. "We felt that we were protected by the great powerful Soviet Union." The events could be understood as a policing action by Georgia. The advance took place as criminal activity was rampant on the railroad that crossed Abkhazia and civil war for control of the government escalated in Georgia. Yet the motivation behind the Georgian advance was not straightforward. "They said that they came to guard the railroad, but how can you guard the railroad with tanks?" was a question commonly asked in Abkhazia.

Related concerns stood out sharply as the Abkhaz navigated uncertainty about the Georgian advance. *Who was threatened, by whom, and to what extent?* If the Georgian action was related to railroad security or the ongoing civil war in Georgia, Georgian troops could have entered Abkhazia to pursue criminal bands or supporters of President Gamsakhurdia ousted from Tbilisi (who were ostensibly hiding in Abkhazia with kidnapped Georgian officials). But the nature of the advance was puzzling. Could Georgian troops have arrived to "settle the problem of Abkhazia once and for all," as one respondent put it, by securing Georgia's control over the territory with armed force? Would Abkhaz leaders come under attack? Would the ordinary Abkhaz and Abkhazia's broader population suffer as a result? Finally, would local Georgians join the advance? Would looming violence be intimate (Fujii 2009), involving Georgian family members, friends, neighbors, and colleagues in what was to come?

Uncertainty over the nature, subject, and object of threat posed the ultimate question. *How to act in response?* The ordinary Abkhaz did not know whether or in what capacity to mobilize on behalf of their group. Many remembered the risks of mobilization from the clashes of 1989. The Georgian capacity for mobilization was vast, and Georgia had a repressive apparatus that could be used against future dissent. While large segments of the population had mobilized in the past, most Abkhaz were not prepared for war, as relative calm prevailed during the three years after the clashes. The core dilemma for the Abkhaz was *for whom to mobilize*. Was one's own or one's kin's safety a priority over that of the Abkhaz group or the population at large, including its Georgian part? "Where could we go, run?," men and women caught up in the turmoil asked. "What to do, whom to tell, how to save, where to get weapons?"

In these conditions, at least one thousand Abkhaz mobilized at the war's onset and up to 13 percent of the population mobilized in the course of the war. This estimate is based on casualty figures. While these figures are contested, the Abkhaz report 4,040 deaths, 2,220 combatants and 1,820 civilians; 8,000 injuries; and 122 missing in action (HRW 1995, 5n1). Over 4,000 deaths, 10,000 injuries, and 1,000 missing are recorded on the Georgian side, with most of the prewar Georgian population of Abkhazia displaced as a result of the war (HRW 1995, 5n1). Mainly, the Abkhaz mobilized on the Abkhaz side when the war began, but many Armenians and other non-Georgian minorities and foreign fighters, particularly from the North Caucasus and Russia, joined in the course of the fighting (Yamskov 2009, 167–168).[7]

Most mobilized spontaneously, but some had been previously recruited into the Abkhaz Guard. A minority adopted support or fighter roles to defend Abkhazia's population as a whole, including its Georgian part, but, in general, individuals joined on behalf of the Abkhaz group. Individuals often left the relative safety of native locales for areas of intense fighting, initially the capital, Sukhum/i, and the western center of Gagra. Others stayed to protect their villages, towns, or cities or their families and friends there. Individuals shifted between these roles as the war went on. Among the people able to fight or otherwise support the Abkhaz, many, however, hid in places of relative safety in Abkhazia; fled, mainly to Russia, with kin or alone; or in rare cases defected to the Georgian side.

Approaches to Civil War Mobilization

These divergent mobilization trajectories cut across individual differences in age, family and occupation; ties to local Georgian communities; and prewar participation in Georgian-Abkhaz conflict. They cannot be explained by preferences developed before the war, as conflict experiences and group loyalty were widely expressed among the Abkhaz, yet their mobilization decisions were distinct.

Historical grievances (Gurr 1970; Horowitz 1985), community norms (Petersen 2001), and social sanctions and rewards (Weinstein 2007; Humphreys and Weinstein 2008) do not fully capture this variation. Nor do material (Weinstein 2007; Humphreys and Weinstein 2008) and security incentives (Kalyvas 2006; Kalyvas and Kocher 2007), regardless of prewar commitments, as the Abkhaz mobilized on the weaker Abkhaz side, often unarmed.

Political, cultural, and economic grievances are central in the *relative deprivation* approach to mobilization. In this approach, the difference between what people expect and what they attain underlies the relative inequality between individuals (vertical) and groups (horizontal) that motivates them to act (Østby 2013). "Large-scale group mobilization—particularly for violent actions—is unlikely to occur in the absence of serious grievances at both leadership and mass level" (Stewart 2008, 12). The risks of mobilization are overwhelmed by shared experiences of injustice (Cederman, Gleditsch, and Buhaug 2013, 25). These experiences could have prompted the Abkhaz to mobilize in 1992.

Indeed, the common themes that the Abkhaz raise when explaining their participation in the war include the change in Abkhazia's political status, Georgian demographic expansion in Abkhazia, and the so-called Georgianization of Abkhazia, which Abkhaz respondents characterize as benefiting the Georgian group relative to the Abkhaz. They note economic deprivation as well: the entity above the Autonomous Republic of Abkhazia in the Soviet state hierarchy, Georgia, controlled most of Abkhazia's economy. Leading economic posts were occupied primarily by Georgians, in part as a result of appointment in the Soviet apparatus and in part due to the small proportion of the Abkhaz in the population.

However, exclusion at the leadership level did not translate to unequal access to regular employment, where Soviet nationalities policy based on group inclusion applied, giving the Abkhaz access comparable to that of other demographic groups, at least in principle.[8] Other grievances were addressed by the Soviet authorities in Moscow and Tbilisi, especially in the last decades of the Union, on a case-by-case basis and with titular quotas favoring the Abkhaz in education and employment. As the Union collapsed, the electoral compromise struck with Gamsakhurdia overrepresented the Abkhaz in Abkhazia's government. Yet, despite the steps taken to remedy Abkhaz concerns, historical grievances remained. Still, these common motivations resulted in highly different mobilization trajectories, both in terms of participation and nonparticipation and in terms of where and for whom people mobilized in the war. How the widely shared grievances mattered in producing variation in Abkhaz mobilization for war is unclear from the theories of relative deprivation.

Whereas the relative deprivation approach struggles to answer why some individuals do not mobilize as part of the group, given common grievances, its alternative, the *collective action* approach, struggles to answer why people participate in collective action at all (Lichbach 1995, 13). This second approach to mobilization is based on the premise introduced by Mancur Olson (1965) that collective action is costly and its benefits are distributed across the relevant group regardless of individual participation. Thus free riding should be expected from individuals, but their participation can be incentivized with selective access to social and material goods. Jeremy M. Weinstein (2007, 8) summarizes the collective action problem as it applies to civil war: "Attracting recruits to participate in civil war is not an easy task. The work of rebellion is difficult and potentially dangerous. And when a rebel group sweeps to power and transforms the political regime in a country, it is difficult to exclude nonparticipants from the new freedoms that come with political change. So while the potential costs of participation make joining unattractive, the promised benefits may not tip the balance." In this approach, people reevaluate the risks of participation in civil war as armed groups motivate participation using material incentives (Weinstein 2007; Humphreys and Weinstein 2008) and social rewards and punishments that relate individual participation to prewar group ties and commitments, especially in strong communities that impose norms of reciprocity (Petersen 2001). Material and social incentives thus could have affected mobilization decisions of the Abkhaz in 1992.

Yet material rewards were unavailable at the time of mobilization. The disadvantage in manpower and arms meant that the Abkhaz saw little prospect of benefit in a dire situation of power asymmetry. With regard to material incentives, looting was observed on the Georgian rather than the Abkhaz side early in the war (HRW 1995, 6). On the other hand, the density and strength of Abkhaz social ties could have affected mobilization. These ties are based on *familia* (family name) relations and traditional Apsuara (Abkhazianness) norms, including that of reciprocity, reinforced by the history of political, demographic, and cultural suppression and the small size of the Abkhaz group. A classic strong community (Petersen 2001), the Abkhaz thus could punish nonparticipation with postwar exclusion. Some evidence of community exclusion exists, as a respondent illustrates: "[Those] who went to fight on the other side or left for Russia or Georgia . . . are traitors. My brother, for example, his wife is Georgian, they went to Moscow after the war began, then she went to Georgia and he returned. . . . I cannot accept him." In turn, participants were rewarded with postwar status and reputation. Many fighters received government posts and were awarded war medals, both highly regarded in Abkhaz society.

Nonetheless, the effects of participation on postwar status were inconsistent: both fighters and those who escaped the war would assume leadership roles. One respondent captures it well: "When they returned after the war, we could not ask them why they left since it is such a sensitive question. But they brought back money ... [and] became leaders." More important, postwar effects do not give a sense of the situation at the war's onset. Then, strong community pressures, passed through the generations in social institutions and reinforced by participation in prewar activism, applied to most Abkhaz, but not all mobilized to fight. The collective action approach leaves unanswered the question of how the social environment drew some but not others to participate in the war.

In response to the collective action program, the third approach to mobilization, what I call *strategic interaction*, posits that participation in civil war is not necessarily riskier than nonparticipation. As Stathis N. Kalyvas and Matthew A. Kocher (2007, 183) argue, "The costs of nonparticipation and free riding often equal or even exceed those of participation: while it is undoubtedly true that rebels run serious personal risks in war zones, war is very dangerous for nonrebels as well." The skills and resources that armed groups provide their members increase the security of participants in this approach and account for decisions of security-seeking individuals irrespective of their prewar preferences (Kalyvas 2006; Kalyvas and Kocher 2007). The Abkhaz could have joined the war effort to gain access to weapons, training, and safe places necessary for their survival.

The Abkhaz army formed during the war could offer these benefits of participation, but they were not available at the war's onset. Access to arms at the Abkhaz Guard barracks or the Gudauta military base was not comparable to that of Georgia's forces. Many Abkhaz mobilized unarmed or with unregistered weapons, mainly double-barreled hunting guns, stored in their homes. As a respondent recalls, "We collected weapons, and those who managed to get them went toward [the Georgian forces].... Of course, tens [of us] who got the weapons were not enough," as the Georgian forces swiftly advanced through the territory. Immediate Abkhaz casualties further showed that mobilizing on the Abkhaz side would not increase fighters' prospects of survival.

Even the guards recruited and trained prior to the war were unprepared for this advance. Most were off duty at the time; those on duty were captured or bypassed by Georgian forces. "I was very troubled," an Abkhaz commander says, "[by] an order a few days before the war to let reservists ... go and seize their automatic weapons" (interview in Khodzhaa 2009, 437). In this situation, defection to the stronger Georgian side would have offered greater safety than mobilization on the Abkhaz side. Still, defection was rare. People mobilized across areas of Abkhaz and Georgian territorial control, despite their limited access to weapons, although they could have joined Georgia, hid, or fled for their own safety.

These three approaches address different aspects of the historical (relative deprivation), social (collective action), and structural (strategic interaction) context of Abkhaz mobilization, but they do not explain the range of mobilization roles. The relative deprivation and collective action approaches shed light on the history of the conflict and the social pressures involved, yet they do not account for why some Abkhaz mobilized and others did not despite shared grievances and social incentives. Strategic interaction suggests why some Abkhaz hid, fled, or defected but struggles with why others joined, as the Abkhaz side was weaker at the war's onset and joining it did not increase but rather jeopardized personal security. How, then, can we understand the mobilization decisions of the Abkhaz?

A Sociohistorical Approach

I find that earlier experiences of Georgian-Abkhaz conflict and social networks at the time of mobilization were central to different Abkhaz decisions. In the context of intense uncertainty surrounding the first days of the war in Abkhazia, Abkhaz men and women turned to their familiar social networks to understand threat and how to act in response. National leaders, respected local authorities, friends, and relatives invoked shared understandings of the conflict to make sense of the Georgian advance. Decades of observing and participating in the conflict, with memories of the 1931 political status change, Georgian demographic expansion in Abkhazia, the closure of Abkhaz schools, and prohibition of the Abkhazian language, meant that the Abkhaz interpreted the Georgian advance as aimed at eradication of the Abkhaz position in society and Abkhazia as a unit separate from Georgia, one with an independent cultural history. As national leaders broadly articulated the threat, which local authorities then typically adapted to the needs of local defense across Abkhazia, these national and local actors produced a collective notion of the Georgian forces as threatening Abkhazia and the Abkhaz.

The emergence of collective threat framing affected how the ordinary Abkhaz perceived the threat of the Georgian advance. People realized that a war had started, rather than a clash similar to that of 1989 or a Georgian policing action, and that mobilization was necessary in response. But they did not know how to act. It was with immediate networks of family and friends that collective threat frames were consolidated into mobilization decisions, from attempts to flee to Russia, hide in Abkhazia, or defect to the Georgian side, alone or together with close family and friends, to collective mobilization to provide support or fight in one's locality or areas of utmost intensity. Small groups who mobilized together directed their mobilization to the protection of those segments of society that they perceived to be particularly threatened, from individual safety to the group at different levels of aggregation. The resulting trajectories were often surprising from the perspective of existing explanations. Directed by close family and friends, many politicized individuals fled Abkhazia to protect their own safety or that of close family and friends, whereas others who had not actively participated in the Georgian-Abkhaz conflict before the war stayed in Abkhazia and mobilized on the weaker Abkhaz side.

What does this mean for our understanding of mobilization and broader processes of conflict? The recognition of uncertainty that regular people experience when violence and war break out in their communities challenges the assumption in existing approaches of potential participants' knowledge of risk and mobilization decisions based on this knowledge. Instead of calculating whether and how to mobilize based on a particular notion of risk, potential participants have to make sense of violence—who is threatened, by whom, and to what extent and for whom to mobilize in response. They come to perceive threat in different ways, and that affects their mobilization decisions. Placing variable threat perceptions at the center of our analysis of mobilization can help explain how individuals with similar backgrounds facing similar structural conditions adopt different roles in mobilization.

Therefore, we need to rethink our approaches to mobilization to better capture the process that relates uncertainty to a range of decisions about whether and in what capacity to mobilize. Prewar conflict experiences and social networks at the time of mobilization are critical in navigating the dilemmas of mobilization. Individuals are not isolated from the history of conflict of which they are a part. Their understandings of conflict and their roles in it change before, during, and after the war, and their social networks can shape distinct perceptions of threat under conditions of uncertainty, even when drawing on the same shared narrative of conflict, to direct mobilization to the segments of society that are perceived to be particularly threatened. Understanding how different threat perceptions emerge and affect mobilization decisions requires attention to sociohistorical factors.

It also requires broadening our concept of mobilization. Mobilization in civil war does not start with the recruitment of fighters into armed groups, but is part of a prolonged social process of observation of and participation in collective action, which spans the pre- to postwar stages of conflict. During the war, it entails not simply a decision to fight or not to fight, but a range of roles from fleeing, hiding, or defecting from one's group to offering indirect or direct support or fighting on behalf of one's group locally or in areas of utmost intensity. These roles can be adopted alone or, most commonly, together with others. Scholars of political violence and war have recognized this variation.[9] I add a previously overlooked dimension of *whom* mobilization decisions are taken for, whether one's own safety or that of family, friends, the community, or the broader group, which can be defined in ethnic, national, or other terms.

This range of roles reflects the difficult dilemmas that people confronted with intergroup violence and war face about whether, how, and for whom to mobilize, especially when their commitments to different segments of society compete for salience. The choice, for example, to protect one's family over the broader group in this context, points to the agency that people exercise over their decisions, even when constrained by armed actors and the social context (Baines and Paddon 2012; Barter 2014). Scholars of mobilization should be attentive to these dilemmas to better grasp different self- and other-regarding motivations underlying various participant and nonparticipant roles.

Understanding how ordinary people adopt a range of mobilization decisions is critical for our analysis of political violence and war in general as these decisions affect the structure, capacity, and patterns of violence by armed groups (Kalyvas 2006; Weinstein 2007; Staniland 2012; Viterna 2013). Why some clashes develop into wars and some killings acquire a mass character cannot be established without a full appreciation of ordinary people's participation in these processes. Had the ordinary Abkhaz not taken up arms, Georgia's advance in 1992 may not have turned into a war that lasted over a year and displaced most of the prewar Georgian population from Abkhazia, with postwar violence and no political resolution in sight.

More broadly, looking closely at mobilization before, during, and after civil war from the perspective of the actors involved provides insight into a range of conflict processes inaccessible through a focus on structural conditions or armed group strategy. How nonviolent contention turns violent and how conflicts unfold over time to transform actors' identities are some of these processes (Tarrow 2007; Wood 2015). In this book, I demonstrate how a detailed study of a single case that is difficult to explain with existing approaches can shed light on the broader processes of transformation of violence and mobilization, which have lasting effects on societies marked by conflict.

1
STUDYING CIVIL WAR MOBILIZATION

> The unique context of a conversational interview—an exchange with a focused listener who is eager to devote time to hearing the respondent's views—allows the respondent to reflect on and even explore her own ideas, to reveal not only strong views but also worries, uncertainties—in a word, to engage human vulnerability.
>
> —Yanow and Schwartz-Shea 2006, 118

Questions of intergroup violence and war are difficult ones to study. We cannot grasp how people arrive at decisions in situations of confusion and shock that these processes bring with them if we rely only on secondary materials, archival or news sources, or elite interviews or infer people's willingness to mobilize from civil war outcomes, observed behavior, assumption of interests, or retrospective assignment of grievances that could have affected these decisions given the history of intergroup conflict. These sources may be essential to the overall research goals, but they rarely document how participants understood the reality they faced. When they do, as in memoirs, these sources are limited to the personal reflections on conflict of a few individuals and do not provide the sufficient comparative basis to make systematic conclusions about the social processes involved.

I turn to field research with the actors in Georgian-Abkhaz conflict to explore the interpretations of conflict experiences by the participants themselves. This research is based on my careful selection of the case of Abkhazia, locales within the case, and participants in the interviews that I collected in these locales. I substantiate and contextualize these interviews with participant observation in Abkhazia, additional interviews that I collected with Georgians displaced by the Georgian-Abkhaz war of 1992–1993 and with experts in Georgia and Russia, and extensive archival, news, and secondary materials. I take seriously ethnographic surprises, or unexpected narratives and observations that emerge systematically yet are unaccounted for by existing theories. I thus arrive at a novel focus in civil war studies, the centrality of uncertainty to mobilization, and the theoretical approach centered on the collective threat framing mechanism that helps account for how ordinary people navigate this uncertainty.

The following sections walk the reader through the research underlying this book, from the research design to the process of immersive fieldwork.[1] I then focus on two ethnographic surprises that drew my attention to the question of uncertainty and the collective threat framing dynamics and give a sense of the materials I use in this book by analyzing a sample interview excerpt.

Research Design

What kind of research design can allow for an in-depth exploration of the process of mobilization? Whereas many studies take a quantitative or cross-case comparative approach to examining civil war mobilization and focus on insurgent leaders,[2] my study's goal is to understand how ordinary people experience mobilization across the prewar, wartime, and postwar stages of intergroup conflict. This book, as a result, is based on a systematic study of a single case that offers wide variation in conflict dynamics across time and space and that existing approaches cannot fully explain. Abkhazia is such a case.

The Case of Abkhazia

A small area along the Black Sea coast, Abkhazia has been a place of imperial conquest, colonial rule, and intergroup conflict for centuries due to its critical geopolitical location at the intersection of the Caucasus, Russia, and the Middle East. It saw striking demographic changes as the Russian Empire established control in the nineteenth century, displacing the majority of Abkhaz. Georgian-Abkhaz conflict evolved in the context of repopulation of Soviet Abkhazia after it was formally integrated into the Georgian state structure within the broader Soviet Union. Daily tensions and episodes of nonviolent and violent contention, such as letter writing to the Soviet center in Moscow, public gatherings, and clashes, characterized the period and culminated in the Georgian-Abkhaz war of 1992–1993. The war displaced most of the Georgian population of Abkhazia and paved the way for the establishment of the contested de facto state supported by Russia. The focus here is on this war.

The term *civil war* is rarely used in Abkhazia. Locals distinguish the broader Georgian-Abkhaz conflict from the war of 1992–1993 but say that the latter was "not a civil war for us at all. There was an element of great civilian suffering— maybe this is a characteristic of civil war. [But we] see it as a clearly ethnopolitical war because the ethnic factor played such a big role here." "It was a political war," they go on to explain, "because it stemmed from the Georgian political elite. The Abkhaz were not the initiator. We simply resisted the ideas and rules imposed by the Georgian center." Indeed, the war set off with the entry of Georgia's forces into Abkhazia and Abkhaz resistance to these forces. But it unfolded with the participation of the local population in Abkhazia, a defining element of civil war, and became internationalized with the engagement of foreign fighters and Russian support on both sides in the fighting (Zverev 1996; Baev 2003).

While some scholars characterize the war as conventional (Kalyvas and Balcells 2010, 419), it presents a much more nuanced picture of warfare across the period of the war and in the areas of Abkhazia that were involved in the fighting in different ways. The war started as a case of irregular civil war in August 1992. It was marked by the relative military asymmetry on the Georgian and Abkhaz sides. Since Georgian forces entered Abkhazia when it was Georgia's autonomous part, the case best resembles other irregular wars "in weak but modernizing states bent on centralization and the subjugation of their periphery" (Kalyvas 2006, 67). Statements by Abkhaz respondents reflect this characterization: "[Georgian leaders, who] thought they were strong, that their hour had come . . . , emulated the image of the [Soviet] empire that created them. They decided that [Georgia was] the secondary imperial center that could afford such actions, but they did not recognize that they had nothing valuable to offer those territories that they were trying to colonize and occupy." As a former Georgian resident of Abkhazia who is now an official in the capital of Georgia, Tbilisi, confirms: "If we ask the Abkhaz now, they say that they wanted to gain state independence [from Georgia]. If you ask Georgians, they say that they wanted to preserve state unity, [with Abkhazia as an autonomous part]."

Indeed, Georgia was modernizing and did not have a regular army when the war began. The National Guard and the Mkhedrioni were "regarded at the time as the core of a future Georgian army," but were best described as a paramilitary rather than a regular force (Coppieters 2000, 21–22).[3] "What was called a Georgian army," Ghia Nodia (1998, 34) says, "was really a bunch of self-ruled . . . 'battalions' comprising both romantic patriots and thugs, whose activities were only loosely coordinated." "When they entered [Abkhazia in August 1992]," Abkhaz fighters confirm, "they started looting . . . , did not subordinate [to their superiors]."

The elements of irregular war, that is, Georgia's preponderance of force and subjugation of the periphery, were evident in the sheer control that these forces established over Abkhazia as they advanced through the territory during the first four days of the war. By August 18, 1992, the east and west of Abkhazia were under Georgian control, with the center left to the Abkhaz side.

A combination of irregular and conventional elements in the fighting defined the war thereafter. Irregular, poorly armed Abkhaz units engaged in the early fighting. At the war's onset, "people without arms began organizing into groups in their villages," respondents report. Some joined the fighting alongside the Abkhaz Guard. This Abkhaz force made up of volunteer groups and Abkhaz guards could not be seen as a regular army. As Christoph Zürcher (2007, 216) captures the early character of the Abkhaz force, "the organization of violence did not initially rely on an 'impersonal' state bureaucracy but, rather, on densely knit, small-scale networks of interaction that facilitated trust and cohesion."

As the Abkhaz regained the area adjacent to Russia's border in October 1992 with the help of foreign fighters, formation of the Abkhaz army formally began and the map of territorial control changed. Conventional battles with clear front lines and heavy weaponry characterized much of the subsequent fighting, including the battle over the capital, Sukhum/i, which ended the war in September 1993. But irregular warfare continued in the east until the end of the war, and the Abkhaz remained a weaker actor until that battle, as observed in the failed attacks on the capital in October 1992 and January and March 1993. This nuanced combination of irregular and conventional fighting and changes in territorial control, which could have affected ordinary people's decisions, make Abkhazia particularly suited to studying mobilization in civil war.

Research Sites

The dramatic differences with which the war began in the east and west of Abkhazia place these areas at the heart of the micro-comparative research design in this book. I leverage variation in subnational structural conditions and territorial control and individual mobilization trajectories to explore these differences. Proximity to the Russian border in western Abkhazia, where people could flee at the war's onset and external help could come from, and the former Soviet military base in Gudauta, where some weapons and a hiding place could be accessed in central Abkhazia, starkly contrasted with the situation in the east, where the administrative border with Georgia facilitated immediate establishment of Georgian control over the area. "Tqvarchal was in the blockade from the beginning of the war. They were isolated right away," respondents say. "We gave in Gagra and Sukhum . . . and had fighting in two directions, east and west, from the headquarters in Gudauta." As a result, "Gudauta and Tqvarchal [were] the only ones that did not suffer as much during the war. We did not let Georgians into these towns." My research ran along the major road connecting these field sites (see figure 1.1 and 1.2).

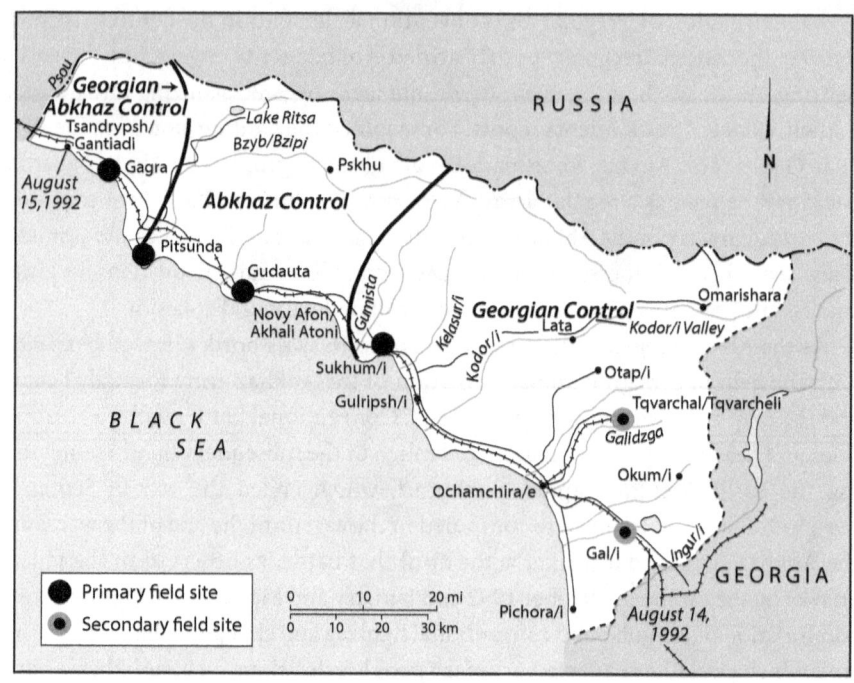

FIGURE 1.1. Research sites.

FIGURE 1.2. The road connecting research sites.

EAST: TQVARCHAL/TQVARCHELI, GAL/I, AND SUKHUM/I

I studied Abkhaz mobilization in the east in response to the Georgian advance from the administrative border near Gal/i, along Tqvarchal/Tqvarcheli, to Sukhum/i that began on August 14, 1992. The districts that these urban centers give name to differed in their demographic makeup, socioeconomic basis, and prewar intergroup conflict (see figure 1.3). I carried out fieldwork in Sukhum/i and collected interviews with former residents and additional data on the less accessible sites of Tqvarchal/Tqvarcheli and Gal/i in other areas of Abkhazia and Georgia.

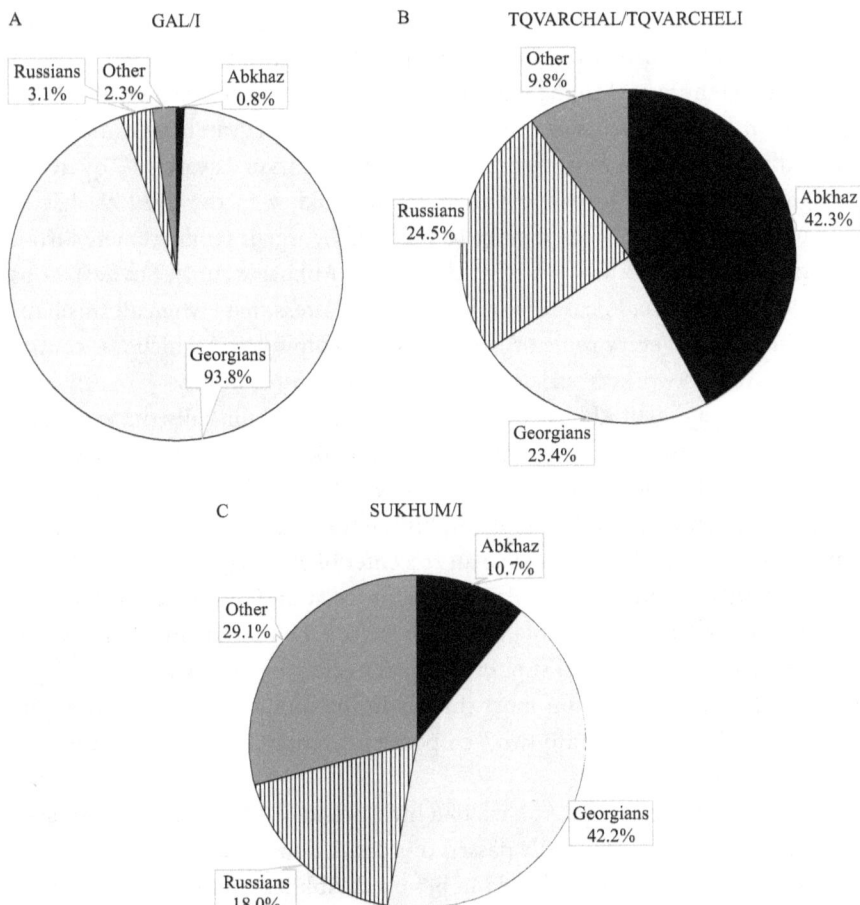

FIGURE 1.3. Prewar demographic composition in research districts: east.

Source: Official census data numbers from Trier, Lohm, and Szakonyi 2010.

Before the war, the Gal/i district was nearly all Mingrelian, a subgroup often recorded as Georgian in the Soviet statistics. An agricultural district, it was "one of the richest in the Union" and "produced nuts, tobacco," former Georgian residents recall in Tbilisi. It was relatively peaceful in the prewar period. "We lived in a very friendly way, including with the Abkhaz," former residents say. But in the 1980s, as intergroup tensions in Abkhazia intensified, the local population became active in the conflict. Georgian movement leaders organized rallies in Gal/i in response to the Abkhaz gathering and the letter to the Soviet center that called for the separation of Abkhazia from Georgia in April 1989 (Lezhava 1997, 1998). In July 1989, Gal/i residents participated in the clashes that started in Sukhum/i and spread across Abkhazia in a spree of localized violence (Sagarija 2002, 10–13).

The Tqvarchal/Tqvarcheli district, by comparison, had an Abkhaz majority and a mining town at its center—"one of the only industrial towns in Abkhazia." As in Gal/i, "there were very few interethnic problems," a former Abkhaz resident tells me in Sukhum/i. "Mining work is such that relations between people shape up differently." The events of 1989, however, involved Tqvarchal/Tqvarcheli in the conflict in a specific way as a mining town. Residents of Tqvarchal/Tqvarcheli brought ammunition to support their fellow Abkhaz in the 1989 clashes in Sukhum/i and used it in the district to hold off Georgian reinforcements from Georgia, Gal/i, and other adjacent districts of Abkhazia, until Soviet troops stopped the violence. Local respondents further stress that "when all this happened in Sukhum, every mine organized a strike committee," which was central to the all-Abkhaz workers' strike that followed the clashes of July.

Lastly, the capital of Abkhazia and the associated Sukhum/i district were relatively diverse yet were dominated by the Georgian population. Sukhum/i was the base of the Soviet government of Abkhazia as well as its intellectual elite, represented by the university, and offered multiple employment opportunities for the mixed urban population. It was also an epicenter of everyday confrontation, political contention, and violent opposition before the war. It was here that the 1989 clashes unfolded and reached high intensity before the war, involving many layers of the city's residents and support from elsewhere in Abkhazia and Georgia. People felt social polarization most sharply in the capital after the clashes. The government "simply split into two," respondents report; so did staff in the university and across vocations.

When the war began, the Abkhaz had little presence in Georgian-dominated Gal/i, and Georgian forces easily passed this district on the way to Sukhum/i. In contrast, guerrilla warfare unfolded in besieged, Abkhaz-dominated Tqvarchal/Tqvarcheli and continued during the war, along with conventional battles in the surrounding area that locals joined after the Abkhaz army was formed. Finally, Sukhum/i underwent the highest-intensity fighting in the war. Irregular Abkhaz units and Abkhaz guards attempted resisting the Georgian advance at the war's onset. The Georgian side then held Sukhum/i in the course of the war. But in September 1993, after a number of failed attacks, the Abkhaz pushed Georgian forces beyond Gal/i.

After the war, Gal/i saw the most postwar violence. Georgian armed crossings of the Ingur/i River to sabotage Abkhaz forces guarding the area, Abkhaz operations aimed at pushing Georgian units out, and underground economic activity that placed local farmers at the center of armed group confrontation in what became known as "nut racket" dominated the borderline district.

WEST: GUDAUTA, GAGRA, AND PITSUNDA

The picture was different in Abkhazia's west. The Abkhaz mobilized in response to the Georgian advance from the sea that began on August 15, 1992. Gagra was soon captured, while the tourist town of Pitsunda was contested due to its proximity to the Gagra front line, and the Gudauta military base remained under Abkhaz control. I lived and worked in each of these three locales.

Like Sukhum/i, Gagra was a mixed urban center before the war (see figure 1.4). A large Armenian presence differentiated it from other districts demographically. Located in the Gagra district, Gagra and Pitsunda attracted Georgian tourists and became sites of everyday arguments and fights between tourists and the local Abkhaz. Due to its location in far western Abkhazia, at the Russian border, the district played a unique role in the Georgian-Abkhaz conflict. Respondents recall flag bearing symbolizing the boundaries of Georgia's territory at Georgian rallies and religious processions held at the border, the Gagra stadium, and Gagra's town center. The Abkhaz here turned to more extreme forms of mobilization, such as hunger strikes. The district hosted a violent wing of the Abkhaz movement, Abrskyl (Prometheus), and a branch of the Mkhedrioni active in Abkhazia since 1989. As a result, the local population on both sides of the conflict was active in the fighting that shifted control over Gagra from the Georgians to the Abkhaz in the course of the war.

In turn, as a traditional Abkhaz enclave dominated by the Abkhaz, the town of Gudauta was a symbolic Abkhaz location. The Lykhnashta field, located nearby in the Gudauta district, was a center where the Abkhaz historically gathered to address the group's concerns. It was here that the Abkhaz came together in April 1989 to call for the separation of Abkhazia from Georgia, setting the course to the July clashes. It was in Gudauta that during the war the Abkhaz had access to some weapons of the former Soviet military base, where the Abkhaz headquarters were established in this Abkhaz-controlled area, where the front lines to the east and west were formed, where the North Caucasus fighters first arrived to support the Abkhaz offensive on Gagra in October 1992, and where the fighting and

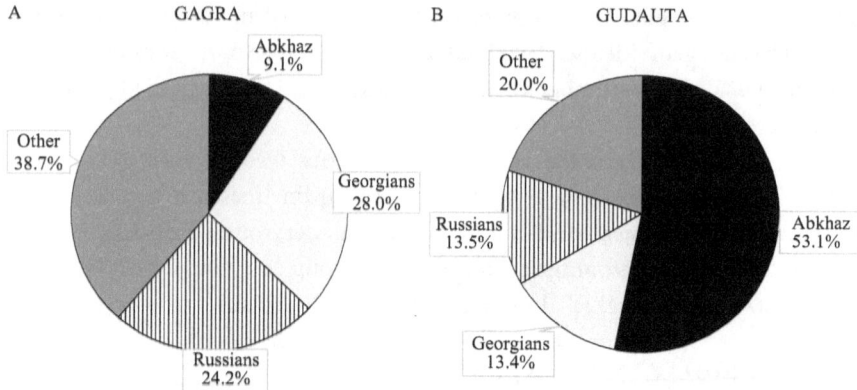

FIGURE 1.4. Prewar demographic composition in research districts: west.
Source: Official census data numbers from Trier, Lohm, and Szakonyi 2010.

support apparatuses of the emergent Abkhaz army were directed from. The heart of the Abkhaz war effort was located in Gudauta.

Variation in these sites helps me understand how, in different ways, Abkhaz men and women might have experienced the prewar conflict, interpreted the Georgian advance and mobilized at the war's onset, and engaged with the conflict thereafter. Despite the differences in structural conditions and territorial control across these locales, I discovered that the process of mobilizing for war was similar in the east and west of Abkhazia.

Research Participants

Who are the people whose life stories underlie this process? The book is based primarily on 150 in-depth, semi-structured interviews with 142 individuals on the prewar, wartime, and postwar Georgian-Abkhaz conflict, conducted mainly in the fall and winter of 2011 in Gagra, Pitsunda, Gudauta, and Sukhum/i (see table 1.1). In each site, I spoke with individuals recruited into Abkhaz movement organizations, particularly the Abkhaz Guard, before the war; those who mobilized for war spontaneously, without prior recruitment into the Abkhaz Guard; and those who did not fight.

The respondents are equally distributed across the locales and mobilization trajectories, with a balance achieved between participants and nonparticipants. Organized and spontaneous fighters constitute 17 percent and 83 percent, respectively, which reflects actual mobilization patterns. The male-to-female ratio captures the gendered nature of mobilization, with fighting dominated by men and women represented in the support and nonfighter roles.[4] To account for age

TABLE 1.1. Research participants

			TOTAL	PERCENTAGE (ROUNDED)
General information	Gender	Male	99	70
		Female	43	30
	Self-identified	Abkhaz	127	90
		Other	15	10
	Age	<50	72	51
		>50	70	49
	Location	Eastern mobilization	45	32
		Sukhum/i	45	32
		Western mobilization	97	68
		Gagra	42	28
		Pitsunda	36	26
		Gudauta	19	14
Prewar	Occupation	State	29	20
		Nonstate	113	80
	Mobilization	Organized	45	32
		Spontaneous	43	30
		None	54	38
Wartime mobilization	Fighters	Organized	14	10
		Combat	13	9
		Male	13	9
		Female	0	0
		Support	1	1
		Male	1	1
		Female	0	0
		Spontaneous	69	48
		Combat	50	35
		Male	50	35
		Female	0	0
		Support	19	13
		Male	12	8
		Female	7	5
	Nonfighters		59	42
	Male		23	16
	Female		36	25
Postwar	Occupation	State	42	30
		Nonstate	100	70
	Mobilization	Organized	59	42
		None	83	58

Source: Reprinted with permission from Shesterinina 2016, 416, table 1.
Note: Based on 150 interviews with 142 research participants.

and status in mobilization for war, I distinguish young adults under the age of thirty at the war's onset from adults over thirty years old, who likely had families and jobs at the start of the war. When the war began, Abkhaz authorities announced a general mobilization of the population, which included individuals between eighteen and forty years old (Ardzinba 2004, 6). However, units of older men between thirty-five and sixty-five years old were formed to carry out some difficult tasks, such as attacks in the open. Losing these older men in battle was perceived to be a necessary sacrifice. A small percentage of individuals under the age of eighteen participated in the war as well, even though Abkhaz authorities included them in the protected persons category and they were not required to join the Abkhaz war effort. The respondents' broad range of backgrounds helps check prewar factors that could shape wartime decisions and postwar allegiances that could influence how people viewed and discussed the conflict with me (see also under "Triangulation").

Examples of mobilization trajectories that emerge from this interview strategy include a teacher who did not participate in prewar Abkhaz mobilization, fled Abkhazia during the war, and stayed in Russia thereafter; a librarian who participated in the prewar all-Abkhaz workers' strike, among other mobilization events, fled Abkhazia during the war, and returned to her post after the war; a student who did not join the mobilization before the war, hid in Abkhazia during the war, and then became an economist; a researcher who was part of the organizing committee of a local Aidgylara (Unity) branch but hid in Abkhazia during the war and became a staff member of a local museum after; a nurse who did not mobilize before the war but joined the war effort as part of the support apparatus and later became an activist; a journalist who was active in Aidgylara and maintained his role as a war journalist to take a leading position in the postwar government; a driver who organized prewar hunger strikes, joined a volunteer defense unit when the war began, and became a leader of a local veterans' group; a policeman for whom mobilization was prohibited before the war but who mobilized on the Abkhaz side to join the security apparatus after; and a tourism worker who joined the Abkhaz Guard after participating in the 1989 clashes, mobilized for war as part of this armed structure, and opened a local business in the challenging postwar climate.

These varied trajectories from no prewar mobilization and prewar activism to a range of nonparticipant and participant roles in the war and postwar periods challenge some of the common explanations that exist in the literature on mobilization. For example, prewar activism deemed to be critical for future mobilization did not always translate into wartime participation or postwar activism in Abkhazia. Of 142 respondents, 20 without prior mobilization joined the war effort and 27 active in the prewar conflict, including leaders of the Abkhaz movement, did not mobilize for war. Similarly, 31 who were part of the Abkhaz army by the end of the war did not continue their mobilization into the postwar period, while 52 maintained their commitment to the cause and 13 who did not participate in the war joined postwar mobilization as part of the Abkhaz police and army active in border defense and military operations, respectively.

This variation in backgrounds and roles in the prewar, wartime, and postwar intergroup conflict that individuals adopted across the research sites allows for systematic study of mobilization inaccessible through a focus on elite interviews, archives, or secondary literature.

Research Process

The conversations that I had with the people who invested valuable time and invited a stranger into their daily lives were formalized as interviews and held informally as part of participant observation and were central aspects of my research process.

My research in Abkhazia began with meetings in the nongovernmental sector, the de facto government, and community groups in 2010. I explored the feasibility of working in an isolated de facto state, finding individuals with distinct mobilization trajectories, and discussing the Georgian-Abkhaz history. I discovered that security limitations on fieldwork existed in the eastern border area, but I could access other sites and individuals needed for the study. I also discovered that people were less willing to talk about postwar violence than prewar and wartime conflict. This careful entry to the field focused my research on the four primary and two secondary sites, which would achieve comparative leverage without compromising my security as a researcher or that of my research participants, and on my interviews on prewar and wartime mobilization appropriate for the local environment. These and other choices that I made before, during, and after my core fieldwork in Abkhazia are part of the overall care and attention with which I have approached questions of research ethics and protected my research participants in an ongoing way across the life span of this research (Fujii 2012).[5]

The insight that I gained during the exploratory trip guided my core fieldwork in Gagra, Pitsunda, Gudauta, and Sukhum/i and collection of primary and secondary materials on Tqvarchal/Tqvarcheli and Gal/i in 2011. I learned that organizational affiliation could raise suspicion in Abkhazia's highly politicized postwar setting and worked unaffiliated, as one of the only solo researchers in Abkhazia at the time. Many locals referred to me as a journalist, but I stressed that I was a university student gathering recollections of the conflict for my doctoral dissertation.

My Russian language ability and Canadian background provided a peculiar balance of proximity and distance, an insider-outsider status, that enabled my research. Had I not been a Russian-speaking foreign woman, I might not have accessed respondents who saw me in distinct ways. Women quickly accepted me as a younger woman, as exemplified by their openness to engage in collective mourning with me—an intimate activity in war-torn Abkhazia. Men treated me as a researcher and disclosed accounts that they would not have shared with other women, as I was invited to join male tables at communal celebrations and male-only gatherings.

As I moved through my field sites across Abkhazia, I gained trust with locals by seeking approval from mayors and police for my fieldwork, which many asked about, and through a prolonged, engaged presence and research activities in each locale. My day was structured around interviews, carried out in the offices of local town halls, respondents' homes, and public areas, including parks and cafés, and archival work. It was important that I was *seen* collecting books, documents, and news excerpts in local libraries, archives, or museums. It was equally important for me to *be present* at the communal or war-related events that I was invited to. To many potential interviewees, this routine meant that I was indeed a researcher with whom they could share sensitive, often appalling, personal stories of violence and war. My unaffiliated status further implied that I did not accede to any position on the conflict and would not challenge my respondents' views.

Local gatekeepers, including members of mothers' and veterans' groups, whom I met during my exploratory trip, introduced me to my first respondents in each field site. These community leaders had the knowledge of local mobilization inaccessible through other sources and would "vouch for [my] legitimacy" (Peritore 1990, 366). Traditional network referrals by the gatekeepers and first respondents provided the initial stage of my interviews in each site.

I located respondents in other ways as my local networks grew. Informal conversations and observation of events pointed to potential respondents who were not identified earlier, such as fighters noted during war-related meetings and events and police officers reported present in the Georgian-Abkhaz border area. I approached these individuals in their workplace as appropriate, in what I call the *targeted selection* strategy. This strategy helped avoid institutional and personal referral biases and characterized the second stage of my interviews.

However, as I sought to fill in a broad range of roles in the mobilization continuum, I added to it new roles that consistently emerged in interviews and participant observation. For example, protected persons whom Abkhaz authorities ordered not to fight in the war were a novel category that required additional interviews. I sought respondents in these roles in the third stage of my interviews.

At each stage, I selected from my multiple network referrals and targeted selection only those respondents who helped achieve a balance across the mobilization continuum.

Interviews

The life histories that these respondents shared with me followed the prewar, wartime, and postwar paths in the context of Georgian-Abkhaz conflict. Our in-depth conversations invited departures from my questions and emphasized my role as an engaged listener: I used the semi-structured interview plan to guide rather than determine the course of the conversation (see box 1 for examples of questions in interviews with former fighters).[6] In response, people conveyed "not only strong views but also worries, uncertainties" (Yanow and Schwartz-Shea 2006, 118). Respondents revealed their personal positions through stories, silences, and physical gestures that signaled their "thoughts and feelings" (Fujii 2010, 232). This discursive dynamic helped me discern the meanings that the ordinary Abkhaz attributed to the conflict, from prewar social interaction, political affiliation, and participation in everyday confrontation, political contention, and violent opposition to the interpretation of the Georgian advance and mobilization at the war's onset and thereafter.

Box 1

Part 1: Childhood

"Where were you born?"
"What stories did you hear from your parents and grandparents when you were growing up?"
"Were you friends with Georgian neighbors and classmates?"
"What language did you learn at school?"
"Did you learn the history of Abkhazia?"
"What traditions do you remember following at home and in your neighborhood?"
"Who came to family gatherings and community celebrations?"
"Did you participate in youth organizations?"

Part 2: Prewar Adulthood

"Where were you before the war?"

"What did you do?"

"Where did you study or work after school?"

"Was it difficult to enrol in a university or find a job?"

"Did you discuss the issues of Abkhazia's status with your Georgian friends and colleagues?"

"Were there tensions between the Abkhaz, Georgian, Russian, and other local residents?"

"Were tensions different with Georgian visitors from outside of Abkhazia?"

"Did you participate in the activities of the Abkhaz national movement?"

"How did you get involved in the Abkhaz national movement?"

"What problems did the Abkhaz national movement raise and how?"

"Did you participate in demonstrations, clashes, and strikes?"

"How did you learn about demonstrations, clashes, and strikes?"

"Who organized and joined demonstrations, clashes, and strikes?"

"Did your friends and colleagues participate in demonstrations, clashes, and strikes?"

"Why was there unrest every ten years in Abkhazia?"

"Why did the situation worsen in 1989?"

"How did the Georgian-Abkhaz clashes of 1989 unfold?"

"How did the clashes affect your relations with Georgian friends and colleagues?"

"Did you join the Abkhaz Guard after the clashes?"

Part 3: The War's Onset

"Where were you on August 14, 1992?"

"What were you doing?"

"How did you learn about the Georgian advance into Abkhazia?"

"What did you do next?"
"Whom did you talk to when you learned about the advance?"
"Did you mobilize alone or together with others?"
"Whom did you mobilize with?"
"Where did you go?"
"How did mobilization take place in your locality?"
"Who organized and joined your fighting unit?"
"Did you have weapons?"
"How did the fighting start?"
"Were there casualties on the Abkhaz side?"
"Did you anticipate the war?"
"How did you understand the risks associated with the war?"
"What motivated you to participate?"

Part 4: Wartime Experiences

"In what capacity did you enter the Abkhaz force?"
"Did you retain your initial role in the fighting when the Abkhaz army was formed?"
"How did your role change?"
"Did you continue fighting with your friends when armed units were restructured?"
"How did the fighting progress?"
"Who participated in the war on the Abkhaz side?"
"Where did weapons come from during the war?"
"Did your Georgian relatives, neighbors, friends, and colleagues participate in the fighting?"
"Which battles were particularly important for you and why?"
"Were there greater losses on the Abkhaz side in some battles than others?"
"How did the war end?"
"Do you regret participating in the fighting?"
"What does the Abkhaz victory in the war mean to you?"

> ## Part 5: Postwar Conflict
> "What happened after the war?"
> "What were your greatest concerns?"
> "Were there killings, robberies, and acts of revenge in the city?"
> "Was the situation different in the border area?"
> "Did you continue participating in the Abkhaz postwar defence?"
> "What was your role as part of the Abkhaz postwar defence?"
> "What groups engaged in clashes, crossfire, and fighting on the Abkhaz and Georgian sides?"
> "How did postwar violence affect displaced Georgians returning to Abkhazia?"
> "How did the postwar situation change over time?"
> "Why did the situation worsen in 1998?"
> "What happened in 2008?"
> "Why was the Kodor/i operation successful in 2008?"
> "How did the 'liberation' of Kodor/i affect the situation in Abkhazia?"
> "Do you anticipate fighting in the future?"
> "Should Georgians displaced from Abkhazia as a result of the war return to their residence?"

The first, childhood part of the interview focused on the stories that Abkhaz respondents recalled hearing at home, in school, and on the street; the relations that they had with their Georgian relatives, teachers, classmates, and neighbors; the language that they spoke (Abkhazian, Georgian, and/or Russian); and the history of Abkhazia as they learned it. How the attitudes on Georgian-Abkhaz conflict formed in the family and local institutions and were reinforced at the national level, including through education policy, became apparent in this discussion (see chapter 3).

The next, prewar adulthood part of the interview focused on the university experience, intergroup relations in the workplace, and participation in the prewar conflict. It was at this stage of life that individuals formed social ties that positioned them differently in the conflict, as nonparticipants or participants in everyday confrontation, political contention, and violent opposition in the context of Abkhaz movement organizations or spontaneous collective action. Through these experiences people formed shared understandings of the conflict and their roles in it, making it a critical part of the interview to understand how Abkhaz men and women in different state and nonstate positions related to the conflict as part of their group before the war (see chapter 4).

The central part of the interview focused on August 14–17, 1992. I asked respondents to reconstruct the events of the first days of the Georgian-Abkhaz war to the finest detail that they could recall, exploring how they learned about the Georgian advance into Abkhazia, whom they talked to when they heard about the advance, and what actions and with whom they took them in response. I followed up with narrative questions on perceptions of the war's onset. "Did you anticipate the war?" "How did you understand the risks associated with it?" "What motivated you to participate or not and in what capacity?" These were among my questions. The result is a richly detailed set of mobilization trajectories, with sequences of individual actions situated in the context of structural differences in the locales, social networks at the time of mobilization, and the broader conflict (see chapter 5).

The last parts of the interview focused on the continued wartime and postwar conflict. Respondents reflected on whether they changed their mobilization decisions in the course of the war after observing or participating in the early or later violence. They discussed how their roles in the war effort and their social ties shifted in the context of the Abkhaz army's formation, as armed units were restructured and the nature of fighting changed. They remembered how the war progressed through the battles that they observed or participated in and the Abkhaz force transformed from the weaker side at the war's onset to push the Georgian force beyond Abkhazia at the end of the war. In the discussion of war-related events, I similarly followed up with narrative questions on the ways in which respondents perceived the risks of continued mobilization and saw particular battles as more or less salient in the context of potential Abkhaz loss in the war (see chapter 6).

The interview concluded with questions on postwar Abkhazia. I asked how respondents perceived the Abkhaz victory in the war and whether and why they participated in the continued Abkhaz mobilization in the Georgian-Abkhaz border area. Those comfortable doing so spoke of postwar violence in the area, including Georgian guerrilla activities, the recurrence of fighting, and ongoing displacement of local Georgians. This discussion was important for understanding the continuation of Georgian-Abkhaz conflict after the war, which is frequently but incorrectly described as "frozen" (see chapter 7).

Participant Observation

Interviews constitute the core of the analysis in this book, and I contextualized them with informal interaction and participation in social rituals, meetings of organizations, and local events in present-day Abkhazia. Participant observation demonstrated the remarkable presence of the war and the intensity with which it is memorialized in everyday life and on special occasions.

Daily rituals of coffee drinking and dinner toast making and conversations at communal celebrations, such as weddings, were an invaluable source of information that helped me better understand what some stories, silences, and gestures might mean in the interview. For example, women's accounts of war participation often focused on fathers, brothers, husbands, and sons and were followed by silence. The consolation that women offered one another after this silence over coffee implied that the telling about men's sacrifice was a way of coping with the loss and the need to ask about women's own participation once these stories were told in the interviews.

Similarly, many men recounted their war paths in great detail, as if they had told the story in the past or prepared for the interview. Table traditions indicated why this was the case, as preservation of war memories was institutionalized in this social setting. Every dinner started with a toast to the Almighty, followed by one to those killed in the war, and invited recollection of the fighting. Corrections of one another's stories, rumors about some men who did not participate in the war, and jokes about others' self-glorifying tendencies that emerged in this and other contexts helped me check and further probe the accounts presented by the relevant individuals in the interviews.

I compared these accounts to the official conflict narrative. For instance, former fighters used the term Patriotic War, I noted, in speeches at war memorials, medal award ceremonies, and victory celebrations, whereas those disillusioned with the war, such as mothers of disappeared fighters or fighters who were not awarded a medal, did not. How people differently affected by the war perceived it was evident in meetings of mothers' and veterans' groups. Injured fighters, for example, created or joined new networks after the war to reflect their wartime experience.

Triangulation

Participant observation thus served as one of my main tools of triangulation, helping me address issues of memory and potential bias in my interviews. In particular, participant observation helped me develop follow-up questions that could get at important aspects of mobilization that respondents would not discuss otherwise, as in the example of women's silences, and cross-check interview responses with my knowledge about people's past that emerged through my daily interactions, as in the example of rumors about men who did not fight, and through the official conflict narrative that became apparent during war-related meetings and events. Respondents often began with the official narrative of the war as a Georgian attack on Abkhazia but then departed from this narrative in their accounts after my follow-up questions. In combination with interviews, participant observation exposed the dilemmas of war participation in the current social context in Abkhazia, focusing my attention on questions of guilt, regret, responsibility, and the moral choices of my respondents (Shesterinina 2019).

Beyond participant observation, my triangulation strategy involved cross-checks within and between the interviews. Combining event and narrative questions about the war that took place twenty years ago helped recover memories from different angles (Viterna 2006). Some respondents left out details and then added them as I shifted between event and narrative questions, such as "How did you learn about the Georgian advance into Abkhazia?" and "Did you anticipate the war?," respectively. For example, a then construction worker in Gagra answered the former question by referring to the televised message of the Abkhaz leadership. "On August 14, the announcement came that a war began between Georgians and the Abkhaz." He went on to discuss Georgian violence at the war's onset. It was after I asked about whether he expected the war that he clarified details of the prewar confiscation of weapons from the population, the village gathering that he went to once he learned about the Georgian advance, and the decision that he made with his friends to work on the fortification of his village when the war began.

Comparison across my interviews and those collected by other researchers at the time of the war and a decade after (Bebia 1997, 2011; Khodzhaa 2003, 2006, 2009) helped me evaluate whether and how wartime processes and postwar affiliation affected what people remembered and told me (Wood 2003). I paid particular attention to how people spoke about their wartime experiences in relation to others and how my respondents who were interviewed by other researchers spoke about their experiences then and now. Respondents referred to one another when discussing their shared experiences of the war, and responses in my and other researchers' interviews were closely aligned, which helped me corroborate and reconstruct my respondents' wartime paths. Individuals in distinct postwar positions recalled the war in similar ways despite their present-day ideological differences, which increased my confidence, in that postwar affiliation did not shape what respondents told me about their trajectories during the war.

Additional primary and secondary materials supplemented these mobilization accounts. Interviews with former Georgian residents of Abkhazia affected by the conflict and academics and policymakers in Georgia and Russia, conducted in the spring of 2013, and a vast array of local studies, documents, and news sources that I collected in libraries, archives, and museums, highlighted inconsistencies in the narratives on the broader Georgian-Abkhaz conflict, which I reconciled through triangulation. For example, reconstructing mobilization in prewar Abkhazia would not be possible without comparing interviews, Soviet criminal investigation reports, and Abkhaz, Georgian, and Russian academic research on these events. Nor would it be possible to trace the patterns of postwar violence without the Abkhaz news archive and the data for internal use that I received access to. Overall, these materials reflected the structural context of mobilization.

Ethnographic Surprises

While secondary materials revealed the contested nature of the history of Georgian-Abkhaz conflict, the most surprising aspect of my research was the consistent narratives in interviews and participant observation, which I did not expect given the existing theoretical knowledge that I consulted in designing my research and drawing my initial conclusions during fieldwork. Lorraine Bayard de Volo (2013, 220) refers to these unanticipated insights as "ethnographic surprises" and focuses on "the implicit meanings associated with activism" that these surprises help uncover. I use ethnographic surprises to distinguish the effects of existing theories and develop an alternative explanation that better captures unexpected yet systematic narratives and observations that emerge during fieldwork. Two such surprises emerged systematically during my fieldwork and shaped the question that I focused on and the theoretical framework that I develop in this book.

Research Question: Mobilizing in Uncertainty

One of the most surprising aspects of my field research was the recurring references to the intense uncertainty that surrounded the Georgian advance into Abkhazia in mid-August 1992. In designing my research, I followed other scholars who understand civil war mobilization as a problem of overcoming the high risks that potential participants face in settings of violence and war (Roger D. Petersen [2001], Elisabeth J. Wood [2003], and Jeremy M. Weinstein [2007]). As a result, I selected the sites with different structural characteristics that could have posed diverse risks to potential participants in the war in areas defined by varied patterns of territorial control by armed actors (Kalyvas 2006).

When entering the field, I expected participants in my research to refer to the wartime risks that they faced, especially in light of the sheer numerical disadvantage on the Abkhaz side in the war and the precedent of the Georgian preponderance of force established during the clashes of 1989. I expected respondents to calculate their mobilization decisions based on these risks and differently so in the east and west of Abkhazia, which were characterized by the distinct access to weapons, escape routes, and hiding places and patterns of territorial control by the Georgian and Abkhaz sides in the war. As one of Doug McAdam's (1988, 70–71) sources describes such calculation when joining the 1964 Freedom Summer in the United States, "What are my personal chances? . . . I shall be working in Forrest County, which is reputedly less violent than Nesoba County. . . . All considered, I think my chances of being killed are 2%, or one in fifty."

None of my respondents or those of other researchers in Abkhazia, however, engaged in such calculation. Instead, respondents described the situation at the time of the Georgian advance as one of intense uncertainty, which suggested to me that they did not have the knowledge of risk that observers often assume or attribute retrospectively. From the first day of my interviews and consistently thereafter, my research participants said that they did not understand what was going on or whether it was a war or simply a clash similar to that of 1989, three years before the war. Most did not believe that a war could possibly start in Abkhazia in the first place.

This consistent, unanticipated insight in the field motivated me to focus on the concept of uncertainty and redefine the question guiding my research, from why individuals mobilize in civil war despite the high risks involved to how ordinary people navigate uncertainty of the war's onset to adopt a range of mobilization decisions. Consequently, along with the questions that I prepared in advance of my field research, such as "Where were you on August 14, 1992?," "How did you learn about the Georgian advance?," and "What did you do next?," I asked about whether respondents anticipated a war and how they saw the risks associated with the advance.

The contrast between the regular pace of life before the advance and the bewilderment and confusion that respondents experienced when they learned that Georgian forces entered Abkhazia was evident across formal interviews and informal conversations, with the exception of a few individuals. Hours before the advance, people engaged in usual activities—they were at the beach, going to work, or visiting parents—and planned their next days. It was "regular life" and "everything was in order," respondents sum up. The "disruption" of this normalized routine by the Georgian advance was conveyed in terms such as "no one expected/understood/realized" what was happening. Many "thought it was a clash/like in 1989." "This cannot be," respondents recall saying to one another as they described their "panic/shock/disbelief" in response to the "outbreak/eruption" that was "sudden/quick/abrupt" with "noise/crowds/leaving work/running to streets/cars stopped/people discussing something emotionally," producing "complete chaos."

Taking seriously how Abkhaz men and women spoke about the war shaped the analysis, in the approach that Edward Schatz (2013) calls "ethnographic sensibility," defined as "being sensitive to how informants make sense of their worlds and incorporating meaning into our analyses" (Simmons and Smith 2017, 126). In particular, I took note of references to the expectation of war, as indicated by prior knowledge that respondents conveyed about the possibility of the Georgian advance and their preparation for it, for example, through the purchase and stockpiling of weapons, and their descriptions of the advance, as exemplified by the terms listed above that respondents repeatedly used to express the sense of uncertainty. I drew on grounded knowledge of these terms that I developed over time to understand who anticipated the war, for whom the war came as a shock, and who did not see the Georgian advance as a war at all. The differences that emerged during my fieldwork challenged the common assumption of a given notion of risk with which potential participants are expected to calculate their mobilization decisions and offered a greater appreciation of variation in the perceptions of risk (see also "Theoretical Framework" below) that exist when violence and war set off in a society. I explore these differences in detail in chapter 5.

Theoretical Framework: Collective Threat Framing

The second ethnographic surprise that emerged in my fieldwork was that so many of my respondents, even if they were highly politicized and participated in Abkhaz activism before the war, fled the territory when the war began, often with their family members and friends. In turn, many others without an activist past remained in Abkhazia and mobilized on the weaker, Abkhaz side in the war, often unarmed. This challenged the key theoretical expectation that I had when entering the field, namely, the importance of prior activism for future mobilization.

As McAdam (1986, 76) writes in his Freedom Summer study, "Activists are expected to be more integrated than nonactivists into networks, relationships, or communities that serve to 'pull' them into activism." High-risk activism in particular "will grow out of a cyclical process of activism and deepening personal and ideological commitment to the movement" (77). Yet variation in the mobilization trajectories that was apparent in interviews and participant observation in Abkhazia put in doubt the expectation of activist history, including participation in the violent Georgian-Abkhaz clashes of 1989, as a predictor of wartime mobilization.

When I drew my initial conclusions during fieldwork, I also expected that grievances (Gurr 1970; Horowitz 1985), social and economic incentives (Petersen 2001; Weinstein 2007), and pleasure of collective action against injustice (Wood

2003) could explain mobilization in Abkhazia. But these factors were similar for many of my respondents, whereas their mobilization decisions were not. What, then, could help me understand how people went from confusion and shock at the war's onset to a range of mobilization decisions, from fleeing to fighting on their group's behalf?

How people spoke about their perceptions of risk that emerged soon after the Georgian advance began gave me an indication of the process that was involved in this transition. The experience of intense uncertainty in my respondents' accounts was repeatedly followed by the depiction of Georgian "forces/troops/marines" as "strong/brutal" and the realization that they "invaded" Abkhazia with "heavy weaponry/artillery/tanks/helicopters," "shooting at the beach and civilians/crushing resistance/taking into captivity/imprisoning" Abkhaz guards in a show of "aggression/violence/attack/military action." "Everything happened so quickly," respondents indicate that they came to terms with the reality of war, Georgian forces "attacked abruptly" and "the war started."

However, where did these perceptions come from? Two paths emerged in the course of my fieldwork, that of a minority who learned about the Georgian advance by virtue of being positioned in its midst, in what I call *situational threat perception*, and that of most respondents who engaged in the complex social process of information filtering, which I call *collective threat framing*. Most men and women in Abkhazia came to understand the anticipated risk, or threat, associated with the Georgian advance as information on the advance filtered across social networks that they interacted with in daily life. This information was articulated and adapted in the national and local settings, respectively, to be consolidated into different and often surprising mobilization decisions at the quotidian level, with immediate social networks of family and friends. As a result, people understood risk differently, as mainly directed to their own safety, that of their families and friends, their locality, or the broader group, and adopted different roles, from escaping the fighting alone to mobilizing to areas of high-intensity fighting together with their immediate social networks, which reflected whom they mobilized to protect.

I traced this mechanism in each interview, paying particular attention to the "sequential processes" in the Abkhaz case (George and Bennett 2005, 13). I noted the source of information about the war and location at the time of mobilization, which suggested the importance of some networks for threat framing and mobilization decisions, for example, those in one's hometown. I noted the content of messages, with a focus on different framings of threat. Threat perceptions were evident in the acknowledgment of this information by use of the terms of alarm listed above. I then differentiated between individual and collective actions taken in response to the received information to chart the organized and spontaneous participant and nonparticipant trajectories.

Uncertainty at the war's onset was in general followed by information filtering from the national to local and quotidian levels and mobilization decisions across a range of participant and nonparticipant roles related to individuals' threat perceptions. In the first step, actors across society addressed each other in an attempt to frame the Georgian advance as threatening the group and its different collective identities. Second, people referred to this framing in how they learned about and perceived the advance. Third, those who reported to have perceived threat as directed primarily to their own safety often escaped the fighting alone. Those who prioritized threat against family and friends, locality, or the broader group mobilized with their immediate social networks to defend these aspects of their group in hometowns or areas of high-intensity fighting, such as the capital. Tracing the sequence of events helped me reconstruct step-by-step individual mobilization trajectories at the war's onset. I aggregated and placed these trajectories in the context of broader pre- and postwar mobilization in Abkhazia in the last stage of analysis.

Sample Interview Excerpt

The sample interview excerpt (see box 2) illustrates how I reconstructed mobilization trajectories from the prewar to war and postwar stages in Abkhazia and placed mobilization for war in the context of the broader Georgian-Abkhaz conflict.[7] The sample is taken from a three-hour interview recorded in a 6,500-word transcript. I present only a short selection here, with any identifiers that could point to the respondent replaced with a two-em dash or general affiliation, location, and time period, a strategy that I follow throughout the book.

Box 2

1. Prewar Stage

Q: Where were you before the war? What did you do?
A: Arabs, Mongols, Greeks, Romans all invaded us and we always won. On the land that our people has lived on for a thousand years, such a people cannot be defeated. We have always fought not for our language or our appearance but for *our territory*.

Note: Begins with the official conflict narrative.

I worked as a history teacher, then headmaster. For a short period I was——of the *gorkom* [city committee] of the Komsomol . . . , then of the Union of Public Education. . . . Division was always present, [for example, in] *appointments of leading specialists*. . . . One cell in the Education Department worked on questions popular in Tbilisi during Gamsakhurdia['s presidency] of *closing of the Abkhaz cultural center*. . . . They antagonized the local population, had meetings about the *removal of the Abkhazian language and closing of the Abkhaz school*.

We did not organize such large meetings. But I was part of the popular forum *Aidgylara*. . . . The steps we took were not militant, but appeals to the [Soviet] center in *letters*. . . . There was some reaction, but due to Georgian influence in Moscow, it was difficult to resist, [particularly] when Shevardnadze was in the Central Committee of the Communist Party.

There were *clashes*, especially when Gamsakhurdia was in power [in Georgia]. They marched from Tbilisi to the river Psou, held a service at [the border], thereby declaring that [Abkhazia] was originally Georgian, that there will be no Abkhaz schools or state language here. In *1989, the events were similar to a war. Many died, were arrested, taken to Tbilisi*. . . . But a large-scale war did not happen then. . . . Nonetheless, those who stood with [Gamsakhurdia] here then got directly engaged in preparing for a war. . . . They *created an armed group* called the Mkhedrioni. . . . The Abkhaz Guard . . . resisted [them] and created a *counterbalance*. . . .

Then the Supreme Council [of Abkhazia] headed by Ardzinba suggested . . . a confederal basis . . . , but there were those who rejected that in Georgia: "Why negotiate when we can simply take [Abkhazia]?" It was fashionable across the Soviet Union to rob trains, and so under this pretense they [advanced]. But *how can you protect the railroad with tanks?* They started preparation and *momentarily this all happened in August*. We suspected something, but even that day when we saw ships, we could not tell—a ship is a ship.

2. Wartime Stage

Q: *Where were you on August 14, 1992? How did you learn about the Georgian advance into Abkhazia? What did you do next?*
A: I was in [the west] that moment. An hour later, *my friend found me and said that the* [Georgian] *marines were landing in* [the west]. *"How the marines?" "The marines!"*

Note: Reenacts reaction with confused facial expression and gestures.

They crossed the border there. By then there was a *message on TV* about the beginning of *aggression*. Tanks crossed [in the east]. Here, the marines. Forty to forty-five of us gathered at the beginning in [the west]. Mostly people had shotguns. Some had hunting rifles. The Abkhaz Guard came. They were from the young generation, eighteen-to-nineteen-year-old boys. . . .

We moved toward Gagra. Here *[the head of] administration* gathered the people . . . [and] said, "There are *battles, shootings, the aviation.* . . ." We decided, given our small numbers, the lack of weapons . . . to *retreat and organize a town defense*. The head of administration held the last negotiations with [Georgians]. They entered the city, encircled the administration. . . .

[I]n three days, we got to [the Gudauta district]. From there the resistance began. . . . We were in a depressing state . . . , defended the front line but did not have enough people. . . .

We *had no regular army* at first. . . . I was in the headquarters from the beginning and fought as a soldier. . . . We had two unsuccessful attempts, but then in one take *freed Gagra*.

When Gagra was freed, a serious preparation for war began. An *army was created*, subdivisions, garrisons, battalions, structures. There were not enough experienced people. But there were professionals who had experience in Russia, served in the Union. . . . Whom we could find . . . , we organized training [with them] to seriously *prepare the resistance*. . . .

3. Postwar Stage

Q: What happened after the war?
A: To say they were cruel and we were not would not be true. It does not work that way. If you are shot at, you shoot.... You have to kill in your war, otherwise you won't win.... *To say that everything was clean after the war, this is impossible.* Imagine the people who returned to their houses, the houses were robbed and burned. And so the resistance to the remaining Georgian population took place..., people were burned alive..., constant raids took place in the Gal district..., killings.... It was difficult the first two to three years....

Note: Transition from the official narrative to the dilemmas of participation.

Military actions... did not only take place during the war, but after the war as well in the Gali district.... In 1998, this was a *small war*, very serious events.... We had enough strength by then. Abkhazia was *not the same with the war experience* and an *understanding of what [Georgian actions] meant.*...

If to think deeply, where did these Georgians grow up? They all came from Georgia in the 1940s. Their children and grandchildren were born here. In the Gagra district, 75 percent of all financial institutions, businesses, when democracy started, were taken by them. All the bars at the resort were under direct control of Tbilisi. *What were they lacking?* ...

Our people won because we *suffered so much throughout history*.... Abkhazia was a republic when it entered the USSR [Union of Soviet Socialist Republics]. In May 1931, we were turned into a [Georgian] autonomy. After the 1940s, the Abkhaz lost our language and schools. My mother, her mother, studied in Georgian schools [to] *Georgianize* us.... *We lived through all this.*

The respondent begins with the official narrative on the Abkhaz belonging to Abkhazia and the history of defending this territory from various aggressors. He then discusses prewar Georgian-Abkhaz conflict, focusing on everyday confrontation in the employment setting in public education, where his Georgian colleagues were appointed to leading state-level positions and advocated the closing of Abkhaz schools and prohibition of the Abkhazian language; political contention reflected in the Abkhaz movement's letter writing to the Soviet center and Georgian marches and demonstrations in Abkhazia; and violent confrontation in the Georgian-Abkhaz clashes of 1989, which demonstrated the Georgian preponderance of force and repressive capacity through the deaths and injuries of some participants and imprisonment of others and led to the formation of armed groups on both sides in the conflict.

The respondent conveys the experience of sheer shock at the war's onset by reenacting facial expressions, gestures, and exclamations, such as "How the marines?" "The marines!" National articulation of the Georgian advance as aggression on television, local adaptation to the needs of Gagra's defense by its head of administration, and quotidian consolidation of the decision to mobilize for town defense with a friend become evident in the account of the war's onset. Transformation of the Abkhaz force through training and battles characterizes the remainder of the war.

However, the dilemmas of participation arise in the postwar stage of the interview when the respondent acknowledges violence by the Abkhaz committed against Georgians during and after the war and contextualizes the Abkhaz victory through the prior history of Georgianization in the social, political, and economic realms. This respondent thus followed the trajectory from prewar membership in the Abkhaz movement to spontaneous mobilization with friendship networks following collective threat framing at the war's onset and a continued role in the nascent Abkhaz army, with the postwar period marked by the defense of its military victory.

In the following chapters, I situate this and other mobilization trajectories conceptually and theoretically and relate the prewar, war, and postwar stages of Georgian-Abkhaz conflict in a detailed case study of Abkhazia.

2
A SOCIOHISTORICAL APPROACH TO MOBILIZATION

> The values, norms, practices, beliefs, and collective identity of insurgents . . . [were] not fixed but evolved in response to the experiences of the conflict itself, namely, previous rebellious actions, repression, and the ongoing interpretation of events by the participants themselves.
>
> —Wood 2003, 19

A common assumption in the literature on civil war is that individuals know the risks involved in mobilization and calculate their decisions to participate or not in the war and in what capacity on the basis of this knowledge. Historical grievances, socioeconomic incentives, and in-process benefits of participation are offered as explanations for why individuals turn to participation, despite the high risks of doing so. Where the assumption of risk associated with participation is challenged, it is because nonparticipation is argued to be as risky as engagement in the fighting, with the expectation that individuals will join the side that provides the skills and resources for survival (Kalyvas and Kocher 2007). In the Abkhaz case, the Georgian advantage in manpower and arms and the precedent of the intergroup clashes of 1989 that demonstrated the preponderance of Georgian force before the war of 1992–1993 would suggest that the Abkhaz should not have mobilized on their group's behalf due to the overwhelming risk of participation in the war. Yet many did, whereas others escaped the fighting. How can we explain this variation?

In my sociohistorical approach, people do not operate with a given notion of risk, but come to understand the anticipated risk, or threat, of mobilization by drawing on earlier conflict experiences and the social networks that they are embedded in. My theory of mobilization in uncertainty thus answers two questions: How are people faced with war related to one another and the history of the conflict of which they are a part? How do these factors interact in mobilization?

I start from a simple premise. Mobilization decisions at the civil war's onset cannot be separated from people's prewar conflict experiences and the social setting in which they find themselves at the time of mobilization. Rarely do people act by forgoing their knowledge of conflict. Yet social networks can channel this knowledge in surprising ways. Those who were not politically active before the war can collectively adopt the roles that place them in the midst of high-intensity fighting, whereas political activists who are expected to mobilize on behalf of their group can turn to the protection of families and flee from violence with them.

These mobilization decisions are often made in small groups that experienced conflict together before the war—experiences that relate individuals to each other in powerful ways. Relatives join armed units together, bound not only by kinship ties but also by a family history of intergroup conflict. Community members form local militias to protect their neighborhoods from imminent violence. University friends, colleagues, and participants in prewar violent and nonviolent events call on each other to defend their collectivity. In each of these cases, people draw on their shared experiences of conflict to navigate the uncertainty of the war's onset.

Combined, prewar conflict experiences and social networks at the war's onset help individuals faced with violence understand who is threatened, by whom, and to what extent and decide for whom to mobilize in response to the violence. This combination of historical and social factors in mobilization helps explain why individuals with similar backgrounds often adopt different roles in mobilization. The collective threat framing that unfolds has implications for how people engage in the continued war and postwar conflict processes.

The argument that I advance calls for a reconceptualization of mobilization to reflect its sociohistorical foundations. The concept that I develop departs from the view of civil war mobilization as isolated from prewar conflict dynamics and thus appreciates it as an ongoing process. It also surpasses the fighter-nonfighter dichotomy that exists in civil war studies by incorporating a range of mobilization repertoires that emerge before the war and a continuum of roles that actors move along during the war and after.

I focus on the process of mobilization to develop a grounded understanding of why so many Abkhaz joined the fighting, whereas others escaped to relative safety. This discussion challenges the assumption of a given knowledge of risk by the potential participants in civil war and places what I call the *collective threat framing* mechanism at the center of how regular men and women come to perceive threat in the uncertainty of intergroup violence and war and how the social construction of threat affects mobilization.

The Concept of Mobilization

Any concept of mobilization should incorporate a discussion of who the participants are, how they relate to one another, and what actions they undertake collectively. I define *mobilization* as an ongoing process involving organization of and participation in collective action (see figure 2.1). This definition captures the ongoing nature of mobilization, the relationship between the actors involved, and the collective action that is the outcome of mobilization. In addressing each of these aspects of mobilization in turn, with illustrations from the Abkhaz case, this discussion clarifies the scope of the book.

Mobilization as an Ongoing Process

The first step in redefining mobilization in this book is the recognition of its ongoing nature. Mobilization in civil war does not start with recruitment of fighters by armed actors, but is a continuation of day-to-day intergroup interaction, political contention, and violent opposition—repertoires (see under "Collective Action") characteristic of societies that experience civil war. This is one of the central ways in which my argument departs from the common view of mobilization in the civil war literature as separate from preceding intergroup conflict.

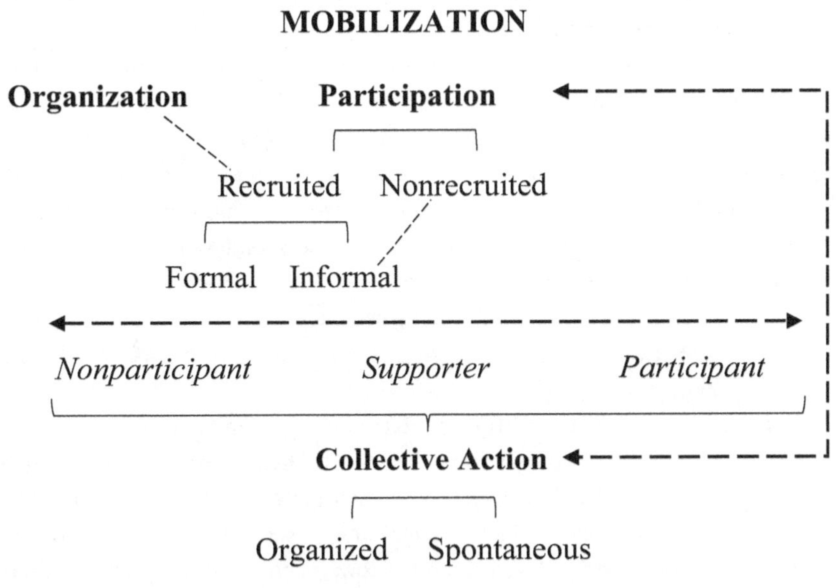

FIGURE 2.1. The concept of mobilization.

This literature in general conceptualizes civil war as a phenomenon that is isolated from broader conflict (Sambanis 2004) and follows a separate logic (Kalyvas 2006). It distinguishes civil war from other forms of violence and political contention writ large (Tarrow 2007; Wood 2015). In his foundational text, for example, Kalyvas (2006, 22) argues that "war and peace are radically different contexts that induce and constrain violence in very different ways." Seen as "armed combat within the boundaries of a recognized sovereign entity between parties subject to a common authority at the outset of the hostilities," civil war differs from contentious action in intensity and form (Kalyvas 2006, 5). In terms of intensity, the losses of life, resources, and infrastructure from the fighting are incomparable to other forms of contention (Gurr 1986). In terms of form, if contention is a challenge to the state with a monopoly of violence, civil war is defined by the breakdown of this monopoly (Kalyvas 2006, 23). As a result, the logic of violence in civil war centers on armed combat over territorial control in a sovereign state.

This underlying characteristic of civil war, Kalyvas finds, shapes civilian collaboration with armed actors, or the support roles on my mobilization continuum (see under "Participation"). It conditions people's choices in ways that align their preferences with wartime patterns of territorial control and distance these choices from commitments and loyalties developed before the war. Civilians support those actors who are in control of the territory in which they find themselves during the war. They provide support irrespective of prewar preferences, as survival is the primary goal of civilians, and armed actors controlling the territory can offer protection in return for support.

In a similar vein, Weinstein (2007) brackets prewar contention and views mobilization as recruitment that takes place during civil war, which, as I show below, is one of the different ways in which individuals mobilize for war. Weinstein argues that due to the risks of rebellion and people's tendency to free ride on its benefits, wartime recruitment depends on the resources that armed groups have at their disposal. Armed groups' economic and social endowments attract low-commitment consumers seeking short-term gains and high-commitment investors dedicated to the cause of rebellion, respectively, and are associated with the different violent strategies that armed groups pursue toward civilian populations (Weinstein 2007, 9).

Civil war is thus seen as a distinct analytical category, a phenomenon sui generis, and is studied in isolation from the broader field of contentious politics (McAdam, Tarrow, and Tilly 2001). How individual preferences (Kalyvas 2006) or armed group resources (Weinstein 2007) are shaped through prewar conflict is not part of the analysis, but, as I discuss below, is central to the organization of and participation in wartime collective action. Looking at prewar contention helps understand why so many Abkhaz mobilized for war in areas where Georgian forces instantly established territorial control, absent the promise of material rewards for participation on the Abkhaz side, which challenges two central aspects of the strategic arguments that bracket prewar processes.

Although civil war differs from prewar contention in intensity and form—it is deadlier and structured around sustained armed opposition—by viewing civil war mobilization as unrelated to prewar contention, we risk overlooking the ways in which prewar conflict is causally related to civil war. "Extreme political violence," Nicholas Sambanis and Annalisa Zinn (2005, 1) rightly point out, "does not occur in a vacuum." Rarely do civil wars break out in societies without a history of intergroup conflict, as exemplified by the mass mobilizations that preceded violence in Yugoslavia, the South Caucasus, and the Baltics as the Soviet Union collapsed (Kaufman 2001; Petersen 2001; Beissinger 2002). As Sidney Tarrow (2007, 589) finds, "Hiving off civil wars from other forms of contention ... downplay[s] the relationship between insurgencies and 'lesser' forms of contention."

This relationship is generally seen as one of escalation of conflict to war. Studies of escalation demonstrate that civil wars can emerge from other forms of nonviolent and violent political contention as they escalate in scale, frequency, or the widening of mobilization repertoires (Sambanis and Zinn 2005; Davenport, Armstrong, and Lichbach 2008; Gutiérrez Sanín and Wood 2014). In the Abkhaz case, the events of 1989 that brought the Abkhaz and Georgians in Abkhazia into face-to-face violent confrontation are typically characterized as part of Georgia's "escalation of tension with the minorities" (Cornell 2000, 151). "The events leading up to the war of 1992–1993 were to follow one another at high speed," Bruno Coppieters (2002, 99) summarizes the escalation to the war.

However, the lens of escalation commonly used to relate prewar processes to civil war falls short in identifying microlevel dynamics of violence and mobilization. That few Abkhaz expected a war despite the clashes of 1989 and few violent events took place in Abkhazia after the clashes, while the conflict continued at the state level, challenges the linear escalation story. The concept of escalation is too broad to capture the nonlinear ways in which prewar conflict affects civil war dynamics, that is, "what kinds of noncivil war contention they come from and how they evolve internally" (Tarrow 2007, 592).

Riots and clashes (Varshney 2002; Wilkinson 2004), demonstrations and strikes (Jasper 1997; McAdam, Tarrow, and Tilly 2001), and everyday resistance (James Scott 1985) can appear at different points in the conflict's history, without escalating to civil war. As Adria Lawrence (2010, 145) captures this complex relationship, "Conflict need not be violent; violence need not reach the level of war; and the causes of violence may differ from the causes of other forms of conflict." Yet forms of nonviolent and violent prewar contention can affect the dynamics of civil war in other ways, for example, by shaping an ideology or a collective identity (Chenoweth and Lawrence 2010).

Drawing on this insight, I argue that each episode of prewar mobilization in Abkhazia had a microlevel dynamic of its own, even if placed in the broader context of the century-long conflict with Georgia (see chapter 3). As a result, events of conflict at the microlevel did not always follow the macrolevel conflict narrative (Kalyvas 2003). For example, while the elite in Georgia and Abkhazia adopted the dominant narrative of Abkhazia's separation from Georgia in the context of the Soviet collapse to describe Abkhaz prewar mobilization, the clashes of 1989 were triggered by the opening of the Sukhum/i branch of Tbilisi State University, rather than the separatist conflict that unfolded at the macro-elite level. Participants on the ground saw the events as an attack on the Abkhaz identity and turned to this shared view at the war's onset to define the Georgian advance into Abkhazia in August 1992 as the continuation of this attack.

What I understand by the ongoing nature of mobilization in this book, then, is not its part in the escalation of conflict to war, but rather the ways in which nonviolent and violent prewar events affect potential participants in the war. These effects are twofold. First, participation in and observation of prewar everyday confrontation, political contention, and violent opposition shape shared understandings of conflict in the group. Second, these repertoires, some of which are organized by political movements, situate potential civil war participants in relation to one another and the broader group, to establish expectations of their roles in the conflict, be it as national or local leaders of the movement, its recruited members, nonrecruited participants directly or indirectly involved in collective action, or nonparticipants observing the events.

These two aspects of conflict identities—shared understandings of conflict and one's role as part of the social networks involved in mobilization—transform through collective action and orient decisions to mobilize at different points in the conflict. The ongoing nature of mobilization thus means that potential participants' identities invoked in wartime mobilization are deeply endogenous to prewar conflict and continue to evolve through collective action before, during, and after the war. The following sections unpack the aspects of organization, participation, and collective action in my concept of mobilization to then relate prewar and wartime factors in the process of mobilization.

Organization

The aspects of organization and participation in my concept of mobilization are broadly associated with two sets of actors, "first movers [and] late joiners," identified in civil war studies (Kalyvas and Kocher 2007, 182; Fearon and Laitin 2003).

Activities of the core group of political activists in the context of intergroup conflict reflect the aspect of organization, which includes formation of movement organizations, accumulation of material and social resources, recruitment of participants, articulation of the program for action and coordination of collective action in advancement of movement goals, and creation of links with other movements at home and abroad (Weinstein 2007; Staniland 2012).[1] As Christian Davenport, David A. Armstrong II, and Mark I. Lichbach (2008, 8) observe, "Active rebels recruit before civil war, practicing rebels instigate others to protest before civil war, experienced rebels attack authorities. . . . Indeed, what is most important about the diverse insurgent strategies . . . is that in every case, pre–civil war behavior . . . is . . . important for understanding latter conflict behavior."

Central to our understanding of wartime mobilization, prewar activities of the activist core, even if not directly related to future rebellion, establish the structure of leadership and membership on which armed groups are modeled at the war's onset. As Paul Staniland (2012, 17) shows, "Prewar political parties, students' and veterans' groups, and religious organizations, among others, are repurposed for rebellion." In particular, leading activists at the national and local levels are expected to become part of the insurgent leadership and local commandership, respectively, and their prewar recruitment and local activism form the basis of armed units that mobilize when civil war begins. "Absent any such 'mobilizing structure,' incipient movements . . . lack the capacity to act even if afforded the opportunity to do so" (McAdam 2003, 289).[2]

Among the prewar organizational activities that contributed to the wartime mobilization capacity of the Abkhaz are formation of Abkhaz movement organizations, above all Aidgylara (Unity); recruitment of fighters into the Abkhaz Guard by Abkhaz political leadership with Aidgylara's active involvement; the efforts that Aidgylara put into the distribution of information in society and coordination of such events as the Lykhny gathering of 1989 seeking separation from Georgia and the strike that followed the clashes of the same year; and attacks on Georgian authorities by the more extremist wing of the movement. Most of the non-Georgian population did not view these actions of the Abkhaz political and intellectual elite as rebel or insurgent and considered Abkhaz officials who were active in prewar organization as a legitimate part of the government. Yet their actions laid the structural and ideological basis of Abkhaz armed forces modeled on the Abkhaz Guard and volunteer groups that mobilized at the war's onset. Activists capture the importance of prewar organization for war: "Information and organization wise, Aidgylara did a lot to unite the Abkhaz people into one fist. . . . The organization was open. It held congresses, [did] explanatory work, improved [Abkhaz] ties with the Adyg people [who supported the Abkhaz during the war]. . . . Apart from the distribution of weapons, ideologically everything was done."

Participation

These activities were far-reaching in the Abkhaz society, as most observed, participated in, or had relatives and friends who participated in the prewar events organized by the movement, especially the Lykhny gathering and the strike of 1989. But surely not all Abkhaz were members of the movement. Some participated in prewar conflict outside movement structure or were touched by it through nonorganized conflict processes, such as everyday confrontation. Experiences of the core group of movement activists, who simultaneously occupy the roles of organizers and active participants in collective action and cross the aspects of organization and participation involved in mobilization, are distinct from and may not convey the effects of prewar conflict on the ordinary men and women who participate in conflict in other ways.

While many Abkhaz were drawn to participation in prewar events by relatives, friends, classmates, and colleagues who were active in the movement, not all participants were formally recruited.[3] Some participated in prewar demonstrations, strikes, and clashes by virtue of being in the midst of these events, situationally. Alternatively, regular Abkhaz with no membership in movement organizations prompted each other to participate informally in daily interactions. For example, parents sent their children to enlist in the Abkhaz Guard when the armed structure was formed. This blessing illustrates another form of participation, direct and indirect support for the cause through symbolic or material contributions. Lastly, many Abkhaz had no prewar experience of mobilization, even if they supported the cause, but observed the conflict in day-to-day life.[4] An individual was thus exposed to the conflict in one way or another by being part of the group.

These forms of prewar participation relate to mobilization in civil war. Individuals who become insurgent leaders and fighters, the categories most studied in civil war research, as well as local commanders (Wood 2015; Hoover Green 2018), participants in the support apparatus (Parkinson 2013), and nonparticipants,[5] less explored in the literature, interact before the war as part of the core group of activists or as participants in or observers of movement activities and conflict processes outside the context of political movement. This range of roles is akin to Petersen's (2001) spectrum of mobilization roles, which includes neutrality, unarmed opposition to the state, direct support for rebels, and membership in a rebel group, particularly as fighters. I add indirect or symbolic support and local command as important separate roles to Petersen's spectrum.[6] As Petersen (2001, 8) says, "A great deal of variation exists in the types of roles that individuals come to play during sustained rebellion."[7]

Not only the roles are heterogeneous, but individuals "often follow multiple paths to the same participation outcome" (Viterna 2006, 1).[8] Mobilization trajectories that extend from prewar participation engage individuals in civil war in different ways. Individuals recruited into prewar organizations typically follow what I call the *organized trajectory*, which gives participants access to the organizational hierarchy, mobilization skills, and resources, including arms in the case of existing armed groups. Those who do not hold membership in prewar organizations or avoid prewar activism altogether but mobilize for civil war follow the *spontaneous trajectory*, which does not give immediate access to the organizational structure available to prewar members.[9] Critically, people with either mobilization past can follow the *participant trajectory*, which includes support and fighting roles on the mobilization continuum, and the *nonparticipant trajectory*, which takes individuals away from the fighting. The latter trajectory suggests a combined effect of prewar and wartime factors in mobilization. Even if individuals share a history of political activism, they can be convinced to flee or hide by the social networks with which they meet the war.

In Abkhazia, the organized and spontaneous trajectories differentiated individuals who were recruited into the Abkhaz Guard before the war of 1992–1993 and mobilized as part of this armed structure when the war began and those who mobilized spontaneously into volunteer defense groups, commonly referred to as *opolchenie* in Russian. Bound by prewar ties, most individuals recruited into the Abkhaz Guard mobilized with other guards under the established command structure when Georgian forces entered Abkhazia. Those who were not recruited into the Guard but nonetheless mobilized did so with groups of relatives and friends who often bonded through participation in prewar activism and violent intergroup opposition.[10] "Many were in the Guard, [and] they were given weapons and uniforms," respondents summarize the difference, whereas others "mobilized with what [they] had. Some went with sticks." The latter either joined Abkhaz Guard units in the fighting or continued to mobilize separately. However, even the most politicized individuals left Abkhazia, most commonly with their next of kin.

Thus, actors can be formally recruited into the movement, join prewar collective action informally, or not participate at all. They can move in and out or combine these roles (Petersen 2001; Parkinson 2013). In the war, the roles transform to insurgent leadership, local command, membership in the fighting and support apparatuses, and nonparticipation. This range of shifting roles along the participant, supporter, and nonparticipant continuum represents the aspect of participation in my concept of mobilization (see figure 2.1).

Collective Action

Collective action is the combined outcome of organization and participation by actors across this range of roles. This aspect completes my concept of mobilization.

	Spontaneous		Organized
	←-------------------------------------→		
Repertoire	Everyday confrontation	Political contention	Violent opposition
Examples	Language use, social customs, jokes, brawls	Written protest, public gatherings, demonstrations, strikes	Intergroup clashes, riots, armed conflict
Social setting	Family, friendship networks, acquaintances, strangers	Elite, public (includes family, friendship networks, acquaintances, strangers), organizations	Organizations (includes elite, public)

FIGURE 2.2. Collective action continuum.

I refer to repeated nonviolent and violent forms of collective action that take place in the course of conflict as mobilization repertoires.[11] These repertoires range from spontaneous to organized depending on the movement's involvement (see figure 2.2). At the spontaneous end of the continuum are the repertoires not organized by the movement but with participation of individuals regardless of whether and how they have been recruited into the movement, whereas those closer to the organized end involve informally and formally recruited participants.

Everyday confrontation lies at the spontaneous end.[12] This widespread repertoire marks people's day-to-day lives in the context of intergroup conflict. Customs excluding individuals and groups from engaging in social activities, the use of jokes and derogatory language, and arguments and brawls among strangers, classmates, colleagues, neighbors, friends, and relatives in public and private settings are examples of forms of everyday confrontation. An observer describes its common occurrence in prewar Abkhazia:

> We had a magnificent bar on the fourteenth floor. Four, five well-dressed Abkhaz men came and began singing an Abkhaz song, when Georgian [tourists] intruded: "You have no right to sing your Abkhaz songs here. This is the Georgian land." Can you imagine this? That in our own home we could not sing our own songs and someone told us not to. . . . The Abkhaz continued to sing. Georgians threw a champagne bottle on the table and a brawl began. They took it outside. Georgians called their own—other tourists; the Abkhaz, their own from Pitsunda. I was afraid that they would smash the windows. They all shouted. One Georgian woman was screaming: "This is our land, our sea!" I called the police. But she denied she said that and they let her go.

The next repertoire, political contention, involves spontaneous and organized elements.[13] Written protest, public gatherings, demonstrations, and strikes attract a wide range of recruits and nonrecruited participants, often coordinated by movement members. The Aidgylara-led Lykhny gathering of 1989 is an example. Activists discuss the events that brought over thirty thousand people, including the elite, to seek the restoration of Abkhazia's status, with a formal letter sent to Moscow and violent opposition that followed:

> We Abkhaz had to preserve ourselves. A question about an Abkhaz plebiscite emerged. On March 18, 1989, we held the Lykhny gathering. The Abkhaz people all came. So many attended that there was no place to stand. Even [Soviet] party [members], whom we did not expect, showed up. We called on Russia to at least merge us with [Russia's] Krasnodar Krai, to save us, [as] we were not Georgian in any way. All [those present] signed [the "Lykhny Letter"]. Once we made this appeal, [Georgians] went out of control. They organized such an event [in Sukhum/i]! All streets were closed. They did the same at the stadium in Gagra on April 9. Our [Aidgylara members] went there, tried closing off the streets, so that no clash would happen. But people clashed anyway.

The collective action closest to the organized end of the continuum is violent opposition. While this set of repertoires involves organization on the part of the movement, especially when it is sustained in the form of systematic intergroup clashes, riots, or civil war, collective action can unfold spontaneously and individuals can begin their participation spontaneously, without formal recruitment into organizations being involved. The clashes of 1989 are exemplary. One instance of this violence began with an attack on an Aidgylara photojournalist, who drove to the Rustaveli Park in Sukhum/i to photograph Georgian demonstrators protesting against the Lykhny gathering. A witness describes what followed: "Georgians attacked [him], beat him up, and took his camera . . . , hit the car with hands, feet, and trash cans. *Milicija* [police] tried pushing Georgian demonstrators away and rolling out the car, when an Abkhaz crowd approached shouting: 'Ours are being beaten!' And that was it . . . , a clash began." Aidgylara messengers then informed those active in the organization across Abkhazia's districts of the violence, and many joined the violence as the clashes continued.

The spontaneous-to-organized continuum of prewar collective action does not suggest a linear pattern of escalation, but reflects complex conflict dynamics where these repertoires can emerge at different times in the conflict, take place simultaneously, often in interaction, and change in the course of conflict. Seen through the lens of everyday confrontation, political contention, and violent opposition, it is clear that prewar conflict dynamics implicate not only members of movement organizations and other active participants in prewar mobilization but also a broad range of groups in society, from families and friends, to neighbors, classmates, and colleagues, to strangers. Bearing witness to and participating in various capacities in these prewar repertoires over time shape how ordinary people across these social groups come to understand the conflict of which they are a part and relate to one another as participants in collective action, movement supporters, or simply members of society exposed to conflict in daily life through intergroup interaction.

The Process of Mobilization

Taken together, these aspects of the concept of mobilization point to the general process of mobilization that spans the pre- to postwar periods. This process involves three main stages: formation of collective conflict identities in the prewar period; their invocation in collective threat framing at the stage of the war's onset, which affects individuals' threat perceptions and mobilization decisions; and their continued evolution in the course of the war, with implications for the ways in which conflict participants treat wartime and postwar outcomes.

Stage 1: Collective Conflict Identities

Viewed as an ongoing process, mobilization begins long before the onset of war, with prewar intergroup interaction that shapes what I call *collective conflict identities*, or self-perceptions in relation to and as part of broader conflict. A collective conflict identity in the context of intergroup conflict is akin to Roger V. Gould's (1995, 13) "*participation identity . . . ,* [or] the social identification with respect to which an individual responds *in a given instance of social protest* to specific normative and instrumental appeals" (emphasis in original). Following Gould (1995, 14), I see a conflict identity as "the particular identity whose normative and practical implications are relevant for successful recruitment." In other words, the concept concerns those aspects of an individual's identity that develop in the course of conflict so as to inform decisions about whether and how to mobilize for war. "Multiple, competing, and interdependent identities . . . , [or] 'role[s]' that an individual plays, such as 'mother,' 'activist,' 'peasant,' or 'youth,'" in my view, are conflict identities insofar as they affect wartime mobilization (Viterna 2013, 44). For example, a mother, while not joining the fighting herself, can play a critical role of blessing her child to fight. In this example, the mother's conflict identity is that of the symbolic supporter in mobilization, an identity that is often adopted with others in a similar position. Mothers' groups that emerge during or after the war, then, serve to sustain this collective conflict identity, where the roles of "war's symbolic supporter," "fighter's mother," or even "bereaved parent" overlap.

I extend this notion in a number of ways. Whereas Gould (1995, 20) stresses "the importance of formal organizations for the creation of *new* collective identities" (emphasis in original), I argue that organizational experience is not necessary for the development of collective conflict identities. Organizations are one, but not the only, context in which people come to form shared understandings of conflict and their roles in it. Staniland (2012) and Sarah E. Parkinson (2013) focus on this context in civil war, arguing that membership in nonmilitant and militant organizations repurposed for or involved in rebellion shapes social ties that structure or sustain armed groups.

As the discussion of participation and collective action shows, however, individuals are exposed to intergroup conflict before the war as part of social networks that stretch beyond organizations. They share prewar experiences of everyday confrontation, political contention, and violent opposition across the quotidian or daily family and friendship ties (Parkinson 2013), local community and organizational affiliation (Staniland 2012), and macrolevel connection to the group's elite. Prewar experiences as part of these multiple social structures shape shared understandings of conflict and people's roles in it that constitute collective conflict identities.

Hence, the Abkhaz came to understand the nature of the Georgian-Abkhaz relations from narratives of conflict that they heard as children and that continued to take shape through daily intergroup interaction within family, neighborhood, organizational, and state settings. As a result of these interactions, the issues of Abkhazia's political status, Georgian demographic expansion, and repression in the Soviet period defined people's perception of the self in relation to the conflict as part of the Abkhaz group that was being dissolved in the Georgian mass. Absorbed early on, this self-perception affected prewar intergroup relations, as the underlying political issues became a taboo in private and public, creating tension between the Abkhaz and Georgians.

This self-perception is not static but evolves in the course of participation in prewar conflict. As Wood (2003, 18) finds in the El Salvador context, through participation in political activity insurgent supporters developed "a new political identity . . . reflecting the fact that once-quiescent campesinos had for over a decade contested the authoritarian practices of landlords and the state." The self-perception in relation to and as part of the conflict in Abkhazia evolved as the Abkhaz participated in repeated arguments and fights with friends and strangers, appeals to the state through letter writing to the Soviet center, demonstrations and strikes, and armed clashes that had at their core the underlying issues of the conflict and over time transformed into a separatist program among the Abkhaz, in part as a reaction to the calls in Georgia in the 1980s to further diminish Abkhazia's status.

Experience of intergroup violence is particularly significant in this process of the evolution of conflict identities. Participation in violence, Fujii (2009) finds, confers powerful identities on individuals as part of the group that enacts it. In the Rwandan case, "acts [of killing] constituted the group as a particular kind of social actor with a particular identity" (175). In Abkhazia, the violent clashes that broke out in 1989 polarized society. Teams split and armed groups were created on both sides in the conflict, with many participants in the clashes joining these groups. Transformation in intergroup relations, from the underlying but largely contained tension to polarization after the clashes, vividly illustrates the evolution of collective conflict identities. Abkhaz respondents are clear that after 1989 their perspective on the conflict and their part in it changed dramatically. "We were woken up in 1989," nearly all respondents say. "We were now certain about their [Georgians'] hatred toward the Abkhaz. This was one of the factors that helped us unite."

Importantly, the prewar experiences on which these identities are based need not be direct, but can involve observation of and ties to others active in mobilization. For example, knowledge gained from interactions with an activist relative or friend can add to one's view of intergroup relations and adoption of roles in the conflict. As McAdam (1986, 69) establishes in the case of the 1964 Freedom Summer in the United States, "In talking with [activists, a potential participant] may well develop a better and more sympathetic understanding of the . . . movement." One of my respondents describes the impact that her sister's activism had on her role as an active supporter of the Abkhaz movement: "I was a regular person. My sister was an activist. I helped her. She was a teacher of physics and mathematics at school. She did not have a husband or children, was not burdened by family. She had time to dive into this head-on. Plus, she was [*pauses*], I cannot say that I was not a patriot, but I was tied hand and foot. I had two little children. But I helped my older sister. . . . She was an important connecting chain in all this work."

Collective conflict identities are thus inherently relational and emerge in interaction with others involved in conflict through conversations, observation of society, and participation in prewar collective action that produce shared understandings of conflict and participant roles. Shared background shapes how conflict participants relate to one another. As these experiences evolve, so do conflict identities. Conflict can be seen as part of daily life, public intergroup interaction, or the realm of the political elite and as nonviolent or violent, stagnant or escalating, and requiring mobilization or not. People can view themselves as active participants, supporters of the cause, and nonparticipants and transition between these roles in the course of conflict.

Stage 2: Collective Threat Framing

Shared understandings of conflict and one's role in it that evolve before the war relate individuals to the group, which can be defined as broadly as the nation (the population of Abkhazia) or its subset categorized by class, gender, or ethnicity (the Abkhaz) or as narrowly as the locality to which one feels belonging (a native village) or one's kin (a *familia* sharing a last name, or a nuclear family). Collective conflict identities therefore reflect "a perception of a shared status or relation [with a broader community], which may be imagined rather than experienced directly" (Polletta and Jasper 2001, 285). In mobilization for war, identities that people develop in relation to these segments of the group before the war "compete for salience" (Viterna 2013, 10). Based on shared understandings of conflict and their part in it, groups of relatives, friends, neighbors, and locals negotiate the mobilizing appeals of the groups' leaders to direct collective action to the different segments of the broader community. In contrast to the distinction commonly assumed between private (mother) and collective (supporter) identities (Kalyvas 2003), these identities intersect as people mobilize to protect their families, localities, or broader group.

This is the second way in which I extend Gould's notion of collective identities. I argue that individuals are not simply recipients of mobilizing appeals with which "actors involved in mobilization . . . convince potential participants that, given their social situation, they are both likely to benefit from and, as a result, obligated to contribute to the collective effort" (Gould 1995, 13–14). Potential participants are active in the negotiation of these appeals, which are often articulated by a group's national or local leadership or organization that individuals are linked to through weak ties or indirect association, but are interpreted and translated into collective action across other social networks that individuals are embedded in, in Granovetter's (1985) term. Based on individuals' distinct prewar conflict experiences, mobilizing appeals can be seen differently in groups tied by strong "everyday kinship, marriage, friendship, and community-based relationships" (Parkinson 2013, 418) and undergo a transition as they are transmitted across these networks.

When the war begins, collective identities are invoked to make sense of violence. Whereas most civil war literature starts with the assumption of the given knowledge of risk on the part of potential participants in the war, I find that distinct conflict experiences and social networks with which people mobilize at the war's onset shape different perceptions of anticipated risk, or threat, of mobilization.

Mobilization decisions vary as a result. As Kalyvas and Kocher (2007, 184) note, "Empirical literature has refrained from engaging theoretically with the assumption that participation in violent collective action is always 'risky,' a risk usually conceptualized as the principal (expected) individual cost paid by rebels."[14]

Weinstein (2007, 21), for example, says that "organizers must motivate and challenge untrained peasants to take up arms and engage enormous risks in fighting for a cause." Risking "lives in battle against a stronger government force" is the main cost for participants associated with rebel recruitment in his analysis (Weinstein 2007, 7). This assumption is supported with the observation of casualties among combatants and supporters of insurgency. As Wood (2003, 9–10) finds in El Salvador, "The risks of participation in the insurgency were evident in the patterns of widespread disappearances of purported activists and the subsequent reappearance of many of their tortured bodies." In deciding whether and how to participate in rebellion, Petersen (2001, 53) concludes, people are "faced with a question: how much risk should I accept?" Kalyvas and Kocher (2007, 184) suggest that there are other "possibilities": "In the first scenario rebel and noncombatant risk is roughly equivalent; in the second the risk to noncombatants actually exceeds that to rebels."

The understanding of risk by the participants themselves, however, is not considered in any of these alternatives, whether participation is viewed as more, equally, or less risky relative to nonparticipation in the analysis. Yet regular people faced with violence do not operate with the notion of risk assumed or assessed by an outside observer retroactively. Their interpretation of anticipated risk, or threat, of civil war and participation in it can differ from that based on the patterns of violence recorded during or after mobilization and from one another. Kalyvas (2006, 207), for example, notes that his theory of civilian collaboration with the war parties "assumes that individuals are good at assessing risk." However, psychological experiments, in particular Amos Tversky and Daniel Kahneman's (1974) seminal study of heuristics and biases in judgment, show that people assess risk subjectively, relying among other categories on those invoked by stereotypes or what is available to memory. "These heuristics are quite useful, but sometimes they lead to severe and systematic errors," or biases in the assessment of risk (Tversky and Kahneman 1974, 1124).

Timur Kuran (1991) links these heuristics to our inability to predict revolutions and the surprise with which they are met by scholars and the participants themselves. He argues that preference falsification, or the difference between the preferences individuals express in public from those they hold privately, is responsible for the surprise (Kuran 1991, 23). "As the public opposition grows, with his private preference constant, there comes a point [called revolutionary threshold] where [an individual's] external cost of joining the opposition falls below his internal cost of preference falsification" (Kuran 1991, 18). The perceived risk of challenging the status quo decreases as a result. In the context of the Eastern European revolution of 1989, "each successful challenge to communism lowered the perceived risk of dissent in the countries still under communist rule" (Kuran 1991, 42). Petersen (2001, 47) advances this argument by showing that "individuals may change their level of risk acceptance (their thresholds) over the course of the sequence of events underlying rebellion or resistance situations." He finds that community norms, such as the norm of reciprocity, can reduce these thresholds and shows that ordinary Lithuanians "were drawn in [anti-Soviet action] through their normative relationships with friends and family" (Petersen 2001, 300).

This work suggests that individuals can gauge the level of risk and that their risk acceptance can change over time, but it does not take into account that the actors involved can interpret what happens in situations of revolution, rebellion, resistance, and civil war differently. Nor does it explain how people come to perceive the anticipated risk, or threat, of mobilization to arrive at variable threat perceptions. My mechanism of collective threat framing captures a social dynamic whereby people come to perceive threat differently based on their prior history and social networks at the time of mobilization and shows that it is not the fact but rather the variable perception of threat that shapes people's mobilization decisions (see figure 2.3). In the conditions of intense uncertainty presented by the onset of war, collective threat framing addresses the questions of who is threatened, by whom, and to what extent and helps ordinary people decide who should be protected as a result. The mechanism follows the steps of *articulation* of threat posed by imminent violence by the national elite, local *adaptation* of national messages that in general shifts threat framing to fit local needs of defense, and *consolidation* of information into collective mobilization decisions within the quotidian networks of family and friends.

Over and again Abkhaz respondents tell how, in the confusion of the Georgian advance, they sought information on the threat posed by the Georgian forces from the social networks that they interacted with and trusted at the time.[15] Families gathered by their television sets to hear the message of the national leaders, who invoked ideas developed in prior mobilization to frame the advance as requiring defensive mobilization.[16] Crowds then poured to village, town, or city administrations and other traditional centers of assembly to seek clarification from the local authorities. Men and women called on relatives and friends to decide how to act in response.

Hence, while a period of relative calm followed the clashes of 1989 in Abkhazia, the Abkhaz viewed the Georgian advance in August 1992 through the lens of collective conflict identities that developed earlier. The themes of intergroup conflict shaped through prewar mobilization did not disappear at the entrance of

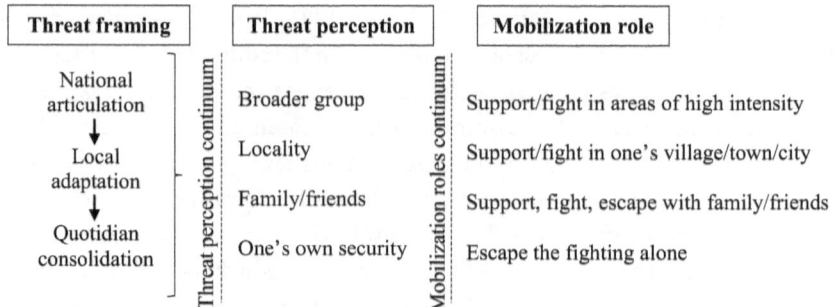

FIGURE 2.3. Collective threat framing.

Source: Reprinted, with modifications, with permission from Shesterinina 2016, supplementary materials, 25: fig. 2.

Georgian forces into Abkhazia, but reemerged to attract regular people to the Abkhaz war effort in powerful ways. It is this shared conflict history that was invoked to make sense of the Georgian advance and underlined with and for whom individuals mobilized in the war. As in other cases of mobilization, men and women who lived in the context of conflict contributed to the armed struggle, informed by their prewar experiences.[17] The account of a woman participant in the war illustrates the importance of prewar experiences: "I participated in the war because since childhood we lived in a society where the Abkhaz were humiliated, eradicated. Our language, last names were changed to Georgian. It has gone on for long. Over the existence of Abkhazia, Georgians attempted to make it so that there would be no Abkhaz, that we became Georgian [along with] Abkhazia—the land that they consider to be their own. But it is our, Abkhaz land. . . . [Therefore], we had to struggle."

Across the social networks with which potential participants found themselves at the time of the Georgian advance, these themes were invoked to make sense of the advance and respond to it. National and local leaders, relatives, and friends appealed to experiences of Georgian-Abkhaz conflict in their interpretations of the advance and thus shaped the ways in which people perceived the threat of Georgian forces. Yet mobilization decisions were negotiated among the immediate social networks—those that people were embedded in *at the time*—to direct protection to families, localities, or the broader group based on who was perceived to be threatened.

Prewar experiences underlie social networks involved in civil war mobilization, both those that structure collective action, that is, who individuals mobilize with, and those that direct mobilization efforts to the segments of society for whom individuals mobilize. People who participate in and are affected by prewar conflict in similar ways are likely to share conflict identities and mobilize for war as part of their social networks. The ways in which people perceive threat as a result of collective threat framing and conflict identities invoked in it are central to how and, importantly, for whom they mobilize. Those who perceive threat as directed primarily to their own safety can hide, flee, or join the stronger side in the war, mainly alone. These trajectories reflect self-regarding concerns of security maximization prioritized in rationalist accounts that view mobilization as a cost-benefit calculation. The more threat perceptions incorporate the broader group, the further they move to other-regarding action, by risking for the sake of the group (Gutiérrez Sanín and Wood 2014).

Individuals concerned with family and friends mobilize on their behalf. These decisions often take an unexpected course, shaped by the social networks at the time of mobilization. For example, by virtue of their embeddedness in family networks at the time of Georgia's advance, some Abkhaz who shared in the collective understanding of the conflict as directed against the Abkhaz group and their participant role in it nonetheless fled with families, to protect children from violence. Even those committed to the broader group thus escape the fighting to protect their kin. If unable, they can fight together with kin or in their home locales.

However, when threat is perceived toward the broader group, individuals mobilize to the areas of high-intensity fighting, such as capitals or contested territory. Abkhaz mobilization generally followed this pattern, demonstrating that self- and other-regarding concerns can be present at the same time in mobilization. Variation in the roles that individuals adopted within each of these trajectories extended beyond the nonfighter, supporter, and fighter categories common in the civil war literature, to include the different segments of society for which mobilization efforts were undertaken (see figure 2.4).[18]

My core addition to theorizing mobilization is the recognition of different subsets of the group that mobilization is directed to. As Gould (1995, 18) finds, "An appeal to solidarity will only succeed to the degree that the collective identity it invokes classifies people in a way that plausibly corresponds to their concrete experience of social ties to others." Hence, memories of prewar repression and intergroup hostility or precedents of intergroup violence suggest who should be protected in civil war. Individual and collective mobilization efforts are accordingly directed to one's own safety or that of close family and friends, local relations in villages, towns, and cities, or the broader group. This places self- and other-regarding concerns at the heart of wartime roles and shows how the two coexist in mobilization.[19]

Mobilization in Abkhazia was directed to the subsets of society that close-knit groups that mobilized together deemed to be particularly threatened by the Georgian advance based on patterns of intergroup conflict that they experienced in the past. Some Abkhaz mobilized to protect the collectivity as a whole, namely,

Self-regarding				Other-regarding
Hide, flee, or join stronger side alone	Hide, flee, or join stronger side with close family/friends	Support or fight on weaker side to protect family/friends	Support or fight on weaker side to protect one's village/town/city	Support or fight on weaker side to protect broader group

FIGURE 2.4. Wartime mobilization continuum.

Source: Reprinted, with modifications, with permission from Shesterinina 2016, 418, fig. 2.

the population of Abkhazia, including its Georgian part, and protected Georgians from both the Abkhaz and Georgian armed forces. To defend the Abkhaz as a group and Abkhazia as their land, others mobilized to the areas of intense fighting, such as the capital. Yet others protected families and friends or their own safety and mobilized in their native localities or escaped the fighting when feasible.

Stage 3: Implications for Wartime and Postwar Outcomes

As individuals adopt different roles in the war, their conflict identities continue to evolve through collective experiences of wartime mobilization. The consequences of potential loss in the war and the salience of their group's success become part of shared understandings of conflict and participants' roles in it. As the war progressed, the Abkhaz envisioned what would happen in the event of Georgian victory. The history of the Georgian-Abkhaz relations, the more recent calls in Georgia to further diminish Abkhazia's status, and the fighting itself, as the Abkhaz observed the brutality of Georgian forces and the mobilization of many local Georgians against them, combined in the view among the Abkhaz that their group would be eradicated if they were to lose the war. "If the events had turned out differently, we would have been liquidated or killed and expelled. We could imagine no other way Georgians would behave on this territory," one respondent captures this common position.

With the group's survival at risk, some instances of the fighting come to be understood as particularly important. Fighters can thus shift in mobilization from defending the hometown to areas that are seen as vital for the broader struggle. The outcomes achieved in the war then become an essential part of collective conflict identities after the war, reflected in mobilization for postwar violence and recurrent armed conflict. The captures of Gagra early in the war to gain access to a lifeline, Russia's border, and of the capital, Sukhum/i, at the end of the war to reestablish the Abkhaz government were critical wartime victories in the Abkhaz context, ones that the Abkhaz protected as they displaced most of the Georgian population of Abkhazia and created interminable obstacles to return, secured the administrative border with Georgia, and fought in the postwar decades for the territory that they considered to be Abkhaz. These themes appear consistently in respondents' accounts of continued postwar mobilization.

The prewar, wartime, and postwar stages are thus intrinsically connected in the process of mobilization. A broader perspective on intergroup conflict gained from this sociohistorical approach suggests that civil war is not an isolated phenomenon but is related to prewar contention and postwar continuation of conflict in important ways. My theory of mobilization in uncertainty specifies the links between these stages by focusing on the formation and evolution of collective conflict identities and their invocation across the social networks with which individuals share their conflict experiences at any given moment in conflict. Collective threat framing is a core social mechanism of civil war mobilization that incorporates these prewar and wartime factors to facilitate individuals' mobilization decisions by making sense of who is threatened, by whom, and to what extent and how to act in uncertainty presented at the time. By looking at civil war mobilization as part of broader conflict, we get a sense of how nonviolent relations turn violent, how ordinary people's understanding of conflict and their role in it change over time, and how these social dynamics of conflict affect civil war and its outcomes.

3
COLLECTIVE HISTORICAL MEMORY

The emergence of the conflict is in the history, language, culture.
—Abkhaz fighter, Pitsunda, 2011

To grasp the collective historical memory of the Abkhaz, we need to understand what historical processes shaped the political status of Abkhazia in the Soviet period, the position of the Abkhaz in the broader population, and the institutional conditions that influenced people's ability to settle, be educated and employed, and develop culturally. The ordinary Abkhaz find explanations to their lived experiences at the intersection of these historical forces. Their shared understandings of the conflict as part of a minority dissolving in the Georgian mass in the course of history are shaped by their interpretation of these processes. As the Georgian-Abkhaz scholar Yuri Anchabadze (1998, 72) writes,

> The historical memory of the Abkhazians still puts the sources of confrontation in the pre-revolutionary period, but the view is that the full offensive by Georgia against Abkhazia came during the Soviet years, reaching its high point during the Stalinist period. This period has been the source of many extremely painful memories in the recent history of the Abkhazians, particularly the successive reductions in the legal status of Abkhazia (a Soviet Socialist Republic in 1921, and an Autonomous Republic as part of the Georgian SSR in 1931), the repressive policy of Georgianization implemented from the end of the 1930s to the beginning of the 1950s, the large-scale colonization of Abkhazian lands during the same period by settlers from Georgia, and the concept of ethnic identity of Abkhazians and Georgians officially approved as a "scientific truth."

This historical narrative is known as the "100-year war" of Georgia against Abkhazia, particularly in the Soviet context (Lakoba 1993). Yet the notion of becoming a minority on the land the Abkhaz feel belonging to, as Anchabadze says, has its roots in an earlier period, that of the Russian Empire.

Pre-Soviet Abkhazia: Russian Imperialism, *Makhadzhirstvo*, and Menshevik Georgia

Parts of this narrative extend beyond the scope of our discussion, but recent historical memory dates back to the nineteenth century. Then, the Russian Empire, in its struggle for control over the Caucasus, colonized and depopulated Abkhazia in mass deportations known as *makhadzhirstvo* (exile)—to give way to the resettlement of the territory, primarily by Georgians, but also by Russians, Armenians, and Greeks (Dzidzarija 1982; Achugba 2010).[1] Abkhazia became Russia's protectorate in 1810 and an administrative unit of the empire in 1864, as the Caucasus War of 1817–1864 ended in Russia's annexation of the Caucasus (see table 3.1 for a list of status changes).[2] Mass deportations occurred in the course of colonization, with major waves following the Abkhaz anticolonial uprising of 1866 and the Russo-Turkish War of 1877–1878.[3] The empire declared the Abkhaz a *guilty* nation for participation on the Ottoman side, a status that was removed for neutrality in the 1905 antitsarist revolution.[4] But approximately 135,000 Abkhaz, most of the Abkhaz population, were deported by then, leaving 59,000 Abkhaz in Abkhazia, according to the 1897 census, and creating an Abkhaz diaspora in Turkey and elsewhere (Dzidzarija in Achugba 2010, 105; Müller 2013).

The prominent Abkhaz historian Stanislav Lakoba (2004) characterizes this as the moment of abolition of Abkhazia's statehood, then a princedom, and the *makhadzhirstvo* associated with this moment is a painful memory in the collective Abkhaz discourse.[5] One respondent, who was a Communist Party worker and regional newspaper editor in the Soviet period, captures this widely shared sentiment: "After the *makhadzhirstvo*, the Caucasus wars, most of the Abkhaz were forced to resettle to Turkey. The lands were emptied, especially central Abkhazia, the heart of Abkhazia. By the end of the nineteenth century, pamphlets appeared among the Georgian intelligentsia, [including] 'Who should be settled in Abkhazia?'[6] The demographic situation in Abkhazia began changing dramatically. As a result, the Abkhaz, the titular nation of this territory, turned out to be a minority."

The gradual resettlement of Abkhazia, largely by the Georgian population, unfolded as a result and was accompanied by one of the most dramatic memories of the Georgian-Abkhaz relations of the time, Georgia's military presence in Abkhazia in 1918–1921. The revolution of 1917 ending Russian imperial rule

TABLE 3.1. Prewar political status of Abkhazia: 1810–1992

ABKHAZIA IN THE RUSSIAN EMPIRE				GEORGIAN CONTROL		STATUS CHANGES IN THE SOVIET PERIOD			PREWAR STATUS	
1810–1864	1864	1880	1907	1917	1918–1921	1921–1922	1922–1931	1931–1990	1990	1992
Russian protectorate	Abkhaz princedom abolished	Abkhaz a *guilty* nation	*Guilt* removed for loyalty in the 1905 revolution	Abkhaz People's Council elected	Georgian governor-generalship, military presence in Abkhazia	SSR of Abkhazia	Georgian-Abkhaz Union Treaty	Autonomous Abkhazia within the Georgian SSR	All-Union referendum votes preservation of the Soviet Union	Reinstatement of the 1925 constitution

Source: I consulted documents and materials in Bgazhba and Lakoba 2007; Kacharava 1959; Lakoba 2004; Lezhava 1997, 1998; Nodia 1998; Osmanov and Butaev 1994; and Shamba and Neproshin 2008, among other sources, in reconstructing the timeline.

enabled the election of the Abkhaz People's Council in Abkhazia, which set a course for self-determination.[7] "Abkhazia's statehood, lost in June 1864, was thus restored," Lakoba (2004, 13) writes, as a result. The council met with representatives of Georgia on February 9, 1918, and agreed on "good-neighbourly relations" (Lakoba 2013b, 90).[8] Soon after, the Georgian side declared the independent Georgian Democratic Republic, which was for the large part led by Mensheviks who questioned the viability of a socialist revolution, and sent its army to help the council establish order, but turned Abkhazia into a governor-generalship (Hewitt 2013, 34–35; Suny 1994, 173, 188). This paved the way for declaring the territory an autonomous part of Georgia in 1919.

These years are marked firmly in the Abkhaz memory as Menshevik Georgia's occupation of Abkhazia (Chirikba 1998, 49–50; Bgazhba and Lakoba 2007, 282–286). Punitive measures against council members and the broader population greatly influenced Abkhaz views of Georgia (Kuprava 2007). The Abkhaz whose relatives the Georgian authorities repressed for dissent had a direct relation to this historical experience of violence. As a descendant of one of the council members recounts,

> It is difficult to tell this. It starts in 1918. The Mensheviks established a nest here. It was horrible. They killed, arrested, destroyed everyone. My uncle was a member of the People's Council. Nestor Lakoba led it. But there were only seven Abkhaz and twenty-eight Georgians there. What kind of a people's council was that? Then they demanded that Abkhazia become an autonomy so that they could send officials from Tbilisi and we would be subordinate. But what they called an autonomy was a fiction. They ruled everything. It was scary. They humiliated us. My uncle was in prison in 1918–1921. He spoke sharply at council meetings and was arrested four times.

People without the family history of Menshevik violence relate their later sentiments to this distant past indirectly. "Tensions were already present at the end of the nineteenth century," a respondent states. "The first Georgian intelligentsia decided to start the colonization of Abkhazia after the Russian *makhadzhirstvo*, and conflict was already very serious in 1918–1919. Thus my grandmother, for example, hates Georgians. Even my father, such an intelligent person, disliked Georgians." The feeling of humiliation by and dislike for Georgian authorities in Georgia and Georgians living in Abkhazia that many Abkhaz developed through direct and indirect experiences of repression in these years was further ingrained as Menshevik symbols resurfaced at the end of the Soviet period. Pro-independence Georgian marches in Abkhazia in the late 1980s featured the Menshevik flag of the early twentieth-century Democratic Republic of Georgia, which "left deep wounds in the Abkhaz," the Abkhaz say. The Abkhaz leadership used the memory of occupation as the basis to declare null and void Georgia's reinstatement of the 1921 constitution in Abkhazia when the Soviet Union collapsed.

The processes that unfolded in Soviet Abkhazia are generally seen as a continuation of what started in this distant past. As a member of an Abkhaz youth organization in the 1980s demonstrates, "It was a program that Georgian Mensheviks began in the nineteenth century. In the 1930s–1940s, it was realized. Georgians resettled, then schools and faculty preparing Abkhaz teachers were closed, then the alphabet was changed. When Georgia had no barriers to realizing assimilation politics they showed what they wanted: that we forgot our language and could not even speak of the Abkhaz people. Georgia's goal was to eliminate the self-conception of the Abkhaz and keep an Abkhaz mass that would eventually dissolve in the Georgian identity. This was frightening." The distinction this respondent makes between Russian and Georgian control is essential to understanding shared Abkhaz views of Georgian-Abkhaz conflict. The abolition of Abkhazia's princedom and the *makhadzhirstvo* stem from the Russian colonial presence in Abkhazia. But what followed Georgia's Menshevik control—further Georgian resettlement, prohibition of the Abkhaz language, the closing of Abkhaz schools, and the rewriting of history to diminish the role of the Abkhaz in Abkhazia's past—undermined an independent Abkhaz identity. Hence, this respondent concludes, "Russia fought in the nineteenth century in the Caucasus and there were catastrophic consequences, but Russia never said Abkhazia did not exist. Russia won territories, but never touched our historical biography. The infringement by Georgia was all the more painful as it related to our identity and the rejection of an independent political and cultural history." The Abkhaz see the Georgian demographic expansion and Georgianization of the population in the Soviet era as the steps in this Georgian program taken toward the dissolution of Abkhaz identity.

Political Changes in Soviet Abkhazia: Autonomous Status of 1931

A single event that enabled these Soviet processes, according to Abkhaz respondents, is the change in the political status of Abkhazia from the Soviet Socialist Republic (SSR) established with the introduction of Soviet power in Abkhazia in 1921 to the Autonomous Soviet Socialist Republic (ASSR) within the Georgian SSR in 1931. To counter Georgia's Menshevik control of Abkhazia, the Abkhaz revolutionary organization Kiaraz (Self-Help) sided with the Russian Red Army in its efforts to establish Soviet power in Abkhazia (Dzidzarija 1963, 346–378; Kuprava and Avidzba 2007). Abkhazia gained an independent status, but soon after, its Communist leaders, under Joseph Stalin's directive, signed the Union Treaty with Georgia; this status was reduced to an autonomy in a decade (Suny 1994, 321; Lakoba 2013b, 94).[9]

Respondents remember the Soviet victory in Abkhazia with great pride. A native of Bzyb/Bzipi in western Abkhazia, for example, praises the influence of his locality on the revolutionary outcome: "The revolutionary unit Kiaraz, a Bolshevik organization that pushed out Menshevik Georgia from Abkhazia with the help of Russia's Ninth Army, was organized from the Gudauta district, so-called Bzyb Abkhazia. Between 1918 and 1921, Abkhazia was occupied by Georgia, but on March 4, Soviet rule was established here." Preservation of this memory is critical for the Abkhaz. "I did a research trip in 1986," a then graduate student says in telling of the importance of establishing the revolutionary record through research. "In every village of Gudauta, I gathered materials about the revolution, the victory." Given this significance, the incorporation of Abkhazia into the structure of Soviet Georgia in 1931 is viewed as the epitome of the infringement on the Abkhaz right to self-determination that was once again restored in 1921 (Lakoba 1991, 328). "We were equals—Abkhazia, Armenia, Azerbaijan, Georgia. In 1931, under a bullet, we were forced to enter the structure of Georgia," respondents stress across the interviews.[10]

This status change placed Abkhazia at the bottom of the Soviet "ethno-federal hierarchy" (Beissinger 2002, 118). The Soviet nationalities policy "granted political status to the major nationalities which composed the Soviet state and ranked them in a hierarchical federal system" (Coppieters 1999, 14). In this system of double subordination, autonomous republics, such as Abkhazia, were dominated by the full republics of which they were part, such as Georgia, yet the highest authority rested with the Soviet center, Moscow (Cornell 2000). "Ruling the vast Soviet territory populated by different peoples was difficult," an Abkhaz professor explains. Thus, "the territory of the Abkhaz ASSR, which [was] the basis of the territorial community of the Abkhaz socialist nation, [became] part of the territory of the Georgian SSR, and the latter an integral part of the entire Soviet Union" (Z. Anchabadze 2011, 193). "This was a way to solve 'the Abkhaz problem,'" the professor goes on.

While the hierarchy was designed to suppress nationalism in the constituent republics of the Union, underlined by the ideology of the "eternal and indestructible friendship" of the Soviet peoples, it left autonomous republics with little political decision-making capacity (Shnirelman 2003, 11). Their titular groups, such as the Abkhaz, were "not granted sovereignty or the right to secede"—in contrast to those of the full republics, such as Georgians, who had "the right to self-determination, up to and including the right of secession" from the Soviet Union (Coppieters 2002, 91).

Quotas prioritizing titular groups aimed to correct this downside of the hierarchical system. In this Soviet affirmative action, titular groups "had definite official and unofficial advantages of representation in the administration, and in a bureaucratic state such as the USSR this was of decisive importance throughout public life" (Gachechiladze 1998, 62). The post-Soviet power-sharing arrangement reached in Abkhazia secured an added quota of Abkhaz seats in Abkhazia's Supreme Council that exceeded that of Georgians and other minorities, entrenching the titular advantage.[11]

The quotas, however, did not prevent discontent among minority groups whose native territories were part of larger republics. The dominant Georgian position in Abkhazia facilitated by demographic engineering and cultural Georgianization was at the heart of this discontent for the Abkhaz. As an Abkhaz philosopher and one of the leaders of the Abkhaz movement since the 1970s captures it, "Other peoples lived here, but Georgians were the main people. They, too, believed in this myth, got used to it psychologically, and started understanding themselves through this prism . . . as superior."

Demographic Changes in Soviet Abkhazia: Resettlement Kolkhozy and Abkhaz Villages

The incorporation of Abkhazia into the structure of Soviet Georgia set off further Georgian demographic expansion. The Georgian resettlement that began with the depopulation of Abkhazia by the Russian Empire took on a different character in the Soviet period. In the late nineteenth century, "a mass of landless peasants from Western Georgia were planted in central Abkhazia, in the depopulated villages" (Lakoba 2013a, 85). As a result, the Abkhaz "were split into two territorially separated groups: the Bzyb in the west and the Abzhui in the southeast," and lived in largely Abkhaz villages (Kokeev 2008, 248). Resettlement of the population from Georgia and other republics in the Soviet period was not only to the areas depopulated in the nineteenth century but also to these Abkhaz villages.[12]

During the first Soviet decade, when Abkhazia was a socialist republic, small numbers of peasants from Georgia arrived mainly to settlements created by their predecessors (Achugba 2010, 198). Mass Georgian resettlement started after the 1931 status change, specifically in the second half of the 1930s, when resettlement kolkhozy (collective farms) were erected on land considered to be undeveloped.[13] The stated purpose of collectivization was to increase economic productivity of Abkhazia by using fertile soil for subtropical crops, such as citrus and tea, and for viticulture.[14] The Abkhazpereselenstroj (Abkhaz Resettlement Office) was responsible for the construction of settlements. New kolkhozy were first established on the outskirts of Abkhaz settlements: "Land plots were taken away from Abkhaz villages, where peasant settlers from different regions of Georgia were settled" (Achugba 2010, 199). Starting in the 1940s, Georgian settlements were also placed within Abkhaz villages.[15]

Although population resettlement was a common economic strategy in the Soviet Union (Viola 1996),[16] the Abkhaz view this process as a means of assimilation by Georgia and the Soviet center. One respondent from western Abkhazia captures the Abkhaz view of resettlement: "In 1939, they started resettling Georgians. Where there were few Abkhaz, Georgians were given land and small houses. The village that you passed when you came to meet me, there were very few Abkhaz there, and so it became a Georgian settlement. [Then Soviet leaders Lavrenty] Beria and Stalin [who were both Georgian] relocated them to destroy the Abkhaz, so that there would be no Abkhaz nation." Abkhaz historians Badzhgur Sagarija, Tejmuraz Achugba, and Valiko Pachulija (1992, 11) draw a similar conclusion, based on the resettlement archives: "The character of compact settlements and the numeric predominance of incomers over locals ... make evident the deliberate assimilation politics of the resettlement campaign in Abkhazia. So does the center [of resettlement] in the Ochamchira and Gudauta districts, where the Abkhaz constituted the overwhelming majority of the population." As many Georgian settlements were created, few Abkhaz villages without Georgian populations remained as a result of the Soviet demographic changes (Achugba 2010, 213; Lakoba 1991, 352).[17]

Resettlement to Abkhaz villages is an especially troublesome memory for the Abkhaz. Due to Russia's imperial policy banning the *guilty* Abkhaz from settling in urban areas, the Abkhaz who were not deported lived in villages.[18] "After the blaming associated with the Caucasus War, we were prohibited from living in cities," an Abkhaz historian reports, so "we all turned up in rural areas." The Abkhaz village served as the key setting of socialization into the Abkhaz culture and continued to be essential for the preservation of intra-Abkhaz ties in the Soviet period. Traditional celebrations and community assemblies were held in villages. These gatherings included weddings and ceremonies reflecting the pagan, Christian, and Muslim elements that could be found in the variations of faith among the Abkhaz and in the institution of collective decision making where major problems were discussed by the elders and broader communities (Krylov 2001; Akaba 2007). As one urban resident illustrates, "We did not study the history of Abkhazia, so the traditions were passed through the family. My father is from the village. We held all holidays there: the Old New Year, Easter, prayer to the god of harvest, killing of a bull.... The Elders Council was in every village."

The village was central to the preservation of the Abkhaz code of conduct, Apsuara (Abkhazianness). This code encapsulates the norms of reciprocity (*aidgylara*), honor (*alamys*), conformity to custom (*acas*), patriotism (*apsadgyl bziabara*), heroism (*afyrhacara*), and masculinity (*ahacara*) (Hewitt and Watson 1994, 5; Maan 2003, 2012, Brojdo 2008).[19] The Elders Council is among the institutions that helped communicate and reinforce this code through the arbitration of disputes and social guidance according to Apsuara. As a villager who migrated to Pitsunda for employment in tourism explains, "The Elders Council was crucial in the village, the region, and the whole republic. At the village level, the council dealt with daily disputes, blood revenge, et cetera. I asked for help with a blood revenge question, for example. At the level of the republic, they intervened in the resolution of national problems. For example, when there was a war, the elders told us how to behave." Thus the *aidgylara* norms—"solidarity, communitarianism, collectivism, mutual help—to this day remain one of the defining features of the mentality of the Abkhaz" (Brojdo 2008, 23). "We do not abandon people in joyful or difficult situations," the Abkhaz say and demonstrate in current social events. "We have very strong family ties. . . . In villages, we have communes. Everyone is close in the holding of weddings or in situations of death. . . . A person is never left alone. There is moral, material, spiritual support of relatives and neighbors." Entire core social units of the Abkhaz, that is, village communes and *familias* (*advla*), or groups of immediate and distant relatives bound by the same family names, came together in these gatherings (Maan 2003, 2007). These cultural institutions ensured the density of ties, regularity of interaction, and reciprocity that lie behind the strength of the Abkhaz community (Taylor 1982; Petersen 2001).

As the Soviet regime targeted local traditions, especially those that appeared contrary to the Soviet ideology, such as blood revenge, kidnapping of brides, and costly festivities, many of these customs survived in the village (Krylov 2001, 81). "During the Soviet Union," a city-based cultural worker confirms, "secret sacrifices were there." The connection that the village provided to the Abkhaz community was preserved as well in the Soviet period. Despite population movement from villages to cities for greater education and employment opportunities, the Abkhaz retained a strong relationship to rural areas where "they have their ancestral countryseat, and numerous kinfolk live" (Y. Anchabadze 2013, 241). As anthropologist Aleksandr Krylov (2001, 84) finds in a study of Soviet Abkhazia, "The vast majority of the Abkhaz continued to live in the countryside, where they absorbed traditional foundations of moral behavior from birth. . . . The situation did not change even after the 1960s, when Abkhaz youth increasingly migrated to the city, as . . . they retained strong ties with their native villages: they necessarily attended family celebrations, often spent holidays in their family homes, and helped relatives with the cultivation of the land."

Those villages where the Abkhaz historically assembled in critical moments for communal, regional, and all-Abkhaz decision making gained particular importance in the changing context of Soviet mobilization (Kuprava 2007). They rose "to prominence as the focus of larger gatherings of Abkhazians drawn from a wider geographic area, including the urban centers" (Clogg 2013, 213). At the events, such as the Lykhny gathering of March 18, 1989, the Abkhaz collectively articulated and institutionalized their concerns and demands regarding the history of injustice (see chapter 4). The consequences of these gatherings on the Abkhaz shared views of the conflict were profound as a result. As a Gagra activist native to an Abkhaz village states, "People's gatherings, of many thousands, that took place in the big village of Lykhny produced letters to [the Soviet center]. Not every people went as far as this. After this we had experience. . . . Our consciousness was very high."

The Abkhaz relate these and other cultural institutions to their belonging to the Abkhaz land, these practices constituting an inseparable part of their group identity. As an Abkhaz elder explains, "We are mostly Christian. Christianity here, however, mixes with paganism.[20] We celebrate both Easter and the Old New Year. For the Old New Year, we make sacrifices . . . by the old, holy trees. Even cows do not go there to eat grass. We value this very much, and when I am asked about Georgian roots here, I respond: 'Where is your grandfather buried?' No Georgian will have his grandfather buried in Abkhazia.[21] But for us this is our land." "Even when we go hunting," the respondent says, speaking of the respect for the land that the Abkhaz learn from early childhood, "our elders give us different names and we are not allowed to call each other in any other way. We walk quietly not to scare away the god of hunting."

Georgian settlements in Abkhaz villages and broader Abkhazia endangered these practices. Over time, resettlement initiated by the Russian Empire and systematized in the Soviet period drastically changed the demographic composition of the territory (see figure 3.1). In the late 1980s, for example, Georgians composed 45.7 percent of the population, with the Abkhaz constituting 17.8 percent. Time and again respondents relate the sense of being a minority in Abkhazia, dissolving in the Georgian mass, and losing their political say and cultural identity to the Georgian demographic expansion that followed the status change of 1931:

> We used to be an independent state before 1931, but were made an autonomous republic. In many ways Georgians were resettled here, there was even the Abkhazpereselenstroj. This deliberate resettlement was so that they were more numerous and we less. . . . We sheltered them, gave them work. . . . As time passed they began working in top positions. The first secretary of the Abkhaz regional branch of the Communist Party was Georgian, only the third was Abkhaz. They imposed their rights on us. We were hosts of our land but without rights.

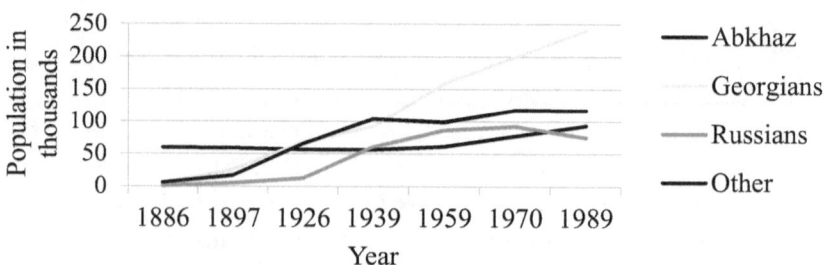

FIGURE 3.1. Demographic changes in prewar Abkhazia: 1886–1989.

Source: Official census data numbers from Müller 2013; I consulted Lakoba 2004 and Trier, Lohm, and Szakonyi 2010 for verification.

Cultural Changes in Soviet Abkhazia: Georgianization of the Elite, Language, and History

As the quotation of a local activist of the Abkhaz movement in western Abkhazia indicates, the Abkhaz understand Soviet-era demographic policies as part of Abkhazia's overall Georgianization directed against Abkhaz political and cultural rights. The interaction of political, demographic, and cultural processes is strong in the Abkhaz discourse. An Abkhaz professor captures this interaction: "When Abkhazia was incorporated into Georgia in 1931, Tbilisi ruled—not militarily, but administratively, via politics. The settlement of Abkhazia was carried out under the pretense of collectivization . . . and then Georgianization of Abkhazia started taking place in all areas." Along with "the dominant presence of the Georgians . . . and the exploitation of Abkhazia's natural resources" for development of the Soviet economy of Abkhazia (Kemoklidze 2016, 133), physical targeting of Abkhaz intellectuals and cultural repression are seen as major components of Georgianization. The professor goes on to summarize the concept of Georgianization as the Abkhaz see it: "Conditions were created to carry out the [Georgianization] policies here without armed force. First, through political repression. Georgians say that such repression was across the Soviet Union, but here repression was ethnic. People were repressed because of being Abkhaz, educated, and in an important social position. Those Abkhaz were supported who did not see themselves as Abkhaz but Georgian. Second, administratively. After people were resettled, Abkhaz schools were closed and the written language, toponyms were changed to Georgian."

Repression

Respondents consistently report the physical repression of the Abkhaz as part of Georgianization. The "mass purge" of the Abkhaz intelligentsia and wealthy peasants in the late 1930s and immense losses in World War II are critical memories of the period (Sagarija, Achugba, and Pachulija 1992, 3). "The mass—most of the elite—was repressed. The rest were taken to fight en masse. Most villages did not have any men left. The draft age was lowered for young boys, raised for older men," a researcher explains. Respondents relate these memories to the Georgian-Abkhaz conflict, rather than Soviet-wide phenomena: "From childhood, I knew that the Georgian-Abkhaz relations were not simple. This touched my family. Beria hated the Abkhaz, could not let us succeed, repressed my grandfather, who lived in Gagra, traded in tangerines, became wealthy, [and] had a house by the sea. This was at the beginning of the 1930s. He stayed in the camps for seventeen years." Although the period of mass repression ended with the conclusion of the Stalinist regime in the 1950s, respondents relate subsequent repression to the expression of Abkhaz political and cultural rights through activism. "My father was a political prisoner," a librarian in western Abkhazia recalls her father's repression:

> In 1967, he got on the blacklist for participation in the protests against the incorporation of Abkhazia into Georgia, resettlement of Georgians to Abkhazia, infringement on Abkhaz rights. There was a sit-down strike by the youth during a demonstration in Sukhum in front of the Philharmonic. My father walked around [among them], so that no one picked up a stick or stone and there was no violence. He had influence, respect. The youth listened to him. This is how he got on the blacklist. He was convicted on economic grounds, with twelve years in prison.

This respondent goes on to link the repression of Abkhaz intellectuals to cultural Georgianization:

> This was an Abkhazia-wide problem in the sense that we did not study the history of Abkhazia, but those of Georgia and the Soviet Union. We very rarely published anything on the subjects of history, archaeology, but in everything that we published we were called a "Georgian branch." There was nothing Abkhaz, it was all a "Georgian branch," including the territory. But we, too, had educated people. Of course, many died in the repression. In Abkhazia, educated people were the focus of repression—those who could do something for their motherland, could change [things in Abkhazia].

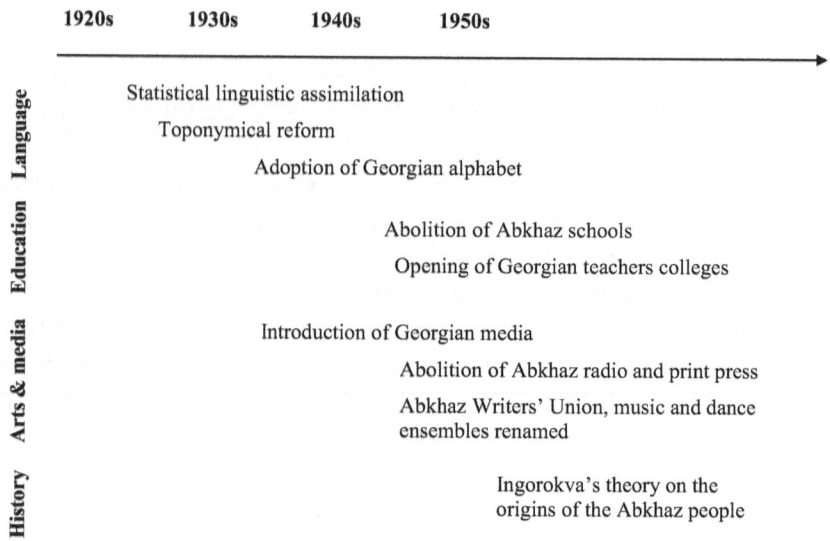

FIGURE 3.2. Timeline of cultural Georgianization: 1920s–1940s.

Source: I consulted respondent recollections and documents and materials in Achugba 2016; Bgazhba and Lakoba 2007; Kacharava 1959; Lakoba 1990; Lezhava 1997, 1998; Maryhuba 1994; Sagarija, Achugba, and Pachulija 1992; and Shamba and Neproshin 2008, among other sources, in reconstructing the timeline.

The absence of the subject of Abkhaz history from the school curriculum and reference to Abkhaz institutions, such as the Abkhaz Writers' Union, as part of a Georgian branch, as this respondent notes, are among the policies of perceived Georgianization that unfolded in the cultural realm, especially in the earlier Soviet decades (see figure 3.2).[22]

Education

For the Abkhaz, family was the major setting in which common historical memory was transmitted. Respondents often tell that they did not learn the history of Abkhazia at school or university, but rather drew on the stories that they heard from their parents and grandparents. "We did not have the subject of Abkhaz history at school," men and women say. "At university, [we] studied history—false interpretations and understandings of Abkhaz history." As an Abkhaz historian explains, "Georgian history was presented as a history of tsars, while the permitted Abkhaz history was a history of the Sovietization of Abkhazia." "Information was hidden," a librarian from Pitsunda concludes: "Grandmothers, grandfathers told us that we are an ancient people, remembering some tales, what the elders said in their time, but nowhere in the written sources could we find this information. We took hints, parts to guess the story." A writer born to an Abkhaz intelligentsia family in the Ochamchira/e region in eastern Abkhazia tells of the imperial wars, the fall of the Abkhaz kingdom, the deportations of the Abkhaz by the Russian Empire, Soviet repression, and Georgianization of Abkhazia—the highlights of the Abkhaz history as it was passed to him by his repressed relative, summarizing shared historical memory:

> This territory was always a field of imperial wars.... For Russia, the Caucasus War lasted one hundred years. The Abkhaz kingdom existed before that and fell apart.... In the second part of the nineteenth century, the main tragedy, the *makhadzhirstvo*, occurred, when no less than 80 percent of the population was sent away from Abkhazia. The whole land was emptied. But those who stayed lived through another big tragedy under the Soviet government, especially during Stalin's repressions.... All our intelligentsia was destroyed. During World War II, Beria announced a general mobilization in the Ochamchira district, where there was a concentration of the Abkhaz.... Then in the [neighboring] Gal region, the Abkhaz population was declared Georgian. Their passports were taken away, [their] last names forcefully changed, 20–30 percent were Georgianized.... They said that the Abkhaz never had a written language.

Language

Language assimilation was central among the Georgianization policies in this shared historical memory. An early form of such assimilation took place in western Abkhazia, where part of the population previously recorded as Abkhazian speaking no longer spoke the language, according to the official Soviet statistics (Achugba 2010, 166–167). This form of assimilation is evident, Daniel Müller (2013, 233) finds, "when we compare 47,307 first-language speakers of Abkhaz ... registered in Abkhazia in 1926 with 58,697 counted in 1897." "Seventy percent of the population of the district who were Abkhaz were recorded as Georgian in the 1930s–1940s," report respondents on Gal/i's continued Soviet-time Georgianization. "Our relatives were Georgianized [in Gal], recorded as Kondzharija, as [spelled in] Georgian, [rather than Kondzharia]." Other forms of language assimilation included the toponymical reform of the late 1920s and shifts between the Cyrillic (Russian), Latin, and Georgian writing of Abkhazian, with the adoption of the Georgian alphabet in the mid-1930s (Grenoble 2003, 119).[23] "All our proper names were erased, changed to Georgian. For example, Tsandrypsh became Gantiadi," a student demonstrates.[24] But the most serious violation of rights, in the Abkhaz view, is the prohibition of the Abkhazian language in schools

(Achugba and Achugba 2015, 126).[25] With the reorganization of the school system in the mid-1940s, "all schools in Abkhazia were Georgianized," a senior respondent recalls and then goes on to explain: "I was born in 1936 in Lykhny. I went to school for the first two grades in Abkhazian. . . . Then Abkhaz schools were closed and changed to Georgian, all subjects. And so, not knowing a word in Georgian, we had to study in Georgian. . . . I finished [at] a completely Georgian school." Other elders similarly say: "Teachers spoke and spoke and we did not understand what they said. I remember them all. They were from Georgia and were forced to come here." They themselves "were uneducated."[26]

This Soviet experiment lasted a decade. "Beria's campaign of overt cultural discrimination against the Abkhaz ended in 1953," after Stalin died, and Beria was arrested to give way to a change in the Soviet leadership (Slider 1985, 54). Most critically, Abkhaz schools were reopened in the mid-1950s and "children could study in their language of choice."[27] As a result, most respondents born after this change report having been taught in primary school in the native language and the remaining years in the common Soviet language, Russian, with the separate subject of the Abkhazian or Georgian language maintained throughout the school years.[28] "When I went to school, it was in the Abkhazian language. There was no repression then anymore," a woman in western Abkhazia describes her studies in the 1970s. "Our parents, though, studied in Georgian." Similarly, "Georgians who wanted to learn in Georgian could go to a Georgian school," and an Armenian respondent in Gagra says he "studied in Armenian at the Armenian school." For the Abkhaz, however, the concern was that "Georgian was [taught as] a native language" in Abkhazia. "The subject of the Abkhazian language was in Abkhaz schools only," a teacher states. "In other schools, Georgian—not Abkhazian—was the subject."

Language assimilation left a significant mark on the collective views of the conflict among the Abkhaz. "They wanted to eradicate the Abkhaz completely—the schools, the language. There was no life for the Abkhaz," a worker in western Abkhazia says. A historian notes the influence of the school reform on the Abkhaz elite: "During Beria's rule, we had a period when Abkhaz schools were closed and we were forced to learn in a different language. This tragically affected the development of our intelligentsia." The influence was equally strong on the regular population. A whole generation did not learn their native language. One senior from Abkhazia's east reports: "I learned Georgian in childhood. We were not allowed to learn Abkhazian. I cannot read Abkhazian." A younger respondent in the west similarly describes the experience and corresponding memory in her family: "I was not born yet, but my older brother and sister told me they went from an Abkhaz school to studying in Georgian. . . . When Stalin was gone and Beria was denounced in the 1950s, we got our Abkhazian back. But even then Georgians wanted to eradicate the Abkhazian language. Georgian would be the state language and we would not be able to speak our native Abkhazian. Everyone was so scared."

As Nodia (1998, 22) says, this "aroused in the Abkhaz fear of extinction as an ethnic group, through forced assimilation." With roots in the school and language reforms, this fear was strongly felt long after as part of Georgian-Abkhaz conflict.[29] A Sukhum/i resident describes this feeling: "Every year I felt the strengthening of the demographic pressure, [as] the Georgian language was more heard on the streets. Everything was going toward our assimilation. If then we were 18 percent [of the population], soon we would be 5 percent and then would disappear.... Many Abkhaz do not know their language. It is a very difficult language, and it went through such traumas ... with the politics of Georgianization. The Abkhazian language was most vulnerable."[30] This vulnerability was especially felt in western Abkhazia. The Gal/i district "had almost no Abkhazian-speaking people by the time of the war—they lost their identity [informally and in official records]." As a then state official active in propaganda confirms, "The Abkhaz were present in Ochamchira, but the spoken language there was Mingrelian." A media worker situates this statistic in Abkhazia today: "Gal is a border district. Georgian influence there is greater—there were many mixed families, people spoke in two languages. But in the 1920s–1930s, people were recorded as non-Abkhaz.... Now many want their identity back. For some it is sincere, for others a way to adapt [to living in postwar Abkhazia]."[31]

Historiography

Along with the language and school reform and other policies undermining Abkhaz cultural rights, such as the shutdown of the Abkhaz print press in the mid-1940s and the absence of Abkhaz broadcasting in the later decades, the problem of historiography, or the origins of the people inhabiting the territory, became a major concern for the Abkhaz in the 1950s. Pavle Ingorokva's (1954) theory rejecting the status of the Abkhaz as indigenous to Abkhazia is one of its highlights (Hewitt 1996; Coppieters 2002). "Even during Beria's time [our] autochthony ... was never disputed," an Abkhaz activist writes (Maryhuba 1993, 16).[32] "It was the last drop when Georgians declared that the Abkhaz people did not exist," respondents recall the Georgian historian's offense. Although its publication was formally criticized in the late 1950s, this version of history was restored and dominated thereafter (Lezhava 1997, 193).[33] "Things were falsified, deformed, silenced," a professor says of the later decades of the Soviet Union. "Two theories dominated: Ingorokva's, that the Abkhaz came down from the mountains (it is still alive); the second, that the Abkhaz are autochthonous to Abkhazia together with Georgians.... Thus the ideological confrontation on the basis of language and history was very sharp."

With the dissolution of the Union and rising nationalism across the Soviet republics in the 1980s, "the theory that the Abkhaz are mountainous tribes who came down from the mountains and occupied an inseparable part of Georgia was reanimated and actively infused" in the population in Georgia and Abkhazia, respondents report. The infamous slogans of the Georgian national movement, such as "Georgia only for Georgians" and "Abkhazia is an inseparable part of Georgia," were part of this revitalization (Lezhava 1997, 227). Time and again Abkhaz respondents relate growing hostility in Abkhazia to these forces. "Nationalism was planted here from Tbilisi," respondents draw implications of this theory for the locals. "Local Georgians living here were never hostile. Then from the outside it was planted that 'the Abkhaz are visitors who . . . took our land.' Georgian youth were educated on that."

A historian thus concludes that "everything was done to assimilate the Abkhazian people at the earliest possible date and to deprive them of their historical memory" (Avidzba 2013, 182). A core element of the group's identity, collective historical memory "was being destroyed" through a range of successive processes, from changes in state statistics in western Abkhazia to those in the writing of proper names, including highly symbolic locations such as the capital, to school reform that shaped a generation of the Abkhaz unable to speak and pass on their language and history, and to demographic engineering that altered the linguistic composition of the territory, with urban centers dominated by Georgian speech due to the continued Georgian demographic expansion.

Economic Changes in Soviet Abkhazia: Georgianization and the Relative Social Status

One way in which Georgianization shaped Abkhaz lived experiences is through limited relative access to status in the society. The Abkhaz relate their challenges in obtaining housing, higher education, and employment to these processes. As a then activist expresses the shared sense of deprivation, "The struggle did not appear out of nowhere. We could not find work in our professions, get apartments, land to live on. Why live if you cannot develop? We had no rights." She further explains:

> If we tried getting into a university, they would not let us. The documents were taken, you could go to [entry] exams, but the commission would give you a C and say you did not have enough points. I tried the first year, the second, and then decided to study in Russia. Many had to do the same. Then we returned as specialists, but again there was no place

for us here. I came to the factory (I received education to work at a factory), but the director, brigade leads were Georgian, while I had to stand in the shop and do manual work. . . . I had to wait three years in line to get land. But all three years I could not get to the head [of the office and had to go] through Georgian relatives. When I was building [my house], I, too, had to go through Tbilisi [to get permits].

This respondent clarifies the Abkhaz view of the housing problem: "The *rajkom* [district executive committee] . . . [worked like] a social organization. Apartments were secured for Georgians who had not even arrived, while the Abkhaz stood in line for years but could not get one, did not have this right, the line did not get to them." As another woman illustrates, "We lived in Sukhum. Only five Abkhaz families lived in our ninety-apartment elite building." "I finished school without Cs and tried getting into the Sukhum Pedagogical Institute. If there were twenty-five spots, twenty would be given to students from Kutaisi or Zugdidi [in western Georgia]," a respondent reinforces the shared notions of limited access to higher education. "I wanted to go to university in Sukhum, passed [the subjects of] language, history of the Soviet Union, English. But they did not let me in." Many studied in Russia as a result: "There was a practice of sending good students to Moscow."

The gravest offense, according to the Abkhaz, however, is that "all key posts were taken by Georgians" and "it was difficult to find a leading position if you were not Georgian." "The lead was theirs, the subordinates ours," people put it simply. "Georgians sent their people to take high posts." Respondents see restricted economic opportunities through the lens of the history of Georgianization. "Abkhazia was cut down: in the 1930s, all the intelligentsia; in World War II, the population. Then Abkhaz schools were closed. Everything was changed from Abkhaz to Georgian. My father served in the army, could have become a scientist, but no one let him." "Georgians took the best positions when Stalin was in power," respondents commonly report. But similar reports continue into the later decades.[34] "I had troubles finding work," a doctor trained in the 1970s states. "There was no Abkhaz surgeon at my hospital. Graduates of the Tbilisi Medical Institute took most of the positions here." "Everyone said there were not enough professionals, but when I came there were not enough jobs [for the Abkhaz]." Whereas some turned to Georgian connections, others managed to get employed in the more Abkhaz-dominated sectors and by merit. "I faced discrimination in hiring. The director was Georgian [and] I got in by protectorate. . . . [Only] two Abkhaz worked at my sanatorium," people of various occupations describe their experience in the 1980s. "I went to Russia for higher education in construction, got two years of work experience. When I returned . . .

privilege was given to the Georgian nationality.... [But] I became head of the construction unit that had more Abkhaz workers, because of my knowledge." "In the prewar times, the economy was in Georgian hands, all factories, companies," respondents capture the view of relative economic opportunities. "Their economic, financial abilities were much higher than ours."

In the 1950s, some of these Georgianization effects were amended: "As a 'titular' group the Abkhaz enjoyed preferential treatment with privileges in terms of high fixed quotas for jobs in the bureaucratic and economic-managerial offices" (Nodia and Scholtbach 2006, 10). Often referred to as part of "Abkhazianization," these quotas favored the Abkhaz in education and employment and overrepresented the Abkhaz in the government (Kemoklidze 2016). As Darrell Slider (1985, 54) explains,

> The policies of the late 1940s and early 1950s were reversed after Stalin's death.... In the 1950s... a policy [was] designed to expand the training of Abkhaz cadres for educational, political and economic posts.... The Abkhaz were also able to reassert themselves politically in the post-Stalin period. Among local party officials and the apparat, the Abkhaz were, in fact, overrepresented in the 1960s.... There was apparently a policy in Abkhazia to promote Abkhaz officials at the expense of the representatives of other ethnic groups.

"There was an employment problem, but it was solved," an Abkhaz historian confirms. "We could propose our candidates [for positions]." "[The Abkhaz] had privileges and support," Georgian respondents in Tbilisi agree. Many Abkhaz report holding leading positions in the political, social, and economic institutions in the second half of the Soviet period. A local of the Georgian-dominated Ochamchira/e district, where Abkhaz leadership would be less likely, states: "I was the assistant of the chairman of the *gorispolkom* [city executive committee], had a leading position, in a word." "In my case getting a job was not connected to the conflict at all," some respondents conclude, especially those in positions protected by titular quotas.

The previous decades of the suppression of Abkhaz intellectuals and the Abkhaz language, culture, and vision of history were damaging in a subtler way, however. "The Abkhaz held some posts," a then Soviet party official explains, "but posts were not the issue. The issue was the attitude toward the Abkhaz." "Who are the Abkhaz? Some tribes that came down from the mountains," respondents say to illustrate the attitude of superiority. Rooted in the Georgian demographic and linguistic dominance and rejection of Abkhaz indigeneity, this attitude strengthened the sense of being a minority among the Abkhaz. "The personnel issue played a big role," a man clarifies, "but more so their perception that Abkhazia does not exist." In the 1980s, when calls to further reduce Abkhazia's status were voiced in Georgia, the Abkhaz summed prior decades as "directed toward annulling the Abkhaz autonomous republic, that the Abkhaz were Georgians, that this land was Georgian, and those who do not want to recognize that should leave." As a then university student captures the Abkhaz view conveyed across the interviews, "From the Georgian side, it was a conflict of interest for the right of owning the land, social positions, political privileges—a conflict aimed at bettering the quality of life. For the Abkhaz, this conflict was about the life or death of the Abkhaz identity. Therefore, the depth of these conceptions of the conflict by the Georgians and the Abkhaz is different."

4
PREWAR CONFLICT IDENTITIES

> In response, we, too, gathered at stadiums, squares, with our flag and our demands.
>
> —Abkhaz activist, Gagra, 2011

What, then, did being a minority mean to the Abkhaz, and how did this relate to the different roles that men and women adopted when the Georgian-Abkhaz war began in 1992? The processes that enveloped the Abkhaz in the early Soviet Union—reduction of the newly acquired political status in the first Soviet decade; the inability to settle in urban areas, especially in central Abkhazia, and the integration of Georgian and other groups in and around Abkhaz villages; repression of the Abkhaz elite and population; loss of the native language and cultural institutions; and the myths surrounding the origins of the Abkhaz on the territory that they felt strong belonging to—meant gradual dissolution of the Abkhaz identity in the dominant Georgian population. Although some of these issues were addressed in the later Soviet period, in part in response to Abkhaz mobilization, memories of Georgianization offered a set of shared understandings of Georgian-Abkhaz conflict as one aimed at the suppression of the Abkhaz in the political, social, and economic realms. Almost all respondents were directly or indirectly touched by these processes and invoked historical memory in the interviews.

These shared understandings lie behind the group's national and local leaders' framing of the Georgian advance into Abkhazia in 1992 as a threat (see chapter 5). But historical memory, on its own, does not explain how this broad framing at the national and local levels translated into distinct mobilization decisions at the quotidian level. Instead, it points to the issues that related the Abkhaz to the conflict and each other in powerful ways, that is, how people understood their roles in the conflict in relation to others. The issues of Abkhazia's political status, the position of the Abkhaz in the population, and institutional opportunities shaped the roles that the Abkhaz assumed in prewar Georgian-Abkhaz relations, from daily life to violent clashes.

Prewar mobilization transformed collective conflict identities. First, intergroup friendship shifted to antagonism as a result of everyday confrontation. Second, appeals to the Soviet center in Moscow to restore the group's rights, including through separation from Georgia, over time drew broad layers of the Abkhaz elite and public into political contention. Third, the first violent clashes split the society, with polarization in institutions and formation of armed groups on both sides in the conflict. These changes redefined the shared understandings of the conflict and one's role in it as part of the social networks with which individuals experienced these processes. Those who avoided sensitive conflict-related topics in everyday relations could no longer do so as intergroup tension intensified; others who were not active in political contention joined collective action organized by the Abkhaz movement; yet others faced with intergroup violence mobilized into armed groups. It is with these social networks that the Abkhaz, in general, mobilized for war after decades of intergroup conflict.

Everyday Confrontation: Intergroup Friendship and Antagonism

What was daily life like for ordinary people in prewar Abkhazia in this historical context? The shared Abkhaz understanding of the conflict as a long-standing program to "flood Abkhazia with Georgians," "mix everyone up and assimilate," and "Georgianize" the Abkhaz did not prevent people from forging close intergroup relationships. As one woman states simply, "On an everyday level, people were friends, because people are people." Ties between Abkhaz, Georgian, and other groups in Abkhazia were strong in neighborhoods, organizations, and families. Respondents tell of reciprocity and mutual help from the moment of resettlement, which in the early Soviet period was often forced, creating a sense of injustice to Georgian incomers.[1] "When land was taken away from the locals and given to Georgians," an Abkhaz librarian says in reciting stories of resettlement, "the locals shared the last piece of *mamalyga* [cornmeal porridge], helped them in every way [as] they had to grow roots. The Abkhaz knew that Georgians were forcefully resettled." An Ossetian senior recalls how an elder of her village in western Abkhazia welcomed Georgian families who arrived in difficult conditions: "Georgians were miserable, poor when they were relocated. A Georgian woman worked with me. She told me how poorly they lived in Georgia.... [In Abkhazia, small] houses were built quickly for them ... and all five, six people had to live in one.... We had an elder, he pitied them. He gathered them, killed a bull and prayed to God for them, so that God gave them plenty." Krylov (2001, 81) interprets such actions as the persistence of Abkhaz customs in the Soviet Union: "Some Abkhaz traditions were further advanced in the Soviet period. This primarily refers to the principle of neighbor solidarity, which was extended not only to the ethnic Abkhaz but also to those who were resettled to rural areas of Abkhazia for permanent residence." Neighborhood solidarity was not limited to the time of resettlement but is reported across the Soviet decades. "As neighbors, we were like the closest relatives, helped each other, were friends," the ordinary Abkhaz tell of intergroup friendship later in the Soviet period. "We lived together with Georgians, Armenians, Ossetians, Greeks as one family. Whether a Georgian or an Abkhaz wedding, we all went."

Friendly intergroup relations were developed not only in the neighborhood but also in organizational settings. Higher education and employment brought people of different backgrounds together in the native locales and in the urban centers to which many people moved.[2] "We had a university where the Abkhaz, Georgians, Russians studied together," respondents describe friendship in these settings. "We were friends, worked together." Intergroup friendship is admitted even at the war's onset. A Georgian official displaced from Abkhazia after the 1992–1993 war tells "for the first time": "My friends (I studied with them at Abkhaz State University) left from my house to fight against me. They came to me, said good-bye, sat a little, played backgammon, and left. They asked if I knew where they were going. I said, 'Yes [to mobilize on the Abkhaz side]. Should I walk you out?' They said, 'No. This might be misunderstood [as friendships with Georgians, especially those who fought on the Georgian side, could be viewed negatively during the war].' Twenty years have passed, why hide these things?"

Importantly, intergroup integration in education and employment settings was common across the seven districts of Abkhazia, including Abkhaz- and Georgian-dominated areas (see figure 4.1).[3] In the west of Abkhazia, in the Gagra district, where the population was mixed and tourism was the core economic activity, a hotel worker recounts: "We lived in such friendship with Georgians, Russians, Armenians. There were [many] hotels. A Georgian woman worked at——, we were good friends, respected, visited each other."[4] "We had an international team. Ethnic diversity was strictly observed," Sukhum/i workers similarly recall. "We did not speak Abkhazian at work out of respect."[5] Other urban centers like the mining town Tqvarchal/Tqvarcheli in the east were engineered so as *to be international.*[6] As a then resident of the town tells, "I worked in Tqvarchal as an engineer, then an instructor of the party *gorkom* [city committee], then the first secretary of the Komsomol. . . . There were few interethnic problems. It was a mining city. It was created to be international: Abkhaz, Georgians, Russians all lived there. Mining work is such that interrelations between people shape up to be more consolidated."

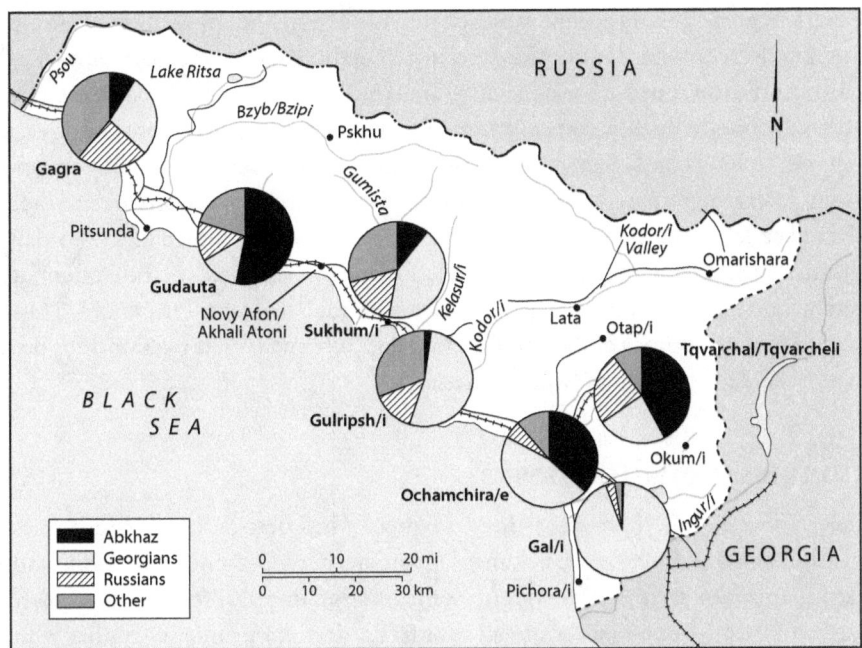

FIGURE 4.1. Demographic composition of Abkhazia by district: 1989.

Source: Official census data numbers from Trier, Lohm, and Szakonyi 2010.

In this context, marriage ties bonded many Abkhaz and Georgians. "Forty percent of families in prewar Abkhazia were mixed," the chairman of the Georgian-Abkhaz Mixed Families Union in Tbilisi reports. "It is difficult to say who is Georgian and who is Abkhaz. Many have old Abkhaz names." Intermarriage had a specific meaning in the Abkhaz social structure: "In a culture that emphasized strong ties with extended family members, for many this meant frequent interethnic interaction in their own homes" (Dale 1997, 79). "There were many intermarriages," the Abkhaz confirm. "We ate, drank together." Georgians displaced from Abkhazia concur even in Georgian-dominated Gal/i: "Gali was the largest Georgian district of Abkhazia. Georgians and Abkhaz lived there with Armenians, Greeks, even Russians. . . . We lived in a very friendly way, including with the Abkhaz. We were friends with the Abkhaz not only in the Gali district but also in Sukhumi. We met at weddings, in cultural places. . . . An Abkhaz woman could be married to a Mingrelian man, or vice versa. We were relatives. I have Abkhaz blood, my great-grandmother was Abkhaz."

As in other diverse societies, local communities in Abkhazia were highly integrated (Varshney 2002). This diverse but integrated nature of intergroup relations is akin to what Fujii (2009, 123) finds in Rwanda, for example: "In their lived experiences, neighbors generally played the role of neighbor, regardless of ethnic identity. Resentments, animosities, conflicts, and disputes were normal, everyday occurrences, but the basis for these antagonisms was generally personal, not ethnic." To settle such private conflicts, Kalyvas (2003) argues, people often co-opt overarching conflict narratives in the context of political violence. But underlying intergroup integration in Abkhazia was a political undercurrent that shaped collective conflict identities rather than simply be co-opted in day-to-day disputes. The character of intergroup relations was conditional on the content of interaction and transformed when sensitive political issues were introduced. Thus shared understandings of the conflict systematically structured relationships between regular people in prewar Abkhazia.

Conversational Taboos

Referred to as "the Abkhaz question," frequently in a derogatory way, the topics of Abkhazia's political status change, Georgian demographic expansion, and Georgianization triggered intergroup confrontation in daily life, only to normalize it over time.[7] Experiences of daily confrontation put people in conflict with each other in familial, neighborhood, organizational, and public spaces. Arguments on political issues, especially the status of Abkhazia, were common even within families. "My wife's mother is Georgian," an Abkhaz intellectual explains in recalling daily familial tensions. "She said 'Abkhazia is Georgia.' How is it Georgia if you take your dead to Mingrelia instead of burying them here?" In general, the Abkhaz believe that people had to make serious choices when forming mixed families: "We felt that we were us and they were them. This did not prevent people from intermarriage, but intermarrying meant that people made a choice, either they are on this side or on the other. If they could not make this choice, the family would break. There are many cases like that." One such choice was to remain in Abkhazia during the war of 1992–1993 and attempt to stay neutral or support the Abkhaz side. "Many Georgians remained on our side. Even until today, there are mixed marriages," respondents praise. Conversely, some blame the Abkhaz who left for Georgia or Russia with Georgian relatives.

Beyond family, everyday arguments and fights emerged during childhood, defining intergroup relations in schools and neighborhoods, the key settings of youth interaction. As a teacher in western Abkhazia says, "There was tension between Georgian and Abkhaz children at school. They had brawls . . . , humiliated each other openly, with open accusations. The political situation at school reflected all that was going on between adults, including fights." "In childhood, I remember," says a man describing a similar state in neighborhoods, "they said, 'We will show you! This is not Abkhazia, this is Georgia!' We fought. There were always clashes." Family upbringing was one source of tension. An educated woman, then a journalist, traces her views to the historical memory passed on in the family: "In my family there was a view that Georgians could do evil—when Abkhazia was occupied by the Mensheviks, for example, . . . I had a very good Georgian friend, but she had different views. It was all calm, but the division existed in our minds."

Arguments between friends, acquaintances, and strangers continued into adulthood. "I was good friends with Georgian fellow students, but [our] friendship ended completely once political subjects were raised," respondents recall the limits on conversations among friends. "The topic of Abkhaz-Georgian relations was taboo. If I said anything, my Georgian friend turned silent. It touched her." "It always related back to political issues. It was difficult to communicate without discussing these issues. As soon as the question of Abkhazia was raised, that was it. Everyday questions vanished," they go on to explain. "As neighbors, directors, coworkers they were wonderful, but as soon as we touched on the topic of nationalism, nothing holy remained in these people." As an Abkhaz activist and intellectual captures the tension behind these conversational taboos despite the apparent calm in intergroup relations, "On the surface it was calm. But inside, due to the unease of historical memory and national values, there was nothing shared. There was peaceful coexistence, but there was always a feeling of two camps. We never discussed the themes that were important to us with Georgians, and vice versa. We could mourn or celebrate together in everyday life. But what concerned us separated us."

Jokes, Insults, and Customs

Not only was tension felt in open arguments on taboo topics, but it was also concealed and manifested in jokes, rumors, insulting questions and passing comments about belonging to the Abkhaz group, and bending of customs in different settings of intergroup interaction. The Abkhaz routinely report these forms of everyday confrontation. "People communicated," a then student comments on the university environment, "but there was suspicion, and so a fence appeared. If you were Abkhaz, you joked [about your Georgian friends], 'He is my friend, but he is of the wrong nationality!' This was on both sides." A woman shows how political issues altered community relations: "My Georgian neighbors quietly stopped inviting us to their weddings." In the context where weddings and other community celebrations lay at the foundation of intra- and intergroup social ties, these exclusionary practices were highly offensive to the ordinary Abkhaz. As one respondent summarizes the situation, "It was apparent that nationalism was present, but was suppressed. It was in our souls and minds."

Insulting comments and jokes were not limited to relations among relatives, friends, and neighbors, but characterized organizational settings where these relations were formalized. The political issues of the status of Abkhazia and the Abkhaz in it ran through interactions in the public-sector, employment, and education spheres. Confrontations ranged from questions of last name attribution to the appropriate language to be spoken in Abkhazia, to the very existence of the Abkhaz as a group and Abkhazia as a Georgian land. A worker illustrates the bureaucratic challenges: "My son was born in Moscow, but we wanted his birth certificate to be from [Abkhazia]. Georgians nearby were fine—got theirs. But we had to work to make it happen.... A Georgian woman worked at the registry office. We used to drink coffee together, knew each other. She asked for my passport. I gave it to her.... When she brought it back, I was recorded as Georgian.... I went back [to the office, where] a Georgian told me, 'What is the difference?' ... Many were rewritten like that." The relative difficulty in resolving the registry issue and the Georgian view of the change from Abkhaz to Georgian identity in the official records as insignificant as described by the respondent point to the entrenchment of the attitude about the Abkhaz as part of the Georgian mass. The situation was similar in the service sector. One western villager tells of her hospital experience:

> There were not many Georgians in my village, a few resettled families. We had good relations. As I began going to Sukhum, Georgians were everywhere. I went to a hospital [where] everyone was Georgian, and there it would start. They looked at my last name, said, "You are Georgian," and spoke to me in Georgian. I responded that I did not know the Georgian language. They replied, "How so, if you live in Georgia?" This is how the conversation with doctors started. Could these doctors treat us after that? This is where my hatred for these people started.

Expression of this attitude extended to strangers in public places—streets, bars, and stores. For example, in the 1980s, "you could not shop in stores if you did not know Georgian," a cultural worker in Gagra remembers. "'We will serve you only if you speak Georgian,' saleswomen said." "They implanted their language. Of course, there will be hatred toward them," the Abkhaz capture the consequence of Georgianization. "The Abkhazian language was driven out. People were ashamed, afraid to speak it." Insulting "rumors, discussions of certain things on the streets" added to intergroup antagonism. This antagonism was acute not only in Abkhazia but also in Georgia proper, as one student recounts his confrontation: "I attended the Sukhum Technical College and had to travel to the Kutaisi automotive factory [in Georgia] for my practicum. I was sitting at the library one day (I was nineteen or twenty years old). Six older Georgians came in and started insulting me. I cried because of my powerlessness."

Low-Level Violence

Over time, intergroup tension was normalized in the prewar Abkhaz society, to the extent that public expression of animosity and low-level violence became systematic. "We had brawls in bars" and "there were small street fights" and "many non–mass clashes," respondents consistently say. As with nonviolent confrontation, taboo questions, customs, and language use lay at the heart of everyday violence. When political topics were not contained, a then university student in Sukhum/i illustrates, arguments turned into brawls, especially in groups of friends facing animosity together: "We tried not talking about politics. Often this question did not let us live, breathe, neither us nor them. They spoke Georgian that we did not understand. We, too, sang and danced. This was grounds for a fight. A conversation would start at a party and transform into outbursts." "In the spring-summer period," other students confirm, "clashes happened all the time, everywhere where there was alcohol." "They always complained about why we did not speak Georgian," Gagra and Pitsunda residents add, "[and we] asked, 'How so that we cannot speak our [Abkhazian] language?!' Clashes followed."[8]

The distinction between local Georgians and those who visited Abkhazia from Georgia proper was sharp in this context. Most violence was reported with the latter, who were seen as "disrespectful in bars, kiosks and often initiated clashes—even local Georgians disliked them." "We had clashes with the locals, but mostly [we clashed] with visitors," then tourist workers tell. "When Georgians came in and said, 'I want to drink for united Georgia,' the Abkhaz heard it and a fight began." A professor and activist explains: "Brawls and then armed clashes were mainly brought in by visitors. The locals did not take up arms, did not get into fights. They lived here, were [our] neighbors . . . , had to come to weddings, funerals, birthdays with us. They did not like that and blamed the politics of Tbilisi."

Low-level violence intensified in the 1980s, in the shifting political climate of Mikhail Gorbachev's perestroika and glasnost promoting free speech.[9] "In Gorbachev's time, it became possible to say what you thought, therefore it started to spill," the Abkhaz recount. "Open confrontation began in 1986," a teacher relates growing animosity to perestroika, and "local Georgians [now] supported visiting Georgians." Yet not all locals were seen in the same way. The Abkhaz differentiate between Georgians who moved to Abkhaz villages and those who were resettled to depopulated areas. The latter "were not friends with the Abkhaz. They did not know us and did not want to. Those who lived here for a long time, they had a completely different attitude toward us," a librarian suggests.

As violence with some local and visiting Georgians became commonplace in the 1980s, its normalization instilled fear in the ordinary Abkhaz. A mother captures this fear: "It was not of large scale, but if a parent was afraid of anything, it was that Georgians would offend the Abkhaz, or vice versa. . . . As there were more Georgians, the threat usually came from them. We were afraid of fights on the streets, based on ethnic humiliation . . . , stereotypes, language, history. . . . We shrank when [Georgian] groups walked around." Daily experiences of fear reinforced the Abkhaz sense of Georgian dominance in Abkhazia. "This was done specifically to strengthen their power and show that they were hosts here," a teacher sums up the general Abkhaz view of the normalization of violence in everyday intergroup relations.

From Conflict Avoidance to Everyday Resistance

The gradual shift from intergroup friendship to antagonism through arguments and taboos, insults and jokes, and normalization of tension and low-level violence before the war of 1992–1993 cemented notions of the Georgian-Abkhaz relations shared among relatives, friends, neighbors, and colleagues as aimed at the dissolution of the Abkhaz identity. Observation of and participation in this daily confrontation, moreover, shaped everyday roles in this prewar conflict, or how people behaved in private and public as part of social networks with similar conflict experiences.

People came to interpret and act on their regular social roles through the lens of intergroup conflict. As the Abkhaz recognized the contested nature of their shared views of the conflict among Georgians, one way to retain close intergroup relations was to avoid sensitive issues. Respondents consistently report adopting this role of conflict avoidance in the prewar period. One woman, then a Sukhum/i university student says, "I managed to keep neutral only by avoiding these discussions." This strategy made friendship and antagonism coexist in the same relationships. The woman goes on to express the distance that it created: "Throughout our lives, it was as if we walked parallel streets. We lived our lives, Georgians lived theirs." As the conflict intensified, avoiding confrontation became more difficult. A then Abkhaz activist illustrates how intergroup interaction changed in the 1980s:

> We confronted each other with words to prove politically our goals and rights. I did that at work. I told everyone, "What Georgians are doing will not lead to any good. Don't do it! Even if Abkhazia is [Georgia's] autonomous [part], we are still hosts and are indigenous to this land. You can live happily here, in peace, but you will not be hosts here. Your ideas will be stopped." I said I will not feed them anymore, as if joking. They laughed. . . . [But outside, in protest, Georgian] women were screaming: "The Abkhaz are nomads. What kind of hosts are they? They lived in the mountains and came down. They are wild."

Many resisted the imposition of the vision of history that appeared to threaten their identity. This resistance, akin to James Scott's (1985) "weapons of the weak," took the form of insisting on the Abkhaz group identification, refusing to speak Georgian, and regarding Abkhazia as distinct from Georgia. The early forms of everyday resistance included students rejecting to go to Georgian schools when the school system was reorganized in the 1940s or to fulfill teachers' requests in the classroom. An elder, who subsequently became an activist in western Abkhazia, reports his resistance in the 1950s: "When we could not learn Abkhazian and learned Georgian, my sister studied in Georgian, but I said I would not go to school. . . . My mother brought me to a Russian school in Bzyb, [where] teachers said, 'Leave this boy with us.' I studied there, but was not in the official records: if the commission had come [to check on the class], they would have said, 'This is an Abkhaz boy!'" Punishment of both the student and the teacher would follow in this scenario, as it did in other cases. An Abkhaz activist recites her siblings' memories of punishment in a reorganized Georgian school: "My brother and sister were not allowed to speak to each other in Abkhazian, even during the break, and were beaten if they did. If they rejected studying in Georgian, children were put in the corner [of the room] on peas, [which was a form of punishment]. Many Abkhaz fought with so-called teachers who were uneducated."[10]

In the later decades, the ordinary Abkhaz were reluctant to learn or speak Georgian given the detrimental effects of the language policy on group identity: "Georgian used to be a mandatory language. People then wanted to learn Russian, rather than Georgian. This, too, was a factor of resistance."[11] As an Abkhaz who decided to study in Tbilisi "to prove we were not worse than them" illustrates: "A rector once came in[to a class] and began speaking Georgian. He said we lived in Georgia and had to learn Georgian and so all his lectures would be in Georgian. I stood up and said, 'I am not Georgian, I am Abkhaz.' He responded, 'What are you talking about?! There is no such nation as the Abkhaz! . . . This is Georgian land, you have to speak Georgian.'" Just as this student rejected speaking Georgian to her professor or adopting a Georgian identity or a view of Abkhazia as an inherent part of Georgia, respondents regularly report resistance in the workplace. "We had disagreements all the time in my unit," a regular Abkhaz worker says. "My last name is———. I know that there are Georgians with this last name. Often at work most of the team was Georgian. They said, 'You are———. You are not Abkhaz. There are no Abkhaz with this last name.' I resisted and said that I was Abkhaz, my passport was Abkhaz, my ancestors were Abkhaz." As a Sukhum/i local summarizes the sense of resistance to Georgianization among the Abkhaz, "Throughout my life, Georgians started speaking Georgian to me, though I did not speak it. They asked, 'Don't you speak Georgian? How so, if you live in Georgia and have a Georgian name?' This was worrisome. My identity protested against that."

Political Contention: From Elite to Ordinary People's Participation

This protest found expression not only in spontaneous everyday resistance but also in decades of organized mobilization by Abkhaz activists and the broader population. Public gatherings where the Abkhaz traditionally made key collective decisions (Kuprava 2007), participation in the Caucasus wars against Russia's imperial control and anticolonial uprisings of the nineteenth century (Bgazhba and Lakoba 2007), and revolutionary mobilization by the Kiaraz (Self-Help) squad (Dzidzarija 1981) are examples of historic Abkhaz mobilization, prominent in the collective memory of defending the group before the Soviet Union was established. The focus here is on Soviet political contention and formation of the Abkhaz national movement with the umbrella organization Aidgylara (Unity).

Two forms of political contention characterized organized Abkhaz mobilization in the Soviet era, the writing of formal letters to the Soviet center in Moscow, first by the activist core, mostly intellectuals, and later by the broader layers of the population, and public gatherings. The Abkhaz raised the issues of the 1930s political status change, the closing of Abkhaz schools, and prohibition of their language and later concerns with the position of the Abkhaz group in Abkhazia's society. Their demands transformed in the shifting Soviet context. The repressive 1930s–1950s marked the struggle for greater cultural autonomy in response to the reforms that inhibited the Abkhaz language and education, ostensibly in favor of the growing Georgian population in Abkhazia. Many of these issues were subsequently addressed, but their long-lasting effects on the Abkhaz group served as the basis for the Abkhaz to call for separation from Georgia through, first, incorporation into the Russian state structure in the 1960s–1970s and, in the 1980s, the return to Abkhazia's short-lived status as a Soviet Socialist Republic (SSR).

Activist Elite and Abkhaz Letters

Letter writing by the Abkhaz political and intellectual elite emerged as the key form of political contention in the period of totalitarian control by Stalin and Beria (1930s–1950s), when participation in collective action was brutally repressed (Sagarija, Achugba, and Pachulija 1992, 4).[12] The double-tier mechanism of appeal to the state in the Soviet hierarchy made Moscow the arbiter of relations between the republics, or SSRs (that is, Georgia), and their autonomous parts, or ASSRs (that is, Abkhazia) (Hewitt 1996; Coppieters 2002). Appeals in formal letters to the Soviet leaders were thus one of the only ways to express Abkhaz discontent, which would likely be (and often was) disregarded by Georgian officials in Tbilisi (Hewitt 1996).

As early as 1921, the chairman of the Revolutionary Committee of Abkhazia sent a letter to the Caucasian Bureau of the Communist Party's Central Committee to secure Abkhazia's SSR status, which was adopted on March 31, but challenged due to "the economic and political inexpediency of the existence of independent Abkhazia" (Achugba 2016, 143). This status did not last, and the author of the letter, Efrem Eshba, was arrested, charged, and executed by the end of that decade in the wave of Stalinist repression that wiped out most of the Abkhaz political leadership (Sagarija, Achugba, and Pachulija 1992). No other Abkhaz letter contested Abkhazia's political status until the Soviet leadership changed in the 1950s.

In the interim, the Abkhaz elite turned to achieving greater cultural autonomy. The Abkhaz Research Institute, now the Institute for Humanitarian Research, became the epicenter of this activism. For example, the letters to the Central Committee of the Communist Party of Georgij Dzidzarija, Bagrat Shinkuba, and Konstantin Shakryl of 1947 and Georgij Gulia of 1954, all members of the institute, voiced the group's grievances over the language, school, and toponymy reforms that prevented Abkhaz cultural development. The authors framed these concerns in terms of Leninist-Stalinist ideology, praising the friendship of the peoples in the republics that was at the core of the Soviet nationalities policy and describing the suppression of cultural rights in Abkhazia as its perversion, which required attention from the Soviet center.

Some of the concerns that the Abkhaz intellectuals articulated were addressed after Stalin's and Beria's deaths in 1953 (Coppieters 2002; Kemoklidze 2016).[13] Abkhaz schools were reopened, a new alphabet based on Russian (Cyrillic) was introduced for the Abkhazian language, and mass layoffs of non-Georgian workers in Abkhazia stopped. Yet these changes were insufficient for the Abkhaz, and their demands intensified with the loosening of totalitarian checks. "After each unrest a special ruling was passed on [our] development, [but such rulings] fooled people by making concessions [instead of true change]," Abkhaz activists recall, "[so that] the [Abkhaz] demands were implemented only partially."[14] Gulia's letter of 1954 thus suggested that "many see a solution in the incorporation of Abkhazia into [Russia]" (Maryhuba 1994, 111). The letters of the 1960s–1970s consistently reiterated this vision.

Broadening Participation and Public Gatherings

Broader segments of the Abkhaz elite and public joined letter writing at this time and public gatherings, a historic form of political contention for the Abkhaz, reemerged, to intersect with formal appeals to the Soviet center. In 1957, in response to the publication in the Georgian journal *Mnatobi* of an article on Ingorokva's denial of Abkhaz roots in Abkhazia, Abkhaz intellectuals, schoolteachers, and party members sent telegrams to Moscow, hundreds of protesters gathered in Sukhum/i and other villages including Lykhny, and university students and cultural figures boycotted planned activities of their respective institutions (Lezhava 1997, 165–166). A decade later, the signatories of the 1967 "Letter of Eight" to the general secretary of the Communist Party, Leonid Brezhnev, included professors of the Sukhum/i Pedagogical Institute, economists, engineers, a school head, and a writer. Professor Shakryl and writer Dzhuma Ahuba introduced the letter at a gathering of student activists, Soviet authorities, and regular people in response to the publication in Georgia of another manuscript that echoed Ingorokva's argument. A mass consultation of up to five thousand people unfolded in the Philharmonic Theater of Sukhum/i from April 7 until a delegation of representatives was elected to sign and deliver the Letter of Eight to Moscow on April 12 (Kvarchija 2011, 139).

The issue of historiography served as a framing device in this and other letters of the decade, but the implication was that "Abkhazia can no longer remain within the Georgian SSR on an autonomous basis" (Maryhuba 1994, 162). A participant explains the importance of the events of 1967: "For the first time, the people said that we could not live in the same state. We held a gathering [in the Philharmonic Theater and] wrote a letter to the Communist Party's Central Committee. There were consultations, but the people and the government did not find a common language." Some signatories were threatened and arrested, yet mobilization continued apace (Kvarchija 2011, 141). "Every ten years there was unrest among the people," most Abkhaz confirm in the interviews.

The spectrum of participants increasingly broadened from the mobilization of the 1960s–1970s to the 1980s. For example, the 1977 "Letter of 130" was signed by party members, academics, schoolteachers, artists, musicians, workers, and World War II veterans, among others. It articulated the Abkhaz grievances voiced earlier on the infringement of Abkhaz rights by Menshevik Georgia in 1918; formation of the SSR of Abkhazia in 1921, reverted by the 1931 status change; repression of the Abkhaz intelligentsia; mass Georgian resettlement to Abkhazia; the language, school, and toponymy reforms of the 1930s; falsification of history; underrepresentation of Abkhaz cadres, including in the political bodies; and the deficiency of educational institutions to prepare such cadres. It described these problems as part of the disproportionate economic and cultural development of Abkhazia and concluded that "at present the situation that developed in Abkhazia requires radical measures for its resolution," that is, Abkhazia's incorporation into Russia (Maryhuba 1994, 176). "This idea," the authors said, "acquired actual meaning today," given the recent adoption of the new Soviet constitution and current constitutional reform in the republics (Maryhuba 1994, 177).

The Central Committee of the Communist Party directed the letter to the authorities in Abkhazia and Georgia for consideration, and its signatories were repressed, which included dismissal from the Communist Party—a significant punishment in the context of the Soviet party system (Lezhava 1997, 194). "All those who signed the letter were repressed," participants recall the consequences. "Many were imprisoned, including in Tbilisi." This sparked mass discontent in Abkhazia. On the one hand, the Abkhaz letters questioned the Central Committee's decision to delegate the issue to local bodies (Maryhuba 1994, 187–189). On the other hand, thousands of participants gathered in Sukhum/i on the arrival of the secretary of the Central Committee, Ivan Kapitonov, in May 1978. Kapitonov rejected the request to integrate Abkhazia into Russia while promising economic concessions for Abkhaz development. Dissatisfied with this outcome, the Abkhaz mobilized across Abkhazia in the summer with slogans such as "Georgians, get out of Abkhazia," and in the fall the Abkhaz activist core organized a two-week strike that disrupted transportation, agricultural production, and other sectors (Lezhava 1997, 204, 196).

Many regular Abkhaz with no prior mobilization experience joined this collective action. A young librarian and member of the Soviet youth organization explains her decisions to participate: "I did not participate in the letter writing [because I] was too young and was in the Komsomol. In 1977, I was already working at a resort library, and when the strike was announced, I did not go to work and wrote an explanatory letter. I said that I was in solidarity with my people and therefore [would] not go to work. My manager refused to take the letter to the head of the resort, saying, 'Write that you got sick!' I rejected [this request]. I was a reading person and knew history a little better." "People were dissatisfied with the existing system of rule," a historian explains, "[with] the prohibition of the native language, the negative attitude to traditions, the suppression of scientific and cultural development, attempts to exaggerate . . . Georgian history . . . as the history of tsars, while the permitted Abkhaz history was the history of Sovietization of Abkhazia." This historical memory was mobilized in the context of the opening in the Soviet system created by constitutional reform. As a prominent activist says, "The events of 1978 are exemplary not because I participated actively, but because they took place [in the context of] democratic transformation, the liberation movement. People picked up on this immediately. To speak against the Soviet Union—what we wrote and demanded [in our letters and at mobilization events]—was not in the spirit of Soviet politics, even though we were *for* the Soviet Union."

Although the core demand to incorporate Abkhazia into Russia was not implemented, the 1977 letter and subsequent unrest prompted a number of

Central Committee resolutions on the situation in Abkhazia (Coppieters 2002). Abkhazia received economic assistance for its future development, Abkhaz State University was opened, replacing the former Pedagogical Institute, and print media and television broadcasts now functioned in the Abkhazian language.[15] "All small, unrecognized people try to get freedom," a participant explains about the importance of these outcomes, "but how [can this be achieved]? TV, radio, newspapers are there to get this message across." Furthermore, "the constitution of 1978 recognized Abkhazian, Russian, and Georgian as the state languages," a journalist says. Finally, imprisoned letter signatories were released. "We managed to return all those who were convicted," one activist says.

The National Movement: Aidgylara

The mobilization of the 1960s–1970s that drew broader segments of the Abkhaz population into collective action paved the way for what became the Abkhaz national movement in the 1980s. The movement started with the formation of a range of student organizations across Abkhazia. Informal discussions among the students of the Sukhum/i Pedagogical Institute on issues of Georgianization, particularly the predominant use of the Georgian language in Abkhazia, led to the creation of a student society, which in 1967 had up to three hundred members, including the Abkhaz studying in Tbilisi (Kvarchija 2011, 131). Similar discussions took place in Pitsunda, where students of the Sukhum/i Pedagogical Institute and other youth from western Abkhazia formed a literary club with elder activists, such as teachers. Abkhaz teachers in particular played a crucial role in this mobilization. "We led educational work on the subject of patriotism in schools," an activist says. "One of our people . . . was a teacher. He developed patriotism in every class at school, explained what was happening. The youth knew, we knew." Beyond the school setting, the club distributed leaflets and information on gatherings in the area. One leaflet read: "If you do not open your eyes, you will die. . . . We are not the hosts of our motherland. . . . Our goal [is to] protect the Abkhaz motherland!!! [He] who deems himself Abkhaz will support us! . . . Behind these leaflets are people willing to sacrifice their lives to save [Abkhazia]. . . . Read, pass [them] . . . to those you consider to be Abkhaz patriots" (Maryhuba 2000, 70–71).

It was these student organizations that were at the forefront of mobilization efforts along with the Abkhaz political and intellectual elite in 1967 and 1977–1978. Members of organizations knew each other and coordinated to notify fellow Abkhaz of the time and location of mobilization. For example, at the height of the decade's wave of Abkhaz unrest in 1967, core activists of Pitsunda's literary club mobilized Gagra, Pitsunda, and Bzyb/Bzipi residents to remove the Georgian toponyms and paint over Abkhaz city, street, and shop names, such as Gagrypsh instead of Gagrypshi (Maryhuba 2000, 73–74). Two participants were arrested and dozens from western Abkhazia gathered in protest in Sukhum/i. This mobilization then merged with the gathering in the Philharmonic Theater, linked via activists of the Pitsunda literary club and the Sukhum/i student society (Kvarchija 2011, 132).

Great pride is associated with this mobilization. "We were persecuted," participants recall, but "Abkhaz mobilization for self-determination" began as a result. "I participated in the formation of the Abkhaz [civil] society," respondents who were then students say. "Can you imagine?! A small nation like the Abkhaz was destroying Soviet ideology from the inside." "It started underground," states one activist in capturing the importance of these efforts, "but what was growing included revolts, people's gatherings, letters. . . . [Now] we could work openly."

Indeed, the major organization of the Abkhaz movement, the National Forum of Abkhazia, or Aidgylara, emerged during Gorbachev's reforms of the late 1980s, with active participation and leadership of former student activists. One activist, Igor Maryhuba, born Marholia, who led the mobilization in western Abkhazia in the 1960s, drafted the "Abkhaz Letter" of 1988 requesting "the revision of the provision for the withdrawal of the Abkhaz ASSR from the Georgian SSR and the return of the status of SSR to Abkhazia" (Maryhuba 1994, 439). The "Letter of Sixty" to the Nineteenth All-Union Party Conference was the catalyst for the formation of Aidgylara and an explosion of Georgian movement activities in Abkhazia by existing organizations, including the Chavchavadze and Rustaveli Societies created in Tbilisi, and new ones, such as Tskhumi, which was formed by Georgian students in Sukhum/i. As the Georgian movement sought independence from the Soviet Union, the Abkhaz aimed to achieve the restoration of the SSR status of 1921–1931 to distance Abkhazia from Georgia's government.

Under the conditions in which perestroika, mainly glasnost policy, "created a public sphere where political ambitions could be voiced and favored the formation of national movements," the signatories of the 1988 letter—party members; academics, predominantly of the Abkhaz D. Gulia Institute of Language, Literature, and History; lawyers; journalists; and writers, poets, actors, artists, musicians, and other cultural workers, in a word, intellectuals—proposed an organization that would advance the goals that they articulated (Zürcher, Baev, and Koehler 2005, 261). As Georgi M. Derluguian (2005, 164, 161) explains the importance of intellectuals in creating civil society organizations across the republics at the time, "[With] Gorbachev's policies . . . the high-status intellectuals in the republics could rapidly transform themselves into the leaders of emergent civil societies. Such societies originated mainly in networks of cultural intellectuals who had known each other for a long time and usually spent their entire lives in the same towns working in interconnected state institutions concerned with national history, culture, etc."[16]

By the end of 1988, Aidgylara was formalized with a charter and program that set as its primary task "advancement of the legal status of Abkhazia" (Shamba and Lakoba 1995; Chumalov 1995, 122). Its structure comprised a congress and government, including a chairman, presidium, and revision commission, with district branches reporting to the central leadership. The organization published the newspapers *Aidgylara* in Abkhazian and *Edinenie* (Unity) in Russian and mobilized the Abkhaz and other non-Georgian populations for key events of the period. "One novelty brought about by democratization," Derluguian (2005, 208) similarly finds in other Soviet republics, "was that national intellectuals now also used discussion clubs, newspapers, and television to foster 'awareness' and mobilize their co-ethnic constituencies." Members of Aidgylara were part of Abkhazia's government and after the intergroup clashes of 1989 were active in the formation of the Abkhaz Guard, which was critical in the war of 1992–1993. A student activist, later an Aidgylara member and government official, charts the organization's path:

> We had a number of chairmen at the Creative Youth Union [who] participated actively in the creation of a political union, and an initiative group appeared. They prepared a charter and, in 1989, we had a congress.
>
> The experience of public discussion on sharp issues, including Georgian-Abkhaz questions, at the Creative Youth Union [was important] when I entered the [National] Forum.... We called it a forum ... so that different communities could unite there, all except Georgian[s].
>
> It was created underground. Then it was made official. Everyone wanted to enter the organization. Our people who wanted to rule, who were assistants to Georgians, did not want to go against their Georgian superiors or lose their positions. But we regular people had nothing to lose. We did propaganda work for the growing generation— [to say] that we cannot live like this. We have to struggle against this rule. Thus, from young to old, we knew what would happen to us if we had stayed in Georgia, especially after the Soviet collapse. Before the collapse, we wrote letters, had gatherings, such as the Lykhny gathering.
>
> When the tension rose in the late 1980s ... bureaucrats here got worried as well. The ethnic division of society did not just touch the lower levels. It also touched the upper levels. People started to also divide there along ethnic lines. Thus Aidgylara quickly grew in power and got support because regular people did not see another power. The Soviet sys-

tem was breaking down and could not protect people anymore. People needed another lively power. And Aidgylara became such a power. People started to unite around this organization. The intelligentsia and the top, some of them started to support the organization.

While earlier mobilization drew individuals into collective action in a variety of ways, from leadership as part of the group's political and intellectual elite to student activism and the decision of regular people to participate based on the collective memory of Georgianization, Aidgylara unified the existing efforts, offered a dominant mobilization channel, and became the epicenter of activism in Abkhazia. Branches of Aidgylara emerged in every district of Abkhazia. "I was part of the national liberation movement, responsible for the Gagra section of Aidgylara. We defended the interests of my people," states a then secretary of a local branch, for example. Other sociopolitical organizations were created in the 1980s, but were typically localized, and the leadership of Aidgylara worked to involve these organizations in their activities. As a member of the Pitsunda Creative Youth Union illustrates, "We had a social organization that dealt with everything from ecology to exposed electricity lines. . . . We wrote letters, statements, sent information to the creative unions. We were also part of the forum [Aidgylara] and helped there. We participated in the events if gatherings were organized."

Based in Sukhum/i, Aidgylara thus had branches across Abkhazia and carried out its work in coordination with other organizations whose aims did not contradict its own. Its members could at the same time hold membership elsewhere. Territorial representation and overlapping membership across organizations facilitated Aidgylara's reach and mobilization capacity. With representatives embedded in nearly every Abkhaz community, the information on collective action spread like fire. One member of Aidgylara who led its press service in Sukhum/i recalls how mobilization took place: "The Abkhaz people were one. A rumor passed that Georgians organized something. Within an hour, the whole of Abkhazia knew to come here [Sukhum/i]. We passed information by phone. There were [Aidgylara] representatives in every district. We called them . . . and momentarily everyone turned out here."

These efforts to consolidate the Abkhaz national movement were not always successful, and some organizations acted outside of Aidgylara's remit. Divisions existed within the organization on the nature and courses of action. "I was in the presidium. We met regularly and discussed important political questions. There were divisions, of course, [for example,] in the work on symbols," a core activist recalls. These divisions led to fragmentation of the movement. A leader of the Gagra union Abrskyl (Prometheus), the extremist wing of the movement and later the Strike Committee, explains:

Aidgylara asked me to work with them. I joined, but did not like it: they only did paperwork, wrote and wrote, but did not get any responses.... [For example,] I told Aidgylara's chairman that Georgians wanted to put up a memorial. He responded by saying that they would write about it. I said, "While you write about it, the monument will already be built." He said, "So what? Always you extremists, you like fighting." We could not work together. I left and ... [with other local leaders] create[d] ... Abrskyl. We were a political organization sanctioned in Gagra.

The archive of the Gagra branch of Aidgylara records this fragmentation. "We are already few and still got disunited by creating a number of streams, organizations," one of the speakers at a local conference notes (Aidgylara 1990, 3). Yet even members of such organizations as Abrskyl and individuals without membership participated in activities coordinated by Aidgylara. "Aidgylara woke Abkhazia up," the ordinary Abkhaz say. "Meetings organized by Aidgylara were a consolidating force for the Abkhaz." One such meeting was the Lykhny gathering of March 18, 1989, which was the first in a series of events culminating in major intergroup violence in Abkhazia.

The Lykhny Gathering of 1989

The Lykhny gathering in Abkhazia took place in the context where nationalist mobilization spread across the Soviet Union's republics, in what Mark R. Beissinger (2002, 36) calls "the *glasnost'* tide of nationalism." In Georgia, this tide initially focused "nationalist consciousness around demands for independence," especially in relation to the constitutional amendments of the time, but then shifted to include Abkhazia's status demands voiced in the Abkhaz Letter of 1988 (Beissinger 2002, 181). Growing nationalist mobilization in Tbilisi intensified after the publication of this letter and surged in Abkhazia, with calls for the independence of Georgia intertwined with those to annul Abkhaz autonomy.[17] By the spring of 1989, an Aidgylara member recalls, "Georgians, including Georgian authorities, openly demonstrated in Abkhazia." In particular, Zviad Gamsakhurdia, who in 1990 became chairman of Georgia's Supreme Council, attracted mass rallies in Georgia and Abkhazia with slogans such as "Georgia only for Georgians" and "Abkhazia is an inseparable part of Georgia" (Lezhava 1997, 227; Kvarchelia 1998, 20). As a then professor active in Aidgylara states, "This view was common among the Georgian intelligentsia and the public." The Abkhaz thus say that Georgians "did not just support Gamsakhurdia, they supported his idea." The Lykhny gathering was in part a response to the calls to abolish autonomous republics in Georgia, which the Abkhaz feared would mean further reduction of Abkhazia's autonomous status to a Georgian province (Lezhava 1997, 230). As activists say, "Our national movement was built on the rejection of Georgian nationalism. In 1988, protests in Tbilisi called to annul Abkhaz autonomy. In 1989, we had the Lykhny plebiscite on the restoration of our status as a full Soviet republic."

Aidgylara organized the event. On March 14, 1989, its leaders sought sanction from the Gudauta District Committee to hold a rally in Lykhny to discuss Abkhazia's political status in advance of the plenum of the Central Committee of the Communist Party on interethnic relations (Lezhava 1997, 220). "We knew that the struggle was necessary," an Aidgylara member explains, "[and] fought by means of popular gathering." Aidgylara's prior integration into the society and its links with other organizations, some of them non-Abkhaz, facilitated mobilization. "The Lykhny meeting took place in 1989," a Russian activist recalls. "We came there [Lykhny] right from Pitsunda. We were invited and went." Over "30,000 people gathered in Lykhny" as a result; "national minorities in Abkhazia, such as the Greek, Armenian and Russian communities, took part in this mobilization" (Coppieters 2002, 97). When asked how they learned about the Lykhny gathering, regular Abkhaz respondents often said: "How could we not find out? This was discussed everywhere. The television showed [and] the Parliament discussed all the actions in Georgia. There was no censorship of journalists—the government was open. All their discussions were shown. The people were in attention, and it was impossible not to know. This was discussed in every kitchen, market, on the street."

Activists, regular people, and even Soviet leaders attended. Aidgylara opened the event, but teachers, professors, students, poets, writers, journalists, army officers, and miners, among others, gave speeches. "I was asked to speak and I did," the aforementioned Russian activist states. "We spoke against the pressure from Georgia . . . , that even leaders of organizations had to be approved in Georgia, there was no self-government, and the Abkhaz had to establish their status. The question of exit from the structure of Georgia [and] independence was raised." The resultant "Lykhny Letter" comprised a statement and declaration to the Central Committee, particularly to Gorbachev, demanding "the return to Abkhazia of the political, economic, and cultural sovereignty . . . [as] an independent Soviet republic" (Maryhuba 1994, 459). All thirty thousand participants signed the letter, among them Communist Party members, including the first secretary of Abkhazia, and over five thousand non-Abkhaz signatories (Avidzba 2012, 49). "In 1989, there was the Lykhny gathering, and we all signed this document," an ordinary woman recalls. "The conflict had been going on for eighty years," an Abkhaz professor explains the importance of the event, and "the Lykhny gathering . . . was a logical conclusion," one of the most vocal acts of resistance in support of the Abkhaz identity. As Maryhuba (1994, 12–13) puts it, "All prior 'Abkhaz letters' are a prologue . . . , [a part of] the gradual crystallization of the key ideas and program goals of the Abkhaz national movement." "Our national consciousness was very high," a journalist and activist concludes. "We said that we did not want to be part of the Georgian nation, we wanted to be Abkhaz, to develop our culture. Georgian leaders did not like that."

Indeed, the gathering led to a dramatic escalation of Georgian mobilization in Georgia and Abkhazia (Hewitt 1996, 205; Francis 2011, 72). Weary of Georgia's looming separation from the Union, Soviet authorities in Moscow disregarded the Lykhny Letter, while Georgian leaders used the Abkhaz demand as an opportunity to organize a wave of mass protests. As a professor explains the situation, "In 1989, it went out of control. By then, it was a period of extreme tension due to Georgia's declaration of exit from the Soviet Union . . . [and] the Abkhaz declaration on returning the 1921 status. Thus the opposition started, when at every square where more than five people could gather, buses were brought in with Georgians [and] local Georgians assembled." Some protests were sanctioned, yet others were not. One unsanctioned event of the Chavchavadze Society, for example, gathered up to fifteen thousand people in Sukhum/i on March 25 and "condemned [the Lykhny gathering] as offensive to the Georgian people" (Lezhava 1997, 225). The first secretary of the Communist Party of Georgia as well openly condemned Abkhaz actions (Avidzba 2012, 52).

Violent Opposition: Toward a Split in the Society

Intergroup tension that intensified with Gorbachev's reforms spilled into violence after the Lykhny gathering. Almost immediately, this violence polarized and militarized the already divided Abkhaz society. The Georgian rally of April 1, 1989, was its first episode. The rally was sanctioned, but should not have exceeded an hour. It took place in Gjachrypsh/Leselidze, the farthest west town of Abkhazia, by the border crossing at the Psou River, which marks the border with Russia. It had "a distinct anti-Abkhaz nature," as "anti-Soviet, anti-Russian slogans and speeches" burst from the tribune, cordoned in order to prevent violence.[18] "There is no such nation as the Abkhaz!," the Abkhaz recall the slogans. "The Abkhaz are visitors from the North Caucasus!" Protesters carried Menshevik flags, a symbol of the Georgian Democratic Republic that left wounds in the Abkhaz collective memory of its military presence in 1918–1921.[19] As the then Pitsunda Kolkhoz chairman, a participant, describes this event,

> It was an invasion! They assembled their people in a column to protest against us. Our youth all gathered. I, too, participated. The assistant min-

ister of internal affairs arrived from Sukhum to calm people down, so that there was no clash between them and us, but Gamsakhurdia went on with the propaganda to Psou, which had a 4,000-large Georgian kolkhoz. He gathered all our local prosecutors, all Georgian bureaucrats, about three thousand of them. He stood on the tribune, made a speech. The first secretary [of Gudauta then] said, "Stop this! Stop the agitation! Do not make the people clash!" But the youth from Georgia were arriving with flags.

At the same time, more and more Abkhaz appeared, and some organized a picket around the area. The rally "ended with a provocative, triumphant passage of protesters waving Menshevik flags."[20]

The first violence broke out soon after: although the leadership of Aidgylara worked to prevent it, the extremist wing of the Abkhaz movement, Abrskyl, gathered its youth in nearby Bzyb/Bzipi, waiting for Georgian protesters to return. "When they passed Bzyb, our boys stopped them with stones," a local witness tells. "We broke down a Georgian bus carrying flags, as they screamed, 'This is our land!' and did not let them through. We finished them off without fear," an Abrskyl leader and participant confirms. Abkhaz cars chased the bus, but the *milicija* (police) dispersed them. Another group attacked a second bus further down the road. Its passengers were not part of the rally, but Georgian students returning to Sukhum/i from a funeral. An Abkhaz truck followed them, trying to run them downhill. Students were beaten up on arrival into Sukhum/i. As Lezhava (1997, 228) summarizes these events, "One bus with protest participants . . . and another random bus with people who did not have any relation to the protest were attacked, resulting in [over a dozen] injured. News of this caused a new wave of [Georgian] demonstrations and rallies [in Abkhazia]."

Georgian protests started on April 2 in Sukhum/i, Gagra, and Gal/i and took place on a daily basis thereafter. The Abkhaz participants in the violence were prosecuted, but the Georgian protesters demanded that "the crimes related to the attacks against the buses on April 1 be considered a nationalist action rather than hooliganism."[21] Georgian university students started a boycott on April 3, calling to end pro-Abkhaz propaganda in the Abkhaz and Russian media, eliminate the subject of Abkhaz history recently introduced into the school curriculum, make the history of Georgia part of university entry exams, and punish participants in the Lykhny and April 1 events.[22] Georgian professors joined the boycott on April 5 and, the next day, proposed splitting up Abkhaz State University, which was the catalyst for further intergroup clashes in July. Boycotters made an ultimatum on the punishment of the Abkhaz Lykhny and April 1 participants. A signatory of the Lykhny Letter, the first secretary of the Abkhaz Regional Committee, was thus dismissed and replaced (Y. Anchabadze 2013, 132).

Tragedy of April 9 and Georgia's Independence Day

The Abkhaz events triggered Georgian mobilization not only across Abkhazia but also in Tbilisi. A rally on April 9 "started with the issue of Abkhazia and then moved to the independence of Georgia," a Georgian expert says.[23] Indeed, in due course, Gamsakhurdia's slogans went from "The Abkhaz nation never existed" to "While there is Soviet power, we cannot abolish the autonomy of Abkhazia" (Lezhava 1997, 235). The Soviet state reacted with force. Troops of the Transcaucasus Military District violently dispersed Georgian protesters, legitimizing Georgia's eventual split from the Communist regime. Ghia Nodia and Álvaro Pinto Scholtbach (2006, 8) capture the consequence of this violence: "The new Georgia starts with the period of *perestroika* and *glasnost* . . . [in particular] April 9, 1989, when the Soviet army dispersed a huge pro-independence rally, leaving twenty people, mostly young women, dead. This tragic event represented the moral death of the Communist regime in Georgia: its legitimacy was fatally injured and never recovered."

This further intensified tensions in Abkhazia. Georgian workers of Abkhazia held a general strike. Students and professors boycotted university activities with a sit-down strike, demanding the opening of the Sukhum/i branch of Tbilisi State University. Aidgylara appealed to Gorbachev on May 11, but Georgia's Council of Ministers approved the branch on May 14. While this ended the Georgian campaign, the Abkhaz gathered to protest the decision on May 15 (Kvarchija 2011, 213). At the protest, the first secretary of the Abkhaz Regional Committee vowed that the branch would not be created, as Georgia's approval was a temporary measure taken to pacify Georgian unrest.

Georgians across Abkhazia mourned the victims of Soviet violence, organized a procession on May 19, and put up a memorial in Ochamchira/e shortly thereafter. They "tried 'burying' those killed with a monument to [April 9]. All the youth went up to it with flowers, although no dead were buried there. It was done to show that they have power here," a local Abkhaz interprets these actions. According to the Supreme Council report on the events, over four thousand Abkhaz gathered in protest, and the Regional Committee decided to take down the memorial (Sagarija 2002, 35).

In this context, Georgia's Independence Day on May 26 sparked more clashes. The Central Committee of Georgia approved celebrations across Georgia, yet the Abkhaz Regional Committee did not, given the escalating tensions in Abkhazia. The Georgian movement held unsanctioned rallies nonetheless. Protesters put up Menshevik flags at Constitution Square in Sukhum/i. "The square was full of flags on each pole," an Abkhaz sports student recounts the situation. "As sportsmen we climbed up and put the flags down. This led to fights," which law enforcement managed to halt.

The Georgian procession continued to Psou, at the border with Russia, to raise a flag at the stela commemorating the proclamation of Soviet power in 1921. "To prove their rights to Abkhazia, they held a rally at the border in Psou with Menshevik flags," an Abkhaz historian explains. "This provoked a reaction from the Abkhaz," the Supreme Council report on the events concludes, "since it is here that the restoration of the Soviet power in Abkhazia began" (Sagarija 2002, 35). The Abkhaz took down the flag with the help of authorities. The situation stabilized, but minor incidents continued.

After these events, in letters to Moscow, Aidgylara worked to distance the April 9 violence from the Lykhny gathering, which was seen as its trigger (Lezhava 1997, 245). The deputy of Abkhazia's Supreme Council, Vladislav Ardzinba, an intellectual who was appointed director of the D. Gulia Institute of Language, Literature, and History in 1988 and, in 1990, became chairman of the Supreme Council of Abkhazia and led the Abkhaz war effort, connected the gathering to decades of injustice in Abkhazia in a speech given at the First People's Deputies Congress in Moscow on May 25. Due to this history, he said, "the Abkhaz consider remaining in the Soviet Union as the sole possible means of preserving their national self-identity" (Maryhuba 1994, 466). Support for Ardzinba skyrocketed as a result. "In times of tension, revolutionaries, leaders are born," an Abkhaz official captures the effect of this speech. "Our leader appeared then . . . [one] who could bravely stand up and say what the true condition of the Abkhaz was, that the rights of the people were infringed. The congress heard him." "Six of us from my neighborhood secretly went to Moscow to hold a hunger strike in front of the congress. Ardzinba spoke there and then," an activist exemplifies this support.

July Clashes: Abkhaz State University

In Abkhazia, however, tension continued rising around the opening of the Sukhum/i branch of Tbilisi State University. The Abkhaz political and activist elite requested a Soviet commission on the university in letters to Moscow.[24] Aidgylara gathered up to one thousand people at the Philharmonic Theater on June 22 and made a statement to the population of Abkhazia (Lezhava 1997, 248). "Let us unite in the struggle against any expression of nationalism and extremism, which are foreign to our common spiritual culture," the statement said, blaming the Georgian movement for splitting up the society (Kvarchija 2011, 219). "The Abkhaz declared a hunger strike by the Philharmonic" and rejected leaving until a Soviet commission arrived, one participant recalls. "We sat there, all of us."

The commission held consultations on July 3 and concluded that opening the Tbilisi State University branch was not acceptable. Yet the Georgian newspaper *Sabchota Abkhazeti* (Soviet Abkhazia) announced admissions to the branch, and "the Abkhaz saw this as a call to action" (Lezhava 1997, 255). Party leaders vowed at another gathering at the Philharmonic on July 7 that the editor of the newspaper made a mistake, but the Tbilisi State University rector approved admissions exams for July 14.[25] "The confrontation was due to the opening of the Tbilisi State University branch and the beginning of admissions exams," an Abkhaz official confirms. An Aidgylara member who worked in the organization's press service and at the university newspaper and participated in the confrontation describes the events in detail:

> All of this began with the division of the university. [Georgian professors and students] wanted to divide it by nationality by creating the Tbilisi State University branch. By a decision from Tbilisi, a ruling came to Abkhazia, and they began this process. We protested, and they had a hunger strike in front of the Georgian Drama Theater. The demonstrations began, [with] protests on the streets.
>
> Admissions exams would take place in the First School. [A messenger] came and told us. At night, we all went there. The Eighth Division [of the Soviet army] blocked it and did not let us in.... People heard about that and started arriving.... We all stood there, when admissions exams were going on, and did not let students in.
>
> [Georgians] gathered in Rustaveli Park. One thousand youth held a protest there. They read something and shouted, "Zviadi![26] This is our land!"——had a camera and went to take pictures of the protest. He is from our village. They noticed him and decided to take his camera. This is why it all started, at this moment, when [Georgians] attacked him. He, of course, did not want to give up the camera. They started beating him. Then the boys I knew—my brother, my husband, and his friends—passed by, saw what was happening, and went to pull them apart.
>
> Within a fraction of a second, someone ran up and told us that ours [Abkhaz] were being beaten, and that was it. [We] ran there, took whatever we could—metal rods, sticks—and a clash began. We beat each other up and went different ways. We all went to the school, to stand there. It was getting darker.
>
> The [National] Forum [Aidgylara] gathered to decide what to do. We knew [Georgians] would come with weapons, knew they were gathering weapons, whereas the forum did not have anything. We made a decision to take people away from the school, at least to the square. Students returned there after the fight in Rustaveli Park.
>
> The square was filled with people. We all stood there and did not know what would happen. People started saying that [Svans from

Svaneti, a province of Georgia, and from the Kodor/i Gorge in Abkhazia] would come and a fight would take place. Someone had to take the initiative. My husband said, "Let's cut down trees, so that they will not get through," and we did. But they appeared on trucks, half naked, wearing white armbands, with guns attached to their trucks.

The only thing that helped us was that the Tqvarchelians [from a mining town in the east] were right on time with their explosives. [The Svans] came by cars and surrounded the circle with the explosives [that the Tqvarchelians made]. [The Svans] did not have time to shoot. They did, once or twice. But when the explosions went off, here and there, they got scared and turned around. After they left, people were there [in the square] the whole night. Representatives of the [National] Forum went onstage and spoke. We had to tell people something, calm them down, tell them what to do.

There was also a clash at the Red Bridge. Our three Abkhaz were killed there trying to get to the square. . . . Rumors went around that Georgians occupied the whole Ochamchira district [and that] the same was happening in Tqvarchal. People were agitated because the whole population able to fight was at the square. A decision was made to transfer people to Gudauta, and that was done. Buses came to get people to Gudauta, and then people from different districts went to Ochamchira and Tqvarchal.

The chairman of the [National] Forum . . . [and] all the activists were writing to Russia the whole night, appealing to save us: "If you do not send the army, there will be no Abkhaz people." And really, . . . when the Russian forces came, the situation more or less calmed down.

Official reports and other interviews support this account.[27] Indeed, Aidgylara activists and regular Abkhaz picketed the school on July 14, then blocked it the next day. When the picketers' demand to cancel admissions exams was not met, the picketers broke in, injuring Georgian students and professors, and damaged admissions documents. In the meantime, a clash broke out in Rustaveli Park over an attack on an Abkhaz cameraman. Picketers were informed and headed to the park with "stones, rails, garden benches, and fences" (Sagarija 2002, 188). It was "a 'wall on wall' clash—the Abkhaz from one side, Georgians from the other," Abkhaz participants tell. "We drove [the Georgians] to the sea with sticks." Over forty people were injured or killed in this episode.

The news spread, and the Abkhaz and Georgians from Abkhazia's districts set out for Sukhum/i. As activists and regular Abkhaz of the Gagra district describe: "A messenger came for me and said, 'A fight is going on in Sukhum between the

Abkhaz and Georgians!' We went"; "We took hunting rifles and went where the protest was in Sukhum. We knew it would not end just like that." Svans, a Georgian subgroup residing in Svaneti and the Kodor/i Gorge, arrived to block the White and Red Bridges on the entry to Sukhum/i and stopped a bus from the eastern Abkhaz village of Kutol, killing and injuring passengers. "Svans studied there [in Sukhum]," an Abrskyl leader explains. "They, too, came here, got involved in armed fights, took defense of the Red Bridge, so that help [for the Abkhaz] would not arrive from Ochamchira." It was the Svans who appeared half naked and armed in Rustaveli Park, but left as Tqvarchal/Tqvarcheli explosives "went off by their truck. Such a fight began that they were beaten to near death," the Abrskyl leader goes on.

To avert passage from Georgian-dominated Gal/i, the Abkhaz placed trucks on the Galidzga Bridge in Ochamchira/e and defended the bridge with stones and other improvised tools. As a leader of Aidgylara's Tqvarchal/Tqvarcheli branch corroborates, "there was nothing to use for defense, no weapons." Weapons were seized from the population in anticipation of clashes and stored at police stations, the prosecutor of the Gal/i district reports (Sagarija 2002, 11). A Gal/i resident, however, was killed, and his body was exhibited in Gal/i to mobilize further support.

Many villages organized road pickets thereafter, and some militias gained access to stockpiled arms in eastern Abkhazia. The Georgian movement brought armed supporters from western Georgia. But clashes ended as soon as the Internal Forces of the Soviet Union arrived in Abkhazia at the request of the Abkhaz activist and political elite. A curfew was imposed across Abkhazia once the situation was pacified, and the police confiscated weapons that had not previously been seized from the population.[28]

The violence resulted in sixteen deaths and up to four hundred injuries; the Prosecutor's Office of Georgia immediately began an investigation (Sagarija 2002, 45; Lezhava 1997, 258). Georgian intellectuals blamed the Abkhaz for the tragedy, and Georgian politicians, linking it to their anti-Soviet claims, "call[ed] on the Georgian nation to refrain from armed conflict, as today we confront not the Abkhaz separatists . . . but the Russian army" (Avidzba 2012, 104). In response to the investigation, Abkhaz leaders wrote a letter to Moscow stating that they would "not recognize an investigation into the events of July 15–16, 1989, by Georgian or Abkhaz law enforcement agencies or with participation of Georgians and Abkhaz" and that a more neutral body would have to undertake this investigation (Lezhava 1997, 258).

The Abkhaz General Strike

Subsequent Georgian and Abkhaz mobilization focused on the investigation process. Georgian demonstrations in Georgia and Abkhazia demanded punishment of the Abkhaz, especially the party members who signed the Lykhny Letter and then assisted fellow Abkhaz in the violence. The Abkhaz defended their leaders and regular participants in the clashes by organizing strikes by workers and hunger strikes, which soon turned into an all-Abkhaz strike, demanding the formation of a Soviet commission to investigate the July events. As the chairman of the newly established Strike Committee, formerly an Abrskyl leader, reports,

> Tqvarchal was the first place that the Abkhaz had to defend. . . . Their intelligentsia . . . could all be repressed, as in 1937, [for bringing explosives to Rustaveli Park. Also], Bagapsh, our second president, then secretary of the Ochamchira district, gave an order to take hunting weapons [from the stockpiles] and shoot. Here, in Sukhum, Ozgan gave an order to break the security in Gudauta and take weapons. They were persecuted for this.
>
> I was called into the Bzyb *sel'sovet* [village council]. There sat [Abrskyl leaders] . . . , the chairman of the council. I was offered to lead this business and become chairman of the Strike Committee in Gagra. Tqvarchelians came. We decided on a general strike across Abkhazia . . . first in Tqvarchal, then in Gagra. We created the Strike Committee [and] prepared a statement.

The Strike Committee had branches in Tqvarchal/Tqvarcheli, where Abkhaz workers dominated, and Gagra, among other sites, but the coordination center was in Sukhum/i, where workers were mainly Georgian. Presented to Abkhazia's first secretary on August 18, the Strike Committee's statement demanded special administration of Abkhazia under direct control of the Supreme Soviet, formation of a commission on the causes of destabilization in Abkhazia, transfer of the investigation on the July events to Soviet bodies, and repeal of the May 14 ruling on the Sukhum/i branch of Tbilisi State University. The demands, it said, "must be implemented by August 25, 1989. Otherwise, the Strike Committee of Abkhazia will declare a general strike on the territory of the republic." The chairman goes on: "It was not enough to write. All the shelves in Moscow were filled with our letters. Aidgylara was writing, too. Thus the Strike Committee went to Moscow with the elders, war veterans, to ask the Central Committee of the Communist Party. Once a week we went to the *obkom* [Abkhaz Regional Committee] with workers' demands, resolved them, and reported back to the people."

When the demands were not implemented, the general strike began in September. Over forty thousand Abkhaz workers joined across Abkhazia.[29] "All factories went on strike," a Tqvarchal/Tqvarcheli participant states, "even the bakery—which supplied bread to civilians while its employees were officially on strike" (Zhidkov 2011, 41). "We had to organize the strikes in a civil manner," the chairman says. "Parallel to these strikes, a hunger strike was announced in Gudauta. But strikes and hunger strikes are very different things. I was against hunger strikes. I eat, I do not walk around hungry. I told them, 'Our status, our sovereignty stretches up to the border. So you boys preserve yourselves for further struggle against [Georgia].'" To the participants and observers, however, the hunger strike meant that "people were ready for the last measure," and this form of collective action spread across the major urban centers of Abkhazia. "Hunger strikes started in Pitsunda, Gagra, every administrative center of Abkhazia," participants explain.[30] Tqvarchal/Tqvarcheli miners similarly went on a sit-down strike underground (Zhidkov 2011).[31] This put pressure on the authorities, and the investigation of the July events was transferred to the Soviet judiciary.

Polarization in Employment, Education, and Government

Although the situation in Abkhazia calmed down after the July 1989 clashes, the violence dramatically shattered the already polarized intergroup relations. "We were woken up in 1989," most Abkhaz say. "We were now certain about their hatred toward the Abkhaz." As a result, "open division began after 1989." Division touched all areas of the society and was acute in the highly integrated employment, education, and government institutions, particularly in urban areas. "There was a split in 1989—teams, hospitals, kindergartens," a then student captures the societal polarization. As a communications operator describes the deterioration of intergroup relations in the workplace, "1989 split our team. We had four Abkhaz girls, Armenians, Greeks, Russians, Georgians, and Mingrelians. Georgians and Mingrelians paired up and all the rest were in the opposite camp. There was nothing like that before. If before we had been close with Georgian girls in the brigade, we now had coldness between us."

When the Sukhum/i branch of Tbilisi State University was opened, students and professors of the university split as well. A then Abkhaz professor characterizes the intergroup tensions in the university:

> All national tensions were reflected at the university. . . . We had the Abkhaz, Russian, and Georgian sectors. Of course, the Abkhaz studied in the Abkhaz sector. The Russian sector was the largest. Georgians studied in the Georgian sector. In the Russian sector, too, up to 60 percent of the students were Georgian.

We young scientists tried talking to our Georgian counterparts, to find some compromise, suggested governance models for a coexisting university, tried convincing them that it was wrong to cut the university team by ethnicity. In 1989, the university split, however. They opened the [Tbilisi State University] branch [and] our department split. Half the philosophy professors were Georgian and went to the branch. Almost all non-Georgian professors remained.

Some wanted to develop the national idea, but others under its guise followed their own interests . . . related to [leading] positions and bribes. [For example], when they opened the branch, they right away opened a Russian sector there, [where students would not] speak Georgian, but would be admitted on a paid basis.

As the society split, the government could no longer hold together. As an Abkhaz official illustrates: "The Supreme Council formed then was half Georgian, half Abkhaz. [It] simply split in two when drafting legislation. The Georgian half would stand up and walk away—and this often happened on serious questions. Can you imagine how legitimate a decision was if it was taken by the minority? There was a battle for every voice. If fifty left and the forty-nine remaining passed a bill, the Georgian part of the population ignored the decision and did not implement it."

The independence campaign in Georgia deepened this split. In November 1989 and March and June 1990, Georgia's Supreme Council declared "null and void all state structures that existed in Georgia from February 1921" and called them the result of occupation through the overthrow of the Georgian Democratic Republic (Lezhava 1997, 267). Georgia thus "annulled all the treaties . . . serv[ing] as a legal foundation for the existence of the Georgian autonomies," including Abkhazia (Zverev 1996, pt. 3). In the summer of 1990, Georgia changed the elections law, precluding candidates from the autonomies from running in Georgia's elections, and made Georgian the only language of the government.

In response, boycotted by its Georgian deputies, the Supreme Council of Abkhazia issued the declaration "On the state sovereignty of the Abkhaz Soviet Socialist Republic" and the resolution "On the legal safeguards for the protection of the statehood of Abkhazia" on August 25, 1990. It made null and void treaties concluded with the Georgian Democratic Republic, called the arrival of its troops into Abkhazia in 1918 a military intervention, and sought restoration of Abkhazia's 1921 status as an SSR. The Georgian Supreme Council declared these documents unlawful, and Georgian deputies of Abkhazia supported the Supreme Council's decision in their separate emergency session.

At the same time, Aidgylara worked to preserve the Soviet Union as a federation based on the equality of subjects and hosted the first Assembly of the Mountain

Peoples of the Caucasus, which then played a role in the war of 1992–1993. It condemned the forceful resettlement and Georgianization of Abkhazia as an act of genocide and the 1931 status change as an act of political aggression.[32]

In this context, the election of Gamsakhurdia in Georgia and Ardzinba in Abkhazia in 1990 hardened the respective self-determination campaigns. Resolutions preparing Georgia to transition to independence were passed on November 14, 1990.[33] Boycotted by the Abkhaz, the referendum of March 31, 1991, unanimously supported Georgia's independence. On April 9, Georgia adopted an act, "On the restoration of state independence of Georgia," proclaiming "the territory of the sovereign Republic of Georgia as one and indivisible" (Lezhava 1997, 291). In turn, the Abkhaz referendum on the preservation of the Soviet Union of March 17, banned by Georgia, received 98.6 percent of the votes in favor among the 52.3 percent of the population that participated, almost all non-Georgian minorities (Hewitt 1996, 213).

This showed that not only the Abkhaz but also other minorities of Abkhazia were reluctant to live in independent Georgia. Pressured by Abkhazia's growing ties with the North Caucasus and Russia and Georgia's war in South Ossetia of 1991–1992, Gamsakhurdia made concessions to the Abkhaz. Elections in October–December 1991 in Abkhazia assumed a quota system, whereby the Abkhaz received twenty-eight seats, Georgians twenty-six, and other minorities eleven (Zverev 1996; Zürcher, Baev, and Koehler 2005). By the time of the elections, Aidgylara consolidated its power among the non-Georgian population, and non-Georgian minorities united in a winning coalition, polarizing Abkhazia's new Parliament.

The collapse of the Soviet Union and the overthrow of Gamsakhurdia by Eduard Shevardnadze and his supporters, the National Guard and the Mkhedrioni (Horsemen), advanced this polarization. In February 1992, Georgia's Provisional Military Council reinstated the constitution of 1921, "which included only a vague clause on Abkhazian autonomy" (Coppieters 2002, 99). The Abkhaz proposed a "confederal-type structure," which Shevardnadze rejected (Francis 2011, 90). On July 23, 1992, Abkhaz and non-Georgian deputies terminated Abkhazia's 1978 constitution as Georgia's autonomous republic and restored the 1925 constitution as an SSR, "independent but 'united with the Soviet Socialist Republic of Georgia on the basis of a special union treaty'" (Cornell 2000, 170).[34] The decision was again made in the absence of Georgian deputies. "From 1989, the political situation worsened," an Abkhaz activist concludes.

Militarization: The Mkhedrioni and the Abkhaz Guard

Polarization in institutions after the 1989 clashes went hand in hand with the creation of Georgian and Abkhaz armed groups in Abkhazia. "The society was militarized," a security official characterizes the situation. The Mkhedrioni and the

Abkhaz Guard were the main armed actors. A Georgian paramilitary unit established in Tbilisi, the Mkhedrioni appeared in Abkhazia after the 1989 violence. "At the end of the 1980s, Gamsakhurdia was forming the Mkhedrioni units here (it means Horsemen)," an Abkhaz journalist says. "The Mkhedrioni were located across Abkhazia. They had pockets everywhere, but the commanders and most men were in Gagra." An Armenian hotel owner confirms: "We are currently sitting where the Mkhedrioni had their headquarters. My whole upper housing sector was the headquarters." A Gagra local explains the composition of the armed group: "Ninety percent were from Georgia, but locals also joined." Many Abkhaz thus say, retrospectively, that "the Mkhedrioni were really preparing Georgians after 1989"; they "created weapons stockpiles in Georgian homes" and "distributed arms to hide in gardens until the time [came]," referring to the war.

The Abkhaz Guard, officially known as the Special Regiment of the Internal Forces (SRIF), emerged in response. An Abkhaz who served in the force captures its rationale: "The Abkhaz Guard was created before the war ... in response to [the formation of the Mkhedrioni] units [in Abkhazia] ..., to defend the population in case the Mkhedrioni turned violent." "I formed [a local unit of] the Abkhaz Guard with residents of Ldzaa [an Abkhaz village] to balance out the Mkhedrioni [in the Gagra district]," an officer confirms. The force was modeled on the Eighth Regiment of the Soviet army, or the Battalions of the Internal Forces of the Russian Ministry of Internal Affairs, which suppressed violence in Abkhazia before the collapse of the Soviet Union and which the Supreme Council of Abkhazia took under its control on December 29, 1991, after the Union collapsed.[35] Because of this history and the Supreme Council's involvement, the Abkhaz Guard was in general viewed as an official force in Abkhazia. "This was an official structure," regular Abkhaz and government officials explain, and "therefore, it had some legitimacy."

Soviet officers willing to stay and reservists across Abkhazia were drafted into the Guard.[36] "I was doing my business and was also in the Abkhaz Guard," the Abkhaz who were drafted report. "Those who served there were typically younger. Those who had already served in the Soviet army were mentors, officers." Up to one thousand reservists and one hundred regulars, including some Soviet officers, were drafted, equipped with weapons and uniforms, and stationed across Abkhazia to guard major infrastructure sites. "They guarded roads, had uniforms, there was internal discipline," regular Abkhaz say. "They had barracks and weapons, were well known, with documents. We knew who belonged to the Guard."

By January 1992, the force guarded the Ingur/i Bridge, a crossing point at the administrative border with Georgia. In February, it resisted Georgian forces that marched through Abkhazia in pursuit of ousted president Gamsakhurdia's supporters (Pachulija 2010, 31). In April, a small-scale clash broke out during another attempted intrusion from Georgia proper (Avidzba 2013, 371–372).

In Abkhazia, the Mkhedrioni "had clashes with the Abkhaz Guard, but tried avoiding armed confrontation," a Pitsunda Kolkhoz vice-chairman reports. The clashes were limited to street fights, like those normalized before 1989, but now involved armed groups. "The Mkhedrioni orchestrated riots, fights in restaurants, such as the Gagrypsh. I was a witness there," the Pitsunda bread factory's director states in summarizing their activities. "They vandalized . . . and walked around in groups to pick fights." These activities were widely seen as criminal. "I encountered events of criminal nature, but not organized violence," an Armenian victim reports. "[To give] an example, a Greek man was fishing," another witness demonstrates, and "the Mkhedrioni came and killed him just like that, for nothing." Reservists of the Abkhaz Guard thus say, "We were finding these Mkhedrioni, beating, disarming them."

No large-scale violence with participation of the broader population, as in 1989, took place until the war of 1992–1993, despite the presence of these armed actors. The Georgian Independence Day could again have resulted in clashes in 1990. As in the previous year, "Georgians marched with flags through the city center [of Gagra]," Abkhaz witnesses recall, "kissed the land at the stadium [where the celebration was held] saying, 'This is our land.'" While Aidgylara appealed to local authorities, Abrskyl organized a hunger strike at the stadium. Video footage of the event shows that the strikers had to flee, but Soviet troops placed between the two sides prevented the violence.[37]

The activists went to Gagra chairman K. D. Kuchukhidze, who sanctioned the event. "My boys . . . and I nailed the door to the *ispolkom* (executive committee), blocked the door to the reception room with a couch, and went to the balcony to wait for what the committee would tell Georgians," a then Abrskyl leader explains. Kuchukhidze resigned (but was later reinstated) and violence was again averted. No other events led to clashes until August 1992, when the Georgian-Abkhaz war began. "We had clashes in 1989, but not after," the Abkhaz consistently report. As Zürcher (2007, 140) corroborates, "Until 1992 there was astonishingly little organized violence between local ethnic groups in Abkhazia." The war, as a result, came as a surprise (see chapter 5).

Mobilization Trajectories

How did the direct and indirect experience of everyday confrontation, political contention, and violent opposition affect wartime decisions? Over time, most Abkhaz were exposed to these repertoires of intergroup conflict as part of their group. When the question of political status became a topic of everyday conversations, it became difficult to maintain friendships across group boundaries. "Our relations were no longer the same," a student reflects on his experience of everyday confrontation. With the deterioration of intergroup relations and the explosion of national movement activity on both sides in the conflict, ordinary people who previously did not participate in political activism joined collective action. "In this atmosphere, the university split, opposition started, there were even those killed. I joined the movement then," explains a now prominent Abkhaz activist on her decision to join. "Everyone my age participated," most Abkhaz in their twenties and early thirties at the time say as a result. Those who faced intergroup violence in particular often joined the armed mobilization that followed the 1989 clashes, which then structured their wartime decisions. As one participant demonstrates, "In 1989, I participated in the Georgian-Abkhaz armed clash.... From the first days of the Abkhaz Guard, [I] joined it with friends ... [and] guarded the Inguri and Okhurej posts. On August 14, [we] defended the Red Bridge" (Khodzhaa 2009, 793–794).

Participation in prewar conflict shaped mobilization trajectories in the war. Depending on whether and how people mobilized before the war, they adopted a range of roles in and outside the structure of the Abkhaz movement at the war's onset. Those who had been active in the Abkhaz Guard typically joined the war effort as part of this organized armed structure, as illustrated above. These individuals followed an organized mobilization trajectory. Those who joined prewar mobilization spontaneously, in general, became defense volunteers. "I participated in 1989 ... [and] on the first day of the ... war joined as a defense volunteer," one fighter explains (Khodzhaa 2003, 117). These individuals followed a spontaneous mobilization trajectory.

However, there was variation in these trajectories. Whereas some individuals who participated in prewar collective action mobilized in support and fighting roles in the war, others hid or fled Abkhazia, and not all fighters had prior mobilization experience. Three women demonstrate the mobilization trajectories that diverge from the predictions that we could make based on their prior mobilization experience. First, instead of joining the Abkhaz support or fighting apparatuses in the war, as we would expect based on her active political past, the secretary of a local branch of Aidgylara hid during the war with the archives of the organization. Second, the librarian who joined the workers' strike following the 1977 Letter of 130, who would be expected to mobilize on behalf of her group based on this experience, fled Abkhazia altogether, as did other Aidgylara activists and participants in prewar collective action who were not members of the organization. Third, one woman whose prewar roles were primarily those of a wife and a mother of two children decided to fight without prior mobilization experience. "Half a year after the war began, my wife joined the war effort. We went together during the offensive on Sukhum," her husband, who fought in the war, corroborates.

Beyond the organized and spontaneous trajectories, prewar mobilization defined the social network basis of wartime mobilization. People who participated together in prewar arguments, rallies, and especially clashes often located each other at the war's onset to discuss how to collectively act in response to the Georgian advance, or consolidate the national and local threat narratives into action, and mobilized together to protect their group at the quotidian, local, or national levels. Thus relatives tied by kinship and common experiences of everyday confrontation, colleagues who joined workers' strikes on behalf of their group, and university friends who clashed with Georgian students over the opening of the Sukhum/i branch of Tbilisi State University in 1989 shared experiences that helped consolidate the notions of threat at the war's onset. Variable threat perceptions emerged as a result, to direct wartime mobilization in different ways.

5
FROM UNCERTAINTY TO MOBILIZATION IN FOUR DAYS

Now we understood what we faced—weaponry, tanks, marauding. They had it all, whereas we had nothing. Our strengths were uneven.

—Abkhaz fighter, Gagra, 2011

How did regular men and women in Abkhazia meet the advance of Georgian forces into Abkhazia? I asked respondents, "Where were you on August 14, 1992?" The conversations that followed demonstrate the immense uncertainty that ordinary people experienced at the outset of the Georgian-Abkhaz war.[1] When the Georgian armed forces entered Abkhazia in mid-August 1992, nearly all of the 142 people who shared their stories with me turned to their social networks to fathom the meaning of the Georgian advance and decide how to act in response. The picture of mobilization that emerges from this analysis is not one of cost-benefit calculation expected from individuals based on their assumed and fixed knowledge of risk. Rather, it is a nuanced account of how collective conflict identities formed through day-to-day exposure to and participation in prewar repertoires of intergroup conflict are invoked at the war's onset and how different framings of the nature of violence filter across society to consolidate among socially embedded actors at the time of mobilization. These priors from the prewar period and situational social network effects at the war's onset often in surprising ways shape how people come to understand anticipated risk, how threat perceptions vary across individuals, and how this variation affects mobilization.

"No One Understood What Was Going On": Uncertainty of the War's Onset

August 14, 1992, began as a regular day for most men and women in Abkhazia. It was a typical instance of the "quotidian," or everyday life, defined by "patterns of everyday functioning and routinized expectancies associated with those patterns" (Snow et al. 1998, 19). In other words, people across the territory set out for their usual activities and made plans for the following days, as troops thousands strong crossed the Ingur/i River to eastern Abkhazia in the morning and advanced toward the capital, Sukhum/i, crushing initial Abkhaz resistance by the eastern center of Ochamchira/e. Some respondents were at work, while others were enjoying a sunny summer day at the beach, tending gardens at home, or visiting relatives in near and distant parts of Abkhazia and expecting to return in time for the work week. A teacher, then on school break, captures the everyday character of life in Gagra in western Abkhazia at the time of the Georgian advance: "When the war began, I was at the beach with my children. We had guests from Kiev, [Ukraine], and were getting ready to make kebab." A mother of two young children conveys the regular pace of family activities and expectations of future days in the east and west of Abkhazia: "On the eve of the war (the war started on Friday), my husband took my oldest, three-year-old son and left for eastern Abkhazia to visit his parents. I stayed with my younger son in Gagra [in the west]. It was just regular life. [My husband] would then come back to go to work."

The events turned out differently, however. The sudden appearance of Georgian troops, first in the east and the following day in the west of Abkhazia, and the news of the violence that spread across the territory interrupted current and planned activities, rupturing the normality of day-to-day life. Traffic stopped, people left work and ran to the streets, and traditional gathering places overflowed with crowds. Profound confusion over the Georgian advance ensued among the ordinary Abkhaz. As in other cases where intergroup violence erupted unexpectedly, the Georgian advance into Abkhazia disrupted everyday routines and expectancies.[2] A university student returning from his trip to Russia recalls the disruption near the border with Russia and confusion among the locals of Gagra who gathered outside of the town's administration building: "The day of the war, in 1992, I was in Sochi, [Russia]. On my way back, I saw that all the cars were stopped and people were discussing something emotionally. I did not know what happened. . . . Everyone at the administration was confused. No one could understand the situation. Many thought it was like [the Georgian-Abkhaz clashes] in 1989." In Sukhum/i, reports evoke images of Georgian helicopters shooting at the beach and the civilian population, with the tourist season still in peak. As an Abkhaz Soviet party member clarifies: "The war started. The first shot [in Sukhum/i] was at 11:30 a.m. from a tank toward the then Supreme Council [of Abkhazia]. After that, helicopters appeared. They shot at the building of the Supreme Council from various directions, aiming at the flag, but hit the beach." Witnesses recurrently describe the panic that this violence triggered on the streets of Sukhum/i. A professor recounts the chaos that overtook the city center near Abkhaz State University: "In 1992, [the troops of] the State Council of Georgia came to the territory of Abkhazia. No one expected that. There were tourists. A helicopter flew over. They started military action against the peaceful population. . . . I left the [university because] there was noise. It was noon on Prospekt Mira [Victory Avenue]. There were many pedestrians. All started running to the sides [of the street]. I saw tracked vehicles coming—armored personnel carriers, infantry fighting vehicles. Our military units that were deployed near Sukhum were retreating to the Gumista [River]. It was complete chaos."

The shock that the Georgian forces produced swept not only ordinary men and women but also government officials and military personnel of the Abkhaz Guard. A member of the Parliament remembers her shock when she saw Georgian helicopters over the Supreme Council building, even though she was informed that the Georgian military was advancing its way to the capital: "We were in shock then, did not expect that. I had my children here [in Sukhum/i]. I was in the House of Government, looked out the window, and saw helicopters coming from the sea and shooting. Can you imagine that? Before that, we had already been told that the Georgian armed forces took into captivity the head of the Ochamchira administration, an Abkhaz. We did not think they would appear here so soon."

The few Abkhaz guards who remained on duty, as most reservists were released from duty shortly before the Georgian advance, were similarly shocked. Georgian troops immediately captured and imprisoned up to ten reservists who guarded a post by the Ingur/i River, along with their commander and the head of the Ochamchira/e administration. Surviving guards say that they did not expect the fighting (Pachulija 2010, 29–30). A commander further along the road to the capital was bewildered by the news of the Georgian advance, so much so that he forgot the relevant command for alerting the guards: "August 14, 1992, was a regular day on duty. . . . Suddenly, [the commander] looked out the window . . . [and] gave a command, 'Alarm.' Not understanding what was happening, I said that everything was in order. But he repeated, '[A]larm.' Realizing that [he meant to issue a] combat alert, I told him to turn on the siren, [as] the button was in his office. As he came to his senses, he gave the signal [to mobilize]" (interview in Khodzhaa 2003, 17).

The confusion over the Georgian advance was only strengthened by the rumors that surrounded Georgian actions. For example, a driver recalls the rumor spreading at the time that Georgian paratroopers were coming to western Abkhazia: "We were told that there would be an air landing, but there was none." Instead, hundreds of Georgian marines landed in the area on August 15 with arms and heavy equipment.

Across the interviews, respondents report that they did not expect the Georgian advance or believe that a war had started in mid-August 1992. "No one thought there could be a military attack," recounts a director of a state enterprise in Gagra of his disbelief in the danger posed by the events. "We did not believe that [Georgian] marines were dropped off [in Tsandrypsh/Gantiadi, near Gagra]. I went there without a weapon." "We suspected something, but even that day when we saw ships [approaching Abkhazia], we could not tell—a ship is a ship," a local teacher concurs. Respondents widely expressed such disbelief: "My sister was visiting, when the phone rang, and we were told that a war began. We thought, 'This cannot be!'"[3]

A worker in Gudauta explains this reaction by the calm that preceded the war: "Between 1989 and 1992, there were no more clashes. The situation did not heat up, and so they attacked abruptly. I went to work, but cars were standing in traffic. [People screamed], 'The war is in Sukhum!' We went there.... We did not know that the case was the same in Gagra." As a result of the relative calm over the three years before the war, "many did not realize that this was a serious war." "We understood that something was happening, but did not think it would be a war," an assistant chairman of a kolkhoz in western Abkhazia reports.

Instead, respondents across occupations and the geographical span of the study interpreted the events as a clash similar to that of 1989. "On August 14, we thought it was a usual, regular clash," a professor caught in Sukhum/i at the war's onset explains. "But a war, of such a large scale? I did not expect that." A youth activist and journal editor in the west similarly reports: "We had a hope that this would be over, that this could not last long. They would make an agreement and it would be over. As in 1989, it would last two, three weeks and that's it."

Only 5 of the 142 respondents say that they "knew about the war, but did not expect it then." "A foreseeing person could see something," these respondents tell, as "there were constant Georgian incursions, visits, [acts of] humiliation of the Abkhaz people." Some claim that they prepared for the imminent violence. A tourist sector administrator in central Abkhazia explains such precautions: "We were civilians in regular professions . . . and understood that if Georgians in Georgia were firing at each other [in the ongoing war with supporters of the ousted president Gamsakhurdia], they would certainly come with weapons to Abkhazia. Every rational Abkhaz understood this. And people were preparing. How? By creating self-defense groups in case of a war." One was a group of university students who set a meeting place in event of a war and headed there at the war's onset.

In each of these cases, the individuals involved were active in the Abkhaz movement and had access to networks that other ordinary people did not have. A member of the university student group that prearranged a meeting place illustrates this connectedness on the day of the war:

> I got stuck in a traffic jam for a long time. I listened to everything [people were saying]. Before that, I had other connections. It was not a militia, but in case of an emergency we [the university student group] knew where to go [*names the place*]. I saw boys there who asked whether [others from the group] were in Sukhum. Everything happened very quickly. There were already battles in the middle of the day [on August 14].... Then [on August 15], we saw the marines, but could not do anything about it.... We knew that, in any case, we could see each other in the [named location]. This was a gathering place.

Another activist's sister corroborates: "My brother felt that there would be a war. He was even called an extremist for it. But he had more information than regular people. [Levan] Gytsba, [Boris] Kikhiripa, [leaders of the more violent wing of the Abkhaz movement, Abrskyl], were all from his circle."

Whereas a few Abkhaz may have prepared for war, most ordinary Abkhaz men and women reacted to the news of the Georgian advance with confusion, shock, and disbelief.[4]

"Now We Understood What We Faced": From Uncertainty to Mobilization

How did the Abkhaz navigate the uncertainty of the Georgian advance to understand the anticipated risk involved and arrive at a range of mobilization decisions from fleeing to fighting on the Abkhaz side? This section traces the process by which regular people in Abkhazia came to view the threat of Georgian forces and the typical mobilization trajectories that followed as a result. I draw on responses in my interviews to the questions "How did you learn about the Georgian advance?" and "What did you do next?" The questions were purposely open-ended to discover the diverse sources and sequencing of information that people sought in the context of intense uncertainty of the Georgian advance and to record individual reactions to this information. What emerged from the responses are detailed accounts of individual mobilization that combine in a common social dynamic of information filtering I call the *collective threat framing* mechanism.

The mechanism captures how different, often competing, framings of threat were transmitted across the social structures with which people interacted on a daily basis and turned to for threads of information when confusion was the order of the day. The first source of information on what had taken place and how to act in response were for most respondents Abkhaz leaders in the government who articulated the broad confines of the threat posed by Georgian forces and called on the population to mobilize. This framing was then adapted at the local level by heads of local administrations, the elders, and military and social movement figures, among other respected community members, to fit the needs of local defense. But these diverse framings were consolidated, and mobilization decisions were typically made with close relatives and friends, the quotidian social networks that enabled the trust essential in the context of uncertainty. Almost all respondents drew on these social interactions to understand the nature of the Georgian advance, the dangers it posed to personal safety and broader groups in the population of Abkhazia, and the actions to be taken in response. A minority who found themselves in the midst of the Georgian advance or were informed by those who did followed the alternative path of situational threat perception.

Situational Threat Perception

Organized fighters previously recruited into the Abkhaz Guard and positioned along the route of the Georgian advance from eastern Abkhazia toward Sukhum/i were the first to face Georgian forces in the morning of August 14. Units of the Abkhaz Guard were stationed across Abkhazia before the war, with guard duties along the road connecting the territory of Abkhazia (see figure 5.1). However, the Ingur/i post at the Georgian-Abkhaz administrative border was discharged and reservists more generally were released on the eve of the advance (Pachulija 2010, 28–29). As reservists who served in the east and west of Abkhazia commonly report: "At one point sometime at the end of July, part of the reservists were dismissed" (interview in Khodzhaa 2006, 34); "for unknown reasons, our unit was demobilized, and when the war began the Abkhaz met it completely unprepared."[5] "I was very troubled," a commander confirms, "[by] an order a few days before the war to let reservists go" (interview in Khodzhaa 2009, 437). Georgian forces thus crossed the Ingur/i River unimpeded and at the next post in Okhurej captured the few reservists and their commander who remained on duty, but met initial armed opposition from Abkhaz guards further along the road, midway to the capital.

These fighters came to understand the Georgian advance as a threat by virtue of carrying out military duties in the midst of the advance, seeing Georgian troops firsthand, or hearing of their movement from other guards or local residents. An operator on duty in the west reports that he learned about the Georgian advance over the night of August 13–14 as he "was receiving radiographs about the disar-

FROM UNCERTAINTY TO MOBILIZATION IN FOUR DAYS   129

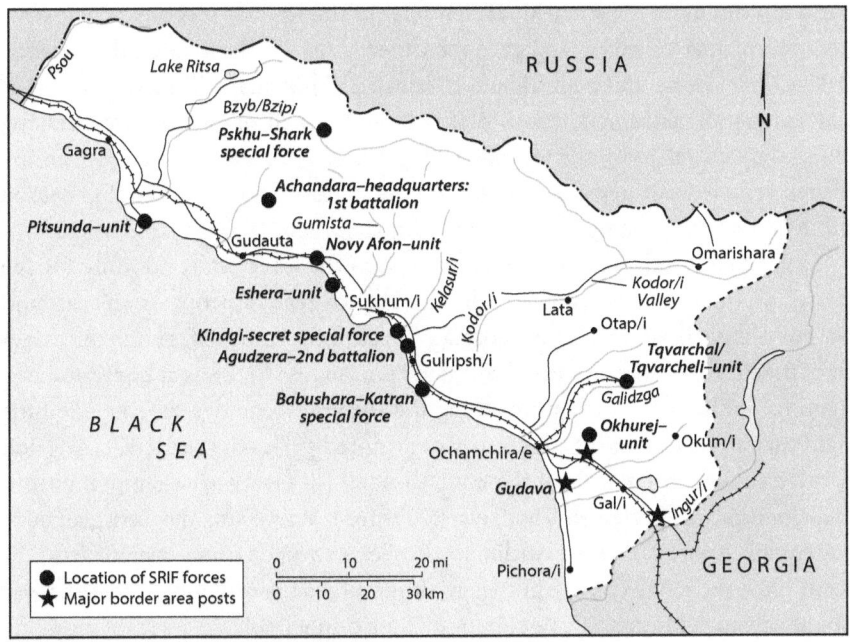

FIGURE 5.1. Military structure of the Abkhaz Guard.

Source: I consulted respondent recollections and the discussion of Abkhaz Guard headquarters, units, and posts in Khodzhaa 2003, 2006, 2009 and Pachulija 2010 in reconstructing the military structure of the Abkhaz Guard.

mament of [guards] at the airport and the attack on the Okhurej unit" (interview in Khodzhaa 2003, 40). One officer in the east realized the threat as he was captured: "In the morning of August 14, platoon commander——came by and said that now we leave for the Inguri [River]. My soldiers and I got into [his] truck and drove to Agudzera to arm. But we did not reach Agudzera because in twenty minutes we collided head-on with the convoy of Georgian occupation troops, who disarmed us and put us in a truck . . . [as] prisoners. . . . Twice Georgian soldiers wanted to kill us" (interview in Khodzhaa 2003, 45–46).

Guards who were not captured recognized the threat when tanks and troops approached them and mounted resistance at their posts or blocked the road further along to halt Georgian movement to Sukhum/i. Informed of the advance by a local, Gudava guards immediately left the post to cut off the road near Ochamchira/e (Pachulija 2010, 34). "On the first day of the war, we were on duty in Gudava," a participating reservist recalls. "We managed to leave Gudava without losses . . . [but] had a minor clash in Merkula" (interview in Khodzhaa 2006, 158). As Georgian forces broke through the roadblock, Abkhaz guards in Agudzera took the first fight, with casualties on both sides. An officer of the Agudzera battalion discusses the situational character of the Abkhaz response: "The deputy commander called . . . and gave the order . . . to set out to close the Kelasuri Bridge. [We] came under attack and returned. . . . [Others] fell into captivity. . . . The convoy of tanks and troops of the State Council of Georgia was moving along the central road and engaged in gunfire. A commander . . . on an armored vehicle went to the crossroads and took the fight. He was shot but caused some losses to the enemy" (interview in Khodzhaa 2003, 57–58).

Situational threat perception characterized the war's onset not only for the guards on duty but also for those off duty and for regular people in the east and west of Abkhazia who ran into Georgian forces in the course of the day. A reservist of the Pskhu unit recalls his encounter: "On August 14, I was at home and had to go to Sukhum. . . . But approaching the [central] road, we barely pulled the right turn to Adzuzhba, as the convoy of armored personnel carriers, tanks, and 'Ural' trucks full of guards of the State Council [of Georgia] was moving from Ochamchira" (interview in Khodzhaa 2003, 163). Witnessing the Georgian convoy equally signaled threat to ordinary people. A sovkhoz (state-owned farm) director who faced the convoy in the east remembers his reaction: "I met the war on the way to Sukhum. . . . The convoy of State Council soldiers was moving along the road. I immediately turned around—went back to the village." A university professor traveling to Sukhum/i from the west reiterates: "Today we have cell phones, everyone knows everything. It might seem strange now that we were not informed right away. Past Gudauta, I noticed a flow of cars away from the city. . . . By Novy Afon, the bus stopped and people were told that the city [Sukhum/i] was bombed." The following day, when Georgian marines landed in the west of Abkhazia, locals recount observing their deployment and thus coming to terms with the threat they posed. One man recalls: "When I saw that armored vehicles were being dropped off, that there was shooting, and the first casualties were appearing, I understood that this was a serious question."

Whereas some Abkhaz resisted or escaped the violence as they recognized the immediate threat posed by being in its midst, most turned to social structures to figure out the content of the threat—who was threatened, by whom, and to what extent—and mobilized based on whom they perceived to be threatened, the self, family, or the larger group.

Threat Framing: Elite Articulation

Most Abkhaz learned about the Georgian advance from an address to the population given by the Abkhaz leader Vladislav Ardzinba, a long-standing defender of Abkhaz rights and the then chairman of the Supreme Council of Abkhazia. Broadcast on national television at midday on August 14, when Georgian forces were already in Sukhum/i, the address rapidly spread across the society. "On August 14, the announcement came that the war began, Georgians against the Abkhaz," respondents say in interview after interview.

Some were simply watching television at the time of the war's onset. "The beginning of the Georgian-Abkhaz war caught me in my native village——, where I worked as a teacher," one man in the east says. "I learned about the occupation of Abkhazia on television.... Personally, I was shocked" (interview in Khodzhaa 2003, 131). Others turned to television in disbelief of the spreading news of the Georgian advance: "That day I was making jam. I stood in the garden and cooked on the fire. We usually make a lot of jam. My daughter ran in and said, 'The war started!' I asked, 'War? With whom?' I froze and went to the TV. Everyone there was saying that the war started." Yet others, often with relatives and friends, gathered by television sets to seek an explanation of the Georgian troops, tanks, and helicopters they saw or heard outside or the rumors of the entry of Georgian forces into Abkhazia. "On August 14 ... I was at work at the sovkhoz," a worker says in telling how the locals of his village turned to the address for an explanation of what they observed. "At 10 a.m. we went outside due to noise. There moved a convoy of tanks, Ikarus buses, State Council troops in vests naked to the waist. The locals watched in amazement and incomprehension. Not understanding anything, we all gathered by the TV. And in the evening—Ardzinba's address, where he spoke on the start of aggression by the Georgian State Council against our republic, the formation of battalions to defend the motherland. The Abkhaz population of——gathered right after" (interview in Khodzhaa 2003, 85–86).

As this worker notes, the address incited further local mobilization that sparked in cities, towns, and villages across Abkhazia. A teacher in the west speaks about the diffusion of the leader's message and its importance for local gatherings: "My classmate ran by: 'War!' Ardzinba's address followed on television: 'The aggression began. The population should come to the defense.' I took my children home and went to the administration." People with and without experience in the Abkhaz Guard similarly reacted to the address. One Abkhaz Guard reservist reports its effect: "On August 14 ... I was at work. Having seen the address of the chairman of the Supreme Council of Abkhazia, V. G. Ardzinba, I left the workplace and went to the regiment of the Internal Forces in the Achandara area" (interview in Khodzhaa 2003, 209).

Ardzinba addressed the nature of the Georgian advance, the threat that it posed, and the necessity of collective response—issues that deeply troubled the Abkhaz in the environment of uncertainty. The leader drew on the history of Georgian-Abkhaz conflict and placed the violence in the context of recent developments in the Georgian-Abkhaz relations at the state level and in the broader political situation in Georgia and the falling Soviet Union. Not since the 1989 Lykhny statement that claimed Abkhaz self-determination had a message so poignantly brought together the common understandings of Georgian-Abkhaz conflict and every Abkhaz's role in it. "Dear citizens of Abkhazia," Ardzinba opened his address to the entire population, with no reference to ethnic difference, "I appeal to you at this difficult time" (Ardzinba 2004, 5). The appeal stressed the offensive nature of the Georgian advance and the lethal danger that it posed: "Our land was invaded by the armed formations of the State Council of Georgia, including the criminal elements that spread death and destruction in our land" (5). Ardzinba signaled the threat to personal safety and that of the Abkhaz as a group and the broader population of Abkhazia: "Of course, it is not easy to speak, when perhaps right now, as I am speaking, our homes are being robbed, people are beaten, and life itself is not guaranteed" (5). He linked the threat to other victims of Georgia's wars taking place in Tbilisi, Mingrelia in western Georgia, and South Ossetia: "The Abkhaz and the entire population of our long-suffering Motherland are being added to the blood of Georgians in Tbilisi and other regions of Georgia, Mingrelians in Mingrelia, Ossetians in South Ossetia, spilled by the [Georgian] leadership" (5).

The address evoked the long-lasting subjugation of Abkhazia in the Georgian-Abkhaz relations that the confederal solution proposed by the Abkhaz elite on the war's eve was intended to overcome: "There is no reason for such a barbaric action on the territory of small Abkhazia. We lived quietly and peacefully in our home, not without controversy, not without problems. But we tried addressing these problems in a peaceful and civilized way. . . . No one started a war when the Russian Federation was created with a federal agreement, and its people found mutual understanding. Our proposals to resolve relationship issues peacefully, in a civilized way, were answered with tanks, planes, guns, murder, and looting" (5).

Ardzinba promised wide condemnation of Georgia and potential outside support for the Abkhaz and suggested the need to mobilize against Georgian forces given the threat that they posed: "The world knows the position Abkhazia is in. The world strongly condemns this barbaric act and will provide its moral and material support. . . . I think that we have to resist at this very difficult time, and we will resist, we will defeat those who sow death and destruction in Abkhazia, who bring hostility between the peoples of Georgia and Abkhazia" (5).

Ardzinba's message was reinforced by the resolutions of the Supreme Council adopted thereafter. The resolution of August 14, "On the mobilization of the adult population and transfer of arms," urged all citizens eighteen to forty years old to mobilize for defense due to "the entry of the armed forces of the State Council of Georgia into the Republic of Abkhazia and the real threat that appeared to the sovereignty of the Republic of Abkhazia [and] the life of the population" (Ardzinba 2004, 6). As Georgian forces laid siege to the area around Tqvarchal/

Tqvarcheli and gained control over Sukhum/i in the east and Gagra in the west on August 18, the council formed the State Defense Committee. Its address of August 19 stressed the threat brought by the forces "who came to us with arms ... [as] enemies of the entire multinational people of Abkhazia" (Ardzinba 2004, 26). By mid-September, the council formally recognized "the armed attack by the troops of the Georgian State Council on Abkhazia of 14 August 1992 and the occupation of part of its territory [referring to besieged Tqvarchal/Tqvarcheli] as an act of aggression against the Republic of Abkhazia" (Ardzinba 2004, 160).

The framing of the Georgian advance as an attack, occupation, and aggression, or a war, stands in sharp contrast to the counternarratives of Georgia's leadership. Russian and Western news agencies recorded on the eve of the advance that "National Guard contingents in Western Georgia set about securing road and rail links on 13 August in the hunt for the security officials taken hostage two days earlier" and ostensibly brought to Abkhazia by supporters of the ousted Gamsakhurdia (Fuller 1992). The secretary of the Okhurej administration reported on August 14 that twice before "a member of the Georgian State Council, [Tengiz] Kitovani, said on Georgian television that he would go to Abkhazia" (interview in Khodzhaa 2003, 61). Once Georgian forces took Sukhum/i, Georgian leaders gave railroad security as an explanation for their presence in the capital: "They arrived ostensibly to 'protect the railway'" (interview in Khodzhaa 2009, 638–639).

This explanation, however, did not reflect the observed reality on the ground, where the railroad was functioning as normal, yet Georgian forces immediately established control over most of Abkhazia. "Georgians came under the pretense of railroad security," respondents say. But this interpretation is seen as "laughable": "It is artificial. There were singular cases that I heard about, [where] a train was robbed. These cases were along the railroad, not only in Abkhazia. And it was not systematic. Not all trains were robbed." Respondents in Abkhazia's east and west find that "it was an argument made to explain the entry of tanks into Abkhazia. In reality, the railroad was functioning fine. In 1992, we had a very good summer. [Abkhazia] was filled with tourists. If the railroad had not been working, we would not have had so many people.... There was also an argument on kidnapping. Yes, officials were kidnapped, but in Zugdidi and Gal. They did not need to send forces to Sukhum to address this. This was simply propaganda." The Abkhaz outside of Abkhazia who learned about the advance were similarly unconvinced: "I was in Perm, [Russia].... On August 15, 1992, I was watching TV with family, and all of a sudden *Novosti* (News) showed how Georgian State Council troops reached Novy Afon to restore order on the railway from the Gumista River, and Gagra was taken from the Psou River. In a word, the whole of Abkhazia was taken, except for the Gudauta district."

The Georgian narrative was further contradicted as people watched the troops' brutality in the areas that they passed and the instant participation of local Georgians on the Georgian side. An Abkhaz woman who hid in Abkhazia during the war states: "Armed Georgians came with tanks, helicopters, bombed [Abkhazia], and the local population joined them. 'Not one of you Abkhaz will continue living here,' Georgians [indicated when they] stood up against their neighbors. In Tsandrypsh (formerly Gantiadi), there lived [an Abkhaz] family of——and a Georgian family. In peaceful times, [they] had coffee at each other's places. Once the war began, the husband in the Georgian family took a canister of gasoline and burned [his neighbors]." Local Georgian participation in the brutality as well as the fighting against the Abkhaz is widely reported, with many Georgian participants known from previous intergroup interactions. As an Abkhaz Soviet official who fought on the Abkhaz side says, "Georgians who in response to the Abkhaz movement formed their own organizations and armed units before the war stood up with weapons against us when the war began. Part of the Gagra population went to guard some positions. . . . We knew who they were. . . . They did not even think of Abkhaz independence."

Selective targeting of the Abkhaz political and social elite and looting of Abkhaz homes and infrastructure more generally, especially in urban centers, are widely reported at the war's onset.[6] "They had lists of whom to kill in Abkhazia," respondents recall, "went house to house looking for the Abkhaz." "We saw how women were raped, houses looted," witnesses in Gagra and Sukhum/i say, "[how] they looted stores and stockpiles." Reports in the east similarly reject the Georgian narrative, first, because of the suspicion raised by *Georgian* looting of trains, with no action from the troops meant to prevent it, and, later, as steps were taken against Abkhaz families and the male population in the area:

> On August 14, 1992, at 11 a.m. panic started in Sukhum: gunshots, screaming. They said Georgian troops invaded our republic, already occupied Ochamchira, and mass Abkhaz executions began. I immediately went to Ochamchira. . . . There were rumors that Georgian soldiers guarded public order, so that no trains were robbed. But on August 16, a huge number of Ochamchira residents [Ochamchira/e was largely Georgian] were actually robbing freight cars the whole day. It felt like a "top" command was given to "rob" to confirm the feeble version of the Georgian State Council on the entry of its troops into Abkhazia, ostensibly for the security of railway routes. They robbed and dragged [goods] all three days, from regular sewing thread to refrigerators, VCRs, TVs, sugar, and flour. This was surprising, as neither the police nor the Georgian army soldiers prevented this robbery. . . . By the end of September,

rumors emerged about the robbery of Abkhaz families. . . . The occupation authorities of the State Council of Georgia banned the male part of the population from leaving the town. . . . It became clear that this was not the establishment of order on the railroad of Abkhazia, but suppression of the Abkhaz people. (Interview in Khodzhaa 2003, 93–94)

The Georgian explanation of the advance did not resonate with regular Abkhaz men and women for more profound reasons. It did not correspond to the history of the Georgian-Abkhaz relations as the Abkhaz perceived it. In contrast, the Abkhaz leaders' framing of the advance as a threat to individuals, the Abkhaz group, and the population drew on the shared understandings of the conflict that developed before the war. In explaining how they viewed the advance, most respondents refer to this collective memory of the reduction of Abkhazia's political status from full to Georgian autonomous republic in the Soviet period and disagreement over this status as the Union collapsed, the demographic expansion of the Georgian population, and the repression of the Abkhaz social, political, and cultural rights associated with these changes.

One woman's recollection, which I return to in the next paragraphs, is representative of the Abkhaz responses. "We were the only Abkhaz family to settle at the Russian-Abkhaz border," the woman, a sales associate in the west, says. "Georgians held [it] as a strategic location. There were no Abkhaz families here, but after ten years [of waiting] we got a place here. They were coming here in crowds, as long as they could increase their population. In 1953, [when] Stalin and Beria [were in power], there were no Abkhaz schools. All had to study in Georgian schools. It was difficult to find a job." Respondents across the interviews share these prewar memories. Most invoke demographic pressure and repression of Abkhaz heritage and relate the Georgian advance to these memories: "They wanted to take everything away from us, from our language to being hosts on our land."

People also recall the everyday confrontation, political contention, and violent opposition that polarized the Abkhaz and Georgians in the political and social realms. The culmination of prewar intergroup mobilization, for the Abkhaz, was the Georgian calls during demonstrations in Tbilisi and Sukhum/i to abolish Abkhazia's autonomous status to make Abkhazia a Georgian province. "The [Georgian-Abkhaz] relations started heating up," my respondent continues:

> Then Georgians held demonstrations. They wanted to abolish Abkhazia's autonomy and create a united Georgia. But the Abkhaz have a language, culture, we are an ancient people. There used to be no Georgians on this land.
>
> In 1989, there was a confrontation between Georgians and the Abkhaz. At work, once they felt the support [of other Georgians], they could

fail you any moment. [Colleagues] told me, "We will come to destroy you anyway." Locals [in the neighborhood] came [to our house] and said, "Go away, it is Georgia here." I responded that it is Abkhazia. They damaged our house, were shooting to scare us. My husband came [home] all beaten up once and died a year after.

"They said that Georgia should become unitary, without autonomies," respondents confirm the latest prewar developments. In this context, a teacher and Abkhaz movement activist explains the reference in Ardzinba's address to the confederal solution that the Abkhaz leadership proposed before the war:

> The Supreme Council headed by Ardzinba suggested the separation of roles among the autonomous republics on a confederal basis. In Georgia, they did not expect that, but paid significant attention. Official meetings began, but there were those who rejected that in Georgia: "Why negotiate when we can simply take it?" It was fashionable across the Soviet Union to rob trains, and so under this pretense they said they needed to protect the railroad. But how can you protect the railroad with tanks? They started preparation and momentarily this all happened in August.

The confederal solution did not take hold, and the Abkhaz leaders restored the 1925 constitution, declaring Abkhazia a Soviet socialist republic shortly before the war.[7] That Georgian forces targeted the building where Abkhazia's state sovereignty was proclaimed was to the Abkhaz indicative of the Georgian intent beyond railroad security. "The first victims were tourists and the building of the Supreme Council. That is where the gathering regarding the recognition of the sovereignty of Abkhazia took place," respondents report.

The mobilization that Ardzinba's address and subsequent Supreme Council resolutions called for in response to Georgian forces was thus seen as a continuation of the prewar Abkhaz struggle and resonated in light of the collective memory of and direct and indirect participation in the prewar conflict, the aspects of the collective conflict identities shared by the Abkhaz. In particular, mobilization against Georgian forces meant state defense for most respondents, with the Abkhaz leadership representing the legitimate government of wartime Abkhazia: "The war accumulated over decades. The Georgian government used the chance when the Soviet Union collapsed. We are a small nation, and they decided to capture our land, to make Abkhazia without the Abkhaz. I could not believe it, how is it that Georgians attacked? Our president told everyone to stand up. Everyone gathered. The Abkhaz rose in spirit because Ardzinba was with us. The [Abkhaz] government was stationed in Gudauta." "The fighting of our people for national self-determination was always ongoing throughout the Soviet period," other respondents similarly contextualize the war. "Georgian forces attacked our motherland without even declaring a war," respondents agree with their leaders' threat framing as a result, "[and] decided that they could settle the problem of Abkhazia once and for all."

The elite threat framing illustrated in Abkhazia is widely recorded in contexts of intergroup violence and war, from interwar Germany (Snyder 2000) to Soviet republics (Beissinger 2002), Yugoslavia (Posen 1993; Roe 2004), and Rwanda (Valentino 2004; Straus 2006; Fujii 2009). Political leaders whose power is challenged, especially in times of political change, such as the dissolution of the Soviet Union, commonly turn to historical narratives and myths to mobilize public support (Kaufman 2001). As Edward D. Mansfield and Jack L. Snyder (2005, 9) argue, "Rallying popular support by invoking threats from rival nations is a common expedient for hard-pressed leaders who seek to shore up their legitimacy." Indeed, the Abkhaz elite was physically and politically threatened by the Georgian advance. Abkhaz deputies were immediately forced from the capital and removed from government control as Georgian troops took the Supreme Council. Ardzinba articulated the threat of the Georgian advance under the direct challenge to his political power.[8]

Yet there is a disconnection between elite threat framing and individual mobilization in the studies that put a premium on manipulation of information by the leaders. Although elite threat framing reaches most individuals, not all mobilize to fight. Some Abkhaz mobilized once they heard Ardzinba's address. As one man in Gudauta illustrates, "When Ardzinba announced general mobilization, I said, 'Everyone, go to Volga!' The headquarters of the military staff was [at the Volga sanatorium]. They separated us into groups." The same evening, the local defense volunteer group that was formed there joined the Abkhaz guards who were holding off Georgian forces at the entry to the capital (Pachulija 2010, 39). Most, however, did not know *how* to act given the broad articulation of threat in the address and headed to local places of assembly, where they sought clarification and further negotiated a collective response to the Georgian threat. As a professor in the west demonstrates, "We realized that the war started, but did not know . . . what to do. I went to the administration of the town. Everyone gathered there and expected a message from the [local] leaders."

Local Adaptation

Whether the news of the Georgian advance reached the ordinary Abkhaz as they observed Georgian troops, tanks, and helicopters firsthand, watched Ardzinba's address on national television, or were informed by relatives, friends, neighbors, and colleagues, people rushed to local places of assembly as soon as they learned about the Georgian advance. Whole neighborhoods, towns, and villages assembled in front of administration buildings, at central squares, or by other gathering places, such as churches and Abkhaz Guard bases. "When the war started, we all gathered at the administration of Bzyb," respondents in the west report. In the east, where Georgian forces immediately blockaded Tqvarchal/Tqvarcheli and the surrounding area, residents fled to neighboring villages and attended local gatherings there. "There was a gathering of the Abkhaz by the Mokva monastery," the locals say, including those "who escaped the town and nearby villages" where Georgian forces established control (interview in Khodzhaa 2003, 67).

The local mobilization dynamics that unfolded from these community gatherings were similar in cities, towns, and villages in the east and west of Abkhazia. The confusion and panic set off by the advance of Georgian forces was vividly manifested as crowds assembled locally. Men and women debated what happened, whether a war indeed began. People expected instructions from the local administrations, as they prepared their statements for residents in the follow-up to Ardzinba's address. Others awaited the arrival of respected local authorities, who included the political elites, social movement leaders, the elders, and military personnel. The messages of the local leaders and the discussions that followed focused on the nature of the Georgian threat to individuals, families, localities, and Abkhazia as a whole and how to act in response. The broad articulation of threat characterizing Ardzinba's address was widely cited to mobilize support, but was not simply adopted locally. Instead, local leaders negotiated collective action with their respective communities to direct it to the local needs of defense. The notion of threat to cities, towns, and villages was often augmented by the unavailability of weapons, and leaders of the local defense chosen from among respected community members developed strategies to attain weapons and defend their localities together with their communities.

As Georgian troops advanced through the east of Abkhazia, local mobilization began in nearly every Abkhaz locality there. Early in the morning, before Georgian forces blockaded the town of Tqvarchal/Tqvarcheli, people gathered by the local Abkhaz Guard base. Ardzinba's message had not been broadcast yet, but the news of the Georgian advance reached residents of Tqvarchal/Tqvarcheli. The status of Abkhaz Guard military leaders played a catalyst role in this local mobilization. One reservist recounts the local character of defense as the commander of the town's Guard unit directed mobilization: "It was about 11 a.m. By then lots of people gathered in front of the military commissariat. Among them were former reservists of the Tqvarchal battalion who had weapons. . . . [The commander] gave the order not to go anywhere, but to organize resistance here locally" (interview in Khodzhaa 2003, 325–326). As the town was besieged, its administration issued a statement that began with the threat to the republic, but emphasized the need to defend Tqvarchal/Tqvarcheli and called on residents to mobilize. The statement was aired on local television as the address of the town defense council:

> Dear Tqvarchelians!
> Dear fellow citizens!
> The republic is in danger!
> Today, at around 10 a.m., troops of the State Council of Georgia, accompanied by tanks, invaded the territory of Abkhazia in order to occupy it. Our forces are uneven. The Okhurej post having been shelled, troops are moving to the interior of the republic. In some parts of the Ochamchira district, battles are breaking out between the occupation forces and the forces of local defense volunteers.
>
> There was an attempt to shell the building of the Supreme Council of Abkhazia. There is cross fire in Sukhum.
>
> Due to the state of emergency in Tqvarcheli, general mobilization of men eighteen to forty-five years of age is declared. The assembly place is the town military commissariat.
>
> In case of the threat of attack on the town, evacuation of the population will be announced. Please be ready for this. We will announce the details of the time and place of gathering.
>
> Dear Tqvarchelians! The town defense council relies on your organization and readiness. Get ready for town defense. Do not panic or trust provocations! (Cherkezija 2003, 84)

The deputy chairman of Aidgylara (Unity), who went village to village to mobilize support in the area, reports on the outcome of the administration's call for general mobilization the following evening: "I went to Tqvarchal. The entry to the town was bustling with work—the boys were mining the road, placing posts. These were volunteer units. A town defense committee had already been created, and a decision was made to defend the town to a victorious end. At the gathering Tqvarchelians said that the town was not giving in ... and [it] became the center around which the entire eastern front was united" (interview in Khodzhaa 2003, 50).

Indeed, local gatherings sparked in most Abkhaz villages in the east, where guerrilla units were formed for village defense. Pakuash, a village near Okhurej where Georgian forces captured the first Abkhaz, held a community gathering, where the local leadership stressed the Georgian threat to the village and its defense was organized. The secretary of the administration recalls: "We were notified that Georgian State Council troops were already in the Okhurej village, had captured the head of the Ochamchira administration ... and with him fighters of the Abkhaz Guard, including natives of our village. ... In the evening, the whole village gathered in the center and elected a village defense council . . . [and] I was appointed head of the headquarters. . . . We organized the line of defense" (interview in Khodzhaa 2003, 100).

The local nature of threat was evident from the violence and military successes of Georgian troops in nearby areas, which suggested that the strengths were uneven, and the imminent arrival of Georgian forces that the local leaders conveyed in their speeches added urgency to local mobilization. As villages in the east held gatherings, appointed local defense leaders, collected hunting weapons, and fortified their localities, a front line emerged, from which future Abkhaz resistance developed. Locally known leaders with social movement organization or military experience played major roles in this process. For example, activists of Aidgylara "went house to house with the locals in search of weapons. [They] gathered village assembl[ies] . . . [and] made a decision . . . to create a partisan formation of residents of the Ochamchira district" (interview in Khodzhaa 2003, 50). Commanders of the Abkhaz Guard "taught local defense volunteers how to defend the village, which hills to select for the watch posts, [and] how to make incendiary mixtures" (interview in Khodzhaa 2003, 52).

The chairman of the Strike Committee describes a similar process in Abkhazia's west, where he played a leading role in the mobilization of the village of Bzyb/Bzipi given his local ties and the reputation he acquired through prewar activism. Before the war, he was among the movement leaders who organized the locals of Bzyb/Bzipi for clashes, demonstrations, and strikes. Participants from his locality developed and took pride in their collective identity as a violent branch of the movement. "We, the Bzyb locals, were considered to be hooligans because we took all the action," the chairman says in explaining how this conflict identity emerged. "We broke down a Georgian bus carrying flags, as [Georgian protesters] screamed, 'This is our land!' and did not let them through" to Bzyb/Bzipi in 1989. As a bus with Georgian protesters "passed Bzyb, our boys stopped them with stones," local residents reiterate the pride with which they viewed these actions at the time. "Some of ours were imprisoned for this."

This leadership role in prewar mobilization positioned the chairman as a respected community member. "We did not know what to start with," he recalls of the day of the Georgian advance, but the locals who gathered by the administration of Bzyb/Bzipi reached out to him for more information. The discussion that followed took Ardzinba's threat framing as a starting point, but channeled collective mobilization to the needs of local defense. The chairman captures the local dynamic: "A group of locals stood by the *sel'sovet* (village council). The war started. Debates were going on. . . . There were people higher [in their sociopolitical status] than me who did more than me. But maybe I was more in contact with the people. And once I came they said, '——is coming. He will tell us something serious.' This is how the war started. At this time, Vladislav Grigorievich Ardzinba, who had big influence, made a speech."

A local force was similarly established near Bzyb/Bzipi as the announcement was made "from the Pitsunda TV tower: 'To the population thirty-five to sixty-five years of age, please gather in the garage of Intourist [Hotel] for the establishment of a battalion.'" "Everything was arranged spontaneously here," Pitsunda locals say in discussing how they came to understand the threat and the steps that they took locally:

> The war started. Prior to August 17, Gagra was still under control of the prewar Abkhaz government. [But this changed because] Georgian marines were dropped off [in the area]. . . . We formed a defense volunteer unit. There were no weapons, [just] who had what, hunting rifles. . . . In the Soviet times, we had [Soviet] army units here, as in all regions. People went there [to get armed]. . . . We collected weapons, and those who managed to get these weapons went toward Georgian marines. This is when the first casualties appeared. Of course, the tens [of us] who got the weapons were not enough.

The Abkhaz further to the west joined this mobilization as their localities fell to the Georgian troops that advanced on the western center of Gagra. Here "[the head of] administration gathered the people . . . [and] said, 'There are battles, shootings, the aviation. . . .' We decided, given our small numbers, the lack of weapons, and [the Georgian] inflow (I cannot say how many [marines] there were, but approximately six hundred people came in at first. They unloaded heavy equipment—tanks, armored personnel carriers, infantry fighting vehicles) to retreat and organize a town defense." The lack of weapons and the observed arrival of Georgian troops augmented the need for local defense. With units emerging across the area, one front line was formed along Bzyb/Bzipi as a result, and another was formed near Sukhum/i when Georgian forces established control of all but central Abkhazia.

Why did men and women head to local places of assembly once they heard the news of the Georgian advance? What gave some community members the ability to direct mobilization to the needs of local defense? The logic of local mobilization by the Abkhaz cannot be grasped without the preceding record of collective action that made local assembly a key setting for the ordinary Abkhaz to turn to in the context of uncertainty and embedded local leaders active in prewar mobilization in their communities. The tradition of collective gatherings in times of crises, when the rights and interests of the Abkhaz are undermined and the Abkhaz elite and ordinary people come together to deliberate a response, figures prominently in my respondents' accounts of their wartime mobilization trajectories. Respondents across the interviews recall the history of collective gatherings.

Communal, regional, and all-Abkhaz assemblies have long served as a site of collective deliberation and decision making in Abkhazia (Krylov 2001, 133). In the Abkhaz customary law, enforcement decisions are made collectively by people's courts and are binding regardless of the status (Brojdo 2008, 21). "If something happens, it is decided by gatherings and judged," respondents confirm. In the Soviet period, public gatherings raised the issues that concerned the Abkhaz. "Before the collapse, we wrote letters, we had gatherings," an activist summarizes. "Every ten years there was popular unrest" as a result. Tejmuraz Achugba (2010, 256–257) outlines the issues voiced at the gatherings and in letters sent to the Soviet center: "The actions of the Abkhaz in 1957, 1965, 1967, 1978–1980, 1989 were unprecedented in the Soviet period. . . . Ending of the demographic expansion of Georgians in Abkhazia, protection of ethnic Abkhaz history, restoration of the native Abkhaz toponymy, preparation of Abkhaz national cadres . . . this is an incomplete list of issues raised by the Abkhaz intelligentsia . . . with active support of the entire Abkhaz people." The gathering at Lykhnashta field in central Abkhazia, where ordinary people, social movement leaders, and government officials came together to demand the restoration of Abkhazia's independent status in the all-Abkhaz plebiscite of 1989, is exemplary. "There the Abkhaz people always gathered when we had critical moments . . . , when we had to discuss the important things," an activist says.

Not all Abkhaz participated in the gatherings, but most knew about them from day-to-day interactions. The Abkhaz concerns articulated at the gatherings shaped the shared view of Georgian-Abkhaz conflict that affected how people understood the Georgian advance and their roles at the war's onset. One respondent, a mother of two, who participated in prewar gatherings and mobilized for war at its outset, captures the importance of local mobilization for the self-understanding of the Abkhaz in relation to the conflict:

> I was raised in the spirit of patriotism [in] a deeply Abkhaz village. I was educated since childhood that we had to struggle. Not once did I speak at Lykhny gatherings. We fought by means of a popular gathering. Internal, external problems—everything was decided not by one or two leaders, but by the people in the historical areas, such as Lykhnashta. Key problems were discussed there. Anti-Georgian demonstrations took place there. I could have lost my life even then [for participation]. . . . This is how we were humiliated. But it only made us stronger. So when the war started, no one had to tell me to [mobilize].

Community members, including those with existing leadership roles in the government or the Abkhaz movement organizations, who actively participated in these gatherings and other forms of prewar collective action, gained an identity as defenders of the Abkhaz rights that others turned to when the war began. It is not surprising that men and women who gathered in the traditional places of assembly at the war's onset expected the local political elite to inform them of the nature of the Georgian advance and the steps to be taken in response. Heads of local administrations were generally highly regarded in the Abkhaz society, especially if they had an Abkhaz background, and were widely known by the locals. As Derluguian (2005, 234) says, "An Abkhaz farmer felt more confident in dealing with an Abkhaz official or policeman not simply because they shared a common culture and language, but primarily because they shared strong ties of ethnic kinship..., because among this small nationality virtually everybody was each other's relative, neighbor, or friend."

But the leaders who were seen as having struggled for their people in the past and even paid for the struggle with imprisonment or removal from office had the heroic status that particularly positioned them to explain the Georgian advance and propose a collective response at gatherings that sparked when the war began. These leaders had often established a precedent of organizing the Abkhaz or supplying information in prewar instances of local mobilization. For example, local narratives consistently refer to the roles that the heads of Gudauta in central Abkhazia and Ochamchira/e in the east played in the Georgian-Abkhaz clashes of 1989. These political elites provided the locals with access to weapons, confiscated and stored in military and law enforcement buildings when the clashes unfolded, and were repressed in the aftermath. Respondents relate their wartime leadership to this precedent across the interviews: "Here, in Sukhum, Ozgan gave an order to break the security in Gudauta and take weapons. Bagapsh, . . . [in] the Ochamchira district, gave an order to take hunting weapons and shoot. . . . They were persecuted for this . . . , [for] doing their part for the motherland"; "After the events of 1989 . . . the first secretaries of Gudauta and Ochamchira were fired. . . . If not for them, Abkhazia would be forgotten by now. [It would be forgotten] that this state existed. These people tried saving the nation, the ethnos. They were not afraid and spoke at gatherings."

Similarly, respondents consistently name activists of Aidgylara and other organizations of the Abkhaz movement as individuals whose prewar struggle for and organization of the Abkhaz people put them in leadership positions during the war. "Zakan Agrba, Levan Gytsba, Boris Kikhiripa did not sleep day and night, gathered the people because of the oppression," Pitsunda residents in western Abkhazia time and again say of their local activists. "They led significant work in our district." "These people were arrested because they acted as leaders," respondents relate these activists' sacrifice for the Abkhaz struggle to their leadership status. "We gathered spontaneously. Our leaders gave us information," the locals recall of the precedent these activists set in the local mobilization for violence in

1989. They recite the activists' speeches from the collective gathering: "Lev Gytsba: 'In 1918, Georgia gained its sovereignty. But Abkhazia was not historically in it. We are trying to do everything peacefully, through negotiations.' Boris Kikhiripa: 'But because Georgians want to celebrate their national day here, we cannot allow this peacefully. As long as Georgians say, "Georgia for Georgians," we will resist.'" As a result, respondents often say that "those who led the people [during the war] were simply leaders in the society, not professional military men." Military men adopted this role along with social and political leaders at the war's onset, especially if they belonged to the Abkhaz Guard, which was viewed as the local counterbalance to Georgian armed groups before the war.

The community ties and experience forged in prewar mobilization provided the basis of local organizational capacity when the war began. Local assembly places repeatedly brought the Abkhaz into the institution of collective decision making in the past and were known in every locality as sites where information could be sought from political, social, and military leaders and collective action could be discussed. Relationships that leaders built with the locals through prewar collective action underlined what Staniland (2012) calls "networks of rebellion," as the Abkhaz mobilization against Georgian forces in general stemmed from this local level. But mobilization decisions did not simply follow from the adaptation of threat to the needs of local defense. They were consolidated with quotidian networks into a range of roles from fleeing to fighting on the Abkhaz side, which sometimes took individuals away from their locality to fight in the areas of highest intensity, including Sukhum/i and Gagra early in the war.

Quotidian Consolidation

As diverse framings of threat posed by the Georgian advance were being transmitted across the national and local levels, men and women in Abkhazia resorted to their families and friends, the quotidian networks that are embedded in "the routines of daily life," to act on the notions of threat that emerged in the Abkhaz society (Snow et al. 1998, 4). Relatives and friends in neighborhood, university, employment, and other daily social settings informed one another of the Georgian advance as they observed the movement of troops or heard about it from the national or local leadership. People urged their relatives, neighbors, and coworkers who were in proximity at the time of the Georgian advance to proceed to local gathering places and often assembled together with these quotidian relations. Others called each other by phone and met in the intimate setting of homes or familiar locations of prior interaction, where families and friends frequently gathered in the past and which were considered to be relatively safe. The discussions that unfolded in this trust-based context consolidated the threads of information that individuals had into shared interpretations of threat and collective mobilization decisions. Small groups bound by quotidian ties typically adopted different roles at the war's onset together as a result.

Very rarely did individuals mobilize alone. Those who did often hid, fled, or defected to the Georgian side.[9] Respondents across this range of mobilization roles report that fear for their lives was their primary concern. People's search for security is a prominent feature of civil war (Kalyvas 2006).[10] Cindy Horst and Katarzyna Grabska (2015, 6) capture this feature in the context of uncertainty: "The radical uncertainty associated with situations of violent conflict, both in the sense of not having access to reliable information about what is happening and in the sense of the extreme unpredictability of the future, severely complicates people's decisions about whether to stay or move. Staying might involve a higher risk than leaving, so moving away from conflict is one way in which people protect themselves and reduce radical uncertainty." By hiding, fleeing, or defecting to the Georgian side, the ordinary Abkhaz were protecting their lives from Georgian violence as it became clear from the demonstration of force and immediate military successes along the route of the Georgian advance that it was a predominantly stronger side at the war's onset. Abkhaz government and social movement leaders sought security from being targeted as organizers and supporters of the Abkhaz struggle in major cities, where many were located at the time of the advance and where Georgian forces soon established control.

A number of possibilities existed at the war's onset for regular people to move away from the fighting that was unfolding in Abkhazia. In the east, where the Georgian side blockaded the area, people hid or fled to besieged Tqvarchal/Tqvarcheli or nearby villages that Georgian forces had not entered for strategic reasons or due to the emergence of guerrilla units there. The Abkhaz refer to the siege of Tqvarchal/Tqvarcheli as occupation by Georgia. "Tqvarchal was occupied," the locals confirm, "but Georgians could not take it because of the partisan [guerrilla] fighting in nearby villages." Due to the siege, the town was poorly supplied, but it was isolated from the fighting, and respondents report to have stayed there for this reason until an opportunity to flee arose. A helicopter transported people from Tqvarchal/Tqvarcheli to Gudauta in central Abkhazia, which remained under Abkhaz control, and to Russia. Regular people were able to board it, especially if they had children. "Tqvarchal was in blockade from the beginning of the war. They were isolated," a woman says in explaining her daughter's path. "My daughter . . . stayed there. On November 27, a Russian helicopter brought her in [to Gudauta]."

In the west, people fled to Gudauta and Russia by land or sea, as this option was still available early in the war. As one respondent who fled to Russia corroborates, "A boat carried all those who wanted to leave from Gudauta to Sochi. . . . [W]e were offered to go to Majkop with the children.... When we went there by sea, we were even attacked by a plane. There was such panic. In Sochi, an Ikarus bus was waiting for us, and we were taken to Majkop.... [M]any left by cars, took whatever they could.... [T]here were tens [of people from Abkhazia in Russia already] when we arrived." According to "the Russian government's State Committee for Emergency Situations," Russia's *Nezavisimaya gazeta* (Independent newspaper) states on August 21, "in the past few days about 10,000 people have been evacuated by sea from the area of Georgian-Abkhaz conflict to Russian territory in Sochi."

Four of my 142 respondents who could have joined Abkhaz mobilization as fighters or in the support apparatus, but instead escaped the fighting alone, adopted some of these options, driven by the fear for their own safety. One respondent reports her perception of the Georgian threat to her life: "I was afraid . . . [and so] went to Gudauta and hid. There was fear for your life and your close ones.... We could be killed any time." The rumors and stories that emerged across my interviews and participant observation surrounding a respondent who escaped the fighting for Russia, but did not acknowledge this choice, suggest that fear was his primary driver.

Among the government and Abkhaz movement respondents, an Aidgylara activist who was responsible for the documentation of meetings and other proceedings of the organization hid in Gagra in order to protect these records as the Georgian side took control of the town. The activist attempted fleeing the town, but faced the Georgian threat then and remained hiding thereafter: "I was hiding for thirty-two days because I had all the documents. I needed to cross to the Bzyb/Bzipi base, but Georgians with rifles sat in high-rise houses, so I crossed through the field, and while crossing, I met a local Georgian. . . . I told him to kill me. But he returned me to where I had been staying, and I continued hiding. In the meantime, [Georgians] entered and searched my apartment. They took the Soviet Union flag that I used for demonstrations."

Similarly, some government officials fled, leaving their families behind. Shocked and frightened by the appearance of Georgian forces in Sukhum/i, one member of the Supreme Council realized the threat to her own life and escaped from the capital to Gudauta without her family. (Gudauta was later fortified and remained under Abkhaz control.) Only subsequently did she recognize the threat to her family, and she took steps from Gudauta to bring them to safety: "We realized that we could all be killed here [in the capital]. Ardzinba gave us an order to go to Gudauta. We got into cars and went there. I was in such shock that I even forgot that my family remained [in the capital]. There was such a horrible situation after that. The mother of one of our deputies was taken captive. . . . And we realized that the same could happen to us all and negotiated that our families be taken out from the city." Finally, a small number of individuals defected to the Georgian side. Reports suggest that fear for their own lives was the driving force behind these individuals' mobilization decisions. Two regulars of the Abkhaz Guard fled and three defected (Khodzhaa 2006, 190–192). The self-regarding motivation of these individuals can be inferred, as their actions commonly compromised other regulars and reservists of the Abkhaz Guard and ordinary people. Reservists, for example, report: "When the Georgian tank approached, our battalion commander . . . ordered personnel to stand right before the tank . . . [and then] disappeared" (interview in Khodzhaa 2006, 58).

Whereas in rare cases individuals hid, fled, or defected alone, these mobilization decisions were typically taken together with families. Quotidian consolidation of information on threat often channeled mobilization in surprising ways. Individuals who were involved in the Abkhaz movement before the war and were touched by the prewar conflict directly or indirectly or who had relatives and friends who participated in the movement could be expected to mobilize in fighter or support roles at the war's onset. Ties with participants in mobilization and prior participation are major predictors of mobilization in the social movements research (McAdam 1986). Yet many individuals with this background escaped the fighting with their families, as they prioritized the threat posed by Georgian forces to their quotidian networks and thus mobilized to protect them. Others who could have fled to safer areas to protect themselves instead stayed to protect their relatives in the areas where Georgian forces established control.

One family's mobilization trajectory captures how people negotiated their mobilization decisions with their quotidian networks to adopt a range of nonfighter roles in the east and west of Abkhazia. The respondent, introduced earlier, whose husband took one of their two children to visit family in eastern Abkhazia, demonstrates how family networks channeled their members' mobilization trajectories to protect their kin rather than participate in the fighting on the Abkhaz side. Her husband, who was able and willing to fight, was convinced to protect his child instead:

> My mother-in-law saw that the ring of encirclement by Georgian forces was getting narrower. She lived in the village of Kutol in the Ochamchira district. . . . [She] took my elder son, ——, and through the back window gave him to my husband and told her son, "Take your child, go to Tqvarchal!"
>
> This town was occupied. It was not taken. You could get there through the nonoccupied part only through secret paths and villages. It was bombed from helicopters, from Su-25 [aircraft]. There was a bread allotment there, one hundred grams of corn cake. People there suffered through famine, the cold, everything. What didn't this town go through?

Somehow, with great difficulty, good people helped [my husband]. Some gave him a ride on a truck. He slept at these and other people's houses. Village by village, he got to Tqvarchal. From Tqvarchal, sometimes a helicopter brought people out of the town . . . , a "helicopter of life," [aboard which] only eighty to ninety passengers could be taken. They went to Teberda [in the Karachay-Cherkess Republic of Russia].

You might have heard, one of the helicopters was shot down. My husband was on the helicopter prior to that. But he was a forty-year-old man [able to fight]. They did not want to put him on the helicopter because he was a man. But he had a child [and] had to take [our son away], because otherwise they would be killed. It was such a burden for a man. But he says that somehow he grabbed the handrail. The child was on his shoulders.

As their quotidian network directed her husband from fighting to fleeing with family from the east of Abkhazia, the respondent herself was in the west with their younger child and could have fled to safer areas to protect him, but stayed with her mother and sister to protect them instead. Another relative, who arrived to pick up her sister, convinced her to leave her mother behind and take the child to relative safety:

When I heard that Gagra was being occupied by Georgians, I did not want to leave. My husband was far away. We would have to travel for two hours to get to where he was. Although Abkhazia is small, it was far for us. And how could I go if my mother and sister——were here? I did not want to leave them and stayed here with a little child.

All of a sudden, a far relative came to take his sister and children to the Gudauta district. He saw me and was stunned. "——, how are you still here with a little child? Quickly, go upstairs and get ready, [then] like a bullet come with your child and things. I will take you to the Gudauta district." I listened to him.

It is good that [he] came. Otherwise, I do not know what would have happened. We could have died. Many people died here. . . . It was scary staying. . . . Georgians already put up a post in Kolkhida [on the way to central Abkhazia]. It was difficult to drive through. They sorted . . . the Abkhaz [from] the others . . . , but still looked through the fingers [as they did so].

He brought us to Bzyb first, and then I got to my relatives in the Gudauta district myself. Bzyb was also constantly under fear. It is located along the road, right after Gagra. My aunt lived there. She was married to——, also a unique patriot, . . . a member of Unity, Aidgylara. I was at their place for a week. He was embarrassed to tell me to move on and told my sister, "What if they break through our Kolkhida block posts and get right away into Bzyb?" He was afraid that I was there with a child. It is more difficult to flee with a child.... "She should go to Achandara [closer to Gudauta]. It is much safer there." And [my sister] brought me to Achandara by car.

Other respondents similarly capture the surprising effect of quotidian consolidation. A native of an Abkhaz village who was willing to participate in the Abkhaz support apparatus in the war was persuaded in the quotidian setting to flee with her children. She recalls the ways in which the prewar conflict affected her and explains why she wished to mobilize: "Our parents studied in Georgian.... I worked at a Russian school. A Georgian teacher, she was a nationalist, made me learn Georgian! Georgian was spoken more often in the cities.... We [Abkhaz] had no right to a voice. Conversations [between Georgians and the Abkhaz] turned into fights at parties. We tried not talking about politics. Often this question did not let us live, breathe, neither us nor them. They spoke Georgian that we did not understand.... We were afraid to speak Abkhazian." This woman's mother blessed her to participate in the war, but other family members and friends convinced her to protect her children instead by taking them to Moscow: "[When the war began], my mother said, 'You just try to return!' [as a blessing to join the war effort]. I did not want to [leave], but was persuaded ... to take the children away from the village [where it was dangerous]. We went to Moscow . . . by boat."

Some mothers hid their sons to protect them from the dangers of the fighting as it became clear that the war began, even if their sons wanted to fight. As one respondent in the west describes, "My twenty-year-old son was serving in the Gudauta army. I came to [visit] him [in the reserve unit's barracks]. He did not like it: 'I am twenty years old, the war is ongoing, but I am lying here, reading books, playing chess, and eating three times a day. Why aren't we fighting?' I told him, 'Stay and read and sit and eat, like everyone.' [Many] were hiding their sons there.... If volunteers came, they were taken to fight. These were not volunteers, however, so they remained [in the reserves] and lived."

Realizing the threat that Georgian forces posed to both their families and localities or the broader group, some stayed to fight and protected their families by sending them away. Fighters who defended Abkhazia's west and east recount their view of the threat and the steps they took to secure relatives who were in Gagra and Sukhum/i, respectively: "There were no weapons. We gave in Gagra because the strengths were uneven. I right away sent my wife and children to Russia while the road was still open." "They wanted to capture the Gumista Bridge past Sukhum. I passed by my house and said, 'Get the children to Gudauta!'"

Not only fighters but also those in the support apparatus protected their families while mobilizing in the rear. As a doctor who remained in the areas of intense fighting, driven by the threat to "his people," demonstrates,

> When the war began, I was here [at the Gagra hospital].... The war began in Sukhum on August 14 . . . , a little later the marines landed here.... The Abkhaz population started to run away. They could not go out to the street. With respect to myself, I sent my family to the other side, across Psou [to Russia], while I still could. Myself, I went to Gudauta. I had to help my people. A normal person has to help his people when they are fine and [when they are] not. I went to the Gudauta hospital because the front line was at Eshera. After the freeing of Gagra, the closest hospital to the front line was opened at Afon. The only place where they brought the injured was the Gudauta hospital.

Most mobilized together with friends and relatives in support and fighter roles to protect their families that remained in Abkhazia, their localities, or the broader group. This was the common mobilization trajectory among the Abkhaz. A fighter who mobilized spontaneously in the west, without prior experience in the Abkhaz Guard, captures the quotidian character of mobilization: "We began calling all of our [sports team] boys by phone . . . [and then] gathered at the sports ground to discuss what to do. My brothers were coming from Gudauta and were shot in Kolkhida. They died. Now we understood what we faced—weaponry, tanks, marauding. They had it all, whereas we had nothing. Our strengths were uneven. The Abkhaz population of Gagra was armed with double-barreled guns and had no structure when the war started. We formed around [our] close ones." An organized fighter in the west who was part of the Abkhaz Guard before the war and mobilized together with his Guard friends, informed of the war by his father, reports a similar trajectory: "I went home. There my dad said, 'Did you hear what happened?' We had two hunting rifles, smoothbore and small-caliber, at home. My father gave me his rifles, cheese, a loaf of bread, and said, 'Go where your friends are,' which meant to Eshera [where the western front line was being formed], and I went. We stood [together], the five of us."

As I discussed above, most Abkhaz mobilization in response to the Georgian advance took place locally. Small groups bound by quotidian ties mobilized to defend families and localities that they perceived to be threatened (see figure 5.2). For example, a spontaneous fighter in the west of Abkhazia mobilized together with his friends from the neighborhood after his family was victimized by Georgian forces. He reports the threat that he realized toward his family and his subsequent mobilization trajectory: "We were very close with our neighbors. And, of course, we had more communication [with each other]. Their

FIGURE 5.2. Locals guarding a village.

Photo by Anastasia Shesterinina, with permission from a private source.

children were already beyond Kolkhida, stood there, [guarding a block post]. When Gagra was freed, I left right away and joined these boys at Eshera. . . . [Georgian troops] cleared out my house, killed my dog, offended my father—all this boiled up and I united people around me to fight." Likewise, an organized fighter in the west joined the Abkhaz side with other Abkhaz guards after his father's house was burned: "Before, I was in the Abkhaz Guard. . . . The house that my father built was the first one to be burned in Gagra. They burned it because they knew my father. We [Abkhaz guards] sat there, hiding. Then we joined the military action. We all participated in the freeing of Gagra, as one group."

Groups within the locality mobilized to protect each other and whole villages. A fighter in the east captures how he mobilized based on the threat directed to friends in his locality: "How [could] I leave my town and the people whom I worked with closely for many years, now that they are in danger?" (interview in Cherkezija 2003, 105). One of my respondents in the west describes mobilizing in response to the perceived threat to his whole village, including to the Georgian population: "We made a decision to guard the village, including the Georgian population. . . . The decision about guarding the Georgian population was made because there were cases of violence against them. This was expected, but we all live in one village. And all our women, children, elders live in this village. Allowing, in these conditions, violence to be perpetrated against our neighbors was unacceptable." Protection of the Georgian communities by the Abkhaz was not a typical outcome as the fighting went on, however. Respondents say that friends and even family members often turned against one another as violence and war unfolded. "My husband's best friend was Georgian," a teacher explains, but "once the war began, they instantly became enemies." Although quotidian ties did not preclude intergroup violence in the war, mobilization decisions were most commonly taken in the quotidian setting.

One town in the west of Abkhazia, Pitsunda, illustrates the quotidian basis of collective local mobilization. A kolkhoz worker who was not part of the Abkhaz Guard describes how the locals, often unarmed, mobilized at the war's onset to protect their locality with close networks: "When the war began, people without weapons began organizing into groups in their villages to patrol the shoreline. Our [group] was in the school. We all knew each other and tried keeping close to one another. We held the Bzyb defense boundary, tried keeping them [Georgian forces] from going to Pitsunda or Gudauta. We asked to be given boats, to transport tourists, children, women to Sochi." A local *milicija* officer (policeman) who, given his official position, was not engaged in prewar Abkhaz mobilization similarly went to fight with his friends in this local setting: "When Georgians occupied Abkhazia, we formed a Pitsunda coy [company]. We were fifteen boys from the village.——was our commander. He worked as the chairman of the kolkhoz, and people listened to him.... Others started to join.... We only had twelve rifles and a grenade launcher. We guarded bridges along the Bzyb River."

Most family members remained in Pitsunda at the war's onset, and the locals, including the youth, followed closely the older fighters they knew, in order to protect their families. A young worker who was recruited into the Abkhaz Guard in Pitsunda recounts his mobilization: "My mother, father were here. Everyone remained, except for wives. I was not married. I joined the Pitsunda battalion. This [mobilization] was spontaneous, without a regular army. It was not professional.... We thought, whatever the older men do, we should do, too. They told us to go into the Pitsunda [or] Bzyb battalion, go into attack to free Gagra, and we went.... This was a people's liberation army. Everyone had something to do. I was a regular soldier."

People who were in Pitsunda at the time but had their close networks elsewhere often left to go where those networks were. As an official who worked in Pitsunda but was rooted in Gudauta describes: "We lived in Gudauta with small children.... Before [the war], I became director of a natural reserve in Pitsunda. All my friends were in Gudauta, however, so I went there. We ... immediately gathered in the center, at first spontaneously creating units out of our own [friends]." One respondent who worked in the tourist sector before the war and mobilized spontaneously when the war began summarizes the friendship-based nature of initial

Abkhaz mobilization in the localities, which lay at the foundation of the Abkhaz army that formed later in the war: "Two, three groups were created on the basis of the Abkhaz Guard. These were the groups who met the first battle with [Georgian] marines. Then the Pitsunda battalion was created. First groups, then a platoon in a month, then a coy already for the freeing of Gagra, depending on the level of armament. . . . The Abkhaz army was formed on the basis of location and friendship ties. You want to have someone close during the war."

However, not all Abkhaz remained in their localities when the war began. A minority of fighters who were from other localities or were not in the areas of intense fighting at the time of the war's onset left their localities to protect the areas that they considered to be most threatened by Georgian forces, namely, the capital and Gagra, even if they had to leave their families and localities behind. Protection of their group and land that they perceived to be threatened by the Georgian advance figures prominently in these fighters' responses. One fighter's brother in the east thus fled the locality to defend the capital: "My younger brother ran away to [Sukhum/i] to fight for the motherland together with his [Guard] friends" (interview in Khodzhaa 2009, 736). A respondent in the west who was not in the Abkhaz Guard before the war but had friends in the armed structure and mobilized to Sukhum/i with other spontaneous fighters likewise reports: "On the fourteenth, in the morning, we took some weapons from the Russian barracks (with some they helped, others we just took, yet others they sold to us). I came to the Guard. My friend——was there. He put together a tank from the old abandoned ones. He sent me to be a commander of the car. We gathered the boys we knew. Right away we were let out with one bullet at the Red Bridge: 'You will get more in the battle.'"

Organized and spontaneous fighters joined Abkhaz Guard units that were the first to mobilize in the areas of intense fighting. "I entered a group of unarmed boys who were standing on the Red Bridge with Abkhaz guards," one fighter without prior Abkhaz Guard experience says of the interaction between Abkhaz guards and spontaneous fighters in Sukhum/i. "I met friends . . . [including] Abkhaz Guard recruits there . . . [and] introduced myself to the military commissar" (interview in Khodzhaa 2009, 760). Since most mobilization in these areas took place as part of and in interaction with the existing armed structure, it could be interpreted that the fighters' strategy was to increase their security in the war through access to the skills and resources of the Guard (Kalyvas and Kocher 2007). Yet neither skills nor resources were available in the context of unanticipated fighting and limited weapons at the war's onset, whereas mobilization in their own communities at least offered a setting where larger numbers of community members could work to protect each other within the locality.

Leaving for Sukhum/i and Gagra or later the front line in the war presented the greatest risk to individual lives, with immediate casualties among these fighters.

As respondents in the west who left for Sukhum/i with their friends as soon as they heard that Georgian forces were in the capital demonstrate: "I organized the boys, told them not to fall in spirit, that something would materialize ... [and] the people would not leave us.... We found a stockpile of pipes. The boys were young. They took the pipes and stood with them at the [entry] to Sukhum.... [O]ur boys died right when [Georgian forces] entered [the city]." When Georgian marines landed in the west, the Gagra locals report, "there stood our boys—some with weapons, others without.... They managed to mobilize to meet Georgian marines. [They] gathered spontaneously, without organization, and stood there. The first casualties were there."

Not only fighters but also individuals in the support apparatus took these risks. "I did not hold a gun, but I held another weapon," recalls a war journalist who shot footage of fighting, "to reflect the real situation on video.... [W]e never kn[e]w which way the bullet would come from." These individuals often mobilized unarmed and observed immediate casualties on the Abkhaz side and therefore realized the risk that fighting for Sukhum/i and Gagra posed to their lives. Yet they prioritized the threat that they perceived to the broader group and the motherland associated with it. "The war started and none of us," a respondent in the west begins, then pauses, as not all Abkhaz mobilized to the areas of intense fighting, and says, "I knew I would be defending the motherland.... And so when [we] went into counterattack the first day of the war, one had a gun, two were unarmed, running behind ... to take the guns of [those] ... injured or killed."

Why did the ordinary Abkhaz navigating the difficult dilemmas of the first days of the war turn to quotidian networks to arrive at collective mobilization decisions? The familial and friendship basis of the Abkhaz mobilization and army formation in the course of the war is rooted in the organization of the prewar Abkhaz society. *Familia*, or a group of relatives bound by a family name, and local friendship are major sources of social support in everyday life. As an Abkhaz historian explains:

> We have very strong family ties. When family celebrations or tragic events happen, the whole *familia* comes together to support each other. In villages, we have communes. Everyone is close in the holding of weddings or in situations of death. Everyone helps and stands by each other's side. This has carried on from ancient times, and we are glad to maintain it. A person is never left alone. There is moral, material, spiritual support of relatives and neighbors. We do not abandon people in joyful or difficult situations.

One respondent captures how this social structure affected mobilization when the war began:

> People in Abkhazia live by neighborhoods. I have one hundred people in my town, we all know each other. It is better to live in peace with each other, so if conflicts arise, we come to face each other with large groups of people, all our friends, and try to settle the issue. We say everything to each other straight. Of course, there are fights, but the end result is that all is said and the issue is settled. . . . There are no clans in Abkhazia, just *familias*. If someone has my last name, even if I do not know them, it automatically means that I will protect and help them if anything happens. . . . People follow each other by *familia* and by friendship. So when the war came, people reported to the army with their friends to fight together. Those who could not fight helped otherwise. After the war, they remained close.

The continuity of friendship ties from the pre- to postwar periods appears across the interviews. It is with these networks that people addressed the problems of everyday conflict and mobilized in the past. "I joined all the clashes," fighters who participated in prewar mobilization regularly report, and "my friends participated in all the strikes." People who mobilized together for war often remained in the same units in the emergent army: "We met three years before the war. We then stayed together in the trenches, in the unit, in the battalion." After the war, this continued among groups whose wartime trajectories were not interrupted by injury or death.[11] The Abkhaz thus see the Abkhaz army as *narodnoe opolchenie* (the people's guard). "People died voluntarily for Abkhazia, no one forced them—they could leave for Russia," an Abkhaz commander explains of the force.

This final stage of the social mobilization process at the war's onset in Abkhazia underlines the intimate character of mobilization under conditions of uncertainty. Mobilization decisions following national and local messages were taken in tightly knit clusters of relatives and friends who fled and fought together and mobilized not only locally but also to the areas of intense fighting in Sukhum/i and Gagra in the east and west of the territory, respectively.

6
FROM MOBILIZATION TO FIGHTING

> Many went to free Gagra with sticks. . . . We went to necessarily free the town. This helped.
>
> —Abkhaz fighter, Gagra, 2011

How did the war unfold after this initial Abkhaz mobilization? I asked participants how the fighting began, whether and how the Abkhaz force changed in the course of the war, and how they viewed the war's outcomes. People's participation in different capacities in the war paved the way for the continued evolution of Abkhaz collective conflict identities. The Abkhaz who remained in Abkhazia and participated in the war as fighters or in the support apparatus, half of my respondents, soon realized the possibility and consequences of losing this war. Meager organization and access to weapons on the Abkhaz side early in the war, the brutality that the Abkhaz observed as the fighting progressed, and the support that many local Georgians offered to the Georgian side during the war meant that the Abkhaz could be dramatically reduced in number and status or eliminated altogether as a result of the war.

As soon as the threat of the Georgian advance was understood and it became clear that the Abkhaz faced a situation of war, the Abkhaz leadership began building an organizational structure to transform into an army the disparate Abkhaz force that mobilized in the first days of the war. In turn, Abkhaz fighters interpreted their role in the war as "defenders" of their collectivity, especially once the Abkhaz Guard and the local defense volunteer units that took the weight of the first days of the war became an army, which gave this role legitimacy. Some battles over the strategically and symbolically important locales of Abkhazia became particularly salient for Abkhaz fighters in this context. The "liberations" of Gagra and Sukhum/i were among these battles, which started and then ended the war, respectively, in success for the Abkhaz. The support of the North Caucasus and

Russia was critical for this outcome, but my focus is on how Abkhaz fighters came to understand the significance of these battles and their ongoing role in the war, informed by their wartime fighting experiences.

The First Months of the Georgian-Abkhaz War

What were the first months of the Georgian-Abkhaz war like for the ordinary Abkhaz who mobilized to protect their own lives and those of relatives and friends, residents of their localities, the Abkhaz group, and the broader population of Abkhazia? In the course of the Georgian advance on August 14–15, 1992, three groups of Abkhaz fighters mobilized: a small number of Abkhaz guards, including reservists, regular soldiers, and commanders, who were on duty at the Okhurej, Gudava, and other posts of the Abkhaz Guard along the main road of Abkhazia; off-duty reservists and regulars who joined at the entry to the capital and Gagra in the west of the territory; and defense volunteers who had not been recruited into the Abkhaz Guard prior to the war but mobilized spontaneously to join the guards by Sukhum/i and Gagra or defend their villages across Abkhazia. This combined Abkhaz force held the Georgian National Guard and Mkhedrioni (Horsemen) units, and the local Georgians who joined them, near Sukhum/i and the Russian border, where Georgian marines landed in western Abkhazia, and around Tqvarchal/Tqvarcheli, which Georgian forces blockaded on arrival into eastern Abkhazia.

Due to a standoff in the initial fighting that broke out on the Red Bridge in the capital, the two sides held negotiations on August 15 and agreed to separate the forces. The Georgian side retreated to the east of Sukhum/i and the Abkhaz side to the Gumista River west of the capital. Similarly, in Abkhazia's west, where Georgian forces crushed resistance by Abkhaz guards and defense volunteers in both directions, to the Russian border and Gagra, a decision was made to retreat from Gagra. Despite the agreement, Georgian forces entered both Gagra and Sukhum/i on August 18. "Once [the sides] were separated, our boys retreated, while Georgians went into [Gagra]," the locals of Gagra and Sukhum/i recall. "On the eighteenth, they fully occupied Sukhum and got to the left shore of Gumista."

Georgian forces thus established control over both eastern and western Abkhazia and cut off Abkhaz access to the border with Russia and the blockaded territory around Tqvarchal/Tqvarcheli. This left central Abkhazia and besieged Tqvarchal/Tqvarcheli under Abkhaz control. To hold on to these areas, the Abkhaz established headquarters in Gudauta, where the former Soviet military base was located, and formed front lines around Gudauta, along the Bzyb/Bzipi River

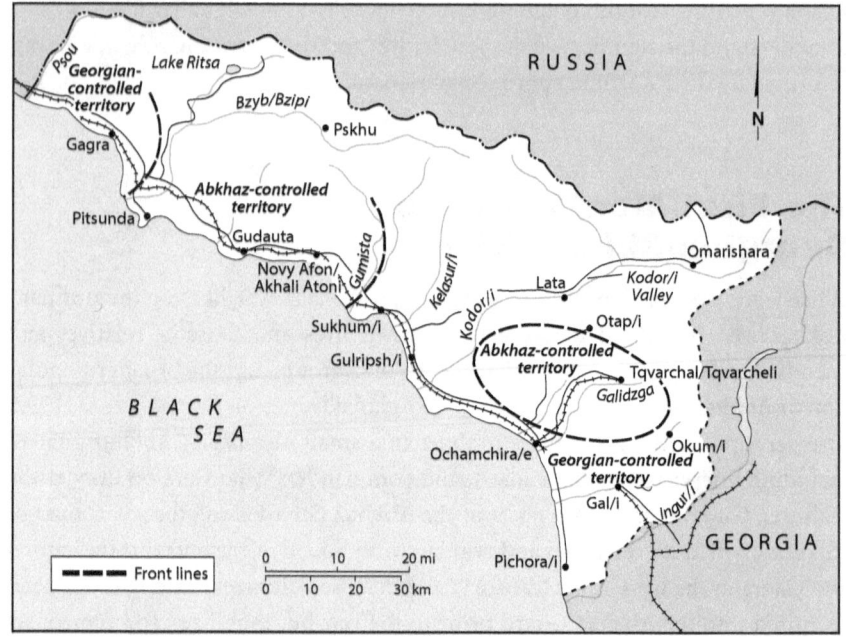

FIGURE 6.1. Front lines: August 18–October 6, 1992.

Source: I consulted respondent recollections and the discussion of fighting in Khodzhaa 2003, 2006, 2009 and Pachulija 2010 in identifying the approximate location of the front lines.

by Gagra and the Gumista River by Sukhum/i, and around Tqvarchal/Tqvarcheli (see figure 6.1).

Western Front-Line Defense: The Bzyb/Bzipi and Gumista Rivers

Some Abkhaz fighters took positions along the Bzyb/Bzipi and Gumista Rivers as soon as the sides retreated from Gagra and Sukhum/i on August 15. "We made a decision for all defense volunteers to retreat from [Gagra] and take positions along the Bzyb," fighters describe the first stage of front-line formation. "Killings [in Sukhum/i] started on the first day of the war. As a result, the front line was formed along the Gumista." These two front lines around Gudauta were then adjusted by military officers and guarded by units, some of which were formed and armed at the Abkhaz headquarters. This was the Abkhaz leadership's initial attempt at organizing the disparate Abkhaz force that mobilized over the previous days.

When the Georgian side entered Gagra and Sukhum/i on August 18, the Abkhaz leadership, which relocated from the capital to Gudauta, issued a resolution, "On the establishment of the State Defense Committee" (Pachulija 2010, 44). Chaired by Ardzinba, the committee subordinated the Abkhaz Guard and Soviet army officers in Abkhazia and appointed personnel to organize defense. "[When] the Georgian side entered Gagra," a former Soviet officer and Abkhaz Guard commander illustrates, "an order came from the State Defense Committee to move the front line beyond the Bzyb" (interview in Khodzhaa 2009, 441). As a result, the fighting position was placed in Kolkhida, right outside Gagra. "The defense boundary was in Kolkhida. This was the Bzyb front line," a local says.

The Abkhaz guards and defense volunteers retreating from Gagra and Sukhum/i and joining mobilization at this time were assigned to front-line units. Some got automatic guns from the Soviet military base, but others went armed with improvised or hunting weapons. "I took my father's rifle and went to Gudauta," a joiner says. "The people's guard was formed at the Volga sanatorium [the Abkhaz headquarters]. We made Molotov cocktails (I made nineteen), self-made grenades. The rest [of the weapons] were double-barreled guns." "We got the order to guard the bridge in Kolkhida," reports one unit fighter, "[so] we guarded it with the weapons we had—hunting weapons for birds. My younger brothers went to the Bzyb, where the [front-line] headquarters was being formed." Some volunteers were assigned there: "We were seventeen [in all] and called each other to go to war. We had two fronts, one at the Bzyb, another at the Gumista. Georgians occupied all territory beyond these points. We went to the Bzyb and there found commanders who assigned us, altogether but with the addition of other men, to fight." By mid-September, the two front lines were fortified and position fighting broke out intermittently. "We defended the Kolkhida front line," a defense volunteer assigned to a front-line unit in Gudauta demonstrates, "so that [Georgian forces] would not go further. We were the first border forces."

Eastern Front-Line Defense: Tqvarchal/Tqvarcheli

The situation was different in the east of Abkhazia, where a loose front line was formed and guerrilla rather than conventional fighting dominated. The front line around besieged Tqvarchal/Tqvarcheli was based on the self-defense organized in nearly every Abkhaz village in the area. As a fighter in one of these villages illustrates: "On the second day [of the war], the youth of the village began gathering, arming themselves with whatever they could: made bottles with incendiary mixtures, got ammonal from Tqvarcheli, and put up a barricade with watch duties" (interview in Khodzhaa 2009, 615). The villages were poorly armed. "We had three automatic guns in the village," one fighter tells, while "others were unarmed or with hunting rifles" (interview in Khodzhaa 2009, 689). Attacks and clashes with Georgia's troops supported by neighboring Georgian-dominated villages were thus common early in the war. "Georgians entered Mokva, burned several dozen Abkhaz houses, killing some civilians," fighters say. "Tsagera, where Georgians resettled in Beria's times, was strongly fortified and armed. And so we had to dig trenches. . . . We had minor clashes" (interviews in Khodzhaa 2009, 683, 550).

Georgian attacks subsided with the upsurge in Abkhaz guerrilla activity. "Almost every night we sabotaged, blew up electricity pylons, attacked Georgian roadblocks . . . to get weapons," fighters describe of this "subversive guerrilla war." "[We] carried out sudden sorties against Georgian units . . . , mined Georgian military vehicle paths" (interview in Khodzhaa 2009, 840, 726). Guerrilla units guarded village defense positions and blocked Georgians from entering mountainous villages and Tqvarchal/Tqvarcheli. "They entered Kutol . . . , burned houses along the road," a villager confirms. "When they met resistance, they did not go into [our] villages anymore." The growing guerrilla presence across this territory strengthened the front line over time. An east front commander describes this process:

> This is how the war started. Tqvarchal was cut off. . . . This meant that the line of resistance from the Kodor River to the Galidzga River was over one hundred kilometers. In places it was broken, in places it stretched through the mountains. This is where we managed to create a resistance boundary in natural places. If there was a mountain peak, a river, we took it and blocked it. . . . In some places we corrected the line [to] get closer to the road . . . [and] any time make sorties, attack Georgian military columns, or blow up bridges. . . . We had position fighting and partisan sorties. The Georgian army held battles across the whole front line and we had to resist.

Early Organization: The People's Guard

Organization of front-line defense consumed the first months of the war for the Abkhaz who joined the war effort in the fighting and support apparatuses. Those in leadership positions, especially local commanders, had the task of building defense with little experience, organizational structure, except for the Abkhaz Guard, or basic resources. As the east front commander above demonstrates, "The frontline did not come together correctly, according to military science. In some places it was instinctive, in others illogical. But we were not war specialists or professional soldiers. Thus, it remained until the end as we built it. . . . We had one problem, lack of weapons and ammunition. We did not have enough medications or bandages. There was a large deficit of food. We had to make use of the whole territory [for supplies] and used every village for corn, meat, milk." "We did not know what to start with," a local commander at the Bzyb/Bzipi front line similarly explains, "[so] we created a headquarters in Bzyb. I was appointed head of the rear [and] knew where more work was needed—weaponry, barricades, bunkers had to be built. We did not have any [of these assets necessary] for contact fights, shoot-outs. It was the worst position. The foreman, an engineer, had to build bunkers, everything for the battle. I, too, [worked] behind him.... I put up refrigeration systems for meat, fuel, so that there was everything [that we needed]. We started selling fish, meat to buy shells from Russians."

For fighters, especially defense volunteers who were not in the Abkhaz Guard, the organization of front lines and units to guard them meant that early spontaneous mobilization assumed structure. "When the front line was shaped," a volunteer reflects, "detachments were organized, commanders chosen, and the military command appeared. Some structure emerged. This is how the war started." Men and women off the front lines participated in this organization. "Pensioners remained to guard the shoreline by Gagra," for example, and women joined the support apparatus in Gudauta. Women report: "I stayed to cook"; "I spent eight months in Gudauta, sew[ing] uniforms for fighters, white overshirts. We were 250 women." A woman active in the support apparatus captures this common experience: "We came to our friend's house in Gudauta. This was a private house. About twenty people lived there packed like sardines. Beds stood in a row at the kitchen. Women sat sewing [tactical] vests for men. Everyone was busy. There was no food, no salary, but people rushed to be of service." Another woman, who wanted to mobilize as a fighter but went into the support apparatus, states: "On the second day, I went to get my daughter at the bank and we went to the headquarters. I asked to be taken to the front, but no one took us. By the evening, a big woman came with a gun. She said a nurse was needed.... She looked at everyone and took me into her team." "There we[re] fighters and everyone else. Fighters f[ou]ght, everyone else help[ed]," a commander describes the resultant *narodnoe opolchenie* (the people's guard).

The Soviet army experience that most Abkhaz men had due to compulsory military service in the Soviet Union helped in this initial organization of defense. As an east front fighter reports, "We did not have professional officers who could correctly create the defense boundary. But we almost all served in the army and with our knowledge began doing all that every one of us could do. As a construction worker, I blocked the main road at the turn to Pitsunda where [Georgian] heavy equipment could break through." "We had tankers, artillerymen who had served [in the Soviet military] before. All this helped in our popular mobilization," western fighters corroborate. Soviet veterans who served in Afghanistan played a particular role in this defense organization "as people with real combat experience" (Brojdo 2008, 151). The eastern village of Mokva, for example, elected an Afganec (a veteran of the 1979–1989 Soviet-Afghan War) to fortify the village and form the front line.

Despite this initial organization, the Abkhaz did not have a functioning army. "There were subdivisions. We said 'coy,' 'battalion,' 'brigade.' But, really, at first we did not have a regular army," fighters across Abkhazia consistently report. "There was self-organization on the Abkhaz side—groups here, groups there. Mostly these were civilians, not a regular army. This was simply popular mobilization." A volunteer who went to Gudauta, only to find little guidance there, captures the situation:

> My cousin and I went to Gudauta. We thought that defense units were being formed there, but nothing was really going on. . . . Slowly, we started getting into the war with the weapons that we had. Of course, in the situation that shaped up, we needed to self-organize. No one would come from the outside and organize us. As a result, territorial units transformed into structural units of the people's guard. Large urban units transformed into companies. Towns transformed into battalions. This way the people's guard was formed [and] took the weight of the first days of the war—daily duties on the front line by Gagra et cetera.

"We started weakly," a commander describes well the first months of the war. "We had many who wanted to fight, but there were no weapons, only hunting weapons. It was difficult to organize."

The Lifeline to Russia and the Survival of the Abkhaz

Organization of and participation in the defense around Gudauta and Tqvarchal/Tqvarcheli in response to the Georgian encirclement of Abkhazia indicated to Abkhaz men and women that the war would be protracted. As a fighter who mobilized spontaneously and entered a Bzyb/Bzipi front-line unit demonstrates, "At first, no one thought the war would be real and would be prolonged to a year and a half. When the first days passed, we started to understand this was serious and not as before, not like the former conflicts that happened on the national grounds all the time." By taking Gagra and the adjacent border area with Russia, Georgian forces blocked Abkhaz access to the lifeline, Russia. "Abkhazia was encircled," one fighter explains, "[and] only mountain passes remained clear. Our communications went through them. The sea route, too, was controlled by Georgia. We could not get support or weapons from the sea, only through mountain passes." Fighters from the North Caucasus thus began arriving "in four, five days by foot through mountain passes" and even "brought a civilian device, a hail rocket, through the mountain passes," Abkhaz commanders remember. Within a month, at least two hundred fighters arrived from Chechnya, Kabardino-Balkaria, and Karachay-Cherkessia, all part of the Assembly of the Mountain Peoples of the Caucasus, which Aidgylara (Unity) helped create before the war (Pachulija 2010, 86). Yet Georgia's forces prevented foreign fighters and the Abkhaz returning to join their group in Abkhazia from passing through the Russian border, which would be essential when winter hit and mountain passes were snowed in. The Abkhaz could not continue fighting in these conditions.

The encirclement produced great fear among the Abkhaz. "What would have happened if they had broken through our Kolkhida block posts and gotten right away into [the village of] Bzyb?" local residents asked. "They entirely closed Kolkhida, so that no Abkhaz could leave, put up concrete structures to block off the area. It was so scary." An alternative that many envisioned was displacement or annihilation of the Abkhaz group. "I thought they would kick us out. We had too few weapons. We prepared to live in the mountains, lead partisan [guerrilla] war," a defense volunteer says, painting a grim picture for the Abkhaz.

Georgian Brutality and Local Support

The brutality and local support of Georgian forces underlined these fears of the Abkhaz. Neither Abkhazia nor Georgia had a regular army when the war began in August 1992, and reports of looting, killing, and torture continued when Georgian forces established control over the east and west of Abkhazia. These forces included the Georgian National Guard and the local and Georgia-based Mkhedrioni, whose legal status as the Internal Troops–National Guards and the Rescue Corps of Georgia, respectively, was formalized in 1990 (Darchiashvili 1997). These and other armed groups that sprouted at the end of the Soviet Union, however, acted outside central control (Driscoll 2015). Insubordination of fighters and disorganization were big problems as a result. As an Abkhaz fighter observes, "Georgian forces that came to Abkhazia were not the same army that Georgia currently has. Today Georgia's army is well trained [and] equipped, [whereas] those forces consisted of crooks. Most were criminals, marauders released from prison to fight in Abkhazia. . . . It was a complete breakdown of the army itself. They did not subordinate to one another."

The first months of the war were wreaked by disorder in the Georgian-controlled territory. Human Rights Watch (HRW 1995, 22) documents the violations by Georgian forces in Sukhum/i: "Within days after Sukhumi was taken by Georgian National Guard troops, and as additional Georgian forces flowed into the city (including the Mkhedrioni), a pattern of vicious, ethnically based pillage, looting, assault, and murder emerged. . . . Although Georgian forces appeared to be operating under no particular command, they did seem to have a clear agenda. They roamed through the city at will, especially at night, looting and pillaging." Locals have similar memories. One woman gasped when she recalled "watching how crazy people, drugged [from] smok[ing] and [shooting up with] needles, were running through our city, getting into our houses to humiliate and kill." Such accounts are common across Abkhazia (Voronov, Florenskij, and Shutova 1993). In the east, "Abkhaz civilians were killed en masse in the Ochamchira region" (Argun 1994, 13). "Marauders were here the first days," residents of the Gagra district say, and "supplies ended, commercial shops were looted." "They robbed, drank, partied, raped women," west front commanders report. "We went to homes where people were robbed, tortured. They hid when we came in," journalists record of the distress.

In this context, the Abkhaz-controlled territory felt relatively safe for the Abkhaz and other non-Georgian minorities who did not want to take the Georgian side or participate in the war. "In Gudauta," a Russian woman who fled from the capital says, "there was a feeling of home, order, it was calm there. No one robbed anyone, there was no horror like in Sukhum." "Armenian village[s] saw horrible destruction. . . . Many came to Gudauta and told me these stories," a member of Abkhazia's presidium says. As a nurse stationed at the Gumista front line from the first days of the war confirms, "I saw how frightened Armenians ran from Sukhum. Georgians gathered all Armenians in a village, said, 'Give us money and you will live.' Armenians gave the money, but then other Georgian groups came. And in the end there was no more money or gold left. They burned some Armenians alive in their houses. And so they ran, and we helped them cross the river."

Whereas some non-Georgian minorities joined the Abkhaz forces as a result, most Georgians supported Georgia (Achugba 2003). As a local of Gagra who formed the Armenian battalion notes, "We know who participated, who did not, who took what measures. Everyone knows what was happening on their street, in their neighborhood, who did what. Gagra is small. About 90 percent [of Georgians], they all supported Georgia, except in different forms. Some stood with a weapon, others with words, others were looting. No matter what they did, about 90 percent participated." Many regular Abkhaz believe that local Georgians prepared for the war. An Abkhaz researcher explains: "After the war, I was looking for [disappeared] Georgians. . . . [Local Georgians] showed me houses where weapons were stockpiled and lists of Georgians, militarized groups, and units that were created. They told me that they prepared before the war, created these lists. Therefore, before the war, they armed their local population to then get support from the inside."

There is a myth that Georgians "happily welcomed the tanks that entered Abkhazia" and "threw flowers" when the war began, and Abkhaz guards report local Georgian participation from the war's onset. "If the first attack was by [Georgia's] Kutaisi battalion [in Sukhum/i], the second involved local Georgians"; "[when] the Abkhaz... retreated from [Gagra] ... Mkhedrioni men and armed local Georgians appeared in the city" (interview in Khodzhaa 2003, 184, 203). More local Georgians were reportedly implicated as the war progressed. Even in Gal/i, which was at first neutral, displaced local Georgians recall, "weapons, money, food, clothes, cigarettes were collected here and sent to the front. Some young even participated."

The implications of local Georgian participation in the war were severe for the Abkhaz. As the Armenian fighter above says, "If local Georgians had not supported the Georgian side, nothing would have happened here." A Georgian who fought on the Abkhaz side concurs: "There would have been no war if the local Georgian population had opposed it." The Abkhaz imagine what would have happened "if residents of the Gal region had stood up and said 'What are you doing?' to their brothers, 'These are innocent people. We live here, too, as one society'"; instead, "Georgians achieved their aims by the hands of locals. There were many groups, organizations in every village, district. They stood up against the Abkhaz people." In this situation, three options existed for local Georgians. "Some openly rejected nationalism and either left or fought with us," a Ukrainian explains, "[but] most... actively supported and were morally on the Georgian side." This affinity with Georgia's goals in the war and participation in the fighting reinforced the Abkhaz fear: "Their brutality made it clear that Georgians hated us."

Georgian leaders added to this fear. On August 15, President Shevardnadze said that "in the struggle for the preservation of the territorial integrity of our state we will not stop before anything. For this we are willing to die ourselves, but also eliminate anyone" (Brojdo 2008, 53). The statement of commander Giorgi Karkarashvili that he would sacrifice "100,000 Georgians [to kill] all 97,000 [Abkhaz]" was aired on television in Sukhum/i on August 24 (Amkuab and Illarionova 1992, 28). Continuing attacks at the Bzyb/Bzipi and Gumista front lines after the signing of a cease-fire agreement in Moscow on September 3 suggested that the Georgian threat would be realized no matter what (Volhonskij, Zaharov, and Silaev 2008, 244–246; Pachulija 2010, 84). "As if it was their country and they could do anything here," west and east front commanders illustrate that nothing could stop Georgia's fight for territorial integrity, "they managed *during the cease-fire* to gain a foothold [and] strengthen their positions." As Anna Brojdo (2008, 52) summarizes the Georgian threat, "The problem of the bio-ethnic survival of the Abkhaz people was very clearly delineated from the first days of the [war]— due to the cruelty of [Georgia's] troops and the local Georgian population in the occupied part of Abkhazia and to official statements of the Georgian leaders."

The Gagra Operation: October 1992

With Abkhazia encircled and the Russian border closed, winter approaching to block mountain passes and prevent support from arriving in Abkhazia, and Georgia's forces, including local Georgians, showing brutality against the Abkhaz, bolstered by their leaders' threats, the capture of Gagra became the priority for the survival of the Abkhaz group. "If Abkhazia was to survive after a month of occupation," a west front commander explains, "we had to free Gagra and get to Psou [the border with Russia] because soon the snow would block the passes." As fighters confirm, "Closer to the fall, as the first snow fell in the mountains, we realized that the situation was worsening. We could find ourselves in a blockade during the winter with closed mountain passes. Thus we had to, at any price, break out of that circle of blockade and free Gagra." This realization of Gagra's significance was a constant theme for participants in west front defense.

Attempts at taking Gagra were therefore made as soon as the Bzyb/Bzipi front line shaped up. For example, on August 25, a former Soviet army major with 150 Abkhaz fighters attacked Gagra and suffered losses (Pachulija 2010, 80). "There were attempts, from our side, of attacks, but this was not organized very well and failed," the fighter above recalls, "[and] then former [Soviet army] officers who lived in Abkhazia, many of [whom] returned and offered their help, began preparing the attack to free Gagra according to military strategy." "By the end of September," a teacher who joined a sabotage unit confirms, "we started preparing the operation to [take] Gagra. We sold cars to buy rifles at the black market. I met [a former officer who] was preparing a reconnaissance and sabotage unit." The unit had to break into the town from the main road. Another fighter reports preparation from the sea: "A week before the beginning of the liberation of Gagra and the Gagra district, I went to the Gagra front line with up to seven of my *familia* members. . . . We knew Gagra, took a position by the poultry farm from the side by the sea. We had only three Kalashnikovs. Our position was far from the main Abkhaz defense line. We were too close to the Georgians. A few times they even kicked us out from our position" (interview in Khodzhaa 2009, 198).

The operation was planned for September 30, but had to be postponed. "We had to go to the town on signal and divert their forces to us from others," the teacher in the sabotage unit remembers. "The operation was canceled, however. They took us to the road in Pitsunda, through gardens, to wait along [house] fences. We had to withhold from talking, smoking, and attack once we heard a shot from the tank. But the tank stalled!" "The main forces were supposed to attack Kolkhida at that time, but something went wrong and the attack was temporarily postponed," a woman recalls her brother's explanation at the time. The next day, however, around six hundred Abkhaz and foreign fighters went on "a three-pronged attack" on Gagra: "One group followed the coastline and attacked [Gagra] from the beach and marsh areas.... The other two ... fought their way through [Gagra] along ... the old and new highways.... By October 2nd Abkhazian units held all the strategic heights" (Billingsley 2013, 150). The Abkhaz force got to the border with Russia a few days later. As the teacher above concludes, "We advanced on Gagra and got to Psou. As we reached the town of Kholodnaya Rechka by the border, we found a column of heavy equipment pointing toward Gagra. Georgians ran away! Even a cigarette was left to burn out on the ground. They left so many weapons, tanks behind."[1]

Participants acknowledge poor Abkhaz organization in the operation: "It was unorganized. We decided by ourselves what positions to take. On the second, third attempt, we managed to enter Gagra. I passed one rifle back and forth with my cousin," a fighter and commander say. "The communication systems were very poor. It was the first attempt at an organized attack [and] I got a serious injury." According to Abkhaz statistics, 108 fighters were killed in the operation, of which only 15 were foreign fighters (Pachulija 2010, 91). This was a big loss for the small Abkhaz force.

Yet fighters stress the significance of taking Gagra, *by any means*. As a local conveys, "We had to free Gagra, as the Abkhaz were squeezed from two sides, Sukhum along the Gumista from the east and here along the Kolkhida line. We ended up inside, separated from everyone. To hope for at least something, we, by any means, had to get to the border with Russia." The sheer significance that fighters attributed to the operation sharpened their understanding of the conflict and their role in it. "If we had not freed the Psou border, there *would not be* this people," a participant underlines, "[as] the freeing of the border was ... the freeing of Abkhazia." The definition of Abkhaz fighters as "national liberation fighters" started with the "liberation" of Gagra as a result.

"We Freed Gagra. From This Moment on, We Were a Real Army": Abkhaz Army Formation

The capture of Gagra and the border with Russia was vital for the Abkhaz force to continue fighting in this war. "The main danger disappeared," one west front commander clarifies, but position fighting continued along the Gumista River. As military expert Dodge Billingsley (2013, 150) puts it, "Once in control of the border and port-facilities ..., the Abkhazian leadership was assured that supplies and manpower would get through. On the other hand, after the loss of Gagra, Georgia could only hope for a break-out on the Sukhum front." Indeed, respondents report the flow of produce and foreign fighters through "the common peaceful corridor" that was established with Russia. Foreign fighters "elevated our spirit, brought weapons, and helped us till the end," Abkhaz fighters explain of the importance of this corridor, and "hope appeared that the war would not last too long, that we were not alone in this world, that there were people on this and other sides of the border who supported us."[2] This support played a pivotal role in the war.

Yet this support, on its own, was insufficient to end the war, as serious Abkhaz losses over the next year indicate. Georgian forces were disorganized and lacked the cohesion that the Abkhaz showed at Gagra, but they still outnumbered the Abkhaz (Billingsley 2013, 155). In addition to the much greater share of Georgians in Abkhazia and Georgia, the Georgian side had fighters from the Baltics and Ukraine, driven by anti-Russian sentiments (Zverev 1996). Moreover, Russia's support was inconsistent and was provided to both sides (Zürcher 2007, 141). As Pavel Baev (2003, 139) finds, "One part of the Russian military, particularly the Command of the Trans-Caucasus Military District, supported Georgia and supplied it with heavy weapons and ammunition. Another part of the Russian military, first of all the forces based in Abkhazia around the airbase in Gudauta, directly supported the Abkhazian side." Other cases of Russian support are known, but were "isolated and more likely reflected freelancing by rogue elements of the Russian military" (Billingsley 2013, 155). "There were multiple layers to Russian involvement in the conflict," an expert in Moscow agrees; military fragmentation was one.

From the Abkhaz perspective, it was the army formation, not only external support, that the Abkhaz needed for victory. Failed attacks and unpreparedness at Gagra demonstrated this need: "As much as we prepared for the liberation of Gagra, we could not say that we had an army. Those who led the people were mostly leaders in the society, not professional military men. They were called commissars but went on naked enthusiasm, rather than knowledge. . . . You can win a battle, but not a war, with enthusiasm. A war is won with military professionalism." As a professor who, with no military experience, was elected to be a commissar at a village gathering illustrates,

> At the beginning of the war, no one was appointed, but we all gathered and chose whom we could rely on and who could be responsible. I was elected to be an assistant to the commander, a commissar, a person responsible for the ideological aspect, the moral psychological spirit of the unit. The fighters were from my village. I knew them all, as I grew up with them. It was a familial environment. My tasks involved supporting the mood, explaining what was happening. I did not let anyone doubt that we were right, that we would certainly win.

To prepare the Abkhaz people's guard for future fighting, on October 11, the State Defense Committee set up the Ministry of Defense to form the Armed Forces of Abkhazia with artillery, tank, navy, air force, and other regular army units. The ministry continued the general mobilization of the population "to defend the independence of [the] motherland" (Pachulija 2010, 249). The resultant army grew from one thousand to twelve thousand participants by the end of the war, with only 10 percent of them foreign fighters.[3]

What did the army formation mean for the ordinary Abkhaz who mobilized on the Abkhaz side? The incorporation of initially mobilized groups of relatives and friends into a larger structure, the official status that this structure received, and the training undertaken to professionalize it gave participants a sense of legitimacy in their defender role. Although some fighters moved between units during the war, fighters stress the importance of preserving the prewar ties underlying the units: "We met three years before the war. We then stayed together in the trenches, in the unit, in the battalion." One defense volunteer's experience exemplifies the continuity of prewar to wartime ties: "I was in the Sharatyn folk ensemble, everyone knew us, [and] we went abroad to perform together. During the war, we went to fight and stayed together." An Abkhaz guard captures the continuity in unit composition during the war: "We all knew each other in the army unit that I joined. First we went to free Gagra with my group. Then we formed a battalion with three groups. . . . [When the army was formed], we became part of the provision platoon responsible for the provision of clothing, food, et cetera."

The process was similar in the east, where guerrilla groups formed at the war's onset were sustained and unified into larger battalions. Fighters joining the Abkhaz side at this time were integrated into these battalions or formed new ones to preserve the unit's composition. "Volunteers [from outside of Abkhazia] were merged with Abkhaz armed units," military historian Valiko Pachulija (2010, 45) explains, and "to create a unified military structure, separate battalions were [also] formed on their basis." The result of this structure of the Abkhaz army was that "the war was a common struggle of close ones," fighters in the west and east stress.

The army gave a formal status to this struggle. Fighters who mobilized for different reasons were now part of the official structure, with the chain of command, subordination, and discipline as its principles and training as a means to prepare fighters for battle. The commanders and fighters of one battalion in the west of Abkhazia demonstrate the transformation. The head of the headquarters of this battalion says: "We had more than four hundred people for reconnaissance. We now had to do everything. . . . Without military preparation we skillfully created a battalion. First we established discipline, then we took the military oath, and then we implemented orders from the highest commanders to the lowest chain. . . . In Gagra, the Gagra district, Bzyb, and Pitsunda battalions were all under the command of the Gagra garrison.... But subordination was to the minister in Gudauta." This battalion's commander explains the organization of training in this transformation: "Former tankers, sappers [in the Soviet military] whom we could find through personnel files organized training to seriously prepare resistance." A former teacher and defense volunteer who joined this battalion corroborates: "After the freeing of Gagra, the Ministry of Defense was created and formation of battalions began. Our group, Abra, where we had twenty-seven people, joined a larger battalion in Gagra. We were part of the Gagra garrison. We formed a regiment and began teaching people how to fight."

This transformation of the Abkhaz force into an army legitimized the fighters' view of their role in the war as defenders from the Georgian aggressor established so strongly at the war's onset. "This was the people's liberation army," fighters characterize their ongoing role. "We did not attack to get others' land. We defended our only motherland and thus had a serious loss in human terms."

Lost Battles: January and March 1993

Indeed, the Abkhaz losses over the next year were dramatic. As the army was being formed during the war, rather than in preparation for it, training during fighting was inadequate to prepare fighters for battle. As a postwar assistant to the minister of defense confirms, "Creating an army is not easy. You need tens of years to create an army. I have been an assistant to the minister of defense for fifteen years, and I can say that something close to an army started to appear only ten years after. It used to be called an army in the past as well, but the qualities necessary to hold fighting operations as an army would require long schooling."

Despite training that began in the east and west of Abkhazia, the transformation into an army was a gradual process, and military failures started right after the successful Gagra operation. By October 13, the Abkhaz took the strategic mountain height of Tsugurovka over the Gumista front line to attack Sukhum/i, but were forced to retreat, with losses. On October 26, the Ochamchira/e operation in the east failed due to weather changes and engine malfunction, delaying support for ground troops from the sea. But the most significant losses were in the January and March 1993 attacks on Sukhum/i.

The Abkhaz planned the January 5 attack on Sukhum/i as the Georgian presence intensified on the east front. The headquarters envisioned a three-pronged attack similar to that at Gagra, with two battalions fortifying the lower and upper bridges across the Gumista River and the third going into battle. Georgian forces, however, prevented the crossing with fire, and some Abkhaz units were late or did not show up for the operation. Those units that crossed the river did not get support, and the operation failed. A fighter at lower Gumista tells, "We sat in ice-cold water for seven hours . . . under sniper cross fire" (interview in Khodzhaa 2009, 48). "We guarded the entire position from Tsugurovka up, but the operation was canceled," a fighter at the upper Gumista says. Thus, thirty-five Abkhaz were killed and dozens injured (Pachulija 2010, 139).

Commanders drew lessons from these losses: "We learned as we went. There were failed attempts from lack of knowledge. For example, in January 1993 we went right to the enemy's front. Many died, many were captured. But the spirit remained. Then we used other tactics, started utilizing [mountain] heights."

In March, a stronger Abkhaz force was to attack the lower and upper Gumista, using the Tsugurovka height. The attack was postponed by a day due to communication issues. When it began on March 15, some units once again were late or did not show up, and a Georgian counterattack forced most Abkhaz to retreat. "We went to the Gumista in March. There was no support, no communication," participating fighters say. "The March attack was the most difficult, [as] they took control of the height, bombed us." Some units broke through, but could not make it to Sukhum/i. As a commander recalls, "All battalion commanders signed orders—at what time one would cross the Gumista River, who would go through to the top. It was a shuttle method—one group from the battalion crosses the river, takes the trenches through battle, and sits there. Then the others cross the river. But the others did not come. If they had come, Sukhum would have been freed that same day. . . . [It] was almost free of Georgians. But we could not manage. The plan died. Many were killed then."

This was one of the darkest episodes in the war for the Abkhaz, with 222 deaths and further injuries (Pachulija 2010, 175). One unit lost half of its fighters, for example. Its commander says: "We went as thirty-one people and came back fifteen. Sixteen remained there injured and dead. We could not take everyone."

The legitimacy that the transformation to an army gave to the Abkhaz force did not translate into military prowess on the ground. Commanders and fighters admit to inexperience and mistakes:

> Before each operation commanders got orders and were supposed to open an envelope [with the orders] at a specific time. But there was inconsistency among commanders. Many were inexperienced, did not implement orders, not everyone opened their orders on time. When we had a task to take a location, we sent a few battalions as cannon fodder, but we should not have done this.
>
> We did not have regular forces, had few weapons, disorganization, even if I do not want to say this. There was no experience. Commanders may have been experienced, but it was not easy to organize fighters. Sometimes commanders said one thing, but the boys did another.

Almost all participants say that they learned from these mistakes and prepared differently thereafter: "We participated in all the attacks—January, March—the unsuccessful ones. Many died. We drew implications and prepared otherwise." Russian training was particularly important in this regard: "We had training with Russian instructors. There our Abkhaz army was really prepared. We were no longer some militia. . . . Those who prepared us said, 'You have to fight not with the number but with the skill.' Because the numbers in our army were not high, the skill brought all the success. . . . This [training] helped with the planning and preservation of the battalion."

The "Liberation" of Sukhum/i: July and September 1993

The Abkhaz leadership took a number of steps in preparation for future attacks on Sukhum/i, drawing on the experience of the January and March operations. Battalions were merged into larger brigades for better coordination, units had training specific to terrain, frontal attacks were avoided, and the headquarters improved communications, while holding attack plans in secret. "Even Adler [a town in Russia] taxi drivers knew about our attacks!," fighters joke. "You could go to the market and hear when and where an attack was going to take place. We learned to keep secrets and use disinformation where necessary. The operations that led to the success were prepared with military strategy." These were the July and September 1993 operations for the "liberation" of Sukhum/i and Abkhazia as a whole.

The operations involved coordinated attacks on the east and west fronts. In the east, the Abkhaz set about to block the Georgian route to the capital along the main road. In the west, the focus was on the heights around Sukhum/i. By July 27, the road in the east and the heights in the west were under Abkhaz control despite serious losses and fighters retreating from shelling and minefields in the mountains. Then the signing in Sochi of the Agreement on a Cease-Fire and Arrangements to Monitor Its Observance stopped the Abkhaz. But their attack continued in September after the break in the fighting that the cease-fire provided.

On September 15, all east front forces launched attacks on the Georgian-controlled villages around Tqvarchal/Tqvarcheli and the road to the capital. The east front forces captured the road with the support of the west front marines, but the fighting continued there until the end of September. In the west, the Abkhaz fought their way to the strategic heights, took the lower and upper Gumista Bridges, and entered Sukhum/i in the face of counterattacks. The fighting racked the city until September 27, when Georgian forces retreated. As the Abkhaz forces moved east thereafter, they broke the Tqvarchal/Tqvarcheli siege, forced Georgian fighters and up to 240,000 local Georgians to flee, and raised the Abkhaz flag on the Ingur/i River on September 30. The Georgian-Abkhaz war of 1992–1993 was over, with the Abkhaz successful.

The preparations that the Abkhaz army made for these operations, including Russian training, was important for this success. The marines, infantry, and mobile platoon fighters regularly note its effects on their performance. But fighters still had massive difficulties in implementing their tasks. In the east, the landing and storming rehearsals helped the west front marines disembark in the seaside village of Tamysh to support the east front units. But it was difficult to hold the village. A local explains: "The village was poorly placed geographically during the war. There goes a road across the village, [and] the sea is close. There are villages all around it. It became a strategic place. Partisan [guerrilla] war took place here. Ours took the village but, because the front was far, had to give it back."

Fighters who took control of the road and villages in this area found themselves surrounded by Georgian forces, with no access to the rest of Abkhazia; the conditions of the siege were severe (HRW 1995). The accounts of a commander, a woman in the support apparatus, and nonfighters below are telling:

> It was impossible to deliver humanitarian aid to us. There were no corridors. Maybe once or twice we got aid, but this was not enough. We had to feed one hundred thousand people, pregnant women, children. It was very difficult.
>
> We did not have electricity, water, gas, produce. We had some reserves of flour and mixed the dough to bake bread—put two bricks together and made a fire to boil water in a kettle.
>
> The rear was so strong, because we stood by the fire and made simple corn cakes and soup. All bulls and cows were killed so that soldiers were fed. We made hundred-liter pots of soup for refugees. . . . Georgians wanted to get into Tqvarchal, but could not. If they had, the situation would have been different. Other areas got weapons from Tqvarchal, [and so] the town was bombed.

But the most painful memory was the attacks on the helicopters that brought in aid and took back women, children, and the injured. "On December 14, a helicopter with children was shot down—eighty-six people, including pregnant women. The youngest was three," a witness remembers. "I was with my son on the second helicopter following it." In Gudauta, these events added urgency to the Abkhaz attacks on Sukhum/i: "Then [after the attacks on the helicopters], everyone lost control. That was it, we had to do something, an operation to kick [Georgians] out of here. How could you burn so many children? The January operation [was undertaken as a result]."

In the west, crossing the Gumista River to get to Sukhum/i was difficult across the front line, but fighters who had to take the strategic heights were in a particularly vulnerable position because so much of the success depended on them and Georgian counterattacks were unforgiving. Fighters on the lower Gumista recount the devastating cross fire at the bridge by the front-line town of Eshera:

> On command, we would leave [to] cross the border [front line] through the bridge at lower Eshera. Our commanders told us that this was the most difficult task. We were called "suiciders." They sent us to die. Going to an open space to attack meant that all Georgian weapons were pointed at us, so we had to dig in every twenty to thirty meters. We came as close as ninety to one hundred meters to their position, went into attack, had a nonstop firefight for days after that. The goal was to send the youth to Sukhum through the mountains. Once they reached that, we also went to join them.

In the mountains, Georgian shelling and minefields drained the Abkhaz regardless of their training. A commander on the upper Gumista tells of the mines, shells, and fire on the Tsugurovka height:

> On May 1, we went to upper Eshera. Everyone got a separate place along the border [front line].... The most critical area was the upper Gumista Bridge, which my fighters controlled and patrolled. We had an observation point there, right above the bridge. From May 1 until September 15, we guarded this territory positionally.... We lost our boys in the [last] operation. When we guarded the territory, a helicopter was shot down in Tsugurovka. Because from our territory we could go to Tsugurovka, I had to go up with sixty-seven volunteers. In advance, reconnaissance reported to us that the place had minefields.... When we went up, another picture appeared—bandages, medications, there were many injured and dead. The atmosphere was difficult psychologically.... I was supposed to enter Tsugurovka and support those who would come to the village from the top. But they could not enter from the top due to the fighting. I got an order to take Tsugurovka. Having studied the terrain, we changed the route and went on command. We entered unnoticed. But then explosions began. My guide, whose parents lived there, blew up on a mine. It became clear [to Georgian forces] that we were there. And the shooting began from all types of weapons. Mines, shells started exploding. Then the fighting really began.

An engineer in the support apparatus corroborates the difficulties of fighting around Tsugurovka: "I got a task to put heavy equipment up the Akhbuk height above Tsugurovka. We had to use explosives to dig up the road. When I was almost done, I got an order to cancel. Tsugurovka had a large concentration of the Georgian army under it. They sensed that an operation was going on. There were very many mines at the height. Despite previous checks by sappers, they could not notice all in the short time that we had. I was injured, my leg was blown off."

Another commander reports the grave result of similar fighting further north in the village of Shroma: "On the first day of the fighting in Shroma, our battalion had 40 people killed and 110–140 injured. A combat-ready battalion lost its strength in a day. Georgian artillery and hail rockets were developed well. They did not leave a stone. They mashed everything that they could." Some fighters had never shot other than during their training before this fighting. The mother of one fighter says: "During the battle at Shroma, when Tsugurovka was burning, my boy was forced to shoot, of course. But this was something scary for him. He could not fall asleep that night. He asked me to go to the church the next day to put up candles for those he killed. He was crying all the while the candles were burning. It was not easy for our children to get over this."

For fighters, however, the liberation of Sukhum/i was an existential necessity, similar to the earlier situation in Gagra. "It was a difficult war," an engineer noted above explains, "but it was our goal, our necessity, we did not have any other idea than freeing our territory. Either self-destruct or free [Abkhazia]. And this is what we did." Fighters grasped the importance of particular tasks in the operations. "The success in the Sukhum direction was the village of Shroma," the commander above explains. "It was impossible to pass the Gumista front line at the lower Gumista because they managed to gain a foothold, strengthen their positions during the cease-fire, [and] created these positions very well. It was impossible to break them, only with air force, but not with tanks."

The liberation of Sukhum/i was seen as the liberation of entire Abkhazia: "We knew, if we freed the capital, the war would be over at that. Getting into Sukhum meant a free country." Thus, when after the Sochi agreement "Ardzinba asked if we should separate Abkhazia into two parts and leave the eastern part to Georgia," the Abkhaz said no, recalls a teacher who mobilized as a defense volunteer and later became a commander. "If once again we had a failed attack, we would be declared political criminals and killed, but otherwise the war would go on for Abkhazia. We decided to fight, breached the agreement, and freed Sukhum in two weeks. . . . Shevardnadze's forces were demoralized and ran away." A professor who followed a similar mobilization trajectory further explains the Abkhaz position: "The Abkhaz could not have behaved otherwise in the situation, when there was an aggressor [Georgia] in front of us that was not happy with the ethnos that lives on this territory or the schemes, such as the federal structure, that we proposed [before the war]."

The realization of what would happen if Georgia remained in control of Abkhazia, even if in part, accumulated over the decades preceding the war, the moment of the war's onset, and now after a year of fighting. "Georgia sent its people to populate Abkhazia long before the war," a veteran disabled by the war recaps, and "in three days [from August 14, 1992], they would take Abkhazia to unite the Georgian people." The sense of attack and aggression by Georgian forces at the war's onset solidified in the course of the war, to define the Abkhaz fighter as Abkhazia's defender. An Aidgylara activist captures the offensive and defensive qualities that the Abkhaz ascribe to the Georgian and Abkhaz sides in the war, respectively: "The Abkhaz, too, had nationalism, but it was defensive, whereas Georgian nationalism was offensive, aggressive." The Georgian attack was primarily directed against the Abkhaz in this assessment. "A five-million-large nation attacked a hundred thousand Abkhaz," fighters and nonfighters repeat over and again. "It was a war against the Abkhaz and for the elimination of the Abkhaz people." The burning of the Abkhaz D. Gulia Institute of Language, Literature, and History in October 1992, where the roots of the Abkhaz national movement and the National State Archive of Abkhazia were located, supported this assessment: "The Abkhazian nation was left with no documentary evidence of its historical past" (Y. Anchabadze 2013, 141; de Waal 2011).

Yet for fighters, the defense was more broadly of the motherland: "We mobilized to defend our land, motherland, our hearth and home"; "we realized that we had to seriously resist, we have no other motherland"; "we had nothing to lose except for our motherland." This differentiated the Abkhaz and Georgian aims in the war: "We fought for our motherland, they did for territorial integrity. This is why they lost. The Abkhaz went to the death. Those who did not feel this way left," fighters explain. "No one forced the Abkhaz to fight for their motherland." As a result, getting to the Ingur/i River at the end of the war was key for the Abkhaz, and those who did not deeply regretted it. "I was injured. This meant that I could not go to the Ingur," say fighters who feel the need to justify their absence. The Abkhaz lived experience of the conflict and war thus sharply contrasts with the common explanation of the Abkhaz success as due to foreign involvement in the war and the common view of the Abkhaz side as separatist. "There is a big difference between separatists and a national liberation movement. We are the latter," fighters stress. The Abkhaz call this war the Patriotic War of Abkhazia, accordingly.

7

POSTWAR ABKHAZIA

Now that we freed Abkhazia, we had to defend it.

—Abkhaz commander, Pitsunda, 2011

What did the victory in the war mean to the Abkhaz, and how did individuals with different mobilization trajectories continue to participate in the ongoing Georgian-Abkhaz conflict? The end of the war brought a period of severe upheaval to Abkhazia. A wave of marauding swept Sukhum/i and other areas that the Abkhaz captured as they advanced to the Ingur/i River. Reprisals against the Georgians who remained in Abkhazia or returned to their homes shortly after the war were reported in the east. Crime and car crashes were rampant in the context of postwar poverty and destruction, reinforced by the economic blockade of Abkhazia, and the trophy weapons and vehicles that were left from the war. While these immediate effects of the war waned in the first postwar years, other systematic forms of violence persisted for over a decade. Low-scale clashes and cross fire characterized the borderline along the Ingur/i River.[1] Georgian guerrillas ambushed Abkhaz security personnel, kidnapped civilians, and met Abkhaz crackdowns that terrorized the returning Georgian population. Renewed fighting took place in Gal/i and Kodor/i in 1998 and 2008, respectively. It was after the "liberation" of Kodor/i—the last area under Georgian control—that Abkhazia was recognized by Russia, among a few other states, and that Abkhazia fortified the Georgian-Abkhaz border area with Russian assistance, to see violence diminish.

This is far from the common depiction of the conflict as "frozen" in Abkhazia. The conflict continued in multiple ways, augmenting the Abkhaz view of the Georgian aggression and their role as defenders of Abkhazia and the Abkhaz. Most Abkhaz were rebuilding livelihoods after the war. Many mobilized as part of the army, police, and irregular forces to defend the Abkhaz victory from further Georgian attacks. All saw establishment of the de facto Abkhaz state as the just outcome of the struggle, despite protracted Georgian displacement and Abkhaz hardship and losses from border violence. The last pages of the Abkhaz narrative turn to this postwar stage of mobilization.

"The War Touched Everyone": Everyday Life in Postwar Abkhazia

What was everyday life like for the ordinary Abkhaz when the war of 1992–1993 was over? The fighting left behind ruins. Mass depopulation, demolished infrastructure and homes, trauma from the firsthand experience of violence and the loss of relatives and friends (sometimes whole families), and fear of local crime and Georgian attacks marked the immediate aftermath of the war. The displacement of most Georgians meant that entire districts of Abkhazia were deserted. "The Georgian population ran in panic when Sukhum was taken," journalists and analysts report, and "while only some Georgians from the Gal region fought, all ran away after the war." As the United Nations (UN) fact-finding mission corroborates: "When [Abkhaz] forces entered Sukhumi on 27 September 1993, the capital had a population of 50,000, down from the previous 150,000. . . . [T]he population of Ochamchira had declined by the end of October 1993 from 85,000 to 8,000. . . . Gali . . . [was] a 'dead city,' in which only some 200 to 300 people were left. Ochamchira and Gali districts, whose inhabitants had been mostly Mingrelian Georgians, were both said to be almost entirely depopulated."[2]

Some Georgians remained in Abkhazia. As a postwar government official in Sukhum/i contends, "It is a myth that all Georgians left Abkhazia in 1993. Many stayed: those who were protected by neighbors, who asserted they were not involved in the war, and who had mixed families. Many wives and mothers of our deputies are Georgian. Georgians live in my building." Others returned soon after the war, particularly to the Gal/i district. "People came back to the border villages right after the war," displaced persons from Gal/i confirm. As an official in Tbilisi clarifies, "Elders returned at first because they had less to risk. They checked the situation there, [and] when it settled down and they learned they could live there, their families returned as well . . . 90 percent returned. Those who did not, crossed a couple of times per year to take care of their houses." Yet others have still been unable to return due to the unwillingness of the Abkhaz to implement the Quadripartite Agreement on Voluntary Return of Refugees and Displaced Persons signed on April 4, 1994.[3] As a result, only around 40,000 Georgians live in postwar Abkhazia compared to 240,000 before the war (Trier, Lohm, and Szakonyi 2010, 21).

Not only Georgians but also other groups, including the Abkhaz, left Abkhazia.[4] As a local official in Tqvarchal/Tqvarcheli explains, "The state of [postwar] Abkhazia was depressing and the state of Tqvarchal even worse so. Imagine, the industries that existed all collapsed in one moment. A huge number of people were left unemployed and without a penny. What were the prospects of such a city? People had to leave, and a mass outflow of the population took place, from twenty thousand to five thousand. People were looking for sources of survival and went to Ochamchira or outside of Abkhazia."

Infrastructure and houses were damaged across Abkhazia, but particularly on the front lines and in the areas of intense fighting, around Gagra and Sukhum/i. "All the houses were burned. We could not come back to our houses," a native of Tsandrypsh/Gantiadi by the Russian border says, estimating that "almost all villages, schools were destroyed." "Gagra was burning in places. The city was empty. The greatest destruction was in Kolkhida, where the invisible front line went," a librarian from Gagra recalls. On the Gumista front line, Eshera by the sea and Shroma in the mountains were destroyed the most. "Not one other territory of Abkhazia got as many shells, as many wounds as Eshera," locals of these fighting spots contend, explaining that "there is no Shroma anymore. You come down and see the Gumista [River]." In Sukhum/i, "the State Archive, the library, the museum—everything was burned." The Government building still stands burned and abandoned. A psychologist working in the east describes the destruction in the area: "There was not as much destruction in Gal. Tqvarchal was a dead city. Ochamchira, too, was greatly destroyed. In Gal, however, schools—centers of activity—were heated with wood. Adults came to throw wood in, put cellophane over the windows. It was impossible to study in these conditions. Everything suffered in these districts—infrastructure, schools."

Survival was the main concern for most Abkhaz. Production stopped during the war, and the Georgian outflow drained the factories. The head of a bread factory in the west explains that "97 percent of [its] workers were Georgian, 70 percent of whom [came] from outside of Abkhazia." Only a few Abkhaz stayed to work there during and after the war. As one of these workers says, "Day and night, we fed everyone, sent bread even to Gudauta. The war was over, but I continued [working at the bread factory]." Agricultural production was suspended as well. "In Abkhazia, the main source of income was agriculture. All of a sudden it disappeared," officials in the east and west say. "There is almost no production. We even do not produce tobacco anymore, the same with tea, only citrus." As a result, many regular Abkhaz sold their only produce at the border with Russia or found alternative produce to buy and resell at the market. "We went to Psou for ten years, sold tangerines," respondents recall, "it was very difficult. Even the tangerines did not help. The salary did not give us anything."[5] A Sukhum/i resident conveys the fear involved in postwar trade: "In 1995, we were thinking of how to survive. My friend watched the children. I went to Gal to buy cigarettes to resell them here. I went at 5 a.m. When I got to Tamsho, where buses were usually robbed, there was such panic. It was easier once we passed that area, but there was tension all the way. People expected to be robbed. I realized I would not go ever again. There were no cigarettes that day, and I was so scared that I never went back."

The situation worsened with the imposition in 1996 of economic sanctions on Abkhazia by the Russia-led Commonwealth of Independent States. This so-called economic blockade banned economic ties with Abkhazia and in particular prohibited Abkhaz men from traveling to Russia.[6] It deepened postwar destruction and poverty and dramatically altered gender relations in the Abkhaz society. Women now traded at the Russian border, while men were left to any work that they could find in Abkhazia. Most Abkhaz women report the acute effects of the blockade on their livelihoods:

> The blockade hit hard here, in Gudauta, Gagra—people starved in the cities.
>
> The blockade made us all think of survival. Eighteen-to-fifty-five-year-old men were not allowed to cross the border. We could not go and buy essential things, and you cannot live long on beans.
>
> All women were forced to trade in tangerines, while men took care of the households.
>
> We went through with the carts . . . , sometimes slept on the bridge. This is how we lived, to buy bread for the children. I was a witness . . . when a woman died. Cars ran over people.
>
> Women raised the Abkhaz economy. They had to stand in daylong lines, carried half a ton, a ton [of tangerines to the border]. This changed the structure of the family, where before the man was the one to get the money. Because there were no jobs [in Abkhazia], the criminal situation worsened.

The unity of the war disintegrated as a result of this hardship. Many people remained armed after the war, and killings, looting, and dispossession became serious problems in the context of depopulation, destruction, and poverty. "There was unity between people in the early postwar period. A car could stop and ask where to give you a lift. Then the blockade started," an Abkhaz activist recounts, "[and] criminality increased, robberies of anyone, not only Georgians." Most Abkhaz kept weapons for fear of future Georgian attacks, and war trophies were widely available. As one Abkhaz official clarifies,

> Abkhazia is packed with guns, this is not a secret. We live by the principle "God helps those who help themselves," and it is difficult to blame

us.... The question was raised [about whether] to take away all the weapons and stockpile them. It was impossible in that situation, not because some would bring them while others would not, but if we disarmed, Georgia would put together terrorist groups and we would remain with nothing. Thus we went along a different track. We had a reservist contingent and registered weapons on hand with permission to hold them at home.

While these weapons were used to defend the territory of Abkhazia from Georgian intrusions, they were also part of the criminal upsurge in the aftermath of the war. Remaining Georgians were often the target. Some Georgians were killed on suspicion of participation in the war. "When the war was over, there were many unjustified cases of violence toward Georgians," an Abkhaz researcher says, and "people who did not participate suffered as well. Men died because they were considered enemies." Others fell victim to revenge by the Abkhaz who returned from the war. The then head of a local police station explains: "Imagine, people returned to their houses that were robbed and burned, whose sons were all killed [during the war]. Confrontation with the remaining Georgian population started.... I sent a *milicija* [police] patrol for every call by Georgians or non-Georgians to stop those people, who returned with nothing, but they were impossible to stop. One family was locked in a house and burned in Tsandrypsh, and those who burned them then lived there."

In most cases, weapons were used to steal or to occupy abandoned houses. "When the Abkhaz took the city," a Russian resident of Sukhum/i tells, "they started doing the same [as Georgian forces did at the war's onset]—robbing everyone, looting Georgian houses." "Some people were killed when we came into the city. Locals told us that the main group passed, then the second column came, and anything could happen," front-line nurses report, "[but] Georgian houses, of course, were empty, and they could come in." "Violence right after the war was related not to the necessity to kick Georgians out but the desire for their property. This was the motivation for robberies, marauding. A few Georgian families were killed then and their apartments were occupied," an Abkhaz activist corroborates.

Not only Georgians but also other groups, including the Abkhaz, were targets of this crime. "Marauders of all kinds got out. They came to steal and did not care if it was a Georgian or an Abkhaz," a librarian in Gagra recalls. "There was chaos. We stole things from each other," a disabled Abkhaz veteran admits, explaining that "it was very difficult after the war." As a Ukrainian local of Gagra attests, "I was robbed. Armed people who live here came in[to my house] and took everything while I was there." The problem of dispossession was acute in the depopulated areas. "Many took others' apartments," a journalist states. A Russian from

Sukhum/i confirms that when she returned to the city in October 1993, her "apartment was occupied, [by] an Abkhaz woman [who] took it [after] her house was hit by a shell."

For some, occupying abandoned homes was unacceptable, even in the direst conditions, for reasons of custom or principle. "It is not in our tradition to live in another's house," the journalist above says. A fighter whose house in Gagra was burned did not take a Georgian house on principle: "I could have taken any house, because I knew them all [Georgians], but I only hoped for my children not to take a Georgian house. I sat them down here, in my burned house, and gave an oath that I will never live in a Georgian house." But others found this practice to be justifiable after the war. "There is nothing to be ashamed of. If the house of an Abkhaz was burned, it was fine for him to take a house of a Georgian," a member of a mothers' organization says. An antiviolence activist explains the repercussions of this acceptance: "Huge buildings, plots of land—everybody took everything. This was a violation of housing and employment that is still influencing us. How long do you guard apartments if people do not return for ten to fifteen years? The housing question is key [in postwar Abkhazia]."

In general, killings, looting, and dispossession reflected the postwar condition where some fighters felt entitlement by virtue of their participation in the war. "The war brings out the good and bad," the antiviolence activist goes on, "[such that] those who were not respected—drug addicts, uneducated people, former criminals—thought they could now be someone." Some youth were part of this problem: "They left home, took guns, walked around as if they were born with a gun. This affected the psyche. They were just boys. It was difficult for them—many went to fight right from school, [and] there was no employment after the war. But now, in a short period, they became important."

Mechanisms existed to curb this behavior, and over time crime subsided.[7] As a military doctor says, "Life was difficult. But in terms of crime, the most difficult time was the first year. Then, of course, the situation improved." On the one hand, familial and communal norms still had some influence. "The Elders Council plays an important role in this respect. There are also family gatherings, when everyone comes together and children who have gone against the law are given counsel, to carry the family name [*familia*] properly. This is worse than punishment by law enforcement," a prosecutor tells. On the other hand, law enforcement worked on a range of issues after the war. For instance, many road accidents were reported. "Fighters took trophy cars and raced without a license, not knowing how to drive. So many died on the road," a member of a mothers' group says. The police became "strict on the roads. They made people buckle up, keep to the speed limit, created block posts," an official tells of some periods. "This disciplined, stopped people. Even criminals started being pressured."[8]

The postwar condition, however, was characterized by deeper, long-term problems. "We thought we could bring order quickly, rebuild. But it is easier to build houses than heal the wounds of the soul. This is the long echo of war," Abkhaz intellectuals say, explaining that "the war—casualties, physical, psychological traumas—then economic sanctions affected the development of the society." Almost all respondents speak of the loss, trauma, and health issues that persist until today. Disability, suicide, and alcohol and drug abuse are common among war participants. "Those who went through the war, no one is healthy. I had a concussion and have had headaches for nineteen years," a front-line nurse tells. "I lost my arm and now cannot dance," laments a member of a disabled veterans association of his past, when he was "a dancer in the famous Sharatyn ensemble." "My son was fighting for a year and six months. He came back ten days after the war," a mother remembers, through tears, a fighter who committed suicide after his friend's death. "He could not stand it any longer and ended his life with one shot."

Families were devastated by these losses. "There is no family that did not suffer from this war. My whole family, men and women, all have diseases now," a nurse says. Another woman states: "On March 16, my younger son, who is now disabled, was injured. . . . On March 17, my older son died while I was caring for my younger son. Our children's, friends', husbands' bodies were considered [to have] disappeared. This is why we rushed to Sukhum when the city was freed on September 27. My son could not be identified. . . . My husband got cancer because of all that."

The postwar government of Abkhazia had little capacity to offer support. "We have such psychological trauma, all of us. We are trying to forget the war, but without treatment we cannot, and there was no treatment, for anyone," a war reporter says. "A center opened by the hospital for HIV, but they treat everyone there, for alcohol, drugs, trauma. These should be separate [issues]," a postwar activist confirms. Interpersonal support was, as a result, the main mechanism to cope with these issues. Fighters and nonfighters created veterans', mothers', and other war-related organizations.[9] "Most of my friends were killed during the war, and so today I turn to new friends in the disabled veterans' association," a former fighter demonstrates. Many women were in mourning for years after the war and reached out to each other to share their grief. As a woman in the west who started a mothers' group illustrates,

> The postwar period was terrible. I wanted to end my life after a year in mourning. I thought I would do everything to mark the year of my husband's and son's deaths, including finishing building our new house, and kill myself. Women started helping me. My sisters came to tell me to stop mourning. I did not listen. Then another woman like me [who

lost her husband and son] came, we spoke, and I gathered all those who were mourning.... We took off the black [for mourning] and put on other colors.... I started helping these women, went to the cemetery, to the parents who live alone.... I wrote a letter to Kislovodsk, [Russia, known for its treatment facilities], took women to treatment [there].

Members of this and other postwar organizations acknowledge that their mobilization helps them endure their loss and hardship. The mothers' group leader above, one woman says, "united, supported us. It is easier when you are together in pain." A woman in the capital similarly explains: "I joined a mothers' movement, learned that I was not the only one like that, started working there, and became part of the core of the movement. We visit military units and check how soldiers are fed. We are always together. This is my second family. If not for the movement, I would be on the other side [of life]. We tell each other [war] stories. This helps."

Wartime Loss and Collective Conflict Identities: Attribution and Memorialization

This mobilization and the loss and hardship that accompanied it after the war had important implications. Everyday postwar experiences of the ordinary Abkhaz who participated in the war in different ways reinforced the Abkhaz views of Georgia as an aggressor and their victory in the war as Abkhazia's liberation from long-lasting Georgianization and the recent attack against their land. Attribution of the Abkhaz loss and hardship to the wartime Georgian aggression and memorialization of the Abkhaz victory and fighters who died for it became part of the Abkhaz collective conflict identities. People maintained their roles in the conflict through these informal and formal mechanisms of attribution and memorialization after the war.

Women who were part of the wartime support apparatus or played the role of symbolic supporters of the Abkhaz war effort by sending or blessing their children to fight, and became mothers of fighters during the war, now sustained their collective identity in the conflict as bereaved mothers. The loss hardened their understanding of the conflict as the Abkhaz defense against the Georgian aggressor. Mothers' groups facilitated women's role to voice this view. A leader of a mothers' group in the capital illustrates this shared understanding and her role in communicating it to her Georgian counterparts: "I meet Georgian mothers and tell them, 'We are consoled only by the fact that our children fought for our land. But you have double grief. Your children had to die for other people's land. Abkhazia was never Georgian land. It was given to us by God, but to you by Stalin.'"

Members of the prewar Abkhaz movement and its core organization Aidgylara (Unity) or of the Abkhaz part of Abkhazia's Parliament often maintained their roles through postwar activism and leadership. This sociopolitical arena became open to fighters, many of whom attained local and national government posts after the war. Some took it as their responsibility to advocate the Abkhaz position on the nonreturn of Georgians who fought against the Abkhaz to Abkhazia and Abkhazia's hard-won "liberation" after decades of Georgian domination and brutality in the war. This includes participants in the unofficial and official peace processes and postwar institution building. As a former Aidgylara member, war journalist, and activist shows,

> Someone starts a war, does something horrible, but is not blamed. We who did not start the conflict have to deal with the consequences. We cannot do that until political questions are addressed, [that is,] Georgia recognizes Abkhazia. Many Georgians returned to the Gal district, but Georgia is not interested in a return to the Gal district or [the return] of a small number of people. Georgia needs a mass return to be able to hold a referendum [on Abkhazia's political status] with a majority of Georgians. If they return, we will have to fight again. This is not possible.[10]

The postwar persistence of collective conflict identities is evident, not only in the organizational setting of activism and leadership, but also more broadly. Many who lost their close ones in the war attribute this loss to the Georgian aggression and speak of hatred and their role in passing it to their children. As one woman explains,

> I have hatred toward them and will always have it. I cannot forgive in my life what they did to us, killing my sister, my cousin. I miss my son. I will pass this at the genetic level to my children. We did not want this war. We were faced with this choice, to hate Georgians. My mother-in-law was Georgian. I loved her very much. But she was one of the few Georgians who knew where they came from, where their grandfathers are buried, who understood that you should not [say] that the Abkhaz came from the mountains or that this is not their land.

This attribution of loss to the Georgian aggression underlies the support of many regular Abkhaz for the nonreturn of displaced Georgians who fought during the war. "Those who did not fight can return," an activist says. Others are commonly referred to as "refugees" who left for their country: "They behaved brutally with the peaceful population. They came to a house, killed the father, the mother. There are witnesses to this. How can we create friendly relations after such brutality? Refugees went to their motherland. They cannot return after this brutality."[11] Respondents relate this brutality not only to the war but also to the

Georgianization of the Abkhaz that preceded it. As one woman shares, "My husband suffered his whole life from Georgians: he was kicked out from school for not [obeying Georgian teachers when the school system was reorganized], [he] left work because of [a Georgian] criminal [whom he arrested and had to release on orders from Georgia], then the war started and he was killed along with his son. How much he suffered from Georgian hands! And why do we pity them [referring to displaced Georgians unable to return to Abkhazia]?"

Jokes, insults, and customs contribute to the persistence of conflict identities in daily life, as in the prewar period. Yet the content of these forms of everyday confrontation changed, as they are no longer enacted in the intergroup context. With most of the prewar Georgian population living outside of Abkhazia, jokes and insults routinely scrutinize Georgian fighters. "The difference between us and Georgians is that they run well" or "Quickly retreated the proud Georgians," respondents laugh, referring to the Georgian retreat from Gagra and Sukhum/i during the war. Myths on Georgian fighters reinforce jokes and insults. As an Abkhaz professor illustrates with the alleged recollections of a Georgian fighter, "During the war, I understood why Abkhazia is not Georgia as I saw how the Abkhaz fought for Abkhazia and how we [Georgians] did. I was not the only one to run, many did. Why fight if it is not our land? The Abkhaz went under the bullets and sang. They went to fight for their territory." Stereotypes of Georgian fighters as weak and feminine are therefore cultivated and passed on in daily conversations and in public. "In spirit, a Georgian is not a fighter, no matter how you equip him," I often heard, or "They can make a toast, dance, sing, but not fight. If you look at the history of Georgia, there are no great victories." These notions reproduce the animosity toward Georgians in daily life.

Intra-Abkhaz customs, in turn, were adapted to praise the Abkhaz victory and commemorate those lost in the war. Stories of Abkhaz bravery and suffering are reproduced in a range of everyday settings, from routine meetings of relatives and friends over coffee or backgammon to reunions of fighters, women's collective mourning, and communal events. Men often retell the same anecdotes of fighting and even laugh at them and tell of others' heroism, rather than their own, in line with the Abkhaz custom. "Even young, fourteen-to-fifteen-year-old boys did such heroic acts, there are many examples," a fighter illustrates. Women speak of the sacrifices that men made in the name of victory. A woman narrates her deceased brother's war trajectory and adds, "Who would defend Abkhazia if not him? Why would he need his life if we or Abkhazia were no longer there?" The sacrifice is thus justified. "We gather every year, remember fellow fighters," men and women stress of their role in passing this memory on, affirming, "we sometimes gather and tell each other . . . the stories we will tell our grandchildren." Table traditions, which the Abkhaz closely observe, institutionalize the commemoration of fighters in daily life. At every gathering, mourning, and celebration that I attended in Abkhazia, the first toast was to God, the second—to those who died in the war. "It is a prayer at the table," the Abkhaz explained to me.

Memorialization of the Abkhaz victory and those who died for it expands beyond storytelling and table culture to every aspect of postwar life. Private memorials of relatives lost in the war are placed in visible parts of homes to reflect informal memorialization practices at the quotidian or individual and family level.[12] Local hotels and businesses are named after the Abkhaz victory in the war, as shown on the banner of an investment and construction company called "Ten years of Victory" (see figure 7.1). War medals, museums, and public memorials, which can be found across Abkhazia, acknowledge fighters' sacrifice formally at the national or societal level, as the Order of Leon awarded for courage, selflessness, and bravery shown during the Georgian-Abkhaz war of 1992–1993 and a public memorial in honor of the natives of Bzyb/Bzipi who died in the war illustrate (see figures 7.2 and 7.3, respectively). "Not everyone acted heroically, but everyone has a medal nowadays," participants in the fighting and support apparatuses reveal of the politics of recognition. Or as one participant says, "If I had fought, I would have died, either as a hero or no one. But no one remembers those who served in the rear, and there are not enough hands to pay tribute to their sacrifice." Recognition, however, is praised in general: "Masculinity, the heroism of many are recognized,

FIGURE 7.1. "Ten years of Victory."

Photo by Anastasia Shesterinina.

FIGURE 7.2. The Order of Leon.

Photo by Anastasia Shesterinina.

FIGURE 7.3. A public memorial in Bzyb/Bzipi.

Photo by Anastasia Shesterinina.

that these boys, defending their motherland at the cost of their lives, went to the end. Many are marked with high awards, many upon death.... The victory and independence are thanks to these men who lost their lives."

Leaders are particularly cherished. Ardzinba, who led the war effort, is cultivated as "a saint, a dome where you have to pray." "He lost all his health, gave his life for this victory," people insist. Streets and buildings carry his name and the names of other leaders. Gagra's central street is Ardzinba Avenue. Gudauta's Museum of the Patriotic War of Abkhazia is named after the head of the wartime headquarters, General Sergey Dbar. These names are engraved in the collective memory through postwar education and war-related events, which constitute a large part of daily life. For example, the twenty-five-year commemoration of the taking of Sukhum/i was celebrated with a military parade, a march, and fireworks, among other activities, on September 27, 2018. The leader of a mothers' group captures the symbolic importance of these activities: "[At the opening of a war memorial], white butterflies surrounded the monument. I finished my speech and they all left. So many of them ... I thought, what are these? It is my husband, who came with his friends. [My friend] said, 'No, it is my husband.' So we could even joke about that. All the dead came with their friends, their names were pronounced, balloons were let go, and they left." These activities embed in day-to-day routines the memory of those lost in the war and formalize the praise of their achievement in the war and the attribution of their loss to the Georgian aggression.

Postwar Threat and Collective Conflict Identities: Defending the Abkhaz Victory

The attribution of Abkhaz loss to Georgia did not end with the war, however. It endured in the postwar period due to the continued threat of attacks from beyond the Ingur/i River and the Abkhaz deaths in the border area. "Georgians, both the local population and the government, openly told us, 'We will return and wipe you off the face of the earth,'" respondents repeatedly convey of the sense of ongoing Georgian threat after the war. "'We will return to win back this territory, we are many,' they threatened." Indeed, Georgian leaders and the opposition voiced a variety of threats after the war. For example, the then chairman of the Georgian Parliament, Shevardnadze, announced on February 26, 1994, that "a renewal of hostilities in Abkhazia was inevitable unless progress was made towards a political settlement of the conflict" (Fuller 1994a). "If no such agreement is reached," experts said subsequently, "Shevardnadze ... may well eventually decide to order the Georgian army to occupy Gali or even to take Sukhumi, thereby precipitating another full-scale war" (Walker 1998, 20–21).[13]

Shevardnadze adopted a conciliatory approach after the wars against ousted president Gamsakhurdia and in South Ossetia and Abkhazia "practically disintegrated" the Georgian army, but others called for the use of force (Fuller 1993).[14] Former defense minister Kitovani, who led the National Guard into Abkhazia in 1992, formed the National Liberation Front with the spokesman for the Georgians displaced from Abkhazia, Boris Kakubava, among others, and "pledged to restore Georgia's territorial integrity" by force (Fuller 1994b). A former fighter of the Mkhedrioni, Dato Shengelia, with his Tkis Dzmebi (Forest Brothers) and other armed groups, such as Tetri Legioni (White Legion), mobilized displaced Georgians for guerrilla warfare in the Georgian-Abkhaz border area (Darchiashvili 2003, 11; Walker 1998, 19).

Abkhazia's information agency, Apsnypress, reported armed Georgian crossings, ambushes, and Abkhaz deaths along the Ingur/i, including those committed by the Forest Brothers and the White Legion, soon after the war and systematically over the next decade and documented occasional demonstrations by displaced Georgians, armed mobilization, and heavy equipment on the Georgian side of the Ingur/i. Word of mouth spread this information quickly in the Abkhaz communities before it even appeared in the news or reached the families of the deceased. As two women who lost their husbands illustrate,

> We thought it was over. Our husbands came back [after the war]. My husband worked as head of the fish factory. Our children were with us. We had to recover. But our husbands were sent to guard the border.... It was horrible at the border. Once [reservists of their team] got caught in the rain and were sent back sick, but our husbands stayed. They had to deliver ammunition.... But they were ambushed.
>
> There was talk that something happened in Gal. I ran to the neighbors. They said that [my friend's] husband died and mine was injured, but [my friend] was told the opposite, that my husband died [and hers was injured]. My mother-in-law said that a boy from [our village] was killed. Everyone knew what was going on, but did not tell us. A crowd gathered outside of my house and I understood [that my husband was dead].

This loss and the threat of another attack associated with it sharpened people's view of the Georgian aggression as the source of Abkhaz suffering. An Abkhaz intellectual captures this view: "We were under the constant pressure and feeling of a direct threat of aggression by Georgia. This is not so much of violence, which was ongoing, but the threat of aggression. We were afraid that Georgia would once again not be able to avoid aggression, because in its political arsenal nothing remained but force. Without force, nothing can return Abkhazia to Georgia."

The threat, moreover, shaped people's roles after the war. Now that the Abkhaz experienced a war, they knew that further fighting was possible. "Abkhazia was not the same with the war experience and an understanding of what this meant," a commander says. With this knowledge, many prepared for a new attack. A woman in Sukhum/i packed her bags to escape with greater ease than in the war:

> It was scary living here, especially with a child. There were constant robberies, marauding, the uncontrolled criminal situation in Abkhazia, on the one hand, and fear that Georgia's forces would enter [Abkhazia] again, on the other. The first years, I remember, I packed my bags, so that there were essential things for the children and I would be ready to leave any minute, because Georgia made constant threats and declarations of the restoration of territorial integrity. They often said that there was an assembly of people in Zugdidi, [a nearby Georgian city]. And as soon as I heard that, I started packing because I thought they would once again attack Abkhazia.

Some became engaged in activism and leadership due to the continued loss from and threat of postwar attacks. The woman above who lost her husband in an ambush after the war became a local leader: "He was not even buried when I was told to take his post [at the fish factory]. A woman would not [typically] take such a high post, [given the] responsibility, but I overcame myself and took it for the children." Others wrote about fighters who died "on duty" and advocated their memorialization. "If [a man] died during the war, he was given a medal. If after, on duty, then no," a bereaved mother explains. Yet others entered into social work in response to the threat: "There was always a threat of another war—ultimatums, warnings, a small war in Gal, Kodor. We understood that for a long time we will remember this, and psychological rehabilitation was needed. Thus my organization works with children with post-traumatic stress disorder—not those who went through the war . . . but those with the transformed fears of their parents."

For Abkhaz fighters, the threat meant that Abkhazia's defense from the Georgian aggressor had to persist into the postwar period. The Georgian armed forces were almost entirely driven out from Abkhazia and no longer had a local support base due to the mass displacement of Georgians. Violence thus concentrated in the border area where some local Georgians returned, and the Abkhaz were unable to establish full control. The Abkhaz and Georgians stationed on the two sides of the Ingur/i River after the war frequently exchanged fire and even engaged in large-scale episodes of fighting, but the activity that regularly took the lives of participants in Abkhaz border defense was infiltration by Georgian guerrillas. "The war ended in 1993, but our borders were still not safe," a border defense participant explains. The Georgian intrusion, from this perspective, was a way to regain the territory that belonged to the Abkhaz and undermine the Abkhaz claims to statehood outside of Georgia. In turn, the Abkhaz postwar mobilization was a way to defend their victory in the war over the territory of Abkhazia and the right to develop independently from Georgia after decades of Georgianization. "They just could not accept that Abkhazia is our territory," fighters assert. "After [the war], Georgians entered our territory, carried out attacks. . . . We were attacked and defended [our territory]."

As the threat originated beyond the Ingur/i River, fighters built defense structures, trenches, and weapon emplacements in the border area as soon as the war was over and mobilized to the Gal/i district to defend what they understood as Abkhazia's state border throughout the postwar period. "The freeing of Abkhazia was along the Ingur. This is *our* territory," fighters demarcate with clarity their conception of Abkhazia's state border, emphasizing, "These are Georgian villages. Here is *our* territory." "[We] went to *guard* the state border," fighters say of the defensive nature of mobilization after the war and stress, "Our function was to *guard* our territory."

They saw this mobilization as defensive even when they attacked Georgian forces, as in the Kodor/i Gorge operation of 2008. This Georgian, particularly Svan-populated, area was seen as a historical part of Abkhazia, but it was controlled by Georgia after the war and therefore had to be "liberated," according to the Abkhaz: "Every little piece of land we have . . . is our territory. . . . How can we give up the boundaries that we have defended for so long?" This mobilization was defensive, the Abkhaz argue, because their forces did not attempt occupying Georgian territory past the Ingur/i River during the postwar fighting. "We did not have military actions beyond Abkhazia. This territory was Georgian," respondents demonstrate, "[so that] when we took Kodor, we could have crossed the Ingur, but we said we could not accept that. . . . We defended *our own* territory."[15]

The Georgian threat diminished with the Russia-assisted "liberation" of the Kodor/i Gorge, fortification of the border area, and recognition of Abkhazia by Russia in 2008. "People were dying from 1993 and until the recognition. The threat of war was present until the recognition," a fighter and local leader corroborates. A war reporter captures how this enduring threat affected the shared understanding of the Abkhaz victory in the war and mobilization of the Abkhaz for border defense: "People understood the end of the war not as a victory per se but [as] something that we completed. This ended, then another period started, a horrible prolonged period. It was very difficult to hold the victory, and the military component was dominant as a result."

Reservists of the Abkhaz army organized during the war and *milicija* officers participated in border defense.[16] "We sent our army and *milicija* to defend [the border]," an assistant head of a local police station tells. The Agreement on a Ceasefire and Separation of Forces signed on May 14, 1994, monitored by the UN Observer Mission in Georgia, and upheld by the Commonwealth of Independent States peacekeepers, who were primarily Russian, prohibited the Abkhaz army from the twelve-kilometer security zone on both sides of the Ingur/i River, and the police took charge in this area.[17] However, some Abkhaz reservists joined the police, and the regular Abkhaz army participated periodically. "As a reservist, I was not allowed [in the border area] often. Only the *milicija* was allowed," a reservist illustrates, "but I changed into the *milicija* uniform and went with them." These forces guarded the area along the Ingur/i River and carried out "cleaning operations" to force Georgian guerrillas beyond the Abkhaz boundary, while the regular army was active in a six-day war in Gal/i in 1998 and the Kodor/i operation of 2008, where Georgia could have established and maintained control, respectively, to then seize the whole of Abkhazia. The next sections focus on how the Abkhaz understood and responded to this threat.

Georgian Guerrillas and Abkhaz Border Defense

As much as the Abkhaz forces attempted fortifying the Ingur/i River when the war ended, this area was difficult to patrol. "The border is long and we were few, there were gaps between us," participants explain. Particularly in lower Gal/i, where the borderline stretches beyond the river and dense forests and marshes characterize the area by the sea, it was possible to cross unidentified and hide in abandoned houses. "It is a wide landscape. There are populated areas and forests, marshes," border guards say, and "there were many abandoned houses. It was easy to hide [and] quickly leave to cross the river back." The Abkhaz did not control the area. "The border there is not along the Ingur. Georgian units control it," participants admit, and "in this part especially they controlled the situation."

Georgian guerrillas thus consistently crossed the river, particularly in lower Gal/i, to destroy infrastructure, place land mines, ambush, and kidnap Abkhaz border guards, Russian peacekeepers stationed in the twelve-kilometer security zone, and Georgians collaborating with the Abkhaz. These activities were called "partisan" in Georgia and "diversionist" or "terrorist" in Abkhazia. "They called themselves partisans," border guards say, "[but] were terrorists, diversionists. They ran over constantly, carried out ambushes, laid mines." In Abkhazia, they were also related to the Georgian state. "The Georgian army was restructured, but these groups were kept to carry out terrorist, diversionist acts in Abkhazia," a regular of the Abkhaz army explains of their link. David Darchiashvili and Ghia Nodia (2003, 18) agree that "until 1998 these groups enjoyed hidden assistance from the Georgian Government. The Abkhaz government in exile openly support[ed them; their leaders promoted their aims in Tbilisi]."

While the Forest Brothers and the White Legion were the umbrella organizations, small groups operated on the ground due to the clandestine nature of guerrilla warfare. "There were a number of groups active in the Gal district, both in the upper area and lower by the sea. These were scattered, small groups, five, six people each," a border guard says. Local knowledge was necessary for these activities, and participation of Georgians displaced from Abkhazia was consistently reported. These groups, participants stress, "were formed from refugees who fought here and ran. . . . Those who ran understood they did not have an option to return peacefully and went into these groups." Georgians who did not fight and returned to their homes in Abkhazia were also implicated. A few joined these guerrilla groups. "Not all locals took our side," border guards clarify, saying that "at night, some changed into uniforms and went against us." Most were forced to collaborate with both sides by providing food, shelter, and local knowledge of where to cross the river and locate armed Georgians and Abkhaz.[18] "The locals told us where someone crossed," an Abkhaz commander confirms. But "the population was unreliable," respondents say in general, since they at the same time assisted the Georgian side.

Of the forty-four reservists and fifteen police officers who participated in border defense and spoke to me, not one took lightly the Georgian guerrilla activity along the Ingur/i River. The threat of an ambush, a mine explosion on the way to the border post, or kidnapping was felt every time a team of reservists and police officers left for their shift of defense duty. "I went with a team in January 1994 and April 1994, ten days at a time, until the next shift came. We were in fear, too. We could have died," a border guard illustrates. When a team drove to the border, it was easy to spot them along the main road to Gal/i, and guerrillas took advantage of this vulnerable position. "It was very dangerous to go to the border, [as] there were mines everywhere," participants remember, saying, "a typical scenario [was that] our group left for the border. They waited by the road to ambush our car, then fired, threw grenades, and used machine guns." "No fewer were killed after the war than in the war. We expected death on every corner" was a common perception among border guards. Their wives corroborate the threat: "My husband is a reservist. He went through the war, has a Leon award [as depicted and described in figure 7.2]. I said, 'If the enemy comes here [Sukhum/i], we will all stand up and fight him. But I will not let you go where the enemy is on every corner.' Although we said so, the border still had to be guarded. *Milicija* officers, reservists, individual patriots and groups—how many died there? Two, three died a week all the time. No one wanted to go, but they all went to preserve life in Abkhazia."

There was a clear threat not only to the lives of border guards but also to the territory of Abkhazia and its potential to become a recognized state. Georgian guerrilla activities undermined Abkhaz control over the border area. "How can you recognize a state that cannot fully control its territory?," respondents spell out the implications. The Abkhaz thus say that the aim of Georgian guerrillas was to "destabilize the situation in Abkhazia, prevent economic development, keep Gal residents in constant fear [and] poverty, thinking that the Abkhaz state cannot protect them, does not have enough power or resources.... Overall, this was done to call Abkhazia a failed state."[19]

The Abkhaz mobilized against this threat. Police officers and reservists engaged in "cleaning operations" akin to counterinsurgency. They combed through select areas to locate and neutralize guerrillas by killing or capturing them or forcing them to flee. A reservist and active participant explains the rationale:

> We never planned operations to cross into Georgia. The only task was to defend ourselves and keep the land we freed untouched. When they infiltrated, we carried out operations to push them out. We did not even say "destroy," but rather "push them out." We had maps marking where they could dig in. According to military strategy, the front group led, the side watch was at the sides, and the main group followed behind them. This is how we combed through the area.... We gave them corridors to leave—to maintain some peace and to not harm our own boys.... If someone appeared, we shot them. Avoiding combat, we moved further on.

This strategy did not achieve its goals, as guerrilla activities continued and the Abkhaz had to adapt: "The first operation [in February 1994] was intended to take them by surprise and squeeze them.... We wanted to close off the Ingur and encircle Gal. This did not happen. We then rarely held large-scale cleanings and moved to local measures, tracking specific individuals ... who carried out [guerrilla activities].... When the tactics changed, we had much greater success." "We had thirty meters between one another and went in different directions, searching for them through tea plantations, in houses," a participating police officer explains of the change. The then Abkhaz deputy defense minister reports its result: "We detained the first diversionist group of the Forest Brothers, five people. I spoke with every one of them. They told us where they were located, what their tasks were, who paid for it." The Abkhaz forces continued these search and capture operations thereafter.

These operations targeted not only guerrillas but also the Georgian locals suspected of collaboration with the guerrilla groups. "Seven people were killed on February 5, 1994. My father was there and died, but the Abkhaz said they only killed partisans.... I escaped to Zugdidi and watched our houses burn," a former Gal/i resident confirms in Tbilisi. In March 1994, the Abkhaz searched lower Gal/i and forced guerrillas and thousands of locals to flee, burning their houses. "Under the pretense of antipartisan operations, they killed everyone" is how displaced Georgians define the Abkhaz operations: "If partisans stayed somewhere and it was found out, not only this house but the whole street was burned." A small war developed in the Gal/i district as the Georgian guerrilla warfare and the Abkhaz cleaning operations became part of everyday life. "After 1993, the war was still ongoing in the Gal district," an Abkhaz police officer says, adding that "until recently, Gal was explosive." The six-day war that unfolded in the context of Georgian-Abkhaz tensions in the area in May 1998 was one of these explosions.

The Six-Day War: Gal/i, 1998

The threat of a Georgian attack was apparent in advance of the Georgian Independence Day on May 26, 1998. After a period of relative calm, the Abkhaz and the international press reported Georgian guerrilla activities in the Gal/i district daily in the lead-up to the event. Some Abkhaz border guards were killed in Mziuri in upper Gal/i on April 28, for example; others were ambushed and kidnapped in nearby Repo-Etseri on May 2 (Apsnypress, *Novosti dnja* [News of the day], no. 66, April 28, 1998; no. 71, May 4, 1998). On May 18, "Georgian guerrillas from the so-called White Legion killed some 20 Abkhaz police officers in a surprise attack" (Fuller 1998b). Georgian guerrilla activities were not the only concern, however.

The Abkhaz intelligence found that the Georgian side was preparing a large-scale attack. A reconnaissance unit deployed to lower Gal/i "reported that Georgians were engineering fortification structures in preparation for an attack" and also that it "had intelligence that [official] Georgian security structures participated." Border guards "reported that Georgians were digging a defense line in the area under peacekeepers' control." "Under the eyes of Russian peacekeepers," a journalist confirms, "Georgians crossed the river and built fortification structures. There was a sense that they closed their eyes to that." In general, the Abkhaz felt that Russia supported Georgia at the time. "Georgia was in all the negotiations with Russia and the UN. They did not let us in," a reservist explains of this position.

In the official Abkhaz discourse, the Georgian aim was to take control over the Gal/i district: "By the Independence Day of Georgia on May 26, the 'White Legion' and 'Forest Brothers' supported by the internal forces of Georgia intended to take the town of Gal by force, detach the Gal district from the Republic of Abkhazia, and place the government of the so-called Autonomous Republic of Abkhazia led by [Tamaz Nadareishvili] in Gal" (Pachulija 2010, 368). But there was a fear that Georgia would go further. A then Abkhaz Gal/i official says, "We knew that it would not stop there." Border guards and regular Abkhaz therefore had a broader sense of threat: "On May 26, the Georgian Independence Day, they wanted to first detach the Gal district or at least get to the channel [from the Gal/i reservoir to the sea, past the town]. If they had gotten to the town of Gal and occupied it, they would certainly have moved on to the Ochamchira district."

The Abkhaz organized a cleaning operation of unprecedented scale to counteract the threat. The fighting broke out on May 19, during a house-to-house search by *milicija* officers. "Our *milicija* went there. When we started pushing Georgians out quietly, the fighting began," a then Abkhaz Gal/i official recalls, "[with] casualties on our side, [and] military events developed from there." By May 22, Abkhaz *milicija* officers, army reservists, and regular soldiers joined forces. "The fighting lasted a few days. The army was stationed beyond the twelve-kilometer distance, but there it had to be incorporated," a reservist explains. The army's involvement indicated to the Abkhaz that this was another war. As a commander says, "When the army is involved, it is a theater of war. A second war, but localized."

Indeed, a cease-fire agreement was signed in Gagra on May 26, recognizing the presence of both Abkhaz and Georgian forces in the security zone.[20] As Abkhaz activist Liana Kvarchelia (1999, 32) writes, "Tbilisi, which had until then distanced itself from the 'partisans,' practically admitted its responsibility for the events by signing an agreement."[21] Yet "hostilities continued for most of that day, with each side accusing the other of violating the cease-fire" (Fuller 1998b). By May 27, the Abkhaz forced Georgian guerrillas and troops to flee. Local Georgians once again were killed or displaced, with their houses burned and then looted. The international media summarizes the losses: "Estimates of casualties differ widely, but it appears that dozens of Georgian civilians have been killed, as well as a similar number of Abkhaz and Georgian combatants. In addition, 30,000–40,000 ethnic Georgian repatriates who returned to the homes in Gali . . . have again sought refuge on the other side of the border" (Fuller 1998b).[22] Despite these losses, this was a major success for the Abkhaz, as they "established control over the 12-kilometer security zone on the Abkhaz side of the border" (Fuller 1998a). There were no further attempts to seize the Gal/i district, and the center of large-scale fighting moved to the Kodor/i Gorge.

The Last Area under Georgian Control: The Kodor/i Gorge, 2008

Georgia still maintained its presence in Abkhazia's northeast. Many Georgians fled in 1993 through the Amtkel/i-Lata escape corridor to the Kodor/i Gorge and from there to the Svaneti province in Georgia's northwest. In March 1994, the Abkhaz captured the village of Lata in lower Kodor/i, but Georgia retained its control over upper Kodor/i beyond Lata and even renamed it Upper Abkhazia. Local Svans did not submit to Georgia's rule throughout the postwar period and mobilized. Emzar Kvitsiani's militia is an example.[23] However, in 2006, under the presidency of Mikheil Saakashvili, Georgia reasserted its control, driving Kvitsiani out and placing Abkhazia's government in exile in the area, with infrastructural development under way. Russian peacekeepers said after the operation that "more than 90 percent of the Georgian troops sent to the gorge remain there" (Fuller 2006).

The presence of the Georgian forces and government in Abkhazia posed a threat to the Abkhaz. Respondents recall their concern at the time and report that Georgia "had very strong fortification," "built their blue and pink houses," and "created a foothold there." While an Abkhaz contingent was deployed to the area, "we fighters were upset our government was passive about it," reservists say. "They created their government agencies [and] the administration of upper Kodor, which used to be located in Tbilisi, with a representative in Kodor," the then deputy minister of Abkhazia's de facto Ministry of Defense confirms of the threat, adding that "in 2006, they officially sent troops and stationed a garrison of three thousand people there, lowered the number to fifteen hundred by 2008, and, in 2008, yet again raised it to three thousand." Indeed, the threat of attack reemerged in August 2008, from Kodor/i, when tension escalated in South Ossetia. As an Abkhaz official clarifies, "We knew that they were supposed to start from Abkhazia and then move to South Ossetia, but at the last moment they changed the plan and decided that South Ossetia could be taken quickly.[24] As a result, a success there would have inspired [further military action] and moral support [of the Georgian population to take Abkhazia by force] if that had happened." The threat was acute not only for participants in border defense but also for the broader population of Abkhazia. "The situation in 2008 was horrifying for the population," an Abkhaz journalist reports. "We felt that the war would start again. My mother stood on the porch and said, 'I am not going to survive this one.' There was no more strength to live through another [Georgian] attack."

The events in South Ossetia, however, radically changed the situation. The Russo-Georgian War that broke out there shifted Georgia's attention to South Ossetia and created an opportunity for the Abkhaz to capture upper Kodor/i. Thus, as Russia crushed Georgian forces in South Ossetia, the Abkhaz forces launched an attack on Kodor/i with Russian support. The gorge made armed combat difficult, and Russia's air force was central to the operation. It "is high up in the mountains [and] difficult to reach and fight there due to the mountainous conditions," Abkhaz commanders explain, adding that "there is simply no place to hold on when you start shooting." "The success there was with the help of the Russian aviation. No one could remain there [after the bombing]," commanders acknowledge. At the same time, the Russian navy prevented an attack from the sea. The journalist above concurs: "We did not even worry about the air. It could be controlled, including by the Russian forces. But the sea was vulnerable. Abkhazia did not have a navy, and we were most afraid of [an attack from] the sea. When Russian ships appeared, people could exhale."

Most Svans, Georgian authorities, and armed forces fled after a warning that Kodor/i would be bombed. "We gave them a corridor, warned that there would be . . . bombing," commanders say, repeating the warning they gave: "'So, please, civilians flee immediately, while the military leaves for your territory [in Georgia].'"[25] Abkhaz reservists and members of the regular army who followed the air force faced no resistance and took Kodor/i with minor losses.[26] "Everything was done with Russia's help before we came," reservists confirm. "The operation ended with no casualties. The army went by air, [and] we went by foot, about forty kilometers. Nowhere was there a military clash. . . . The whole operation took place without a shot. The Kodor Gorge was cleared over three days. We used aviation and artillery on the day that the [escape] corridor expired. The [Georgian] military stockpiles and headquarters were destroyed."

"Our Struggle Did Not End in 1993": The Recognition of 2008

The outcome of the Kodor/i operation was that, for the first time after the war of 1992–1993, the Abkhaz controlled the whole territory of Abkhazia that they consider to be historically Abkhaz. "For many, it is not significant. What difference does it make that the Abkhaz freed a part of their territory?," officials of the de facto Ministry of Defense stress of the importance of the Kodor/i operation. "We are finally controlling the whole territory of Abkhazia." The Abkhaz see the establishment of the historical boundary of Abkhazia and the recognition of Abkhazia as a state by Russia that followed as a logical conclusion to the Abkhaz struggle for independence.[27] "We freed all the borders of Abkhazia. As a result, we restored the Abkhaz statehood," a participant in the operation affirms.

While in Georgia these steps are condemned as part of Russia's "occupation" of Abkhazia, the Abkhaz associate Russia's recognition on August 26, 2008, and the subsequent fortification of the border area with the beginning of a peaceful time.[28] "On August 26, we were recognized. Every day before that, we were provoked. After that, Russia sent its subdivisions to the border. A peaceful time began," Abkhaz reservists say. "When we started guarding together with the Russian border forces in 2008, people felt protection and could lead their lives." Georgian guerrillas could no longer operate in the border area, and the threat of attack declined. "It became more difficult to attack Abkhazia," I often heard, and "after 2008, there were no more outbreaks of violence." Yet this "peace" hangs on the Russian protection from Georgia. Russia "recognized us and supports us, so that Georgia does not tear us into pieces, [as it] is ready to wipe us off the face of the earth any time," respondents admit. "Today we are recognized by five states. But Georgia is still certain that Abkhazia is part of Georgia. . . . We were pressured from all sides—the Russian [economic] blockade, Georgian diversionists—so that we would give up. But now we are developing in all spheres."

This dependence on Russia is evident not only in the military but also in the social, political, and economic spheres. Most Abkhaz hold Russian citizenship, Russia is a political force in the Abkhaz elections, and Russian trade, investment, and tourism sustain Abkhazia's economy (ICG 2010).[29] "How can we speak of sovereignty when Russia is given such liberties here?," regular people argue, saying, "Russia recognized us, but this means that full independence does not exist here." This dependence and the displacement of Georgians and the loss of Abkhaz life that preceded the recognition, however, are seen as a necessary price to pay for developing independently from Georgia. "Through all these sufferings, Russia recognized us and life is getting better," respondents affirm over and again, and "We have elections of deputies, the president. There is opposition, power, people." But since the victory in the war and the postwar recognition are seen as the restoration of "the Abkhaz as the only legitimate power in Abkhazia," these institutions are dominated by the Abkhaz in a monoethnic fashion.[30]

Despite the exclusion of non-Abkhaz groups living in Abkhazia from postwar politics, this outcome is viewed as the utmost achievement in Abkhazia's recent history, representing the symbolic and actual restoration of justice for which the Abkhaz fought for over a century (Shamba and Neproshin 2008). The recognition brought full circle the aim of what the Abkhaz understand as their national liberation struggle, from the prewar demographic, political, and cultural Georgianization of Abkhazia, to wartime opposition to the Georgian aggression, to postwar defense of the preceding victories from the ongoing threat of Georgian attacks. As a prominent intellectual and political leader in the postwar Abkhaz society says, "The Abkhaz culture is the culture of a people who received independence. It is impossible to understand the Abkhaz identity without understanding the national liberation struggle."

Conclusion
UNCERTAINTY AND MOBILIZATION IN CIVIL WAR

> [The existing] collection of theories just scratches the surface of the recruitment of fighters and organization of civil warfare. This area remains one of the most promising and understudied areas in the literature on conflict.
>
> —Blattman and Miguel 2010, 21

When I began this project, I was puzzled by the mobilization of a relatively small group in a war against a significantly larger and better-armed state opponent. Not only were the Abkhaz at a disadvantage in manpower and arms when the Georgian-Abkhaz war of 1992–1993 began, but also intergroup clashes before the war in Abkhazia demonstrated the dominance of the Georgian group and the repressive capacity of the Georgian state to crush Abkhaz dissent. Only Soviet troops could stop the violence in July 1989, and the subsequent dissolution of the Soviet Union added to the futility of Abkhaz resistance to the Georgian advance into Abkhazia in August 1992. Mobilization in the Abkhaz case should not have been expected (Beissinger 2002, 222). It was too risky for Abkhaz men and women to pick up what arms they had, and they should have instead acquiesced to Georgia, especially in the areas where Georgia immediately established territorial control. Yet at least 13 percent of the entire population mobilized on the Abkhaz side—a substantial proportion compared to other civil wars of the time (Lacina 2006, 279). Moreover, the Abkhaz army formed in the course of the war succeeded in driving out Georgia's armed forces and the Georgian population, most of whom cannot return, and defended this victory long after the war, as an official structure of the emergent de facto state of Abkhazia.

While I expected existing research on mobilization in general and Georgian-Abkhaz conflict in particular to provide some answers to my puzzle, what became clear as soon as I started fieldwork in Abkhazia was that this literature did not sit comfortably with what participants in my research told me about their mobilization trajectories. Most theories start with the assumption that individuals make decisions during the war with a given knowledge of risk involved in mobilization and go on to isolate factors that might drive individuals to accept the high risks of joining an armed group. However, rather than risk, most participants in my research spoke of the intense uncertainty that characterized the war's onset. Most did not understand who was threatened, by whom, and to what extent or whether it was a war. When they did, they understood risk in different ways, as directed to their own safety or that of their families and friends, their localities, or the broader group. Mobilization decisions reflected this variation as individuals fled, hid, or joined the fighting alone or with others, to protect the segments of their group or the group as a whole that they perceived to be threatened.

Revisiting Alternative Explanations

Existing theories of mobilization cannot explain this outcome. While explanations focused on historical grievances (Gurr 1970; Horowitz 1985) and social norms (Petersen 2001) overpredict the Abkhaz mobilization in August 1992, those focused on economic incentives (Weinstein 2007; Humphreys and Weinstein 2008) and security maximization (Kalyvas 2006; Kalyvas and Kocher 2007) underpredict it. As the discussion of prewar collective conflict identities (chapters 3 and 4) in this book demonstrates, the memories and experiences of Georgianization during the Soviet decades and duties to the fellow Abkhaz applied to all members of this traditionally strong community, but not all mobilized on behalf of their group. Many escaped the fighting in and outside of Abkhazia, even if they shared in the collective historical grievances, and some returned to leadership positions in postwar Abkhazia, in contrast to the prediction of the social reputation costs of nonparticipation in the war. However, most respondents spoke of the prior conflict and Abkhaz norms in their accounts of the war. The history of intergroup conflict and the social ties that positioned individuals in relation to one another as part of the broader group thus shed light on the structural context of mobilization, but do not explain why many Abkhaz *did not* participate in collective action when the war began.

If structural explanations suggest that more Abkhaz should have mobilized given the pervasive historical grievances and social norms, economic and security explanations struggle to answer why any Abkhaz mobilized *at all* given the absence of these incentives at the time of mobilization. The discussion of the war's onset (chapter 5) shows that the Abkhaz group was weak in resources that it could offer or promise to its fighters and military capacities or skills that could increase the safety of fighters relative to nonparticipants. Only a minority of the group belonged to the prewar armed structure the Abkhaz Guard, most of whom were released from duty, and weapons were collected from the population on the eve of the war, leaving most Abkhaz unarmed. However, that did not prevent ordinary people from mobilizing en masse at the war's onset, often with hunting weapons and even sticks. The economic and security incentives could explain why some Abkhaz escaped the fighting in and outside of Abkhazia and, rarely, defected to the Georgian side or joined later in the war, after the first Abkhaz military success and formation of an army with support from Russia and the North Caucasus, which could provide the skills and resources necessary for survival, but they do not help understand the mass mobilization of the Abkhaz when the war began.

Similarly, the literature on Georgian-Abkhaz conflict emphasizes these external factors in explaining the case. The Russian and North Caucasus assistance (Zverev 1996; Coppieters 2000; Cornell 2000; Baev 2003) and disorganization of Georgian forces (Darchiashvili 1997; Zürcher, Baev, and Koehler 2005; Zürcher 2007; Billingsley 2013) during the war and Russia's ongoing influence (Lynch 2004) and Georgia's state weakness (Darchiashvili and Nodia 2003; Nodia 2004) after the war are prioritized over local factors in these explanations. It was the Russian armament and strategic aid and foreign fighters, particularly from the North Caucasus, that determined the course of the war in the context of fragmentation and indiscipline of Georgia's troops; it was the inability or unwillingness of the Russian peacekeepers to contain border violence after the war that maintained instability in Abkhazia in the context of breakdown of state authority in Georgia, in this line of argument.

Yet the discussion of the war (chapters 5 and 6) in this book demonstrates that the Russian support was unclear and divided between the Abkhaz and Georgian sides during the war, especially at the time of mobilization, and foreign fighters participated on both sides in the fighting. While the remaining Russian personnel of the former Soviet base in Abkhazia gave or sold some arms to the Abkhaz, Georgia received a large amount of Soviet weapons in the Transcaucasus Military District, which ensured its military preponderance at the war's onset. As the war unfolded, Russian support arguably tilted to the Abkhaz side, even though forces within Russia remained split on this issue.

The Russian strategic aid, the arrival of fighters from the North Caucasus, and the Georgian disintegration mattered in the course of fighting, but could not explain why the Abkhaz mobilized when these factors were not present or help understand how the Abkhaz perceived their continuing roles in the war as the Abkhaz force transformed into an army and their defense of wartime victory after the war. The discussion of the war and postwar dynamics (chapters 6 and 7) shows that these external factors did not avert significant losses among the Abkhaz fighters during wartime battles, many of which ended in failure for the Abkhaz side, and during postwar border defense from the ongoing Georgian threat and attacks.

Had Georgia been fatally weakened by the Russian support to the Abkhaz, there should not have been lost battles on the Abkhaz side. Had foreign fighters fought these battles, there should not have been substantial injuries and deaths among the Abkhaz. Had the Russian peacekeepers incited postwar violence by Georgian guerrillas, there should not have been casualties among the peacekeepers. Alternatively, had Russia been invariably on the Abkhaz side, Abkhazia would not have endured the economic blockade or exclusion from the negotiations table after the war. More importantly, the ordinary Abkhaz continued to mobilize during and after the war despite the risks of injury and death that became apparent in the course of wartime and postwar violence. The literature that focuses on external factors cannot account for these local dynamics of mobilization.

Overall, the existing mobilization theories do not explain why the ordinary Abkhaz adopted *different* mobilization trajectories, from prewar activism to participation in the Abkhaz war effort and defense of the Abkhaz victory after the war. These trajectories varied dramatically at the war's onset as people hid, fled, or joined the fighting alone or with others in their locales or areas of high-intensity fighting. These mobilization decisions cut across differences in prewar backgrounds that could have variably pulled or pushed individuals into mobilization, and even prewar activism, the key predictor of subsequent mobilization in the social movement research, did not invariably draw individuals into mobilization when the war began (McAdam 1986; Viterna 2013). Individuals with both similar grievances that accumulated during preceding conflict and social ties at the war's onset adopted different roles along the mobilization continuum, from fleeing to fighting on the Abkhaz side. The fighter units that emerged at the war's onset incorporated men and women of different social status and prior mobilization experience. Even the most politicized participants in the Abkhaz movement fled when Georgia's forces entered Abkhazia, yet others who were not part of the social movement mobilized on the Abkhaz side. Some individuals remained in their localities to protect families and neighborhoods, yet others who had families left home for strategic sites, often marked by utmost fighting, to protect Abkhazia as a whole. Structural characteristics of the environment, particularly access to weapons, the armed structure, and hiding places or proximity to the borders for escape routes, did not preclude these mobilization trajectories across the areas of differential territorial control.

This variation shows that risk was not the decisive factor in the Abkhaz mobilization: it did not yield the same cost-benefit calculation, but was variable in the uncertainty of the war's onset. Had it been decisive, we should have observed few Abkhaz joining the Abkhaz war effort given its futility, with little or no effect of push and pull factors of prior conflict. Those Abkhaz who had no other option but to fight should have stayed in their locales for relative safety. Yet many did not.

Toward a Theory of Mobilization in Uncertainty

How is it possible that risk did not drive mobilization? Why did so many Abkhaz mobilize in such different ways in response to the Georgian advance into Abkhazia despite the apparent high risk involved in mobilization? To understand variation in individual mobilization trajectories at the war's onset, we need a theory of mobilization that places individuals in the context of history of intergroup conflict and social networks that relate people to one another as part of their group and appreciates the uncertainty of violence onset that can drive people to adopt mobilization decisions surprising from the perspective of the existing theories that assume individuals' knowledge of risk in mobilization and their decisions about whether and how to mobilize based on this knowledge.

I show that ordinary people do not make cost-benefit calculations to select from a range of options given the knowledge of risk in civil war. Instead, they face intense uncertainty and have to navigate it with the social networks in which they are embedded at the time of mobilization. Even after decades of intergroup conflict—for example, in the post-Soviet cases, such as Chechnya, Nagorno-Karabakh, Transnistria, and Ukraine; the wars in former Yugoslavia; and those outside of Europe, such as in Indonesia, Rwanda, South Sudan, and, most recently, Syria—violence and war can come as a shock, and uncertainty rather than risk-based cost-benefit calculation characterizes the context of mobilization. I will briefly note the utility and applicability of the argument developed in this book beyond the case of Abkhazia in the historical case of the Rwandan civil war and genocide and the contemporary Syrian uprising, where the nature of prewar conflict and the scale and dynamics of violence were different, but the uncertainty was comparable. As Scott Straus (2006, 65) describes the situation in Rwanda in 1994, "The president's [Habyarimana's] assassination and the resumption of war ruptured the preexisting order, creating a feeling of intense crisis and uncertainty in local communities." In a similar vein, "extreme uncertainty" marked initial mobilization in Syria (Baczko, Quesnay, and Dorronsoro 2017, 73).

This form of uncertainty is distinct from the classic understanding of the term as "general unreliability of all information" in war or "inability to anticipate what the future holds" in general (Clausewitz 1976, 140; Best 2008, 355). This notion relates uncertainty to risk in that actors do not know the outcome, but make choices among a range of possibilities and their probability of success (Knight 1921; Bas and Schub 2017). Rationalist models of war therefore postulate that uncertainty dissipates when relevant information becomes available (Fearon 1995). However, misperception, among other cognitive constraints, might challenge decision making under strain (Tversky and Kahneman 1974; Jervis 1976).

If the classic understanding of uncertainty is rooted in the assumption of rationality, even if bounded, and focused on the outcome, for example, of war, another understanding that differs from my use in this book is of ongoing uncertainty. This form of uncertainty applies to ordinary people's experience, rather than wartime strategies in the Clausewitzian sense. It is normalized in everyday life through the culture of fear as in Guatemala (Green 1999), violence in the realm of the ordinary as in India (Das 2007), and existential stress as in northern Uganda (Finnström 2008) in the context of intergroup conflict. Similarly, expectations are developed as the new social order is normalized in the course of protracted civil wars as in Colombia (Arjona 2016). My core argument on how individuals navigate the war's onset will not apply to these contexts of ongoing uncertainty since the nature of uncertainty changes as people adapt to the war. Whereas prewar life in Abkhazia and institutions of the emergent Abkhaz army during and after the war were characterized by such ongoing uncertainty, which was nonetheless accompanied by a sense of order, the sudden Georgian advance into Abkhazia broke down everyday order and put unprecedented pressure on the Abkhaz.

This intense uncertainty associated with the outbreak of violence, including the war's onset, disrupts everyday life, exposing regular people to different, often conflicting, meanings of violence. As Lee Ann Fujii (2009, 78) shows in the Rwandan case, "A picture of daily life [was] suddenly transformed by civil war." Similarly, in Syria, as Adam Baczko, Arthur Quesnay, and Gilles Dorronsoro (2017, 73) discuss, "the institutional routines, which would have reduced uncertainty at the individual level, had either weakened or disappeared . . . [when] the mobilization phase began in early 2011." The Abkhaz case adds to this assessment that people can understand violence in multiple ways, rather than know its nature and potential associated outcomes. The initial interpretation by many Abkhaz of the Georgian advance as a clash, rather than a war, is a vivid example. As Peter J. Katzenstein and Lucia A. Seybert (2018b, 44) capture this point, "Crises are generators of uncertainty rather than risks with associated probabilities that are known or knowable."

Because the nature of violence is unknown, the intense uncertainty of violence onset puts a premium on the urgency of decisions in response. Recent sociological studies of violence pay close attention to this urgency (Viterna 2013). For example, Randall Collins's micro-sociological theory identifies mechanisms by which tension of fear explodes into violence. Based on different forms of violence, Collins (2008, 8) finds that "people are tense and often fearful in the immediate threat of violence—including their own violence; this is the emotional dynamic that determines what they will do if fighting actually breaks out." I take a step back from this work to show how people come to understand the meaning of violence to make different mobilization decisions in the context of uncertainty.

When the onset of violence ruptures the preexisting order and flow of everyday life, people ask difficult questions about the nature of violence, in particular, who is threatened, by whom, and to what extent and what actions to take in response and for whom, one's own safety or that of the family, friends, the community, or the broader group. As Omar S. McDoom (2012, 155) demonstrates, in some areas of Rwanda, "Hutu and Tutsi . . . were uncertain as to what was happening and what to do." The absence of precedents and inexperience raised similar issues as "the Syrians who took to the streets were demonstrating for the first time, in a country where public protest is rare" and mere discussion of current events is a crime (Baczko, Dorronsoro, and Quesnay 2013, 5). Different answers to these questions emerge as people appeal to their shared visions of the conflict and social networks at the time of mobilization in an attempt to decide how to act. "It is clear that actors *want* to do something in response to the uncertainty that surrounds them," Katzenstein and Seybert (2018a, 84) agree. "What *should* be done, however, is typically unknown. Actors do their best, guessing and coping" (emphasis in original).

In Abkhazia, this decision making followed a general logic, a social process of information filtering captured by the national, local, and quotidian interaction in collective threat framing. This process did not apply to a few individuals who faced the Georgian troops and tanks firsthand and perceived the threat by virtue of being in the midst of violence, due to situational threat perception. Otherwise, the confusion, shock, and panic that enveloped the Abkhaz society when Georgian forces entered Abkhazia was remedied in the course of the first days of the war by appealing to the messages of the national leadership, which shifted in content at the local level, and interpreting the threat of the Georgian advance within the quotidian networks of family and friends as directed to the different segments of the group that ordinary men and women then mobilized to protect.

As in Rwanda, where the Tutsi threat was framed in the elite messages on the radio, but was translated into action at the local level, the national leadership articulated the threat of the Georgian advance as aggression against Abkhazia, but this framing was adapted to the local needs of defense in villages, towns, and cities, where local leaders called on the population to protect their localities (Fujii 2009; McDoom 2012). Had the threat framing by national elite been the full story, we would see most Abkhaz mobilizing to the capital and other areas of high-intensity fighting. Likewise, had the local threat framing been the full story, we would see most Abkhaz remaining in their localities. But there was variation in these mobilization trajectories, and it was at the quotidian level that threat frames were consolidated into mobilization decisions. The quotidian consolidation thus took place in interaction with the national and local information filtering as the Abkhaz navigated uncertainty.

As a result of collective threat framing, people interpreted the Georgian advance as a war, rather than a clash or policing action, came to perceive risk in different ways, and mobilized based on this perception, whether to protect their own safety by fleeing, hiding, or defecting to the stronger side in the war; the safety of their families and friends by fleeing, hiding, or joining the fighting together with these segments of their group, often in their home locales; or the broader group by mobilizing into areas of high-intensity fighting that the overall outcome of the war depended on. Since this protection was directed in some cases to the self, and in others to the different segments of the group, the effects of security seeking coexisted with collective and social motivations for mobilization. As Macartan Humphreys and Jeremy M. Weinstein (2008, 437) argue in the case of Sierra Leone's civil war of 1991–2002, "Different logics of participation may coexist in a single civil war."

In isolation, these effects are expected by applying certain motivations to actors who should then mobilize due to these motivations. Individuals should weigh the risks of mobilization against, for example, the social reputation costs of nonparticipation or the economic benefits of participation and then make their decisions about mobilization. But actors often make mobilization decisions in the quotidian friendship and family setting that direct them away from these predictions and toward protecting different segments of their group. Because of this, prewar activists sometimes flee the war to protect their families and others leave their families in the wake of violence to protect the overall group. This is the force of the collective threat framing mechanism, which filters information from national, through local, to quotidian levels, to define who should be protected from threat and how.

Trust is essential for people to make these decisions under conditions of intense uncertainty. Relatives, friends, and neighbors often turn against each other in times of violence, as the Rwandan case demonstrates. People could not foresee the violence before it began, but were not surprised by the betrayal of close ones when it set off (Fujii 2009, 90–91). Yet it is in these quotidian networks that mobilization for violence and war takes place, because "concrete personal relations" engender trust (Granovetter 1985, 490). Sarah E. Parkinson (2013), for example, shows how trust-based kinship, marriage, and friendship ties connected organizational cells of Palestinian militants in Lebanon, this bridging role primarily played by women as men were confined to their neighborhoods. In Soviet Lithuania, "the individual's set of closest connections, his community, became the key source of information" in mobilization against the repressive Soviet state (Petersen 2001, 2). "The level of absolute trust," Roger D. Petersen (2001, 73) points out, "is less likely in a group of twenty or thirty than in a group of five or ten." Such small quotidian groups constituted the scale of mobilization in Abkhazia.

Individuals learned about the Georgian advance from the national and local leaders, but discussed their framing with small groups of relatives and friends that often mobilized and stayed together during the war.

In Syria, "the existence of a space of trust" similarly enabled small-group mobilization, and this mobilization resembled the process that we observed in Abkhazia (Baczko 2013, 7). Baczko, Quesnay, and Dorronsoro (2017, 73–74) call this process in Syria "mobilization by deliberation," where small groups met in "semi-private spaces . . . that provided a degree of safety" and exchanged information to "define the meaning of the conflict . . . [and] a shared 'moral grammar' . . . [that] defined which arguments were acceptable, which objectives were legitimate, and which methods were permissible for achieving these objectives." Whereas in the Syrian case, this deliberation, at least initially, drove actors to adopt and maintain "a peaceful repertoire of actions" despite violence and repression, in Rwanda and Abkhazia peaceful solutions were rejected, to respectively frame the entire Tutsi group as an enemy and the Georgian advance as a war, which required defensive mobilization (Baczko, Quesnay, and Dorronsoro 2017, 74; McDoom 2012).

This highlights the importance of prewar dynamics for mobilization. The social process of information filtering underlying mobilization at the war's onset does not exist in isolation from the history and experiences of intergroup conflict. In this process, people rely on shared understandings of conflict and their roles in it, or collective conflict identities, that emerge before the war. Some threat frames succeed over others as they resonate with these shared understandings. Whereas protesters in Syria constructed their collective identity around slogans for inclusiveness in "a shared vision of the Syrian nation-state" drawing on the revolutions in Tunisia and Egypt, in Abkhazia and Rwanda intergroup polarization, rather than inclusion, was the driving prewar dynamic (Baczko, Quesnay, and Dorronsoro 2017, 75). People of different, sometimes overlapping, group identities were relatives, friends, and neighbors, but underlying these everyday roles was the historical experience that could drive them apart. McDoom (2012, 122) notes that "historical references to Hutu oppression at the hands of the Tutsi" were mobilized to frame the latter as an enemy. In Abkhazia, the memories and experiences of Georgianization in the Soviet period shaped how the Georgian advance was framed at the war's onset. This history was seen as one of the dissolution of the Abkhaz in the dominant Georgian group, and it therefore made sense to the regular Abkhaz that Georgian forces came to Abkhazia to conclude this process or eliminate the Abkhaz, rather than police the territory—one of the Georgian counterframes that did not resonate due to this history.

This history had concrete manifestations in the lives of most Abkhaz, as most were exposed to intergroup conflict before the war. For many, this exposure centered on the organizations of the Abkhaz social movement. Leaders of these organizations were involved in political contention as they voiced the group's concerns in formal letters to the Soviet center; organized public gatherings, demonstrations, and strikes; mobilized the broader population to join the movement organizations; and actively participated in Abkhazia's government when the Soviet Union collapsed. Leadership and membership in the movement organizations were not the full extent of exposure to intergroup conflict. The regular Abkhaz who were not recruited into these organizations observed movement activity and often contributed to it informally, by joining prewar mobilization. Some participated in intergroup clashes, which put the groups in prewar Abkhazia in violent opposition against each other and polarized and militarized the society. In general, people faced everyday confrontation by merely living in the context of intergroup conflict. Conversational taboos, derogatory language use, arguments, and brawls were common and over time created a distance between the groups.

Collective historical memory evolved through the observation of and participation in these forms of collective action before the war, to shape collective conflict identities among networks of relatives, friends, neighbors, and colleagues who experienced the conflict together as part of their broader group. These memories and experiences positioned individuals in relation to the history of intergroup conflict and social networks at the war's onset and formed the foundation for how the threat of the Georgian advance was interpreted in these networks and why threat frames resonated with the regular Abkhaz. The historical narratives of oppression played a similar role in Rwanda.

The ways in which threat is framed at the war's onset influences how people understand their roles during and after the war in the context of social networks that mobilize together. "Once they joined in the violence," Fujii (2009, 154) demonstrates clearly in Rwanda, "Joiners continued their participation because 'working' in groups conferred powerful group identity onto Joiners, who then re-enacted the specific practices constitutive of the group's identity." In Abkhazia, fighters' identity as defenders informed by the framing of Georgian forces as an aggressor was reinforced during wartime battles and postwar border violence as people continued to mobilize against the ongoing Georgian threat. Taken together, these aspects of prewar, wartime, and postwar mobilization by the Abkhaz were understood as part of the broader national liberation struggle, which culminated in the recognition of Abkhazia, despite persistent exclusion of the Georgian population from the de facto Abkhaz state.

Mobilization is therefore an ongoing process, in which collective threat framing helps grasp individual decisions in the uncertainty of violence onset, but which extends beyond this moment to prewar everyday confrontation, political contention, and violent opposition that inform collective action when the war begins and wartime and postwar participation in the conflict where collective conflict identities transform as people adapt to the new realities of intergroup conflict.

Future Research

This book tells the story of mobilization in intergroup conflict from the perspective of its very actors in the understudied context of Abkhazia, but this story has important lessons for future research on conflict. I demonstrate the inherently relational nature of mobilization in uncertainty as people come to terms with violence and war to make difficult mobilization decisions collectively based on shared understandings of conflict and their roles in it. Future research should extend this logic beyond the context of civil war to mobilization short of war where violence is not expected, from everyday resistance to demonstrations, protests, strikes, clashes, and riots.

This would require broadening the concept of mobilization from recruitment into an armed group to organization of and participation in diverse forms of collective action, including repertoires of everyday confrontation, political contention, and violent opposition, which characterize intergroup conflict. Mobilization into these forms of collective action spans from spontaneous to organized, depending on how individuals join collective action, without prior organizational experience or as formally or informally recruited members of organizations. During the war, mobilization should be understood not simply as a decision to fight or not to fight made spontaneously or as part of preexisting organizations but as a continuum of roles, from hiding or fleeing to participation in the support or fighting apparatuses in home localities or areas of high-intensity fighting, in the rear or at the front. These roles position individuals differently in relation to the conflict, from self- to other-regarding motivations, based on whom they mobilize to protect. If the war changes its course or ends, the experience of prior mobilization will shape whether and how people continue to participate in the conflict to defend wartime outcomes.

Understanding mobilization in this way shows that civil war is not an isolated phenomenon, but is related to the prewar and postwar conflict dynamics in important ways. I identify one mechanism—collective threat framing at the war's onset, which draws on the prewar and has effects on the wartime and postwar processes. Conflict scholarship should further advance our understanding of how civil war is causally related to the broader conflict beyond the logic of escalation common in conflict studies. This can help not only to better explain how nonviolent conflict unfolds into civil war to change actors' identities but also to find opportunities in the local dynamics of conflict that could be used to positively transform it and facilitate demobilization of actors.

These actors follow a number of paths to wartime mobilization informed by varied motivations. Theorized in this way, alternative explanations revisited above apply to different decisions in the same moment of mobilization based on whom people perceive to be threatened and mobilize to protect. The self-seeking, security logic applies to those who view their own safety as paramount and protect themselves in these circumstances. The more people seek to protect the broader group, the more their mobilization is other-regarding, collective and social. "Not all combatants fight for instrumental reasons," Francisco Gutiérrez Sanín and Elisabeth J. Wood (2014, 220) observe in a similar way, as "some join for normative reasons." Starting from the point of uncertainty, rather than risk, and acknowledging that people can come to perceive risk in different ways can help distinguish between these effects.

Yet uncertainty is not a static condition; context and experience change it. People develop new routines and expectancies as they adapt to protracted violence and war based on observation of and participation in these processes. Future research should come to terms with this complexity. In this, rigorous, immersive fieldwork can help get at complexity from the perspective of participants in these processes, and understudied cases, such as Abkhazia, can offer opportunities for theoretical innovation. This will benefit not only conflict studies but also research in politics and international relations, where conflict is pervasive and actors face difficult dilemmas in navigating uncertainty.

Notes

INTRODUCTION

1. Abkhazia's 8,700 square kilometers stretch over 170 kilometers along the coast of the Black Sea and 66 kilometers from the coastal south to the mountainous north of the territory (Dbar 2013, 23). This territory is smaller than Cyprus.

2. I introduce the centrality of uncertainty in the study of civil war mobilization in Shesterinina 2016.

3. On forced recruitment through abduction or press-ganging, see D. Cohen 2016; Gates 2002.

4. Underlying most of these studies is the collective action problem articulated in Olson 1965. As participation in civil war is dangerous and its benefits will be distributed across society, individuals should be expected to free ride.

5. I draw on the insights developed by Gould 1995, Wood 2003, and Viterna 2013 on insurgent identities.

6. For further discussion of the demographic situation in Abkhazia, see Trier, Lohm, and Szakonyi 2010.

7. Lists of casualties on the Abkhaz side include at least 150 local Armenians (Menakeci 2009) and 140 foreign fighters from the North Caucasus and 100 from Russia (Pachulija 2010, 507–544). Khalidov (2014, 56–57) provides a higher estimate of casualties, including at least 200 foreign fighters from the North Caucasus and 200 from Russia. Other casualty lists that I used are included in Khodzhaa 2003, 2006, 2009.

8. The unemployment rate in Abkhazia was in general higher than in other republics of the Soviet Union, but that did not account for the unofficial economic activity that was prevalent, especially in rural areas (Derluguian 2005, 234).

9. For example, in Soviet Lithuania, some regular Lithuanians were active in resistance to the repressive Soviet rule, whereas others held neutrality (Petersen 2001). In El Salvador in the 1970s–1980s, many peasants provided support to the Front for National Liberation (FMLN), whereas others, including women, joined the guerrilla army as fighters (Wood 2003; Viterna 2013). In Lebanon in the 1980s, most male cadres of the Palestine Liberation Organization (PLO) "were deported, imprisoned, confined to their homes, or forced deep underground," while women were central to sustaining the organization through their participation in the information, finance, and supply apparatus (Parkinson 2013, 418). In Rwanda, in the violence following the assassination of President Juvénal Habyarimana in April 1994, "Some people refused [to take part]. Others found ways to avoid participating. Many, however, joined the killings" that resulted in one of the gravest events of political violence in history, the Rwandan genocide (Fujii 2009, 2; Straus 2006). Most recently, while thousands fled from the fighting in Ukraine and Syria, others joined different armed groups that emerged in these contexts (Zhukov 2016; Baczko, Quesnay, and Dorronsoro 2017).

1. STUDYING CIVIL WAR MOBILIZATION

1. I discuss fieldwork logistics, procedures, and protocols in greater detail in Shesterinina 2016.

2. Important exceptions include Petersen 2001, Wood 2003, Parkinson 2013, and Viterna 2013, among others.

3. The formation of Georgia's army began when the Mkhedrioni received legal status as the Rescue Corps of Georgia and the Law on Internal Troops–National Guards was adopted in 1990, but these forces often acted outside state control.

4. The table includes fighters and nonfighters. The figures here are calculated based on the number of fighters only. Of 83 fighters, 14 (17 percent) were organized and 69 (83 percent) mobilized spontaneously.

5. I discuss questions of research ethics in depth in Shesterinina 2019.

6. I provide a small number of questions in box 1 as compared to that in an actual interview where I asked multiple questions that were specific to the experiences of a particular interviewee. See also Shesterinina 2019, online appendix titled "Replication Data under Supplemental Material.".

7. I thank Elisabeth J. Wood for the suggestion to include an interview excerpt.

2. A SOCIOHISTORICAL APPROACH TO MOBILIZATION

1. See McCarthy and Zald 1973, 1977 on resource mobilization.

2. As Robert J. Sampson and colleagues (2005, 679) argue, "The capacity for sustained collective action is conditioned mainly by the presence of established institutions and organizations that may be appropriated in the service of emergent action." On political opportunity, see especially Tilly 1978; McAdam 1982; Tarrow 1998; McAdam, Tarrow, and Tilly 2001.

3. The importance of friends and acquaintances (Granovetter's [1985] "weak ties") in formal and informal recruitment into activism is a central finding in the social movements literature. See Oberschall 1973, 1994; Snow, Zurcher, and Ekland-Olson 1980; McAdam 1986; Gould 1991, 1993; John Scott 2000, 2012. See Diani and McAdam 2003 for a review.

4. Nonparticipation of individuals who support the cause or consider themselves to be affected by the underlying conflict is the core problem of collective action research (Olson 1965). Some attribute this outcome to biographical unavailability, or alternative daily commitments that prevent individuals from participation (McAdam 1986, 70).

5. Studying nonparticipation is motivated by a simple principle: as "instances of violence cannot be considered independently of instances where violence does not occur" (Kalyvas 2006, 48), "we cannot adequately explain those who join in violence without also examining those who do not" (Fujii 2009, 16).

6. Whereas Petersen assumes the existence of a rebel group, I find that prewar mobilization can occur in other types of movement organizations and that participation in such organizations may not be viewed as rebel by the participants.

7. Genocide studies capture a broader variety of roles that are outside the scope of this study. These include leaders, namely, instigators (Mandel 2002) and administrators (Brown 2003), perpetrators (Browning 1993), collaborators (Wiesen 2000), bystanders (Hilberg 1993), rescuers (Mildarsky, Fagin Jones, and Corley 2005; Suedfeld and de Best 2008), and survivors and resisters (Davidson 1985; Tiedens 1997; Finkel 2017). For example, in the case of Rwanda, "in addition to Joiners, leaders, and collaborators," Fujii (2009, 16) identifies "those who did not lead, collaborate, or join in the violence in any way. These actors include those who were the primary targets of violence (survivors); those who helped to save Tutsi (rescuers); those who evaded participation (evaders); those who witnessed but did not take part in the genocide (witnesses); and people who refused or resisted pressures to participate in the violence (resisters)."

8. Analyzing prewar background, Jocelyn S. Viterna (2013, 82) identifies "politicized, reluctant, and recruited" paths to mobilization by women into the guerrilla army in El Salvador.

9. The spontaneous trajectory is akin to that of Fujii's (2009, 15) "Joiners," who "did not lead or organize the genocide but were responsible for carrying out much of the violence . . . [with] no prior military or police training. . . . Joiners were, in every sense of the term, 'ordinary' men and women of their communities."

10. This outcome of mobilization with quotidian networks of family and friends is observed across multiple violent contexts. See Petersen 2001; Aspinall 2009; Staniland 2012; Parkinson 2013.

11. Charles Tilly (1978, 5–14) coined the term *repertoires of collective action* to describe the forms of action routinely used to achieve collective objectives. Amelia Hoover Green (2018, 5) advanced and applied the term *repertoire of violence* to the context of civil war as "the forms of violence frequently used by an actor, and their relative proportions." I use the term *mobilization repertoires* broadly to refer to repeated nonviolent and violent forms of collective action that take place in the course of conflict.

12. I draw on James Scott's (1985) concept of "everyday resistance" in introducing this repertoire.

13. Political contention is the subject of the vast literature on social movements. See McAdam, Tarrow, and Tilly 2001.

14. In his study of high-risk activism in the case of Freedom Summer, McAdam (1986, 67) differentiates between "risk" and "cost" and argues that "the term 'cost' refers to the expenditures of time, money, and energy that are required of a person engaged in any particular form of activism. . . . As an analytic dimension, 'risk' is very different from cost. Risk refers to the anticipated dangers—whether legal, social, physical, financial, and so forth—of engaging in a particular type of activity." He identifies low- and high-cost/risk forms of activism and suggests that recruitment is affected by the different levels of cost and risk involved.

15. Lisa Wedeen (2019, 79) points out a different context, in which uncertainty is "cultivated by an excess of information." Here I focus on a context of limited information and competing narratives on the meaning of violence.

16. Paul Almeida (2019, 53) similarly finds in the context of social movements that threats drive defensive collective action. Almeida draws on the tradition of social movement scholarship that views threats as actual or perceived attempts to "reduce [a group's] realization of its interests" (Tilly 1978, 133). He addresses structural threats, such as economic problems and erosion of rights. By contrast, I focus on threats "to a group's existence" and those of "engaging in a particular type of activity," namely, mobilization to fight, in the context of civil war (McDoom 2012, 131; McAdam 1986, 67).

17. For example, Wood (2003, 19) observes a similar pattern in El Salvador, where land issues were at the heart of some of the campesino support for the FMLN: "Landlessness initially motivated some campesinos; recalcitrant opposition to land redistribution motivated state repression; access to abandoned land provided the autonomy that made possible insurgent collective action for many; and moral outrage at the injustice of landlessness and the brutal measures taken to ensure it fueled mobilization."

18. Petersen (2001) extends this categorization to neutrality, unarmed opposition, support, and membership in the rebel organization, with the flip side of the spectrum reflecting varied support for the state forces. Parkinson (2013) adds the behind-the-lines supply, financial, and information roles to the support category. Carolyn Nordstrom (2004, 256) further advances the variation in fighter roles, as "soldiers range from formal allies through hired mercenaries to largely uncontrolled militias and profiteers fighting alongside national troops or guerrilla and rebel forces."

19. Self- and other-regarding mobilization broadly corresponds to Weinstein's (2007) two types of recruits that differentiate armed groups, the "consumers" and "investors," respectively. I find that both can be present in the same armed group. This argument

advances the recent move in the civil war literature that recognizes that "not all combatants fight for instrumental reasons: some join for normative reasons . . . [and] act on sincere beliefs and other-regarding preferences" (Gutiérrez Sanín and Wood 2014, 200, 222). This trend in the civil war literature echoes an earlier call by James D. Fearon and Alexander Wendt (2002) to appreciate the complexity of motivations in international relations.

3. COLLECTIVE HISTORICAL MEMORY

1. It was favorable for the empire to populate Abkhazia with Russians, but the difficult living conditions made the area unattractive to Russians until the Soviet period. Other *friendly* populations, such as Armenians and Greeks, established settlements, and Georgian settlement, primarily from the province of Mingrelia, began in the 1860s (Achugba 2010, 114–144).

2. Prior to Russian control, Abkhazia experienced the rule of the Ottoman Empire and other imperial powers of the time. On February 17, 1810, a charter by Alexander I granted Georgij Shervashidze, the hereditary prince of Abkhazia, the Supreme protection of the Russian empire" (Shamba and Neproshin 2008, 60; Lakoba 1991, 161; Lakoba 2004, 25). The princedom retained "autonomous control" and "conducted . . . [its] own affairs" (Lakoba 1991, 181; Hewitt 2013, 24). A decree of the governor-general of the Caucasus, Grand Duke Michael, of June 26, 1864, on "the introduction into Abkhazia of Russian rule" abolished the princedom (Shamba and Neproshin 2008, 63).

3. The uprising opposed the abolition of the princedom and agrarian reform that ignored the Abkhaz class structure (Lakoba 1990, 33–34). The feudal nobility was at its top; free peasants, their servants, and slaves were at the bottom. But institutions of integration existed, such as *atalychestvo* (adoption of children), as the nobility's children were brought up by free peasants (Maan 2007, 2012). With these lose ties to the nobility, Abkhaz peasants were landowners and rose up to redeem their lands (Suny 1994, 109).

4. As a *guilty* nation, the Abkhaz were denied the hereditary right to land and the ability to return if deported or to settle in central Abkhazia (Bgazhba and Lakoba 2007, 236–240). The remaining Abkhaz did not join the 1905 revolution in this context.

5. Zurab Papaskiri (2010, 118–140) shows the princedom's ties to Georgia and debates its statehood independent of Georgia.

6. Jakob Gogebashvili's famous article "Kem zaselit' Abhaziju?" (Who should be settled in Abkhazia?) was published repeatedly in *Tiflisskij vestnik* in 1877. The author's answer was that Mingrelians, a subgroup of Georgians, should settle in the emptied areas of Abkhazia.

7. The council issued a declaration and constitution and declared sovereignty on June 2, 1918, as Abkhazia joined the independent Mountainous Republic of the North Caucasus. See documents in Osmanov and Butaev 1994, 79–83.

8. Avtandil Menteshashvili (1990) finds that Abkhaz autonomy in Georgia was proposed, but did not become part of the agreement.

9. On March 31, 1921, Abkhaz leaders announced the establishment of the SSR of Abkhazia. Vladimir Lenin granted the status. On May 21, 1921, the Revolutionary Committee of Georgia issued a declaration on the independence of the Abkhaz SSR (Lakoba 1991, 328). The Union Treaty was signed on December 16, 1921 (see text in Kacharava 1959, 177–178). Abkhazia was formally integrated into the Georgian SSR on February 19, 1931 (Nodia 1998).

10. "The Georgian side, contradicting Abkhaz claims, denies that these changes of status were made under pressure" (Zverev 1996, pt. 3). "After the revolution, Abkhazia was separated and then returned in 1931," a former Georgian official tells me in an interview in Tbilisi. "Not returning to these facts is impossible."

11. In the October–December 1991 elections in Abkhazia, the Abkhaz, then 18 percent of the population, would gain twenty-eight seats in the Parliament, Georgians (46%) twenty-six seats, and other minorities (36%) eleven seats (Zverev 1996; Zürcher, Baev, and Koehler 2005).

12. Daniel Müller (2013, 236) supports the importance of resettlement for demographic changes in Abkhazia: "Numerically, there were 48,172 [Georgians] more in Abkhazia in 1959 than would be expected through natural growth since 1939." Similarly, an increase in the population of Russians and Armenians was largely due to their resettlement to Abkhazia, while the Greek population increased through natural growth (Achugba 2010, 198).

13. Between 1937 and 1940, seven kolkhozy were built "that settled 609 peasant families" (Achugba 2010, 199).

14. See Resolution 13 of the People's Commissars of the Abkhaz ASSR and the Bureau of the Abkhaz Regional Committee of the Communist Party of Georgia, January 11, 1941 (Sagarija, Achugba, and Pachulija 1992, 82–90). Cattle breeding, tobacco cultivation, mining in Tqvarchal/Tqvarcheli, and electricity production in Gal/i were introduced as well.

15. Resolution 13 notes that eleven hundred Georgian households are to be "added" to the existing Abkhaz kolkhozy in 1941.

16. See, for example, Resolution 1447 of the Council of People's Commissars of the USSR, "On organizational issues of resettlement policy under the Soviet People's Committee of the USSR," from September 14, 1939, which established the parameters of the resettlement policy in the republics of the Soviet Union (Sagarija, Achugba, and Pachulija 1992, 22–23).

17. For the distribution of the population by village, see Trier, Lohm, and Szakonyi 2010, 183–189.

18. Of the urban population of 23,168 people in early Soviet Abkhazia, only 1,065 were Abkhaz (Müller 2013, 230).

19. The name of the umbrella organization of the Abkhaz national movement Aidgylara (Unity) derives from the broader and contested term *aidgylara*, which is literally translated as "unity" and "solidarity" as a noun and "to be together," "to unite," and "to support each other" as a verb (Kaslandzija 2005, "Áidgylara"). The "norm of reciprocity" widely discussed in the literature on rebellion and civil war captures the meaning of this term.

20. Estimates of affiliation vary, with 20–40 percent Muslim and the remainder Christian (Clogg 2013, 205). But most Abkhaz report rituals around nature and death: "We do not have a name for our religion, but it exists. It is not simply paganism."

21. In line with traditional practice, many Abkhaz "continue to bury their dead in the yard" of their homes, for example.

22. In a letter to the Soviet authorities of 1977, the Abkhaz elite say that "there is no course or . . . textbook on the history of Abkhazia for either schools or universities" (see this and other letters of the period in Shamba and Lakoba 1995). One of the first textbooks on the history of Abkhazia for the school curriculum was published in 1991 (Lakoba 1991).

23. For example, the resolution of the Central Executive Committee of the Soviet Union "On the correct spelling of names of settlements," from August 16, 1936, stipulated a change from "Sukhum" to "Sukhumi" (Sagarija, Achugba, and Pachulija 1992, 488–489).

24. The differences between the Georgian and Abkhaz versions and spelling of proper names remain highly contentious. For example, no Abkhaz respondent referred to Tsandrypsh as Gantiadi, while it is the town's proper name in Georgia.

25. See the resolution of the Abkhaz Regional Committee of the Communist Party of Georgia "On measures to improve the quality of educational work in the schools of the Abkhaz ASSR," from March 13, 1945 (Sagarija, Achugba, and Pachulija 1992, 484–485).

The document stipulates changes to the existing school system, where first to fourth grades were taught in Abkhazian and fifth to tenth in Russian. This system was deemed to reduce the success rate among Abkhaz students, and the medium of language instruction was transferred to Georgian.

26. In contrast to later decades, reports on the 1940s–1950s reiterate the poor quality of teaching in the reorganized schools. Georgian teachers colleges were opened across Abkhazia in 1945–1946 to address this issue (Sagarija, Achugba, and Pachulija 1992, 485).

27. Following the resolution of the Presidium of the Central Committee of the Communist Party of the Soviet Union "On the errors and shortcomings in the work of the Central Committee of the Communist Party of Georgia," from July 10, 1956, the Council of Ministers of the Abkhaz ASSR and the Abkhaz Regional Committee adopted the resolutions "On the transfer of teaching in primary grades of the reorganized schools to the Abkhaz language" and "Measures to improve the teaching of the Abkhaz language and literature," from August 15 and 29, 1956 (Achugba and Achugba 2015, 314–315).

28. One downside, according to the Abkhaz, was that there were "no textbooks on chemistry, physics, et cetera, in Abkhazian."

29. Yet for Georgian respondents, "Georgianization of Abkhazia [was] just like Russification of all," a parallel process.

30. As a Georgian official explains, "In 1954, when the Abkhazian written language changed for the fifth time, from Georgian to Cyrillic, [as part of the efforts to address the effects of Georgianization], the Abkhaz resisted this, not because they wanted the Georgian script, but because [changing the alphabet once again meant that their language] could not develop."

31. In contrast, the view in Georgia is that the Abkhaz "always admitted that Gali was a Georgian district." In the 1980s, a displaced Georgian recalls, "everyone was recorded as Abkhaz. When I was fifteen, they asked if I wanted to be recorded as Abkhaz. I said my parents were Georgian. Why would I say I am Abkhaz? The same was when I was getting my passport." Hence, Georgian respondents conclude, "Gali historically was ruled by either the Abkhaz or Georgians, and the border was often moved. People who lived between the two rivers [Galidzga and Ingur/i] identified themselves differently based on who ruled then."

32. The *Great Soviet Encyclopedia* of 1949 calls the Abkhaz "ancient inhabitants" of this territory (Maryhuba 1993, 16). However, "according to the Georgian history that was created then," a Georgian official says, "if you reject that you are Georgian [in Abkhazia and insist that you are Abkhaz], then you are a resettler and not an aboriginal [because only Georgians were seen as aboriginal in that version of history]. This created discontent among the Abkhaz."

33. The resolution of the Bureau of the Georgian Central Committee of the Communist Party "On the wrong debate in 'Mnatobi' on P. Ingorokva's 'George Merchule,'" from April 12, 1957, criticized the publication (Sagarija, Achugba, and Pachulija 1992, 561).

34. Abkhaz letters to Moscow raise this issue every decade. In the 1970s, for example, Abkhaz activists report that only 25.6 percent of kolkhozy directors and 8.4 percent of engineers were Abkhaz, while 74.4 percent and 44.7 percent, respectively, were Georgian (Chumalov 1995, 19–34).

4. PREWAR CONFLICT IDENTITIES

1. Müller (2013, 236) describes this resettlement vividly as "Kartvelians [Georgians, Mingrelians, and other speakers of Kartvelian languages] being, often against their will, dumped in truckloads by Beria's henchmen in the Abkhazian countryside."

2. The only university in Abkhazia, the Sukhum/i Pedagogical Institute, which became Abkhaz State University in 1979, was in the capital (Kemoklidze 2016, 135). Labor-based migration was common within and outside of Abkhazia.

3. Driven by the Soviet ideology of the friendship of peoples, intergroup integration was institutionalized through the state's efforts to increase national representation of the republic in education and employment and through the quotas for the Abkhaz as the titular group of Abkhazia introduced in the later Soviet period (Nodia and Scholtbach 2006, 9).

4. In 1989, the population of the Gagra district was 28 percent Georgian, 24 percent Russian, and 9 percent Abkhaz; the remainder was a mix of the population.

5. The Gudauta district to the west of Sukhum/i had an Abkhaz majority; the Sukhum/i district was Georgian-dominated.

6. Tqvarchal/Tqvarcheli was Abkhaz-dominated, while neighboring Gulripsh/i, Ochamchira/e, and Gal/i were largely Georgian.

7. "The Georgian communist leadership . . . tried to avoid further conflicts by making the Abkhazian question taboo. . . . Forbidding public discussion of the Abkhazian question, however, did not prevent it" (Coppieters 2002, 96).

8. Respondents note that "there were [few] fights in Gudauta . . . because [most] of the population there was Abkhaz."

9. On perestroika reforms, see Beissinger 2002; Cornell 2000; Nodia and Scholtbach 2006; Matsaberidze 2011.

10. The general perception among the Abkhaz was that "they sent shoemakers, market workers who could count to one hundred, to become teachers." "Georgian teachers had three months' training . . . , to have the Georgian language [introduced as a subject] in all village schools," a de facto Ministry of Culture representative explains.

11. Over time, Russian thus "replac[ed] Georgian . . . as the second language for the Abkhaz" (Cornell 2000, 133).

12. Letter texts of 1937–1953 and 1947–1989 can be found in Sagarija, Achugba, and Pachulija 1992 and Maryhuba 1994, respectively. Earlier materials are available in Kacharava 1959. Achugba 2016 provides a chronology.

13. The resolution of the Presidium of the Central Committee of July 10, 1956, "On the errors and shortcomings in the work of the Central Committee of the Communist Party of Georgia," blamed Beria for the problems of Georgianization.

14. The Abkhaz view this unrest as part of their struggle against Georgianization, yet in Georgia it is seen as a reaction to the anti-Russian protests in Tbilisi, such as the March 1956 events against de-Stalinization (Kemoklidze 2016, 130).

15. See the resolution of the Central Committee of July 1, 1978, "On the future development of the economy and culture of the Abkhaz Autonomous Soviet Socialist Republic," in Maryhuba 1994, 275–278.

16. On the importance of intellectuals in Georgian-Abkhaz conflict, see also Coppieters 2002.

17. The State Program of the Georgian Language adopted in November 1988 was one result of this mobilization. It aimed to make Georgian the state language, including in Georgia's autonomous republics, which grossly angered the Abkhaz.

18. See the report to the Supreme Council on the situation in Abkhazia, "Development of the Sociopolitical Situation in the Abkhaz ASSR in the Period from December 1988 to Now," in Sagarija 2002, 23–38.

19. Aidgylara to Gorbachev, telegram, March 25, 1989, available in Lezhava 1997, 226–227, Chumalov 1995, 154–155.

20. See report to the Supreme Council, in Sagarija 2002, 23–38.

21. See report to the Supreme Council, in Sagarija 2002, 23–38.

22. See "Demands of a Group of Students of the Georgian SSR Georgian by Nationality," in Sagarija 2002, 16–17.

23. See "Our Demands," in Sagarija 2002, 18–20. See also Cornell 2000, 148–149; Zverev 1996, pt. 3.

24. See, for example, letters to Gorbachev of June 23, 1989, V. A. Mihajlov of June 24, 1989, and the Central Committee and High Council of the Soviet Union of June 27, 1989, in Kvarchija 2011, 219–220; Chumalov 1995, 170–171, 176–179.

25. See "On results of the investigation of events that took place in Sukhumi, other cities, and regions of the Abkhaz ASSR 15–16 July 1989," in Sagarija 2002, 188–225.

26. "Zviadi" refers to Zviad Gamsakhurdia.

27. See "On results of the investigation of events that took place in Sukhumi, other cities, and regions of the Abkhaz ASSR 15–16 July 1989," in Sagarija 2002, 188–225; "Reference to chronicles of events of 15–17 July 1989 in the Gali district," by the police, in Sagarija 2002, 10–13; and resolution of the Presidium of the Supreme Council of the Abkhaz ASSR of July 15, 1989, "On the significant aggravation of interethnic relations in the Abkhaz ASSR due to illicit attempts to form in Sukhumi a branch of TSU [Tbilisi State University]," in Chumalov 1995, 190–193.

28. See the resolutions of the Supreme Council of Abkhazia "On the introduction in the cities of Sukhumi and Ochamchira and the Gulripshi region of the Abkhaz ASSR of the special curfew provisions," July 16, 1989; "On the events in the Abkhaz ASSR," July 17, 1989; and "On the introduction of a special regime of behavior of citizens throughout the territory of the Abkhaz ASSR," July 18, 1989, in Sagarija 2002, 45–50.

29. See National Forum of Abkhazia to Central Committee, telegram, September 1989, in Chumalov 1995, 210.

30. Hunger strikers sent a telegram to Gorbachev on September 14, 1989, and an appeal to the Supreme Soviet on September 25, 1989, seeking the formation of a Soviet commission to investigate the July events. See texts in Chumalov 1995, 207–208.

31. Aidgylara's Russian-language *Edinenie* (Unity) newspaper features photographs of miners during the underground sit-down strike in Tqvarchal/Tqvarcheli and hunger strikers in Gagra. The photograph of the miners' strike shows ten men sitting in mining gear with the banner "My za ravnopravie nacij" (We are for the equal rights of nations) in the background. The photograph of hunger strikers shows seven men sitting and reclining on mattresses and throws by the walls of the Rustaveli Cinema. Author's personal archive, *Edinenie* (newspaper of the National Forum of Abkhazia), no. 1 (October 25, 1989).

32. See Aidgylara's second declaration and resolution of February 3, 1990, in Chumalov 1995, 218–220.

33. See resolutions "On changing the designation" and "On the transitional period," in Lezhava 1997, 284.

34. The legality of this action is debated. Svante E. Cornell (2000, 170) argues that "a quorum of two thirds was needed for such a decision, which was not the case as a simple majority had been present."

35. See the resolutions of the Supreme Council of Abkhazia "On the deployment of military units, institutions of border and internal troops, naval forces and amending their functioning on the territory of Abkhazia" and "On the formation under the chairman of the Supreme Council of Abkhazia of the Provisional Council for the coordination of activities and resubordination of military and police units deployed in Abkhazia," in Volhonskij, Zaharov, and Silaev 2008, 120–121. On the formation of the SRIF, see also Pachulija 1997; Avidzba 2008, 2013; Khodzhaa 2009; Achugba 2011.

36. Supreme Council resolution of March 31, 1991, "On conscription for military service and measures for compliance with the law 'On general military duties' on the territory of the Republic of Abkhazia," in Volhonskij, Zaharov, and Silaev 2008, 124.

37. Video footage of Georgia's Independence Day celebration at the Gagra Stadium on May 26, 1990, from the author's archive, shows one episode, in which over thirty men wearing green Soviet uniforms with helmets and holding shields form a line and separate

people toward opposite sides of a bus with two Menshevik flags on the outside. The committee of the Gagra union Abrskyl states in an open letter to members of the Bureau of Regional Party Committee of Abkhazia of June 23, 1990, that the event "did not reach tragic consequences thanks to the units of the [internal] troops of the USSR" (Gyts 2014, 208). This letter, which was at first banned but later published in the newspaper *Avangard* (Avant-garde), sparked criticism from local authorities and a discussion was published subsequently in *Avangard* (Achugba and Achugba 2015, 462–468).

5. FROM UNCERTAINLY TO MOBILIZATION IN FOUR DAYS

1. My respondents' location during the Georgian advance could have been different than it was at the interview. This distinction is important given the territorial control in the east and west that was established at the war's onset.

2. Nordstrom (2004, 6–8) observes a similar dynamic in the Sri Lanka riots of 1983, for example, where she "watched thousands of people act and react to the events at hand, each in his or her own unique way.... No one knew the violence was about to erupt as they said goodbye to one another [after attending a religious festival the night before] and began their journeys home."

3. There was disbelief even among the top Abkhaz leadership. A reservist in the east who witnessed Georgian tanks and air force called Ardzinba's office, but was told "that Vladislav Ardzinba spoke to Eduard Shevardnadze on the phone, and that the entry of the Georgian State Council troops is impossible" (interview in Khodzhaa 2003, 62).

4. Kuran (1991, 8) describes a similar reaction to the revolution of 1989 in Eastern Europe: "the revolution came as a surprise even to leading 'dissidents.'"

5. Due to the challenges of field research in the east of Abkhazia, most responses reported for this area are from the interviews collected by Ruslan Khodzhaa (2003, 2006, 2009).

6. Local and external sources document these forms of violence. See, for example, HRW 1995; Argun 1994; Voronov, Florenskij, and Shutova 1993.

7. As Georgia's Provisional Military Council declared Soviet laws null in 1992 and reinstated its 1921 constitution, the Abkhaz restored the 1925 constitution, which stated that Abkhazia "was not part of Georgia" (Nodia 1998, 31). This act was not supported by Georgian deputies of the Supreme Council of Abkhazia and was not recognized in Georgia.

8. The Abkhaz case departs from the common pattern identified in the literature where the threat from one group is framed as requiring a response from another. Ardzinba stressed the threat and the need to mobilize among the population as a whole, rather than its Abkhaz part. Later, on August 24, the council relocated to Gudauta in central Abkhazia and called on local Georgians to maintain neutrality to prevent their participation in the war: "Only in this case will the moral responsibly of the Georgian population for the tragedy in Abkhazia be removed" (Ardzinba 2004, 40).

9. During my research in Abkhazia, I did not have access to individuals who defected to the Georgian side in the war, but relied on reports of other researchers, particularly Khodzhaa 2006, and respondents who adopted other roles during the war.

10. On civilian self-protection strategies in civil war, see Baines and Paddon 2012; Barter 2014.

11. Those injured often built new networks in postwar Abkhazia to reflect their distinct wartime experiences.

6. FROM MOBILIZATION TO FIGHTING

1. The scare that "seven thousand Chechens gathered around Abkhazia," fighters say, appears to have contributed to this outcome.

2. "Although Abkhazian veterans claim that there were only 300 combatants on their side, it is more realistic that their numbers exceeded 500" after the taking of Gagra (Billingsley 2013, 155).

3. Human Rights Watch (HRW 1995, 5n1) records over 4,040 deaths and 8,000 injuries on the Abkhaz side in the war, most incurred after October 1992. Over 200 foreign fighters from the North Caucasus and over 200 from Russia were among these casualties (Khalidov 2014, 56).

7. POSTWAR ABKHAZIA

1. In Georgia, the borderline is called the "administrative border" or "administrative boundary line" to define Abkhazia as an autonomous republic of Georgia regardless of the outcome of the 1992–1993 war and Abkhazia's recognition by Russia in 2008. In Abkhazia, it is seen as the state border.

2. UN Security Council, *Report of the Secretary-General's Fact-Finding Mission to Investigate Human Rights Violations in Abkhazia, Republic of Georgia*, S/26795, annex, para. 36 (November 17, 1993), https://undocs.org/S/26795. On the importance of demographic changes, see Nodia 1998; Zürcher 2007.

3. The agreement specified that displaced persons/refugees could return in principle, except those who were guilty of war crimes, crimes against humanity, or serious nonpolitical crimes committed in the context of the conflict or who were serving in armed formations and preparing to fight in Abkhazia again. See UN Security Council, *Declaration on Measures for a Political Settlement of the Georgian/Abkhaz Conflict Signed on April 4, 1994*, S/1994/397, annex II (April 5, 1994), https://undocs.org/S/1994/397. For discussion, see Gegeshidze 2008.

4. The population of Abkhazia dropped from 525,000 in 1989 to 215,000 in the 2000s (Upravlenie 2010).

5. The average salary was 84.5 rubles per month in 1996, enough to buy up to two kilograms of produce (Upravlenie 2002).

6. On the economic sanctions and other forms of isolation used against Abkhazia, see Coppieters 2000; Gegeshidze 2008.

7. Murders and attempted murders dropped from 156 in 1995 to an average of 50 per year in the 2000s, and robberies fell from 261 in 1994 to an average of 121 per year in the 2000s (Upravlenie, 2003 and 2010).

8. Car crashes remain a significant problem, with similar occurrences across the postwar period, from 69 deaths and 282 injuries in 136 accidents in 1994 to 66 deaths and 232 injuries in 152 accidents in 2016, as reported by the de facto Ministry of Internal Affairs of Abkhazia (Ministerstvo vnutrennih del Respubliki Abhazija 2016).

9. See Mikhelidze and Pirozzi 2008. On citizens' peace initiatives, see Garb 1999; Gurgulia 1999; Nan 1999.

10. For the Abkhaz and Georgian positions on this issue, see Kvarchelia 1999; Nodia 1999. See also HRW 2011.

11. While the dominant position is that Georgians who lived in Abkhazia and participated in the 1992–1993 war should not return, many express regret for this outcome. I explore themes of responsibility, betrayal, regret, and violence in Shesterinina 2019.

12. One private memorial I describe in my field notes is an arrangement on an ornate carved wood chest of drawers of six photographs of a lost son as a student, a young professional, and a fighter in a uniform depicted alone and together with friends during the war. The black and white and color photographs of varying sizes, two of which are framed, are surrounded and supported by vases of artificial flowers.

13. The UN-sponsored Geneva talks began in October 1993 and stalled over the issues of the return of displaced Georgians and the political status of Abkhazia. In April 1994,

Shevardnadze "ceded to Abkhaz demands that no Georgians actively involved in last year's fighting should be permitted to return," and the gradual process of return started, with significant difficulties imposed by the Abkhaz side (Fuller 1994b). The status of Abkhazia remains contested up until today. For further discussion, see J. Cohen 1999; Coppieters, Darchiashvili, and Akaba 2000; Cornell 2000; Nodia 2004; Hewitt 2013.

14. This disintegration of the security apparatus and internal political fragmentation reflects the broader problems of state weakness in Georgia at the time (Darchiashvili and Nodia 2003, 18; Nodia 1998; 2004, 12; Zürcher 2007, 147).

15. Note that in March 1994, the Abkhaz briefly occupied two villages in Georgia during a search and capture operation.

16. The postwar standing force included up to 2,000 regular soldiers and an "estimated 15,000 to 25,000" reservist contingent (ICG 2006, 14). See Pachulija 2010, 358–506; IISS 2005, 423; Matveeva and Hiscock 2003, 106.

17. See S/1994/397, annex I. On Russian peacekeeping strategies in Abkhazia, see Lynch 1999. See also ICG 2007.

18. I discuss local Georgian collaboration with both sides and the locals' fear experienced as a result in Shesterinina 2015.

19. See UN Security Council, *Report of the Secretary-General, concerning the Situation in Abkhazia, Georgia*, S/1995/10, para. 28 (January 6, 1995), https://undocs.org/S/1995/10; Khintba 2003; Lynch 2004; Markedonov 2008. See also Shesterinina 2015.

20. See the Gagra Protocol on Ceasefire, Separation of Armed Formations and Guarantees on Inadmissibility of Forcible Activities, in Volhonskij, Zaharov, and Silaev 2008, 385.

21. Georgian officials acknowledged the involvement of Abkhazia's government in exile, units of the Georgian internal troops, and the former Mkhedrioni in the fighting (Fuller 1998c; Krutikov 1998).

22. The Georgian prosecutor general, Djamlet Babilashvili, reported that "35 Georgian civilians and 17 Interior Ministry troops were killed . . . and 1,695 Georgian homes burned" (Fuller 1998d).

23. Shevardnadze integrated Kvitsiani into official Georgian structures, and his militia participated in the fighting against the Russian and Abkhaz forces together with Chechen rebels who crossed into Kodor/i in 2001 (Marten 2012, 89–90).

24. On the shift in focus from Abkhazia to South Ossetia, see Popjanevski 2009, 149. See Cornell and Starr 2009 on the events of 2008 more broadly. The Georgian intention to capture breakaway territories by force in 2008 is contested.

25. Almost all locals fled Kodor/i and only gradually returned thereafter. See Marten 2012, 97; UN Security Council, *Report of the Secretary-General Pursuant to Security Council Resolutions 1808 (2008), 1839 (2008) and 1866 (2009)*, S/2009/254, para. 40 (May 18, 2009), https://undocs.org/S/2009/254.

26. According to official Abkhaz statistics, one Abkhaz fighter was killed and seven were injured (Pachulija 2010, 404).

27. Along with the Russian Federation, Nicaragua, Venezuela, Nauru, and, most recently, Syria recognize the independence of Abkhazia as of 2020, while Vanuatu and Tuvalu withdrew their recognition in 2013 and 2014, respectively.

28. On September 17, 2008, Russia and Abkhazia signed the Agreement on Friendship, Cooperation and Mutual Assistance, followed by agreements on joint efforts in border defense (April 30, 2009), military cooperation (September 15, 2009), and a Russian military base in Abkhazia (February 17, 2010), among others, strengthening Russia's presence in the area.

29. On Abkhazia's postwar politics in general, see Bakke et al. 2014; O'Loughlin, Kolossov, and Toal 2011; Caspersen 2011. On pluralism and the competitiveness of presiden-

tial and parliamentary elections in particular, see Ó Beacháin 2012. On gender representation, see Ó Beacháin Stefanczak and Connolly 2015. On the economy, see Prelz Oltramonti 2015.

30. Prospective presidential candidates must be of Abkhaz origin, according to the Constitution of Abkhazia, and the Parliament is overwhelmingly Abkhaz, with a small number of Armenian, Georgian, Russian, and other candidates (Ó Beacháin 2012, 167, 173). On the postwar demographic heterogeneity of Abkhazia, see Trier, Lohm, and Szakonyi 2010.

References

Achugba, Tejmuraz. 2003. *Otechestvennaja vojna Abhazii i "gruzinskie bezhency."* *Dokumenty i materialy*. Sukhumi: Abhazskij institut gumanitarnyh issledovanij im. D. I. Gulia.
——. 2010. *Jetnicheskaja istorija abhazov XIX–XX vv. Jetnopoliticheskie i migracionnye aspekty*. Sukhumi: Abhazskij institut gumanitarnyh issledovanij im. D. I. Gulia.
——. 2011. "V. G. Ardzinba i voprosy gosudarstvennogo suvereniteta Abhazii." In *Materialy pervoj mezhdunarodnoj nauchnoj konferencii, posvjashhennoj 65-letiju V. G. Ardzinba*, 55–62. Sukhumi: Abhazskij institut gumanitarnyh issledovanij im. D. I. Gulia.
——. 2016. *Istorija Abhazii v datah: Spravochnik. Izdanie vtoroe, dopolnennoe*. Sukhumi: Dom pechati.
Achugba, Tejmuraz, and Daur Achugba. 2015. *Stranicy gruzino-abhazskoj informacionnoj vojny. Dokumenty i materialy*. Sukhumi: Abhazskij institut gumanitarnyh issledovanijim. D. I. Gulia.
Aidgylara. 1990. Protocol of October 30, 1990. Branch archive, Gagra, Abkhazia.
Akaba, Lili. 2007. "Tradicionnye religioznye verovanija." In *Abhazy*, edited by Yuri Anchabadze and Yuri Argun, 356–366. Sukhumi: Abhazskij institut gumanitarnyh issledovanij im. D. I. Gulia.
Almeida, Paul. 2019. *Social Movements: The Structure of Collective Mobilization*. Oakland: University of California Press.
Amkuab, Guram, and Tatiana Illarionova. 1992. *Abhazija: Hronika neob"javlennoj vojny*. Sukhumi: Press-sluzhba VS Respubliki Abhazija.
Anchabadze, Yuri. 1998. "Georgia and Abkhazia: The Hard Road to Agreement." In *Georgians and Abkhazians: The Search for a Peace Settlement*, edited by Bruno Coppieters, Ghia Nodia, and Yuri Anchabadze, 71–79. Cologne: Bundesinstitut für Ostwissenschaftliche und Internationale Studien.
——. 2013. "History: The Modern Period." In *The Abkhazians: A Handbook*, edited by George B. Hewitt, 132–146. New York: Routledge.
Anchabadze, Zurab. 2011. *Izbrannye trudy v dvux tomax. Tom 2, Ocherk jetnicheskoj istorii abhazskogo naroda. Stat'i*. Sukhumi: Abhazskij institut gumanitarnyh issledovanij im D. I. Gulia.
Ardzinba, Vladislav. 2004. *Te surovye dni. Hronika Otechestvennoj vojny naroda Abhazii 1992–1993 gg. v dokumentah*. Sukhumi: Dom pechati.
Argun, Aleksej. 1994. *Abhazija: Ad v raju ... (Besedy s pogibshim synom Batalom)*. Sukhumi: Alashara.
Arjona, Ana. 2016. *Rebelocracy: Social Order in the Colombian Civil War*. New York: Cambridge University Press.
Aspinall, Edward. 2009. *Islam and Nation: Separatist Rebellion in Aceh, Indonesia*. Stanford, CA: Stanford University Press.
Avidzba, Aslan. 2008. *Otechestvennaja vojna (1992–1993 gg.): Voprosy voenno-politicheskoj istorii Abhazii*. Sukhumi: Abhazskij institut gumanitarnyh issledovanij im. D. I. Gulia.

——. 2012. *Abhazija i Gruzija: Zavtra byla vojna (O abhazo-gruzinskih otnoshenijah v 1988–1992 gg.)*. Sukhumi: Abhazskij institut gumanitarnyh issledovanij im. D. I. Gulia.
——. 2013. *Problemy voenno-politicheskoj istorii Otechestvennoj vojny v Abhazii (1992–1993 gg.)*. Sukhumi: Abhazskij institut gumanitarnyh issledovanij im. D. I. Gulia.
Baczko, Adam, Gilles Dorronsoro, and Arthur Quesnay. 2013. "Mobilisations par délibération et crise polarisante." [Mobilizations as a Result of Deliberation and Polarising Crisis: The Peaceful Protests in Syria (2011)]. *Revue française de science politique* 63 (5): 1–25.
Baczko, Adam, Arthur Quesnay, and Gilles Dorronsoro. 2017. *Civil War in Syria: Mobilization and Competing Social Orders*. Cambridge: Cambridge University Press.
Baev, Pavel. 2003. "Civil Wars in Georgia: Corruption Breeds Violence." In *Potentials of Disorder: Explaining Conflict and Stability in the Caucasus and in the Former Yugoslavia*, edited by Christoph Zürcher and Jan Koehler, 127–144. Manchester: Manchester University Press.
Baines, Erin, and Emily Paddon. 2012. "'This Is How We Survived': Civilian Agency and Humanitarian Protection." *Security Dialogue* 43 (3): 231–247.
Bakke, Kristin M., John O'Loughlin, Gerard Toal, and Michael D. Ward. 2014. "Convincing State-Builders? Disaggregating Internal Legitimacy in Abkhazia." *International Studies Quarterly* 58 (3): 591–607.
Barter, Shane. 2014. *Civilian Strategy in Civil Wars: Insights from Indonesia, Thailand, and the Philippines*. New York: Palgrave Macmillan.
Bas, Muhammet A., and Robert J. Schub. 2017. "Theoretical and Empirical Approaches to Uncertainty and Conflict in International Relations." In *Oxford Research Encyclopedia of Politics*, 1–35. Oxford: Oxford University Press. http://oxfordre.com/politics/view/10.1093/acrefore/9780190228637.001.0001/acrefore-9780190228637-e-537.
Bayard de Volo, Lorraine. 2013. "Participant Observation, Politics, and Power Relations: Nicaraguan Mothers and U.S. Casino Waitresses." In *Ethnography: What Immersion Contributes to the Study of Power*, edited by Edward Schatz, 217–236. Chicago: University of Chicago Press.
Bebia, Ekaterina. 1997. *Dorogami geroev*. Kiev: VIR.
——. 2011. *Zolotoj pamjatnik Abhazii–Bzypta*. Ankara: Korza Yayincilik.
Beissinger, Mark R. 2002. *Nationalist Mobilization and the Collapse of the Soviet State*. Cambridge: Cambridge University Press.
Best, Jacqueline. 2008. "Ambiguity, Uncertainty, and Risk: Rethinking Indeterminacy." *International Political Sociology* 2 (4): 355–374.
Bgazhba, Oleg, and Stanislav Lakoba. 2007. *Istorija Abhazii. S drevnejshih vremen do nashih dnej*. Sukhumi: Alasharbaga.
Billingsley, Dodge. 2013. "Military Aspects of the War: The Battle for Gagra." In *The Abkhazians: A Handbook*, edited by George B. Hewitt, 147–156. New York: Routledge.
Blattman, Christopher, and Edward Miguel. 2010. "Civil War." *Journal of Economic Literature* 48 (1): 3–57.
Brojdo, Anna. 2008. *Projavlenija jetnopsihologicheskih osobennostej abhazov v hode Otechestvennoj vojny naroda Abhazii 1992–1993 godov*. Moscow: RGTEU.
Brown, Paul B. 2003. "The Senior Leadership Cadre of the Geheime Feldpolizei, 1939–1945." *Holocaust and Genocide Studies* 17 (2): 278–304.
Browning, Christopher R. 1993. *Ordinary Men: Reserve Police Battalion 101 and the Final Solution in Poland*. New York: HarperCollins.
Caspersen, Nina. 2011. "Democracy, Nationalism and (Lack of) Sovereignty: The Complex Dynamics of Democratisation in Unrecognised States." *Nations and Nationalism* 17 (2): 337–356.

Cederman, Lars-Erik, Kristian Skrede Gleditsch, and Halvard Buhaug. 2013. *Inequality, Grievances, and Civil War*. New York: Cambridge University Press.
Chenoweth, Erica, and Adria Lawrence, eds. 2010. *Rethinking Violence: States and Nonstate Actors in Conflict*. Cambridge, MA: MIT Press.
Cherkezija, Leonid. 2003. *Tkuarchal: 413 dnej blokady*. Sukhumi: Alasharbaga.
Chirikba, Viacheslav A. 1998. "The Georgian-Abkhazian Conflict: In Search for Ways Out." In *Georgians and Abkhazians: The Search for a Peace Settlement*, edited by Bruno Coppieters, Ghia Nodia, and Yuri Anchabadze, 45–55. Cologne: Bundesinstitut für Ostwissenschaftliche und Internationale Studien.
Chumalov, Mihail, ed. 1995. *Abhazskij uzel: Dokumenty i materialy po jetnicheskomu konfliktu v Abhazii*. Tom 2, *Narodnyj forum Abhazii "Aidgylara" i ego sojuzniki (1989–1990 gg.)*. Moscow: Institut jetnologii i antropologii RAN.
Clausewitz, Carl von. 1976. *On War*. Edited and translated by Michael Howard and Peter Paret. Princeton, NJ: Princeton University Press.
Clogg, Rachel. 2013. "Religion." In *The Abkhazians: A Handbook*, edited by George B. Hewitt, 205–217. New York: Routledge.
Cohen, Dara Kay. 2016. *Rape during Civil War*. Ithaca, NY: Cornell University Press.
Cohen, Jonathan, ed. 1999. "A Question of Sovereignty: The Georgia-Abkhazia Peace Process." Special issue, *Accord*, no. 7.
Collins, Randall. 2008. *Violence: A Micro-sociological Theory*. Princeton, NJ: Princeton University Press.
Coppieters, Bruno. 1999. "The Roots of the Conflict." In "A Question of Sovereignty: The Georgia-Abkhazia Peace Process," edited by Jonathan Cohen. Special issue, *Accord*, no. 7: 14–19.
———. 2000. "Western Security Policies and the Georgian-Abkhazian Conflict." In *Federal Practice: Exploring Alternatives for Georgia and Abkhazia*, edited by Bruno Coppieters, David Darchiashvili, and Natella Akaba, 21–58. Brussels: VUB University Press.
———. 2002. "In Defence of the Homeland: Intellectuals and the Georgian-Abkhazian Conflict." In *Secession, History and the Social Sciences*, edited by Bruno Coppieters and Michel Huysseune, 89–116. Brussels: VUB University Press.
Coppieters, Bruno, David Darchiashvili, and Natella Akaba, eds. 2000. *Federal Practice: Exploring Alternatives for Georgia and Abkhazia*. Brussels: VUB University Press.
Cornell, Svante E. 2000. *Small Nations and Great Powers: A Study of Ethnopolitical Conflict in the Caucasus*. Richmond, UK: Curzon Press.
Cornell, Svante E., and S. Frederick Starr, eds. 2009. *The Guns of August 2008: Russia's War in Georgia*. Armonk, NY: M. E. Sharpe.
Dale, Catherine. 1997. "The Dynamics and Challenges of Ethnic Cleansing: The Georgia-Abkhazia Case." *Refugee Survey Quarterly* 16 (3): 77–109.
Darchiashvili, David. 1997. *The Army-Building and Security Problems in Georgia*. Tbilisi: Caucasian Institute.
———. 2003. "Power Structures in Georgia." In *Building Democracy in Georgia: Power Structures, the Weak State Syndrome and Corruption in Georgia*, Discussion Paper 5, edited by David Darchiashvili and Ghia Nodia, 8–15. Stockholm: International Institute for Democracy and Electoral Assistance.
Darchiashvili, David, and Ghia Nodia. 2003. "The Weak State Syndrome and Corruption." In *Building Democracy in Georgia: Power Structures, the Weak State Syndrome and Corruption in Georgia*, Discussion Paper 5, edited by David Darchiashvili and Ghia Nodia, 16–22. Stockholm: International Institute for Democracy and Electoral Assistance.
Das, Veena. 2007. *Life and Words: Violence and the Descent into the Ordinary*. Berkeley: University of California Press.

Davenport, Christian, David A. Armstrong II, and Mark I. Lichbach. 2008. "From Mountains to Movements: Dissent, Repression, and Escalation to Civil War." Unpublished manuscript.

Davidson, Shamai. 1985. "Group Formation and Its Significance in the Nazi Concentration Camps." *Israeli Journal of Psychiatry and Related Sciences* 22 (1–2): 41–50.

Dbar, Roman. 2013. "Geography and the Environment." In *The Abkhazians: A Handbook*, edited by George B. Hewitt, 23–36. New York: Routledge.

Derluguian, Georgi M. 2005. *Bourdieu's Secret Admirer in the Caucasus: A World-System Biography*. Chicago: University of Chicago Press.

de Waal, Thomas. 2011. "Abkhazia's Archive: Fire of War, Ashes of History." *Open Democracy*, October 22. https://www.opendemocracy.net/democracy-caucasus/abkhazia_archive_4018.jsp.

Diani, Mario, and Doug McAdam, eds. 2003. *Social Movements and Networks: Relational Approaches to Collective Action*. New York: Oxford University Press.

Driscoll, Jesse. 2015. *Warlords and Coalition Politics in Post-Soviet States*. New York: Cambridge University Press.

Dzidzarija, Georgij. 1963. *Ocherki istorii Abhazii: 1910–1921*. Tbilisi: Sabchota Sakartvelo.

———. 1981. *Kiaraz*. Sukhumi: Alashara.

———. 1982. *Mahadzhirstvo i problemy istorii Abhazii XIX stoletija*. Sukhumi: Alashara.

Fearon, James D. 1995. "Rationalist Explanations for War." *International Organization* 49 (3): 379–414.

Fearon, James D., and David D. Laitin. 2003. "Ethnicity, Insurgency, and Civil War." *American Political Science Review* 97 (1): 75–90.

Fearon, James D., and Alexander Wendt. 2002. "Rationalism v. Constructivism: A Skeptical View." In *Handbook of International Relations*, edited by Walter Carlsnaes, Thomas Risse, and Beth Simmons, 52–72. London: Sage.

Finkel, Evgeny. 2017. *Ordinary Jews: Choice and Survival during the Holocaust*. Princeton, NJ: Princeton University Press.

Finnström, Sverker. 2008. *Living with Bad Surroundings: War, History, and Existential Uncertainty in Northern Uganda*. Durham, NC: Duke University Press.

Francis, Celine. 2011. *Conflict Resolution and Status: The Case of Georgia and Abkhazia, 1989–2008*. Brussels: VUB University Press.

Fujii, Lee Ann. 2009. *Killing Neighbors: Webs of Violence in Rwanda*. Ithaca, NY: Cornell University Press.

———. 2010. "Shades of Truth and Lies: Interpreting Testimonies of War and Violence." *Journal of Peace Research* 47 (2): 231–241.

———. 2012. "Research Ethics 101: Dilemmas and Responsibilities." *PS: Political Science and Politics* 45 (4): 717–723.

Fuller, Liz. 1992. "Georgian National Guard Launches Hunt for Hostages." *Radio Free Europe/Radio Liberty News Briefs*, no. 155 (August 14). http://www.friends-partners.org/friends/news/omri/1992/08/920814.html(opt,mozilla,unix,english,,new).

———. 1993. "Update: Georgia and Abkhazia." *Radio Free Europe/Radio Liberty News Briefs*, no. 201 (October 19). http://www.friends-partners.org/friends/news/omri/1993/10/931019.html(opt,mozilla,unix,english,,new).

———. 1994a. "Abkhaz-Georgian Talks Deadlocked." *Radio Free Europe/Radio News Briefs Liberty*, no. 40 (February 28). http://www.friends-partners.org/friends/news/omri/1994/02/940228.html(opt,mozilla,unix,english,,new).

———. 1994b. "Repatriation of Georgian Refugees Gets Under Way." *Radio Free Europe/Radio Liberty News Briefs*, no. 195 (October 13). http://www.friends-partners.org/friends/news/omri/1994/04/940405.html(opt,mozilla,unix,english,,new).

———. 1998a. "Abkhaz Expel Georgian Guerrillas from Gali." *Radio Free Europe/Radio Liberty Newsline*, May 27. http://www.friends-partners.org/friends/news/omri/1998/05/980527I.html(opt,mozilla,unix,english,,new).
———. 1998b. "Abkhaz Offensive Ruins Peace Prospects." *Radio Free Europe/Radio Liberty Newsline*, May 28. http://www.friends-partners.org/friends/news/omri/1998/05/9805 28I.html(opt,mozilla,unix,english,,new).
———. 1998c. "Controversial Georgian Paramilitary Organization Still Active." *Radio Free Europe/Radio Liberty Newsline*, May 28. http://www.friends-partners.org/friends/news/omri/1998/05/980528I.html(opt,mozilla,unix,english,,new).
———. 1998d. "Two More Civilians Killed in Abkhazia." *Radio Free Europe/Radio Liberty Newsline*, June 8. http://www.friends-partners.org/friends/news/omri/1998/06/9806 08I.html(opt,mozilla,unix,english,,new).
———. 2006. "Are Georgian Forces Leaving Kodori?" *Radio Free Europe/Radio Liberty Newsline*, July 31. https://www.rferl.org/a/1143684.html.
Gachechiladze, Revaz. 1998. "Geographical Background to a Settlement of the Conflict in Abkhazia." In *Georgians and Abkhazians: The Search for a Peace Settlement*, edited by Bruno Coppieters, Ghia Nodia, and Yuri Anchabadze, 56–70. Cologne: Bundesinstitut für Ostwissenschaftliche und Internationale Studien.
Garb, Paula, ed. 1999. *Rol' Neofitsial'noj Diplomatii v Mirotvorcheskom Protsesse. Materialy gruzino-abhazskoj konferentsii mart, 1999, g. Sochi*. [The Role of Unofficial Diplomacy in the Peace Process. Materials of the Georgian-Abkhaz Conference March, 1999, Sochi]. Irvine: University of California.
Gates, Scott. 2002. "Recruitment and Allegiance: The Microfoundations of Rebellion." *Journal of Conflict Resolution* 46 (1): 111–130.
Gegeshidze, Archil. 2008. "The Isolation of Abkhazia: A Failed Policy or an Opportunity?" In "Powers of Persuasion: Incentives, Sanctions and Conditionality in Peacemaking," edited by Aaron Griffiths and Catherine Barnes. Special issue, *Accord*, no. 19: 68–70.
George, Alexander L., and Andrew Bennett. 2005. *Case Studies and Theory Development in the Social Sciences*. Cambridge, MA: MIT Press.
Gould, Roger V. 1991. "Multiple Networks and Mobilization in the Paris Commune, 1871." *American Sociological Review* 56 (6): 716–729.
———. 1993. "Trade Cohesion, Class Unity, and Urban Insurrection: Artisanal Activism in the Paris Commune." *American Journal of Sociology* 98 (4): 721–754.
———. 1995. *Insurgent Identities: Class, Community, and Protest in Paris from 1848 to the Commune*. Chicago: University of Chicago Press.
Granovetter, Mark S. 1985. "Economic Action and Social Structure: The Problem of Embeddedness." *American Journal of Sociology* 91 (3): 481–510.
Green, Linda. 1999. *Fear as a Way of Life: Mayan Widows in Rural Guatemala*. New York: Columbia University Press.
Grenoble, Lenore A. 2003. *Language Policy in the Soviet Union*. Dordrecht: Kluwer Academic Publishers.
Gurgulia, Manana. 1999. "Citizen Diplomacy: Reality and Illusion." In *The Role of Unofficial Diplomacy in a Peace Process*, edited by Paula Garb. Irvine: University of California.
Gurr, Ted R. 1970. *Why Men Rebel*. Princeton, NJ: Princeton University Press.
———. 1986. "The Political Origins of State Violence and Terror: A Theoretical Analysis." In *Government Violence and Repression: An Agenda for Research*, edited by Michael Stohl and George A. Lopez, 45–72. Westport, CT: Greenwood Press.
Gutiérrez Sanín, Francisco, and Elisabeth J. Wood. 2014. "Ideology in Civil War: Instrumental Adoption and Beyond." *Journal of Peace Research* 51 (2): 213–226.

Gyts, Aspa. 2014. *Odnazhdy v 1989 godu*. [In Abkhazian.] Sukhumi: Abgosizdat.
Hewitt, George B. 1996. "Abkhazia: A Problem of Identity and Ownership." In *Transcaucasian Boundaries*, edited by John Wright, Suzanne Goldenberg, and Richard Schofield, 190–226. London: UCL Press.
———. 2013. *Discordant Neighbours: A Reassessment of the Georgian-Abkhazian and Georgian–South Ossetian Conflicts*. Leiden: Brill.
Hewitt, George B., and Elisa Watson. 1994. "Abkhazians." In *Encyclopedia of World Cultures*, vol. 6, *Russia and Eurasia/China*, edited by Paul Friedrich and Norma Diamond, 5–10. Boston: G. K. Hall.
Hilberg, Raul. 1993. *Perpetrators Victims Bystanders: The Jewish Catastrophe, 1933–1945*. New York: HarperCollins.
Hoover Green, Amelia. 2018. *The Commander's Dilemma: Violence and Restraint in Wartime*. Ithaca, NY: Cornell University Press.
Horowitz, Donald L. 1985. *Ethnic Groups in Conflict*. Berkeley: University of California Press.
Horst, Cindy, and Katarzyna Grabska. 2015. "Introduction: Flight and Exile—Uncertainty in the Context of Conflict-Induced Displacement." *Social Analysis* 59 (1): 1–18.
HRW (Human Rights Watch). 1995. *Georgia/Abkhazia: Violations of the Laws of War and Russia's Role in the Conflict*. HRW Arms Project 7. Helsinki: HRW.
———. 2011. *Living in Limbo: The Rights of Ethnic Georgian Returnees to the Gali District of Abkhazia*. New York: HRW.
Humphreys, Macartan, and Jeremy M. Weinstein. 2008. "Who Fights? The Determinants of Participation in Civil War." *American Journal of Political Science* 52 (2): 436–455.
ICG (International Crisis Group). 2006. "Abkhazia Today." *Europe Report*, no. 176 (September 15): i–28. https://www.crisisgroup.org/abkhazia-today.
———. 2007. "Abkhazia: Ways Forward." *Europe Report*, no. 179 (January 18): i–33. https://www.crisisgroup.org/europe-central-asia/caucasus/abkhazia-georgia/abkhazia-ways-forward.
———. 2010. "Abkhazia: Deepening Dependence." *Europe Report*, no. 202 (February 26): i–18. https://www.crisisgroup.org/europe-central-asia/caucasus/georgia/abkhazia-deepening-dependence.
IISS (International Institute for Strategic Studies). 2005. *The Military Balance 2005–2006*. London: Routledge.
Ingorokva, Pavle. 1954. *Giorgi Merchule*. Tbilisi: Sabcota mcerali.
Jasper, James M. 1997. *The Art of Moral Protest: Culture, Biography, and Creativity in Social Movements*. Chicago: University of Chicago Press.
Jervis, Robert. 1976. *Perception and Misperception in International Politics*. Princeton, NJ: Princeton University Press.
Kacharava, Yuri, ed. 1959. *Bor'ba za uprochenie Sovetskoj vlasti v Gruzii. Sbornik dokumentov i materialov, 1921–1925 gg*. Tbilisi: AN Gruz. SSR.
Kalyvas, Stathis N. 2003. "The Ontology of 'Political Violence': Action and Identity in Civil Wars. *Perspectives on Politics* 1 (3): 475–494.
———. 2006. *The Logic of Violence in Civil War*. Cambridge: Cambridge University Press.
Kalyvas, Stathis N., and Laia Balcells. 2010. "International System and Technologies of Rebellion: How the End of the Cold War Shaped Internal Conflict." *American Political Science Review* 104 (3): 415–429.
Kalyvas, Stathis N., and Matthew A. Kocher. 2007. "How 'Free' Is Free Riding in Civil Wars? Violence, Insurgency, and the Collective Action Problem." *World Politics* 59 (2): 177–216.
Kaslandzija, Vladimir. 2005. *Abhazsko-Russkij Slovar'*. Sukhumi: Olma-Press.

Katzenstein, Peter J., and Lucia A. Seybert. 2018a. "Protean Power and Uncertainty: Exploring the Unexpected in World Politics." *International Studies Quarterly* 62 (1): 80–93.

———. 2018b. "Uncertainty, Risk, Power and the Limits of International Relations Theory." In *Protean Power: Exploring the Uncertain and Unexpected in World Politics*, edited by Peter J. Katzenstein and Lucia A. Seybert, 27–68. Cambridge: Cambridge University Press.

Kaufman, Stuart J. 2001. *Modern Hatreds: The Symbolic Politics of Ethnic War*. Ithaca, NY: Cornell University Press.

Kemoklidze, Nino. 2016. "Georgian-Abkhaz Relations in the Post-Stalinist Era." In *Georgia after Stalin: Nationalism and Soviet Power*, edited by Jeremy Smith and Timothy K. Blauvelt, 129–145. London: Routledge.

Khalidov, Denga. 2014. *Severnyj Kavkaz v Otechestvennoj vojne Abhazii (1992–1993 gg.). Istorija, sovremennost' i problemy osmyslenija*. Sukhumi: Mezhdunarodnyj centr kavkazovedenija.

Khintba, Iraklij. 2003. *K voprosu o sovremennom jetape gruzino-abhazskogo protivostojanija*. Doklad.

Khodzhaa, Ruslan. 2003. *Put' bessmertija. Abhazija. Otechestvennaja vojna 1992–1993 gg.* Sukhumi: Alasharbaga.

———. 2006. *Batal'ony idut na shturm*. Sukhumi: Dom pechati.

———. 2009. *Put' k pobede*. Sukhumi: Alasharbaga.

Knight, Frank H. 1921. *Risk, Uncertainty and Profit*. New York: Hart, Schaffer and Marx.

Kokeev, Aleksandr M. 2008. "Abkhazia: Towards National Rebirth—or an Ethnocratic State?" In *Nationalism in Late and Post-Communist Europe*, vol. 3, edited by Egbert Jahn, 248–267. Baden-Baden: Nomos.

Krutikov, Yuri. 1998. "Tbilisi Can Blame Moscow for Its Defeat: The Latest Military Failure in Abkhazia Took Georgian Politicians by Surprise." *Sevodnya*, May 28. Reproduced in *Current Digest of the Post-Soviet Press* 50 (21), 24 June 1998, 22–23.

Krylov, Aleksandr. 2001. *Religija i tradicii abhazov (po materialam polevyh issledovanij 1994–2000 gg.)*. Moscow: Institut vostokovedenija RAN.

Kuprava, Arvelod. 2007. "Narodnye shody i oratorskoe iskusstvo." In *Abhazy*, edited by Yuri Anchabadze and Yuri Argun, 331–338. Sukhumi: Abhazskij institut gumanitarnyh issledovanij im. D. I. Gulia.

Kuprava, Arvelod, and Aslan Avidzba, eds. 2007. *Uchastniki osvoboditel'nogo dvizhenija v Abhazii (1917–1921)*. Sbornik dokumentov. Sukhumi: Dom pechati.

Kuran, Timur. 1991. "Now Out of Never: The Element of Surprise in East European Revolution of 1989." *World Politics* 44 (1): 7–48.

Kvarchelia, Liana. 1998. "Georgia-Abkhazia Conflict: View from Abkhazia." *Demokratizatsiya: The Journal of Post-Soviet Democratization* 6 (1): 17–27.

———. 1999. "An Abkhaz Perspective." In "A Question of Sovereignty: The Georgia-Abkhazia Peace Process," edited by Jonathan Cohen. Special issue, *Accord*, no. 7: 28–34.

Kvarchija, Valerij. 2011. *Iz istorii nacional'no-osvoboditel'nogo dvizhenija abhazskogo naroda 1967–1992 godov (vospominanija, primechanija, materialy)*. Sukhumi: Dom pechati.

Lacina, Bethany. 2006. "Explaining the Severity of Civil Wars." *Journal of Conflict Resolution* 50 (2): 276–289.

Lakoba, Stanislav. 1990. *Ocherki politicheskoj istorii Abhazii*. Sukhumi: Alashara.

———. 1991. *Istorija Abhazii. Uchebnoe posobie*. Sukhumi: Alashara.

———. 1993. *Stoletnjaja vojna Gruzii protiv Abhazii*. Gagra: Associacija "Intelligencija Abhazii."

———. 2004. *Abhazija posle dvuh imperij. XIX–XXI vv.* 21st Century COE Program, Slavic Eurasian Studies 5. Sapporo: Slavic Research Center, Hokkaido University.
———. 2013a. "History: 18th Century–1917." In *The Abkhazians: A Handbook*, edited by George B. Hewitt, 67–88. New York: Routledge.
———. 2013b. "History: 1917–1989." In *The Abkhazians: A Handbook*, edited by George B. Hewitt, 89–101. New York: Routledge
Lawrence, Adria. 2010. "Driven to Arms? The Escalation to Violence in Nationalist Conflicts." In *Rethinking Violence: States and Non-state Actors in Conflict*, edited by Erica Chenoweth and Adria Lawrence, 143–172. Cambridge, MA: MIT Press.
Lezhava, Grigorij. 1997. *Mezhdu Gruziej i Rossiej. Istoricheskie korni i sovremennye faktory abhazo-gruzinskogo konflikta (XIX–XX vv.)*. Moscow: Centr po izucheniju mezhnacional'nyh otnoshenij Instituta jetnologii i antropologii RAN.
———. 1998. *Jetnopoliticheskaja situacija v Gruzii i abhazskij vopros (1987–nachalo 1992 gg.). Ocherki, dokumenty*. Moscow: Centr po izucheniju mezhnacional'nyh otnoshenij Instituta jetnologii i antropologii RAN.
Lichbach, Mark I. 1995. *The Rebel's Dilemma*. Ann Arbor: University of Michigan Press.
Lynch, Dov. 1999. *Russian Peacekeeping Strategies in the CIS: The Cases of Moldova, Georgia and Tajikistan*. London: Macmillan.
———. 2004. *Engaging Eurasia's Separatist States: Unresolved Conflicts and De Facto States*. Washington, DC: United States Institute of Peace Press.
Maan, Omar. 2003. *Socializacija lichnosti v tradicionno-bytovoj kul'ture abhazov (vtoraja polovina XIX–nachalo XX vv.)*. Sukhumi: Alashara.
———. 2007. "Osnovnye cherty social'nogo stroja." In *Abhazy*, edited by Yuri Anchabadze and Yuri Argun, 322–330. Sukhumi: Abhazskij institut gumanitarnyh issledovanij im. D. I. Gulia.
———. 2012. *Apsuara v social'nyh otnoshenijah abhazov (XVIII–pervaja polovina XIX vv.)*. Sukhumi: Abhazskij institut gumanitarnyh issledovanij im. D. I. Gulia.
Mandel, David R. 2002. "Instigators of Genocide." In *Understanding Genocide: The Social Psychology of the Holocaust*, edited by Leonard S. Newman and Ralph Erber, 259–284. Oxford: Oxford University Press.
Mansfield, Edward D., and Jack L. Snyder. 2005. *Electing to Fight: Why Emerging Democracies Go to War*. Cambridge, MA: MIT Press.
Markedonov, Sergey. 2008. "Abkhazia as the Theatre of Georgia's Terrorist Activities and Sabotage." *Strategic Culture Foundation*, October 31.
Marten, Kimberly. 2012. *Warlords: Strong-Arm Brokers in Weak States*. Ithaca, NY: Cornell University Press.
Maryhuba, Igor. 1993. *Ob abhazah i Abhazii (istoricheskaja spravka)*. Sukhumi: Adygeja.
———, ed. 1994. *Abhazija v sovetskuju jepohu. Abhazskie pis'ma (1947–1989 gg.). Sbornik dokumentov i materialov*. Sukhumi: Akua.
———. 2000. *Ocherki politicheskoj istorii Abhazii*. Sukhumi: Akua.
Matsaberidze, David. 2011. *The Conflict over Abkhazia (1989–2010): The Interaction of Georgian-Abkhazian Nationalisms and the Role of Institutions in the Post-Soviet Developments*. Saarbrücken: Lambert Academic Publishing.
Matveeva, Anna, and Duncan Hiscock, eds. 2003. *The Caucasus: Armed and Divided*. London: Saferworld.
McAdam, Doug. 1982. *Political Process and the Development of Black Insurgency, 1930–1970*. Chicago: University of Chicago Press.
———. 1986. "Recruitment to High-Risk Activism: The Case of Freedom Summer." *American Journal of Sociology* 92 (1): 64–90.
———. 1988. *Freedom Summer*. New York: Oxford University Press.

———. 2003. "Beyond Structural Analysis: Toward a More Dynamic Understanding of Social Movements." In *Social Movements and Networks: Relational Approaches to Collective Action*, edited by Mario Diani and Doug McAdam, 281–298. New York: Oxford University Press.
McAdam, Doug, Sidney Tarrow, and Charles Tilly. 2001. *Dynamics of Contention*. Cambridge: Cambridge University Press.
McCarthy, John D., and Mayer N. Zald. 1973. *The Trend of Social Movements in America: Professionalization and Resource Mobilization*. Morristown, NJ: General Learning Press.
———. 1977. "Resource Mobilization and Social Movements: A Partial Theory." *American Journal of Sociology* 82 (6): 1212–1241.
McDoom, Omar S. 2012. "The Psychology of Threat in Intergroup Conflict: Emotions, Rationality, and Opportunity in the Rwandan Genocide." *International Security* 37 (2): 119–155.
Menakeci, Vagan. 2009. *Zvezdy ne gasnut*. Sukhumi: Dom pechati.
Menteshashvili, Avtandil. 1990. *Iz istorii vzaimootnoshenij gruzinskogo, abhazskogo i osetinskogo narodov (1918–1921 gg.)*. Tbilisi: Obshhestvo Znanie.
Mikhelidze, Nona, and Nicoletta Pirozzi. 2008. "Civil Society and Conflict Transformation in Abkhazia, Israel/Palestine, Nagorno-Karabakh, Transnistria and Western Sahara.: MICROCON Policy Working Paper 3. MICROCON, Brighton, UK.
Mildarsky, Elizabeth, Stephanie Fagin Jones, and Robin P. Corley. 2005. "Personality Correlates of Heroic Rescue during the Holocaust." *Journal of Personality* 73 (4): 907–934.
Ministerstvo vnutrennih del Respubliki Abhazija. 2016. "Statistika DTP s 1994 g. po 25 oktjabrja 2016 g. Analiticheskaja spravka shtaba MVD RA." http://mvdra.org/statistics/5586/.
Müller, Daniel. 2013. "Demography." In *The Abkhazians: A Handbook*, edited by George B. Hewitt, 218–240. New York: Routledge.
Nan, Susan Allen. 1999. "Civic Initiatives." In "A Question of Sovereignty: The Georgia-Abkhazia Peace Process," edited by Jonathan Cohen. Special issue, *Accord*, no. 7: 50–57.
Nodia, Ghia. 1998. "The Conflict in Abkhazia: National Projects and Political Circumstances." In *Georgians and Abkhazians: The Search for a Peace Settlement*, edited by Bruno Coppieters, Ghia Nodia, and Yuri Anchabadze, 15–44. Cologne: Bundesinstitut für Ostwissenschaftliche und Internationale Studien.
———. 1999. "Georgian Perspectives." In "A Question of Sovereignty: The Georgia-Abkhazia Peace Process," edited by Jonathan Cohen. Special issue, *Accord*, no. 7: 20–26.
———. 2004. "Europeanization and (Not) Resolving Secessionist Conflicts." *Journal on Ethnopolitics and Minority Issues in Europe* 5 (1): 1–15.
Nodia, Ghia, and Álvaro Pinto Scholtbach. 2006. *The Political Landscape of Georgia. Political Parties: Achievements, Challenges and Prospects*. Delft, the Netherlands: Eburon Academic Publishers.
Nordstrom, Carolyn. 2004. *Shadows of War: Violence, Power, and International Profiteering in the Twenty-First Century*. Berkeley: University of California Press.
Ó Beacháin, Donnacha. 2012. "The Dynamics of Electoral Politics in Abkhazia." *Communist and Post-Communist Studies* 45 (1): 165–174.
Ó Beacháin Stefanczak, Karolina, and Eileen Connolly. 2015. "Gender and Political Representation in the De Facto States of the Caucasus: Women and Parliamentary Elections in Abkhazia." *Caucasus Survey* 3 (3): 258–268.
Oberschall, Anthony. 1973. *Social Conflict and Social Movements*. Englewood Cliffs, NJ: Prentice-Hall.

———. 1994. "Rational Choice in Collective Protests." *Rationality and Society* 6 (1): 79–100.
O'Loughlin, John, Vladimir Kolossov, and Gerard Toal. 2011. "Inside Abkhazia: Survey of Attitudes in a De Facto State." *Post-Soviet Affairs* 27 (1): 1–36.
Olson, Mancur. 1965. *The Logic of Collective Action: Public Goods and the Theory of Groups*. Cambridge, MA: Harvard University Press.
Osmanov, Ahmed, and Magomed Butaev, eds. 1994. *Sojuz ob"edinennyh gorcev Severnogo Kavkaza i Dagestana (1917–1918 gg.), Gorskaja Respublika (1918–1920 gg.): Dokumenty i materialy*. Makhachkala: Dagestanskij nauch. centr Rossijskoj akademii nauk, In-t istorii, arheologii i jetnografii.
Østby, Gudrun. 2013. "Inequality and Political Violence: A Review of the Literature." *International Area Studies Review* 16 (2): 206–231.
Pachulija, Valiko. 1997. *Kniga vechnoj pamjati: O voinah Abhazskoj Armii, pogibshih za svobodu i nezavisimost' Respubliki Abhazija*. Sukhumi: Ministerstvo oborony Respubliki Abhazija.
———. 2010. *Gruzino-abhazskaja vojna 1992–1993 gg. Boevye dejstvija*. Sukhumi: Alasharbaga.
Papaskiri, Zurab. 2010. *Abhazija. Istorija bez fal'sifikacii*. Tbilisi: Izdatel'stvo Suhumskogo gosudarstvennogo universiteta.
Parkinson, Sarah E. 2013. "Organizing Rebellion: Rethinking High-Risk Mobilization and Social Networks in War." *American Political Science Review* 107 (3): 418–432.
Peritore, N. Patrick. 1990. "Reflections on Dangerous Fieldwork." *American Sociologist* 21 (4): 359–372.
Petersen, Roger D. 2001. *Resistance and Rebellion: Lessons from Eastern Europe*. New York: Cambridge University Press.
Polletta, Francesca, and James M. Jasper. 2001. "Collective Identity and Social Movements." *Annual Review of Sociology* 27 (1): 283–305.
Popjanevski, Johanna. 2009. "From Sukhumi to Tskhinvali: The Path to War in Georgia." In *The Guns of August 2008: Russia's War in Georgia*, edited by Svante E. Cornell and S. Frederick Starr, 143–161. Armonk, NY: M. E. Sharpe.
Posen, Barry R. 1993. "The Security Dilemma and Ethnic Conflict." *Survival* 35 (1): 27–47.
Prelz Oltramonti, Giulia. 2015. "The Political Economy of a De Facto State: The Importance of Local Stakeholders in the Case of Abkhazia." *Caucasus Survey* 3 (3): 291–308.
Roe, Paul. 2004. *Ethnic Violence and the Societal Security Dilemma*. New York: Routledge.
Sagarija, Badzhgur, ed. 2002. *Vazhnaja veha v istorii Abhazii. X sessija Verhovnogo Soveta odinnadcatogo sozyva i prinjatie Deklaracii o suverenitete Abhazii 25 avgusta 1990 g. Sbornik dokumentov i materialov*. Sukhumi: Dom pechati.
Sagarija, Badzhgur, Tejmuraz Achugba, and Valiko Pachulija, eds. 1992. *Abhazija: Dokumenty svidetel'stvujut (1937–1953)*. Sukhumi: Alashara.
Sambanis, Nicholas. 2004. "What Is Civil War? Conceptual and Empirical Complexities of an Operational Definition." *Journal of Conflict Resolution* 48 (6): 814–858.
Sambanis, Nicholas, and Annalisa Zinn. 2005. "From Protest to Violence: An Analysis of Conflict Escalation with an Application to Self-Determination Movements." Unpublished manuscript.
Sampson, Robert J., Doug McAdam, Heather MacIndoe, and Simón Weffer-Elizondo. 2005. "Civil Society Reconsidered: The Durable Nature and Community Structure of Collective Civic Action." *American Journal of Sociology* 111 (3): 673–714.
Schatz, Edward. 2013. "Ethnographic Immersion and the Study of Politics." In *Ethnography: What Immersion Contributes to the Study of Power*, edited by Edward Schatz, 1–22. Chicago: University of Chicago Press.

Scott, James. 1985. *Weapons of the Weak*. New Haven, CT: Yale University Press.
Scott, John. 2000. *Social Network Analysis: A Handbook*. Newbury Park, CA: Sage.
———. 2012. *What Is Social Network Analysis?* New York: Bloomsbury Academic.
Shamba, Sergey, and Stanislav Lakoba. 1995. "Narodnyj forum Abhazija i ego celi." In *Abhazskij uzel: Dokumenty i materialy po jetnicheskomu konfliktu v Abhazii*, tom 2, *Narodnyj forum Abhazii "Aidgylara" i ego sojuzniki (1989–1990 gg.)*, edited by Mihail Chumalov, 9–16. Moscow: Institut jetnologii i antropologii RAN.
Shamba, Taras, and Aleksandr Neproshin. 2008. *Abkhazia: Legal Basis of Statehood and Sovereignty*. Moscow: Open Company "In-oktavo."
Shesterinina, Anastasia. 2015. "Border Violence in 'Post-Conflict' Abkhazia." *Forum of EthnoGeoPolitics* 3 (3): 69–92.
———. 2016. "Collective Threat Framing and Mobilization in Civil War." *American Political Science Review* 110 (3): 411–427.
———. 2019. "Ethics, Empathy, and Fear in Research on Violent Conflict." *Journal of Peace Research* 53 (2): 190–202. https://www.prio.org/utility/DownloadFile.ashx?id=74&type=replicationfile.
Shnirelman, Viktor. 2003. *Vojny pamjati: Mify, identichnost' i politika v Zakavkaz'e*. Moscow: Akademkniga.
Simmons, Erica S., and Nicholas Rush Smith. 2017. "Comparison with an Ethnographic Sensibility." *PS: Political Science and Politics* 50 (1): 126–130.
Slider, Darrell. 1985. "Crisis and Response in Soviet Nationality Policy: The Case of Abkhazia." *Central Asian Survey* 4 (4): 51–68.
Snow, David A., Daniel M. Cress, Liam Downey, and Andrew W. Jones. 1998. "Disrupting the 'Quotidian': Reconceptualizing the Relationship between Breakdown and the Emergence of Collective Action." *Mobilization* 3 (1): 1–22.
Snow, David A., Louis A. Zurcher, and Sheldon Ekland-Olson. 1980. "Social Networks and Social Movements: A Microstructural Approach to Differential Recruitment." *American Sociological Review* 45 (5): 787–801.
Snyder, Jack L. 2000. *From Voting to Violence: Democratization and Nationalist Conflict*. New York: W. W. Norton.
Staniland, Paul. 2012. *Networks of Rebellion: Explaining Insurgent Cohesion and Collapse*. Ithaca, NY: Cornell University Press.
Stewart, Frances, ed. 2008. *Horizontal Inequalities and Conflict: Understanding Group Violence in Multiethnic Societies*. Basingstoke: Palgrave Macmillan.
Straus, Scott. 2006. *The Order of Genocide: Race, Power, and War in Rwanda*. Ithaca, NY: Cornell University Press.
Suedfeld, Peter, and Stefanie de Best. 2008. "Value Hierarchies of Holocaust Rescuers and Resistance Fighters." *Genocide Studies and Prevention* 3 (1): 31–42.
Suny, Ronald. 1994. *The Making of the Georgian Nation*. Bloomington: Indiana University Press.
Tarrow, Sidney. 1998. *Power in Movement: Social Movements and Contentious Politics*. New York: Cambridge University Press.
———. 2007. "Inside Insurgencies: Politics and Violence in an Age of Civil War." *Perspectives on Politics* 5 (3): 587–600.
Taylor, Michael. 1982. *Community, Anarchy, Liberty*. Cambridge: Cambridge University Press.
———. 1988. *Rationality and Revolution*. Cambridge: Cambridge University Press.
Tiedens, Larissa Z. 1997. "Optimism and Revolt of the Oppressed: A Comparison of Two Polish Jewish Ghettos of World War II." *Political Psychology* 18 (1): 45–69.
Tilly, Charles. 1978. *From Mobilization to Revolution*. Reading, MA: Addison-Wesley.

Trier, Tom, Hedvig Lohm, and David Szakonyi. 2010. *Under Siege: Inter-ethnic Relations in Abkhazia*. New York: Columbia University Press.
Tversky, Amos, and Daniel Kahneman. 1974. "Judgment under Uncertainty: Heuristics and Biases." *Science* 185 (4157): 1124–1131.
Upravlenie gosudarstvennoj statistiki Respubliki Abhazija. 2002. *Abhazija v cifrah 2002*. Sukhumi.
——. 2003. *Abhazija v cifrah 2003*. Sukhumi.
——. 2010. *Abhazija v cifrah 2010*. Sukhumi.
Valentino, Benjamin A. 2004. *Final Solutions: Mass Killing and Genocide in the Twentieth Century*. Ithaca, NY: Cornell University Press.
Varshney, Ashutosh. 2002. *Ethnic Conflict and Civic Life*. New Haven, CT: Yale University Press.
Viola, Lynne. 1996. *Peasant Rebels under Stalin: Collectivization and the Culture of Peasant Resistance*. New York: Oxford University Press.
Viterna, Jocelyn S. 2006. "Pulled, Pushed, and Persuaded: Explaining Women's Mobilization into the Salvadoran Guerrilla Army." *American Journal of Sociology* 112 (1): 1–45.
——. 2013. *Women in War: The Micro-Processes of Mobilization in El Salvador*. New York: Oxford University Press.
Volhonskij, Mihail, Vladimir Zaharov, and Nikolaj Silaev. 2008. *Konflikty v Abhazii i Juzhnoj Osetii: Dokumenty 1989–2006 gg*. Moscow: Russkaja panorama.
Voronov, Jurij, Pavel Florenskij, and Tatjana Shutova. 1993. *Belaja kniga Abhazii. Dokumenty, materialy, svidetel'stva (1992–1993)*. Moscow: Tipografija No. 7.
Walker, Edward. 1998. "No Peace, No War in the Caucasus: Secessionist Conflicts in Chechnya, Abkhazia and Nagorno-Karabakh." Strengthening Democratic Institutions Project. Belfer Center for Science and International Affairs, John F. Kennedy School of Government, Harvard University, Cambridge, MA.
Wedeen, Lisa. 2019. *Authoritarian Apprehensions: Ideology, Judgment, and Mourning in Syria*. Chicago: University of Chicago Press.
Weinstein, Jeremy M. 2007. *Inside Rebellion: The Politics of Insurgent Violence*. New York: Cambridge University Press.
Wiesen, S. Jonathan. 2000. "German Industry and the Third Reich: Fifty Years of Forgetting and Remembering." *Dimensions: A Journal of Holocaust Studies* 13 (2): 1–8.
Wilkinson, Steven. 2004. *Votes and Violence: Electoral Competition and Ethnic Riots in India*. Cambridge: Cambridge University Press.
Wood, Elisabeth J. 2003. *Insurgent Collective Action and Civil War in El Salvador*. Cambridge: Cambridge University Press.
——. 2015. "Social Mobilization and Violence in Civil War and Their Social Legacies." In *The Oxford Handbook of Social Movements*, edited by Donatella della Porta and Mario Diani, 452–466. Oxford: Oxford University Press.
Yamskov, Anatoly. 2009. "Special Features of the Changes in the Ethnodemographic Situation in Abkhazia in the Post-Soviet Period." *The Caucasus and Globalization: Journal of Social, Political and Economic Studies* 3 (2–3): 166–176.
Yanow, Dvora, and Peregrine Schwartz-Shea. 2006. "Assessing and Generating Data." In *Interpretation and Method: Empirical Research Methods and the Interpretive Turn*, edited by Dvora Yanow and Peregrine Schwartz-Shea, 115–126. Armonk, NY: M. E. Sharpe.
Zhidkov, Spartak. 2011. *Zjorna mjatezha. Ocherki istorii nacional'no-osvoboditel'noj bor'by v g. Tkvarcheli (1977–1991 gg.)*. Sukhumi: Abhazija print.
Zhukov, Yuri M. 2016. "Trading Hard Hats for Combat Helmets: The Economics of Rebellion in Eastern Ukraine." *Journal of Comparative Economics* 44 (1): 1–15.

Zürcher, Christoph. 2007. *The Post-Soviet Wars: Rebellion, Ethnic Conflict, and Nationhood in the Caucasus*. New York: New York University Press.
Zürcher, Christoph, Pavel Baev, and Jan Koehler. 2005. "Civil Wars in the Caucasus." In *Understanding Civil War: Evidence and Analysis*, edited by Paul Collier and Nicholas Sambanis, 2:259–298. Washington, DC: World Bank.
Zverev, Alexei. 1996. "Ethnic Conflicts in the Caucasus 1988–1994." In *Contested Borders in the Caucasus*, edited by Bruno Coppieters. Brussels: VUB University Press. http://poli.vub.ac.be/publi/ContBorders/eng/ch0101.htm.

Index

Note: Information in figures and tables is indicated by *f* and *t*, respectively.

Abkhaz Guard, 6, 9–11, 128, 129*f*, 131, 156–157, 159–162, 202, 221n9; Abkhaz force and, 21; and access to arms, 14; adaptation and, 138–140, 144; Aidgylara and, 104; Mkhedrioni and, 118–121; mobilization and, 150–153; organization and, 53; participation and, 54–55; research participants in, 26; shock on part of, 125

Abkhazia: autonomous status of, 72–74; as case, 19–21; demographics of, 5; general strike in, 115–116; intergroup conflict in prewar, 5–8; postwar, 177–200, 187*f*–188*f*; power of, 8; in pre-Soviet period, 69–72, 70*t*; recognition of, 199–200; in Soviet period, 5–7, 68, 72–77, 78*f*, 102–104

Abkhazianization, 86

"Abkhaz Letter," 103, 106

Abkhazpereselenstroj, 75, 77

Abkhaz Research Institute, 99

Abkhaz State University, 90, 102, 109–114, 125, 218n2

Abrskyl, 25, 105–106, 109, 114–115, 120, 127, 221n37

Achugba, Tejmuraz, 75, 142

activism, 28, 79, 140, 185, 191, 204; collective conflict identities and, 60; collective threat framing and, 40; ethnographic surprises and, 38; mobilization and, 121; organization and, 53; participation and, 14, 54–55, 98–108; risk *vs.* cost in, 215n14; social networks and, 214n3

adaptation, 63, 64*f*, 137–144

Agrba, Zakan, 143

Ahuba, Dzhuma, 100

Aidgylara, 7, 53, 57, 102–107, 109–115, 117–118, 139–140, 163, 185, 217n19

Almeida, Paul, 215n16

alphabet, 72, 80*f*, 81, 99, 218n30

Anchabadze, Yuri, 3, 69

antagonism, intergroup, 89–97, 91*f*

April 9 rally, 57, 110–111

Ardzinba, Vladislav, 7, 111, 118, 130–133, 136–138, 159, 189, 221nn3,8.

Armed Forces of Abkhazia, 53, 169–170

Armstrong, David A., 53

attribution, of victory and loss, 184–189, 187*f*–188*f*

Babilashvili, Djamlet, 223n22

Baev, Pavel, 168

Bayard de Volo, Lorraine, 38

Beissinger, Mark R., 106

Beria, Lavrenty, 75, 79, 81–83, 98–99, 135, 160, 218n1, 219n13

Billingsley, Dodge, 167

border defense, 29, 191–197, 198, 203, 222n1, 223n28

Brezhnev, Leonid, 7, 100

Brojdo, Anna, 165

brutality, 66, 134, 156, 163–166, 185–186. *See also* violence

Bzyb/Bzipi, 102, 109, 140–141, 158–159

car crashes, 177, 182, 222n3

casualty figures, 11, 171, 213n7, 222n3

Caucasus War, 69, 75, 81

Chavchavadze Society, 108

Chechnya, 163, 205

civil war, 19–20, 47; as isolated phenomenon, 50–51. *See also* intergroup conflict

collective action: activism and, 121; approach, 13–14; collective conflict identities and, 3, 60; collective historical memory and, 210; collective threat framing and, 40–41, 61; confrontation and, 56, 56*f*; continuum, 56*f*; in future research, 211; in mobilization concept, 14–16, 49, 49*f*, 52, 55–58, 56*f*, 141; organized, 49*f*, 56*f*; prewar, 142, 144; prewar conflict identities and, 89; prewar experiences and, 64; repertoires of, 215n11; spontaneous, 49*f*, 56*f*; threats and, 215n16

collective conflict identities: attribution and, 184–189, 187*f*–188*f*; defined, 2; intergroup conflict and, 3, 63–64; intergroup integration and, 92; memorialization and, 184–189, 187*f*–188*f*; mobilization and, 58–61, 89, 136,

collective conflict identities (*continued*)
    209; outcomes and, 66; postwar threat and, 189–199
collective threat framing, 48, 207–208; defined, 2; mobilization and, 5, 19, 48, 58, 61–66, 64*f*, 66*f*, 127–128; social networks and, 41, 46, 61; as theoretical framework, 40–42
collectivization, 74–75, 78
Collins, Randall, 206
Colombia, 206
Commonwealth of Independent States, 4, 180, 193
conflict avoidance, 96–97
conflict identities, 52. *See also* collective conflict identities; prewar conflict identities
confrontation: collective action and, 56, 56*f*; everyday, 2, 24, 31, 52, 54–59, 56*f*, 89–97, 120–122, 135, 210–211; prewar conflict identities and, 89–97, 91*f*. *See also* violence
consolidation, 63, 64*f*, 144–155
conversational taboos, 92–93, 210
Cornell, Svante E., 220n34
crime, 10, 109, 120, 132, 175–178, 180–182, 191, 222nn3,7
cultural changes, 78–87, 80*f*
customs, prewar conflict identities and, 93–94

Davenport, Christian, 53
demographics, 5, 23*f*, 26*f*, 27*t*, 74–77, 78*f*, 91*f*
Derluguian, Georgi M., 103–104, 143
D. Gulia Institute of Language, Literature, and History, 176
displacement, 11, 17, 19, 66, 90, 163, 178–179, 190–191, 200, 222n3, 222n13
Dzidzarija, Georgij, 99

economic changes, 84–87, 179–180, 222n5
economic sanctions, 180, 183
education, 80–81, 90, 102, 116–118, 218n25–26
elite articulation, 63, 64*f*, 130–137
El Salvador, 59, 62, 215n17
employment, 12, 24, 46, 86, 90, 116–118, 182, 213n8, 219n3
ethnographic surprises, 38–46
everyday confrontation, 2, 24, 31, 52, 54–59, 56*f*, 89–97, 120–122, 135, 210–211

Forest Brothers, 190, 194, 195–196
Freedom Summer, 39–40, 60, 215n14
friendship, 89–97, 91*f*, 154–155. *See also* social networks
Fujii, Lee Ann, 3, 206

Gagra, 22*f*, 25–26, 26*f*, 29, 44, 119, 166–167
Gal/i, 22*f*, 23–25, 23*f*, 81, 83, 114, 196–197
Gamsakhurdia, Zviad, 7–8, 10, 106, 118, 126, 220n26
genocide, 118, 205, 213n9, 214n7, 215n9
Georgia: independence of, 7; Menshevik, 69–72, 70*t*, 100, 110; power of, 8; in Soviet period, 68, 72–73
Georgian-Abkhaz war: casualties in, 222n3; clashes before, 120; first months of, 157–162; front lines of, 158*f*; Gagra in, 166–167; lost battles in, 170–172; Sukhum/i in, 172–176
Georgian Independence Day, 110–111, 120, 196–197, 220n37
Georgianization, 6, 78–87, 80*f*, 84–87, 97, 105, 202, 219n13
Germany, 137
glasnost, 95, 110
Gorbachev, Mikhail, 95, 103, 107–108, 110, 220n30
Gould, Roger V., 58
government: Aidgylara in, 7, 104; fighters in, 13; polarization, 24, 116–118; postwar, 183; Soviet collapse and, 12
Grabska, Katarzyna, 145
Granovetter, Mark S., 3
Guatemala, 206
Gudauta, 8–9, 14, 21, 22*f*, 25–26, 26*f*, 29, 44, 75, 145–146, 157–158
guerrillas, 193–196
Gulia, Georgij, 99
Gumista River, 158–159, 170–171
Gytsba, Levan, 143

historiography, 83–84, 100
Horst, Cindy, 145
Humphreys, Macartan, 208
"100-year war," 68–69

Indonesia, 205
infrastructure, 50, 119, 134, 178–179, 193, 198
Ingorokva, Pavle, 83, 99–100
Institute for Humanitarian Research, 99
insults, 93–94, 186
intergroup antagonism, 89–97, 91*f*
intergroup conflict: collective conflict identities and, 3, 63–64; collective historical memory and, 210; future research in, 211; information filtering and, 209; in prewar Abkhazia, 5–8
interviews, in research process, 31–35, 42–46

jokes, 93–94, 186

INDEX   241

Kakubava, Boris, 190
Kalyvas, Stathis N., 50, 62, 92
Kapitonov, Ivan, 101
Karkarashvili, Giorgi, 165
Kiaraz, 6, 72–73
Kikhiripa, Boris, 143
Kodor/i Gorge, 113–114, 192, 197–199
Kuchukhidze, K. D., 120
Kuran, Timur, 62–63
Kvarchelia, Liana, 197
Kvitsiani, Emzar, 198, 223n23

Lakoba, Stanislav, 69
language, 72, 80f, 81–83, 94–103, 117, 218nn25, 27, 30, 219nn10,17. *See also* alphabet
Lawrence, Adria, 51
Lebanon, 213n9
Lenin, Vladimir, 216n9
"Letter of Eight," 100
"Letter of 130," 100
Lichbach, Mark I., 53
Lithuania, 213n9
Lykhny gathering, 53, 57, 77, 106–108
"Lykhny Letter," 107–108

makhadzhirstvo, 69–72, 70t
Mansfield, Edward D., 137
marriage, 6, 61, 91–92, 208
Maryhuba, Igor, 103, 107–108
material incentives, 13
McAdam, Doug, 39
McDoom, Omar S., 207, 209
memorialization, 184–189, 187f–188f
Mensheviks, 69–72, 70t, 93, 100, 110
militarization, 108, 118–120, 164, 210
Mingrelian, 24
mining, 90
Mkhedrioni, 6, 8, 20, 118–120, 163, 214n3
mobilization: activism and, 53; adaptation and, 137–144; alternative explanations of, 202–204; approaches to, 11–15; broadening of concept, 16; collective action approach to, 13–16, 49, 52, 55–58, 56f, 141; collective conflict identities and, 58–61, 89, 136, 209; collective threat framing and, 5, 48, 58, 61–66, 64f, 66f, 127–128; as concept, 49–58, 49f, 56f; consolidation and, 144–155; continuum, 66f; defined, 49; elite articulation, and, 130–137; field research on, 3–5; from, to fighting, 156–176, 158f; future research in, 211–212; local, 150–152, 151f; as ongoing process, 3, 49–52, 49f, 210–211; organization in, 49f, 52–53; outcomes and, 66–67; participation in, 49f, 54–55; prewar experiences and, 64–65; process of, 58–67, 64f, 66f; puzzle of, 2, 201; relative deprivation approach to, 12–13; repertoires, 48–49, 56f, 56–58, 123, 215n11; social structures and, 154–155; sociohistorical approach to, 15–17, 47–67, 49f, 56f, 64f, 66f; spontaneous, 26, 27t, 46, 49f, 56, 56f, 121–122, 150, 211, 215n9; strategic interaction approach to, 14; threat perception and, 65; trajectories, 28–29, 54–55, 120–122, 127, 147–148, 204; in uncertainty, 38–40, 205–211; from uncertainty to, 123–155. *See also* participation
mothers' groups, 58–59, 183–184
Müller, Daniel, 81, 217n12, 218n1

Nadareishvili, Tamaz, 196
Nagorno-Karabakh, 205
National Guard, 8, 20, 163
Nauru, 223n27
Nicaragua, 223n27
Nodia, Ghia, 110
nonparticipation, 41–42, 49f, 52, 54–55, 61–62, 202, 214nn4–5

Ochamchira/e, 22f, 75, 86, 110, 113–114, 124–125
Olson, Mancur, 13
organization, in mobilization, 49f, 52–53
organized trajectory, 55–56, 56f, 57, 98
Ottoman Empire, 216n2

Papaskiri, Zurab, 216n5
Parkinson, Sarah E., 59, 208
participant observation, in research process, 36
participant trajectory, 55
participation: in concept of mobilization, 49f; forms of, 54; identity, 58; in mobilization, 49f, 54–55; mobilization trajectories and, 121, 204; nonparticipation, 214nn4–5; nonrecruited, 49f; recruited, 49f; risk and, 62. *See also* mobilization
perestroika, 95, 110
Petersen, Roger D., 38, 208
Pitsunda, 22f, 25–26, 26f, 29, 102–103, 152–153
Pitsunda Creative Youth Union, 105
polarization, 8, 24, 108, 116–118, 135, 209–210
political contention, 2, 24, 31, 49–52, 56f, 57, 59, 89, 98–108, 210–211
population declines, 178–180, 222n4. *See also* demographics
postwar Abkhazia, 177–200, 187f–188f
preference falsification, 62–63

242   INDEX

prewar conflict identities: conflict avoidance and, 96–97; confrontation and, 89–97, 91*f*; conversational taboos and, 92–93; customs and, 93–94; insults and, 93–94; jokes and, 93–94; low-level violence and, 95–96; militarization and, 118–120; mobilization trajectories and, 120–122; polarization and, 116–118; political contention and, 98–108; resistance and, 96–97; social split and, 108–120; strike and, 115–116; violent opposition and, 108–120
prewar experiences: intergroup conflict and, 5–8; in interviews, 32, 43–44; mobilization and, 16, 28, 48, 64–65; participation and, 54; social networks and, 59, 64–65
purge, 79

quotas, 12, 74, 86, 118, 219n3

relative deprivation, 12–15, 94
religion, 25, 53, 217n20, 221n2
repression, 9, 59, 65, 71, 78–82, 88, 99–100, 135, 209, 215n17
research design, 19–29, 22*f*–23*f*, 26*f*, 27*t*
research participants, 26–29, 27*t*
research process, 29–38
research sites, 21–26, 22*f*–23*f*, 26*f*
resettlement, 69, 72–77, 78*f*, 89–90, 100, 118, 217n12, 217n16, 218n1
resistance, 138, 140; futility of, 8–9; Lykhny gathering and, 107; prewar conflict identities and everyday, 96–97
Revolutionary Committee of Abkhazia, 99
risk: assumption of, 2, 47; collective threat framing and, 48, 62; cost *vs.*, 215n14; participation and, 62; violence and, 2, 62
rumors, 125–126
Russia, 162–167, 192, 203–204, 223n28. *See also* Soviet Union
Russian Empire, 6, 19, 69–72, 70*t*, 74, 77, 81, 216n2
Russo-Turkish War, 69
Rustaveli Society, 103
Rwanda, 60, 91–92, 137, 205, 207, 210, 213n9, 214n7

Saakashvili, Mikheil, 198
Sagarija, Badzhgur, 75
Sambanis, Nicholas, 51
Sampson, Robert J., 214n2
sanctions, economic, 180, 183
Scholtbach, Álvaro Pinto, 110
Scott, James, 97, 215n12

Seybert, Lucia A., 206
Shakryl, Konstantin, 99–100
Shervashidze, Georgij, 216n2
Shevardnadze, Eduard, 8, 43, 118, 165, 175, 189, 190, 222–3n13, 223n23
Shinkuba, Bagrat, 99
sites, research, 21–26, 22*f*–23*f*, 26*f*
situational threat perception, 41, 128–130, 207
six-day war, 193, 196–197
Snyder, Jack L., 137
Sochi, 145–146
social networks: collective threat framing and, 41, 61; conflict identity and, 52; mobilization and, 2–3, 16, 64; prewar experiences and, 59, 64–65; prewar mobilization and, 89, 122; quotidian, 59, 63, 128, 144–155; in sociohistorical approach, 15, 47–48; threat perception and, 63; uncertainty and, 205. *See also* friendship
social status, 84–87, 204
social structures, 154–155
sociohistorical approach, 15–17, 47–67, 49*f*, 56*f*, 64*f*, 66*f*
South Ossetia, 7, 118, 132, 190, 198, 223n24
South Sudan, 205
Soviet Union, 5–7, 12, 68, 72–73, 90, 101–104, 201
spontaneous mobilization trajectory, 26, 27*t*, 46, 49*f*, 55–56, 56*f*, 121–122, 150, 211, 215n9
Sri Lanka, 221n2
Stalin, Joseph, 6, 73, 75, 81–82, 99, 135, 184
Staniland, Paul, 53, 59, 144
storytelling, 186–187
strategic interaction, 14–15
Straus, Scott, 205
strike, 51–54, 56*f*, 57, 79, 101, 110–112, 115–116, 120–122, 210–211, 220nn30–31
Sukhum/i, 22*f*, 23–25, 23*f*, 29, 52, 57, 90, 114, 170–176
Syria, 205, 209, 223n27

taboos, conversational, 92–93
targeted selection strategy, 30
Tarrow, Sidney, 51
Tbilisi State University, 7, 52, 110–112, 115–117, 122, 220n27
Tetri Legioni. *See* White Legion
threat(s): adaptation of, 63, 64*f*, 137–144; collective action and, 215n16; consolidation of, 63, 64*f*, 144–155; elite articulation of, 63, 64*f*, 130–137; framing of, 130–137; mobilization and, 65; perception of, 2, 41, 128–130. *See also* collective threat framing
Tilly, Charles, 215n11

titular group, 69, 73–74, 86, 219n3
Tkis Dzmebi. *See* Forest Brothers
Tqvarchal/Tqvarcheli, 8, 21–25, 23f, 90, 113–116, 138–139, 145, 159–160, 179, 219n6
Transnistria, 205
triangulation, in research process, 36–38
trust, 208–209
Tsugurovka, 174–175
Turkey, 69
Tuvalu, 223n27

Uganda, 206
Ukraine, 205
uncertainty, 2–3; defined, 205; mobilization in, 38–40, 205–211; from mobilization to, 123–155; violence and, 16, 48, 205; of war's onset, 10–11, 124–127

Vanuatu, 223n27
Venezuela, 223n27
violence: collective conflict identities and, 2, 60–61; collective threat framing and, 61–63, 65; low-level, 95–96; meanings of, 206; postwar, 29, 35, 38, 66, 204; in postwar Abkhazia, 190–192; prewar conflict identities and, in opposition, 108–120; prewar conflict identities and low-level, 95–96; risk and, 2, 62; uncertainty and, 16, 48, 205. *See also* brutality; confrontation
violent opposition, 2, 24, 31, 49–52, 56f, 57, 59, 108–120, 135, 210–211
Viterna, Jocelyn S., 214n8

Wedeen, Lisa, 215n15
Weinstein, Jeremy M., 13, 38, 208
White Legion, 190, 194, 196
Wood, Elisabeth J., 38, 47, 212, 214n7
World War II, 79, 81, 85, 100

Yugoslavia, 51

Zinn, Annalisa, 51
Zürcher, Christoph, 21, 120
Zviadists, 8

www.ingramcontent.com/pod-product-compliance
Lightning Source LLC
Chambersburg PA
CBHW022005220426
43663CB00007B/964